FINE WINE
EDITIONS

THE FINEST WINES OF
CALIFORNIA

A Regional Guide to the Best Producers and Their Wines

STEPHEN BROOK

Foreword by Hugh Johnson | Photography by Jon Wyand

UNIVERSITY OF CALIFORNIA PRESS
Berkeley | Los Angeles

University of California Press,
one of the most distinguished university presses in the United States,
enriches lives around the world by advancing scholarship
in the humanities, social sciences, and natural sciences.
Its activities are supported by the UC Press Foundation and by
philanthropic contributions from individuals and institutions.
For more information, visit www.ucpress.edu

First published in
North America by
University of California Press
Berkeley and Los Angeles, California

Fine Wine Editions
Publisher Sara Morley
General Editor Neil Beckett
Editor David Williams
Subeditor David Tombesi-Walton
Editorial Assistants Clare Belbin, Jeanette Esper, Piers Gelly
Map Editor Jeremy Wilkinson
Maps Tom Coulson, Encompass Graphics, Hove, UK
Indexer Ann Marangos
Americanizer Christine Heilman
Production Nikki Ingram

Library of Congress Control Number: 2010931618

ISBN 978-0-520-26658-2 (paper : alk. paper)

Manufactured in China

10 9 8 7 6 5 4 3 2 1
17 16 15 14 13 12 11

Preface

by Stephen Brook

California is as large as many a country, so it is unreasonable to expect its wines to have a single identity, however vaguely expressed. Yet certain conditions do seem to apply statewide. The first is sunshine. In most parts of the state, winters are mild and often wet, and summers are steadily warm, with sunshine rarely interrupted by rain. Fall is more capricious, and in some years the harvest season calls for steady nerves, but most French or German wine growers would laugh at the notion that California autumns are difficult.

Steady sunshine is necessary to ripen the grapes. But like all of the world's great wines, California's are determined by moderating influences. The hottest and driest part of the state is the immense Central Valley, but no one would claim that it is a source of outstanding grapes: constant heat gives high sugars but low acidities, and that means no light and shade in the wines. What moderates the California climate, and makes possible the production of world-class wines, is the Pacific Ocean. Cooling breezes course down the Salinas Valley in Monterey; morning fog can carpet the valley floor in Napa or Sonoma; maritime influences decide which section of the Santa Ynez Valley in Santa Barbara is best for Burgundian varieties and which for Syrah or Bordeaux varieties.

California's growers and winemakers have had decades to work out what grows best in each region and subregion. As in other New World countries, winemakers here choose their profession, whereas in Europe their counterparts have usually inherited the family property. So most California winemakers are technically competent, their vineyards are well maintained, their owners' bank balances sufficiently cash-crammed to allow the purchase of the best presses and the best barrels.

In the 21st century, few would dispute that Napa's Cabernets, Sonoma's Pinot Noirs and Zinfandels, Santa Barbara's Chardonnays, and Paso Robles's Syrahs are capable of standing side by side with some of the world's best expressions of those varieties. (Zinfandel, California's unique calling card, stands alone, of course.) There are many who still look down their noses at these wines, but their disdain seems rooted in snobbery. It was not that long ago that a distinguished British wine writer refused to rate California wines on the grounds that the vines were too young, unaware of the acres of centenarian Zinfandel, Mourvèdre, and other varieties in various parts of the state.

No, California has nothing to apologize for. There is, it is true, no template of tradition to determine the most acceptable styles, no equivalent of a Chevalier-Montrachet or Pomerol plateau or La Morra. There are no rules and no limits. This is liberating, and it would indeed be absurd to tell growers what grapes they are required to plant in what spot, and to tell winemakers how and for how long their wines are to be aged. The consequence of this liberty is that the wines of California are subject to trend and fashion. "Too much oak!" cry the critics, and the order for 100 percent new barrels is canceled. "Too lean and herbaceous!" declare the same critics, and in comes the mantra of phenolic ripeness and a whole raft of overripe jammy wines with headache-inducing alcohol levels. But for every action, there is a reaction, and I sense that the wines have never been better balanced or more drinkable than they are today. Excesses remain, but they are ever more widely perceived as such.

Myself, I am a committed lover of European wines and worship at the shrine of terroir. In California I find other qualities: lush textures, generosity of fruit, and a pioneer's swagger. I believe that the wineries selected in this book reflect the very best of this hedonistic state.

Of Sun and Fog

The wines of California are true reflections of the image of California as a whole: laid-back, hedonistic, sun-worshipping, emblems of unconstrained New Age freedoms rather than Old World restrictions, and bristling with international influences while mostly content to remain within their own borders. The analogy can be stretched too far, but when you are lolling beside a pool in the Hollywood Hills or on the slopes above Healdsburg, a steely Chablis, tannin-laden Barolo, or chewy Aglianico doesn't quite measure up. The climate demands a lush Sonoma Chardonnay, a super-ripe Santa Barbara Syrah, or the heady excesses of an Amador Zinfandel, once the grill is fired up.

Sunshine comes easily in this western state, but great wine, as opposed to quaffable wine, demands more than mere ripeness. Nuance, in California, is provided by those elements that fight the unrelenting sunshine. In much of the state, this means maritime influence. Anyone who has visited San Francisco in August will recall rummaging through the luggage for clothing that will protect you against the chill of the Pacific fog that coats the city for much of the day. Those same coastal fogs take advantage of the moments when the heat of the interior rises; then swirling maritime mists will wriggle through any gap in the coastal hills, through the San Pablo Bay into Napa, through the Petaluma Gap into southern Sonoma, while other entry points into the Salinas and Santa Maria valleys allow cool winds to refresh the balmy hillsides.

There's an approximate altitude above which the fog cannot rise, known as the fog line, and those heights—the Mendocino ridges, Sonoma Mountain, Howell Mountain, or the Santa Cruz Mountains—contribute an alternative constraint on glaring sunshine: elevation. Height brings cooler nights and slower ripening; impoverished mountain soils, in sharp contrast to the alluvial richness of valley floors and benchlands, bring to wines a distinct tannic structure. In contrast, maritime influence retains acidity. The best of California's sites do more than ripen grapes; they give the wines complexity.

Left: The California sun remains a crucial influence on its wines
Over: Elevation and fog are both helpful mitigating factors

It is no coincidence that California's cheap high-volume wines—those hearty "Burgundies" of yore and other concoctions marketed under bogus Italian names to conjure up memories of Nonno Giuseppe's gutsy home brews made in laundry rooms in Brooklyn or Chicago—tend to come from the baking Central Valley, a flat expanse where maritime influence is yearned for but never experienced, and where elevation is only perceived on a distant horizon. Here, ripeness is all; tannin is unwanted, and acidity is often provided by acid adjustment or judicious blending of varieties high in acidity, such as French Colombard or Barbera.

Climate versus terroir

Where Europe has terroir—studied, experienced, and analyzed over centuries—California has climate. Wine literature is full of information about the various soil types of the state's wine regions: the Haire and Diablo clay loams of Carneros, the Goldridge sandy loam of Russian River Valley, and so forth. What is less clear is the correlation, if any, between those soil types and the quality and typicity of the wine founded in them. Soil types can be analyzed in terms of nutrients, water retention, fertility, and other factors, all important for understanding the kind of wine likely to issue from them, but I believe that understanding of terroir is still at an elementary stage. This is not intended to be patronizing. Much the same is true of some of the most minutely examined terroirs of the Old World. Most Burgundy lovers agree on the glorious quality of wines from grand cru Musigny but are hard pressed, as are the growers, to explain precisely why Musigny is almost always a notch higher in intrinsic quality than its illustrious neighbors such as Les Amoureuses and Clos de Vougeot. So it is hardly

surprising that California growers are scarcely more advanced in their understanding of native terroir. Nor are the accepted descriptors of great use. Much is written of Rutherford dust, but after decades of tasting, and greatly enjoying, Rutherford Cabernets, I still find it hard to perceive any quality that differentiates them from counterparts grown in, say, Oakville or St. Helena.

Nor does the primacy of the winemaker over the grape farmer improve the likelihood that any nuances of terroir are going to emerge. The situation is less black and white than 20 years ago, when it was the grower's job to provide grapes and the winemaker's job to make the best of them. Today, conscientious winemakers also spend time in the vineyards, assessing the quality and nature of the fruit before it arrives at the winery. Nonetheless, the California winemaker is equipped with a full bag of tricks: must-watering, microoxygenation, tank-bleeding, tannin and color additives, cultivated yeasts, acid adjustment, enzyme additions, a panoply of oak sources and toasts, stirring and rolling regimens in the barrel room, reverse osmosis, and spinning cones. This is not the place to argue whether these technical aids are positive or negative; I merely observe that their frequent use can sometimes smooth out the differences that make wines interesting and specific. Delicacy and finesse are not qualities much revered by most American wine critics and consumers, though this generalization is less true than it used to be.

The land of the free

California wines also benefit from the industry's lack of regulation. There are rules to regulate labeling, but in general a grower can grow what he wants where he wants, and a winemaker can use any grapes he fancies and do with them what he will. This enviable freedom has led to the swift evolution, and diversification, of the wine industry. Want to try your hand at growing/vinifying Fiano? Go ahead! Some winemakers, such as Kenneth Volk formerly of Wild Horse Winery, established their reputations by producing wines from obscure varieties. On the whole, though, American consumers are not hugely receptive to innovation of this kind; conservative drinkers for the most part, they prefer to stick to their Cabernet or Sauvignon or Zinfandel. For all the talk of and by Rhône Rangers, the amount of Marsanne and/or Roussanne in California is small.

There is no equivalent of the French Institut National de l'Origine et de la Qualité (INAO) or other similar regulatory bodies in California, but the market itself is a form of regulator. Cabernet is king in Napa Valley, for instance, so this variety fetches the highest prices for growers. Twenty years ago, Napa was also home to Zinfandel, Riesling, Muscat, Chenin Blanc, and many other varieties. No longer. Why grow Chenin, however delightful the results, when Cabernet will bring you five times the price? Thus, there is a tendency of some wine regions to become monovarietal—but then the same is true of many parts of Europe.

The nature of the industry makes the task of selecting its top wineries particularly difficult. Here, I have considered quality the most important but not sole criterion. I have looked more indulgently on wineries that make considerable volumes of excellent wine than on boutique operations that do one small thing very well. I believe track record is important. To turn out consistently good wines over three decades is more impressive than winning brief acclaim for some opening vintages.

The industry is also inherently unstable: wineries expand or shrink (or go bust); winemakers flit from employer to employer; grape sources can charge markedly from year to year, affecting the portfolio offered; the understandable journalistic tendency to applaud the latest hot winery can leave hot wineries of previous years on the sidelines or even consigned to oblivion. So my final choices have been hard to make—but they are mine alone.

From Mission to Grand Ambition

Throughout the Americas, missionaries from Spain were the first to import and plant vines. Those early plantings look good on a time chart but count for little if we concern ourselves with what can loosely be called fine wine. Priests and rabbis need wine for sacramental purposes—quality is hardly an issue. There was a Spanish mission in San Diego in 1769, but no one knows if vines were planted. By the end of the century, there were more than 20 missions in California alone. Where grapes were planted, the variety was usually Criolla (the same as the Pais of Chile), eventually renamed Mission in California. Some Mission vines survive in the Sierra Foothills, and a handful of wines are made from these grapes, but the reader who has never sampled a bottle has not missed much. After the missions were secularized by the then-Mexican government in 1833, winemaking ceased to be the preserve of the Catholic Church.

A Bordelais immigrant, appropriately named Jean-Louis Vignes, planted vinifera vines in Los Angeles on the site of what is today the elegant Union Station. Vignes also ran a successful cooperage business for many decades. And he was not alone. There were vineyards close to present-day Disneyland, as well as in a dozen other spots around the city.

Meanwhile, in northern California, there were missions in San Rafael (1817) and Sonoma (1824). Immigrants were also planting vineyards for domestic consumption. Wine production was given a huge boost after General Mariano Vallejo was commissioned by the Mexican government to secularize the missions and dispense immense land grants. He kept one of the best for himself, but another, Rancho Caymus, went to George Yount of Missouri in 1836. This immense tract of land includes most of Napa Valley, and Yount (memorialized in the gastro-village of Yountville, north of Napa) was swift to plant vines, though he chose the Mission grape. By the late 1840s, the new class of landowners had established vineyards in many parts of the state, including what is now the East Bay. Cuttings were imported from the East Coast, so planters were not restricted to the wretched Mission. JW Osborne planted 60 acres (24ha) of other varieties in Napa Valley, and a four-year tax holiday, declared by the state legislature in 1859, encouraged vineyard expansion.

The more spacious hillsides and valleys of Sonoma County were even more hospitable to vines than the steeper, narrower confines of the Napa Valley, and expansion was swift. The Gold Rush brought prospectors and their hangers-on to the Sierra Foothills, and vineyards, some of which are still alive and well today, were planted so as to slake the thirst of these armies of optimists. A proper wine industry had come into being, with growers in Los Angeles, Sonoma, Santa Clara, and Sacramento selling their grapes to larger companies for blending and commercialization. By the end of the 1860s, there were some 2,000 acres (800ha) planted in Napa, though this was small-scale compared to Los Angeles's 10,000 acres (4,000ha). But disaster would strike southern California in the 1880s, when Pierce's disease, which is still a threat to vineyards throughout the state, wiped out these plantings.

To the hills

By this time, immigrants were arriving in Napa, Sonoma, and the Santa Cruz Mountains—newcomers who had considerable experience of grape farming in their native lands, and thus sought out comparable conditions. More vinifera varieties were available than earlier in the century, and Cinsault, Riesling, and Zinfandel began to proliferate. It was not only the valley floors that were being planted. Vineyards sprouted on steep hillsides that may have seemed reminiscent of

Right: Vines arrived with missions, like this one in San Francisco, but the church lost its monopoly on viticulture from 1833

RANCISCO, CAL.

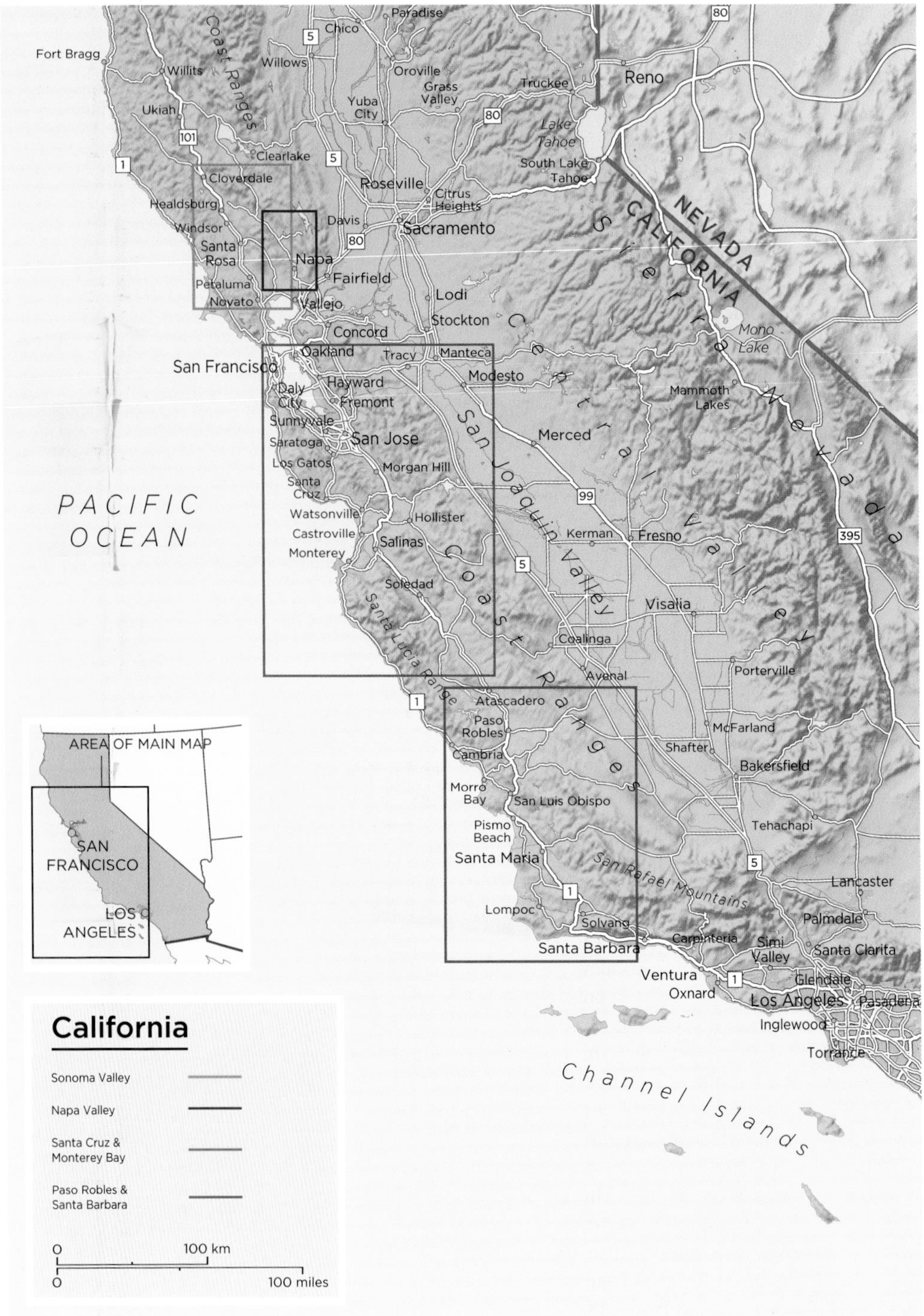
California
Sonoma Valley
Napa Valley
Santa Cruz & Monterey Bay
Paso Robles & Santa Barbara
0
100 km
0
100 miles
AREA OF MAIN MAP
SAN FRANCISCO
LOS ANGELES
PACIFIC OCEAN
Channel Islands
NEVADA
CALIFORNIA
Coast Ranges
Sierra Nevada
Central Valley
San Joaquin Valley
Santa Lucia Range
San Rafael Mountains
Lake Tahoe
Mono Lake
Fort Bragg
Willits
Ukiah
Willows
Chico
Paradise
Oroville
Grass Valley
Yuba City
Truckee
Reno
Clearlake
South Lake Tahoe
Cloverdale
Healdsburg
Windsor
Santa Rosa
Petaluma
Novato
Napa
Fairfield
Vallejo
Davis
Roseville
Citrus Heights
Sacramento
Lodi
Stockton
Concord
Oakland
San Francisco
Tracy
Manteca
Modesto
Daly City
Hayward
Fremont
Sunnyvale
Saratoga
San Jose
Los Gatos
Morgan Hill
Santa Cruz
Watsonville
Hollister
Castroville
Salinas
Monterey
Soledad
Merced
Mammoth Lakes
Kerman
Fresno
Visalia
Coalinga
Avenal
Porterville
Atascadero
Paso Robles
Cambria
McFarland
Shafter
Bakersfield
Morro Bay
San Luis Obispo
Pismo Beach
Santa Maria
Tehachapi
Lompoc
Solvang
Santa Barbara
Carpinteria
Lancaster
Palmdale
Simi Valley
Santa Clarita
Ventura
Oxnard
Glendale
Pasadena
Los Angeles
Inglewood
Torrance
1
5
80
101
99
395

the Vaud or Asti or the Saar. In Napa, Charles Krug established a winery in the 1850s, and it was soon doing a roaring trade. Jacob Schram founded his Schramsberg winery near Calistoga in 1863, and the wineries of Beringer, Inglenook, and Greystone soon followed, the latter being established by 1889. The sheer size of the existing Inglenook and Beringer wineries demonstrates how important the industry had become in Napa Valley. Other, if much smaller, stone wineries on the slopes and mountainsides on all sides of the valley are reminders that artisanal wine production flourished in the same area. Though these wineries were remote, their owners knew that elevation diminished the risk of frost, which was a constant threat on the valley floor.

The valley-floor plantings, as well as the wineries, were on a grand scale. A grower by the name of HW Crabb planted hundreds of acres in Oakville. The site, still known by the name he gave it—To Kalon—is a sea of vines, owned mostly by the Robert Mondavi winery. Because the plantings were substantial in area, growers such as Crabb were able to experiment with different varieties. In adjacent Rutherford, William Watson planted what soon became the Inglenook vineyard, which was bought in 1879 by wealthy Finnish sea captain and trader Gustave Niebaum. It was he who built the magnificent winery that is today part cellar, part museum on Francis Ford Coppola's Rubicon Estate. Niebaum also expanded the range of varieties in the vineyard and bottled his own wines rather than sell the grapes or wines to wholesalers. So Napa Valley began to appear on wine labels, giving recognition to this still young area.

The Sonoma industry was, in contrast, dominated by a single individual—the flamboyant Hungarian poseur Agoston Haraszthy, who invented a noble and military background for himself. After a spell as an adventurer in the Midwest, he came to California in 1848. He dabbled, not very successfully, in vineyards in San Diego and San Mateo but fared better with a vineyard in Sonoma that he named Buena Vista. Well connected politically, he persuaded the governor of California to send him to Europe to look into contemporary viticulture. After a wide-ranging tour, Haraszthy returned with 100,000 cuttings from more than 1,000 varieties—or so it is claimed. As an ampelographer and nurseryman, Haraszthy was disorganized, so no one is quite sure what varieties he imported and where the cuttings were planted. This may explain why some of the more ancient vineyards of California still contain rows of vines that have resisted identification. Haraszthy ran into financial difficulties, which could surely have surprised no one, and went off to pursue new ventures in Nicaragua, where in 1869 he vanished and, it is assumed, died.

Sonoma takeover

Sonoma's vineyards leapt ahead of Napa's in area, and by the mid-1870s, they were producing more wine than any other county in the state, with Los Angeles close behind. Sonoma's topography lent itself to large-scale plantings, such as the famous Italian-Swiss Colony at Asti in northern Sonoma, which was founded in the 1880s; half a century later, it was the country's largest winery. Italian immigrants were quick to establish vineyards as part of mixed farms throughout the county. In southern California, new ranches in areas like Cucamonga replaced the vanished vineyards of Los Angeles, and by the time of Prohibition, they were of considerable economic importance.

It is hard to say how good these early wines were. The climate must have posed a challenge to white-wine producers, and it's likely they were made in an oxidative or fortified style. Inferior red varieties would have led to many mediocre reds, but robust varieties such as Zinfandel and Carignane should have resulted in decent enough wines from experienced winemakers. All the same, stuck fermentations must have been a common complaint, and high volatile acidity must often have led to spoilage. So bad and adulterated were some of the wines that the state legislature had to pass laws to ban the worst practices. On the other hand, proprietors with deep pockets, such as Gustave Niebaum and Charles Krug, were able to invest in such innovations as grape sorting and hygienic practices that prevented the spoilage that damaged many other wines. The noble varieties, however, were slow to make an appearance, and the first varietal Cabernet Sauvignon was not recorded until 1882 in Sonoma.

The first exports

By 1869, a rail network was in place that would transport wines, usually in barrel, to other parts of the country, and this provided a major economic boost to the industry. In the decades that followed, California entrepreneurs were able to sell the state's wines to parts of the world as remote and disparate as Australia and East Asia. This, in turn, encouraged further vineyard expansion, and by 1887 there were almost 17,000 acres (6,900ha) under vine in Napa alone. However, in a scenario that was to be repeated almost a century later, growers were encouraged to plant vines on a supposedly disease-resistant rootstock. This was an error, and the dread phylloxera louse was soon munching its way through the valley. Thousands of acres succumbed, and some of them would not be replanted until long after Prohibition ended. Yet viticulture survived, and growers who had the means and the motivation to replant, did so, employing the latest techniques, such as trellising along wires. Better varieties were being planted, too: Frenchman Georges de Latour, who came to Napa in 1899 and founded Beaulieu a decade later, brought native varieties such as Sauvignon Blanc, Pinot Noir, and Cabernet Sauvignon. A shortage of supply led to higher prices, yet that seemed to do the reputation of Napa wines no harm. In 1900, wines from California and other states won medals at the Paris Exposition.

Just as recovery was getting under way, there were two major setbacks. The first was an act of nature, while the second was a fit of morality that overcame the American people. The San Francisco earthquake of April 1906 did terrible damage to warehouses there, and many millions of gallons of wine were lost. Outside the city, wineries were damaged, too, and some carefully nurtured inventories, such as at the Paul Masson winery, vanished overnight.

But Prohibition would prove a far greater obstacle. Alcohol and alcoholism were undoubtedly genuine problems, though bourbon and rye probably accounted for more drunken shoot-outs in the saloons than Alicante Bouschet or Riesling. The temperance movement did not make such fine distinctions, however, and a decade before Prohibition became law, many states were already dry, and restrictions on the consumption of alcoholic drinks were widespread.

Prohibition

Enacted in 1919, Prohibition was to prove a long-term disaster; but in the short term, many people, and not only bootleggers, did rather nicely out of it. The sale of wine (and other alcoholic beverages) may have been prohibited, but there was nothing in the law to prevent grapes being cultivated. Vineyard expansion continued unabated, at least until the mid-1920s. It remained legal to produce your own fruit juice at home—up to 200 gallons (750 liters) per year; and to make grape juice, you needed grapes, or at least grape concentrate, which was more transportable. Enormous quantities of these raw materials were shipped from California to the cities of the Midwest and the east, so it's no wonder that vineyards continued to flourish. Not all varieties

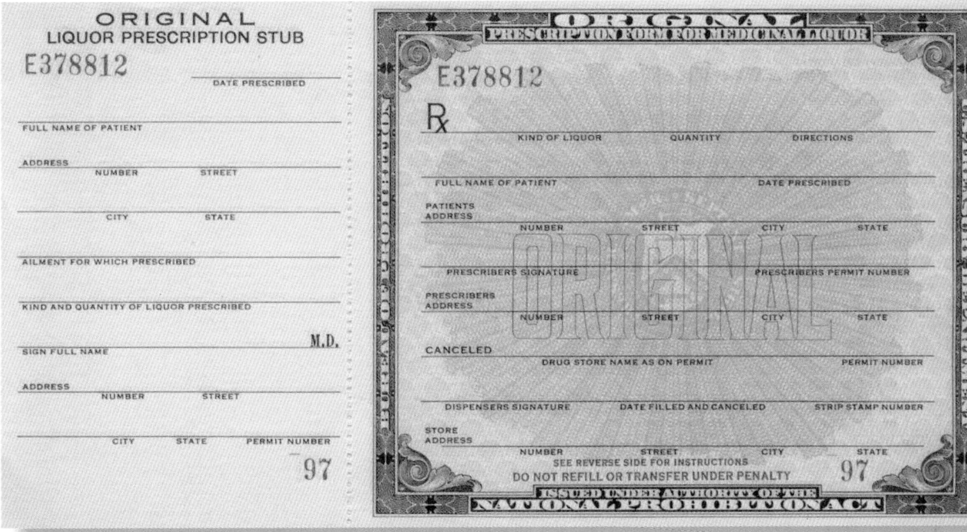

ORIGINAL
LIQUOR PRESCRIPTION STUB
E378812
DATE PRESCRIBED
FULL NAME OF PATIENT
ADDRESS NUMBER STREET
CITY STATE
AILMENT FOR WHICH PRESCRIBED
KIND AND QUANTITY OF LIQUOR PRESCRIBED
SIGN FULL NAME M.D.
ADDRESS NUMBER STREET
CITY STATE PERMIT NUMBER
97

ORIGINAL
PRESCRIPTION FORM FOR MEDICINAL LIQUOR
E378812
Rx
KIND OF LIQUOR QUANTITY DIRECTIONS
FULL NAME OF PATIENT DATE PRESCRIBED
PATIENTS ADDRESS NUMBER STREET CITY STATE
ORIGINAL
PRESCRIBERS SIGNATURE PRESCRIBERS PERMIT NUMBER
PRESCRIBERS ADDRESS NUMBER STREET CITY STATE
CANCELED DRUG STORE NAME AS ON PERMIT PERMIT NUMBER
DISPENSERS SIGNATURE DATE FILLED AND CANCELED STRIP STAMP NUMBER
STORE ADDRESS NUMBER STREET CITY STATE
SEE REVERSE SIDE FOR INSTRUCTIONS
DO NOT REFILL OR TRANSFER UNDER PENALTY
97
ISSUED UNDER AUTHORITY OF THE
NATIONAL PROHIBITION ACT

Above: Wine may still have been available for medicinal purposes, but fine wine suffered serious setbacks during Prohibition

were equally suitable for long-term shipments, so thick-skinned varieties such as Alicante Bouschet and Petite Sirah were preferred to the more fragile Cabernets and Riesling. As American winemaker and writer Philip Wagner put it, "Prohibition proved merely to be a ban on superior wines" (*American Wines and Wine-Making*, p.51).

Wine could also continue to be sold for sacramental purposes. Although there was a finite supply of Catholic priests who needed wine to administer communion, the number of potential rabbis, who also need wine for religious ceremonies, was infinite. Just as cannabis, in some states of the Union, is legal when used for medicinal purposes, so in the 1920s medicinal wine was permitted. Paul Masson's "Medicinal Champagne," among other similar products, proved very popular.

The vineyard boom was over by the mid-1920s, and despite all the loopholes, Prohibition was biting hard by the early 1930s, so Repeal in 1933 came none too soon for the ailing industry. Surviving wineries such as Beaulieu, Inglenook, and Louis Martini were able to resume production, but many wineries had folded for good. The pool of good-quality wine grapes had shrunk severely, and wineries were crammed with outdated, rusting, unhygienic equipment. Moreover, with the Great Depression under way, few had the means to invest. In any case, there was little market for fine wines. For nearly 15 years, the American wine-drinking public had made do with rotgut or switched to spirits. Sweet and fortified wines seem to be what the consumers of the 1930s wanted, and that is what the wineries provided. Sherry- and Port-style wines, as well as Muscats, would dominate the market until the late 1960s.

Varietal wines remained a tiny corner of the market, and larger wineries specialized in proprietary blends such as Martini's Mountain Red. Vintage, variety, and origin counted for nothing. Such wines may have been drinkable, but they did little to nurture the kind of wine culture that

California required if high-quality wines were to find a market. Surviving wine connoisseurs looked to Europe rather than California.

The road to recovery

There were glimmers of light in the gloom. The enology department at the University of California at Davis continued its research and was able to recommend appropriate varieties and yeast selections. Russian-born André Tchelistcheff came to Beaulieu in 1936 and created one of America's finest wines, the Georges de Latour Private Reserve. Excellent though this wine was, the winemaker's importance went far beyond the confines of Rutherford. He trained generations of younger winemakers, consulted for 80 wineries, and brought up-to-date technology to California. He introduced temperature-controlled fermentation and was also one of the first to understand the importance of malolactic fermentation. He retired from Beaulieu in 1973 but lived well into his 90s, continuing to consult and advise. He died a revered figure in 1994. At the other end of the production line, wine importer Frank Schoonmaker was encouraging wineries to adopt varietal and regional labeling. In the 1940s, he would distribute and give nationwide recognition to the best wines that California was producing.

A handful of other forceful personalities kept the cause of fine wine alive. One of them was Martin Ray, who bought the Paul Masson winery in 1936. He insisted on making 100 percent varietal wines at a time when only half a bottled wine needed to be produced from the variety identified on the label. Enthusiastic winemakers such as James Zellerbach at Hanzell, Fred McCrea at Stony Hill, and Lee Stewart at Souverain were making very good wines, but volumes were small. The major producers were cooperatives and companies such as Gallo. Indeed, in 1952, Gallo purchased the total production of the Napa Cooperative Winery, an organization that was vinifying almost half the total production of the valley. In Sonoma, some of the old Italian wineries had kept going: Foppiano, Sebastiani, Pedroncelli, and Simi. In the East Bay, Wente and Concannon had also survived Prohibition.

California redux

Napa finally hauled itself out of stagnation in the 1960s. Plantings increased—and with more noble varieties. There were more than 10,000 acres (4,000ha) under vine in Napa, but this was half the surface planted in the 1890s. In 1960, there was a grand total of 25 wineries in Napa Valley, but gradually new wineries were being established, and not just on a tiny scale, at Schramsberg, Heitz, Freemark Abbey, Mayacamas, and Sterling. Large beverage companies began to take an interest in Napa Valley, and Heublein bought (and later came close to destroying) the legendary Beaulieu in 1969. Inglenook, too, was sold and later came into the hands of Heublein, which increased production of this once revered name to 4 million cases—hardly any of it, of course, from Napa Valley.

Vineyards were expanding, and not only in Napa, but so were centers of population. Vineyards and housing developments were incompatible, and it was usually the vines that lost out. Old-timers can recall celebrated sites that once flourished in Santa Rosa that have long been concreted over. The vineyards of Santa Clara would soon vanish as Silicon Valley expanded. Some far-sighted Napa growers and wineries realized that their comparatively small valley, a mere hour's drive from San Francisco, could easily suffer the same fate, becoming a community of dormitory towns at the expense of vineyards. Property developers were able to make offers that grape farmers found increasingly difficult to resist. The battle for Napa was resolved in 1968, when the valley was designated an Agricultural

Preserve. This placed restrictions on urban development and, in effect, protected vineyards from the grasp of financial speculators. The Napa communities have continued to maintain a fine balance between providing the hotels, restaurants, tasting rooms, and resorts that tourists require, and preserving the vineyards on which the valley's economy depends.

Sonoma, too, was reborn, about a decade later than Napa. In the mid-1970s, wineries such as Jordan, Chateau St. Jean, and Matanzas Creek, all making wines of fine quality, were established by wealthy investors. In Santa Cruz, Ridge and Mount Eden were already producing memorable wines. Away from the North Coast, untested areas such as the Salinas Valley in Monterey were being opened up for vineyard development by schemes that were essentially tax shelters. Some poor decisions were made by people who knew more about dollars and cents than agriculture, but eventually the growers of Monterey worked out what to plant and where to plant it. Santa Barbara was also seeing vineyard expansion: in the warm Santa Ynez Valley, where Firestone was proving to be a commercially successful winery; and in the cooler Santa Maria Valley, where Au Bon Climat and others were making headway with Burgundian varieties.

The Chardonnay boom

Chardonnay was becoming increasingly popular in Napa and Sonoma, with Chateau Montelena and Heitz making great strides with a variety that was little known in California. James Zellerbach sought to imitate white Burgundy at his Sonoma Valley estate, Hanzell, in the late 1950s. So swift was its expansion and so popular were the wines that, by the 1980s, Chardonnay had become synonymous with white wine. It even spawned its own rather snobbish backlash movement—ABC, Anything But Chardonnay—from drinkers weary of its ubiquity.

Wineries were springing up all over the place in the late 1960s and 1970s, but by far the most significant was the founding of a new winery by Robert Mondavi in 1966. The Mondavi family had been involved in winemaking since the 1930s, but a monumental quarrel between Robert and his brother Peter led the former to head off on his own and, with much help from outside investors, set up his own business in the heart of Oakville. Although Robert Mondavi was Californian to the core, he knew that its wines would always be held up for comparison against the classic wines of France. Mondavi, driven by a thirst for perfection, allowed his team to experiment with the latest ideas in viticulture and winemaking. He spent large sums studying barrels—their origins, their coopers, their toasts. Remarkably, when he and his team reached a conclusion, they were happy to share the results with other winemakers, thus allowing California as a whole to raise its game.

The Judgment of Paris

Much has been written of the celebrated Judgment of Paris tasting in 1976, but it was truly a moment of enormous, if unexpected, importance. Steven Spurrier, an enthusiastic and open-minded English wine merchant who was occupying himself in Paris by teaching the French to appreciate their own wines, decided it would be interesting to taste the best of California alongside the best of France. By keeping his ear close to the ground, he knew, or at least got to hear about, the most exciting wines emerging from California. The distinguished French judges, as is well known, made fools of themselves, discerning indisputably French finesse in wines that would turn out to be from California. In short, the French wines were trounced (and when the blind-tasting of the red wines was repeated in 2006, I, alongside most other judges, still gave the highest scores to some of the California entries). Had it not been

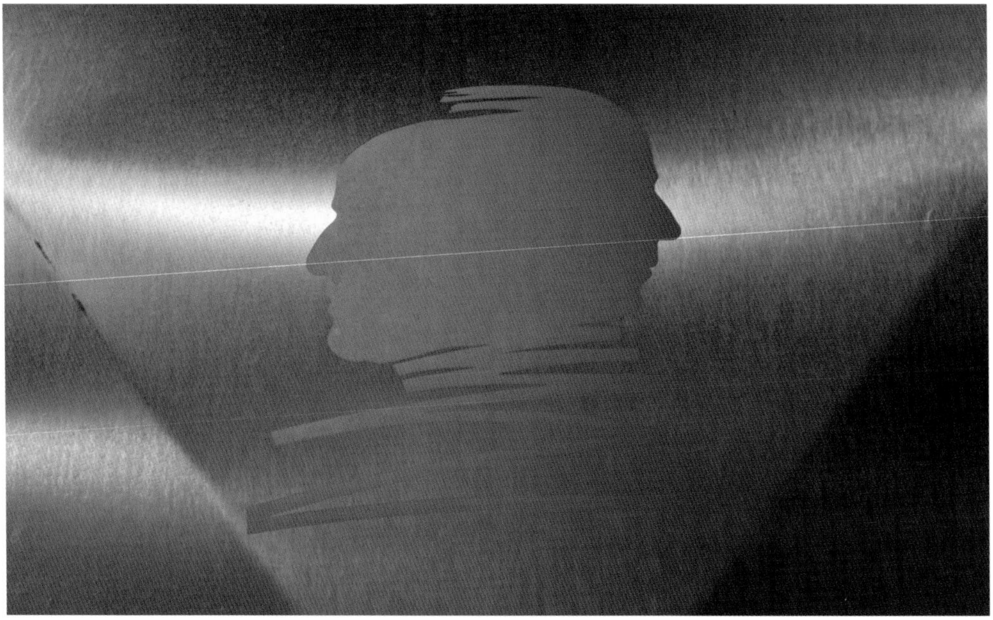

Above: The Opus One logo—on tanks, as well as on labels—affirmed the equal status of its American and European partners

for the almost accidental appearance at the tasting of *Time* magazine's Paris correspondent George Taber, the event might have gone unnoticed, but thanks to Taber's eye for a good story, Spurrier's fine idea—and its outcome—became an international sensation.

A new gold rush

The significance of the Paris tasting was not that California wines were demonstrably better than the first growths of Bordeaux; it was that the California bottles could be spoken of without condescension in their company. The results must have gratified Paul Draper at Ridge and Warren Winiarski at Stag's Leap Wine Cellars; but they must also have encouraged other investors and winemakers, who were not slow to recognize the enormous potential of California's vines and wines.

Some of those investors were European. The Skalli family from southern France developed the large St. Supéry Vineyards & Winery in Napa. Christian Moueix from Libourne, a graduate of Davis, created Dominus in Yountville. The Woltners of La Mission Haut-Brion made an admittedly brief appearance on Howell Mountain. The German Racke family acquired Buena Vista in Carneros. The Japanese Mercian company bought Markham in Napa Valley in 1988. Beringer, Chateau St. Jean, and Meridian are all owned by the Australian Foster's Group. Swiss magnate Donald Hess bought the former Christian Brothers winery and made it his own. None of this came as much of a surprise, since the example had been set by two of the grandest names in the wine world—Baron Philippe de Rothschild and Robert Mondavi—when they created Opus One, striking the deal in 1978. The significance was enormous, since it was seen as a marriage of equals, an impression confirmed by the label featuring the profiles of both men. Nor could it conceivably be perceived as an act of condescension by the Frenchman, since in the early years at any rate, most of the grapes for Opus One came from the Mondavis' own vineyards.

College education

The evolution of the industry was stimulated by the educational programs of the viticulture and enology departments at Davis and also at Fresno.

UC Davis professors created the heat-summation scale, dividing California's wine regions into five zones, depending on how much sunshine each received. It would later prove to be a rather crude measuring stick, but it was at least a step in the right direction in deciding what should be planted where. With many new vineyard areas appearing in the 1970s, such knowledge was indispensable.

There is some truth to the accusation that the teaching at Davis was designed to benefit the large companies that needed squads of technically proficient winemakers, rather than those who conceived of winemaking as an art. Davis taught its students to play safe, not to take chances with hard-to-control "natural" fermentations, and to centrifuge and filter to ensure the cleanest juice and, some would argue, the most characterless wine. One veteran winemaker told me his first task with young recruits was to undo everything they had been taught at Davis. Nonetheless, many of California's most distinguished and adventurous winemakers have been Davis graduates. It's arguable that, without the secure technical basis of a Davis education, they may have lacked the courage to take their own winemaking skills and techniques in a different direction.

The university performed another useful role in propagating and supplying virus-free clones. Many of these clones were selected for their productivity or their resistance to disease rather than for the quality of the wines they were likely to produce, but exactly the same was still true of many European research institutes and nurseries at this time.

Phylloxera strikes again

Davis did, however, make one enormous error, when it recommended the use of the AxR-1 rootstock for new plantings, even though it was not proven to be entirely resistant to phylloxera. When phylloxera returned in the 1980s, the vineyards planted on AxR-1 were swift to succumb, while those planted on less highly recommended St. George rootstock weathered the outbreak.

The economic cost of the return of phylloxera was enormous, since huge tracts of vineyard had to be replanted. On the other hand, it allowed viticulturists and wineries to start from scratch, doing a better job of adapting variety to site, choosing sagely from a wider selection of clones, revising ideas on spacing and trellising, and so forth. What emerged from the disaster of phylloxera was a modern vineyard fully able to compete on many levels with those in the rest of the world.

Expansion and consolidation

Throughout the 1990s, wineries mushroomed all over the state. Their number had risen from 27 in 1966, to more than 800 by 1995. Some were created by growers who decided it was more profitable to bottle and market their own wines than to sell to other wineries. Others were lifestyle acquisitions, allowing very rich men and women to pursue a fashionable retirement project. Many were carting away from Silicon Valley immense fortunes they were eager to invest in enjoyable ways. Some labels were primarily known through the annual Napa Valley Wine Auction, a charitable event that encouraged American wine lovers to bid enormous sums for collectible wines in the full gratifying glare of publicity. Bill Harlan—the owner of Napa's Meadowood Resort, as well as his eponymous winery and label—created the Napa Valley Reserve, a kind of timeshare vineyard and restaurant; its members were recruited from the super-wealthy, who could fly in with their friends for a weekend, prune their rows of vines, and then enjoy a fine dinner with the costliest wines, including their own wine (made for them by the Reserve's resident winemaker), with their name on the label.

As long as you had the money, it was not difficult to achieve the social glory of being a Napa producer.

All that was required was a small parcel of well-located vines, preferably Cabernet Sauvignon; a prestigious consultant winemaker, who would not only make your wine but ensure it was reviewed by the best-known critics; and a mailing list through which to sell the deliberately limited production. The combination of good Cabernet vines and a famous name at the winemaking helm made it more probable than not that the wine would achieve a high score. This would then justify a high price tag and give the wine the celebrity it needed to become sought after. There was no need to build a winery; there were plenty of facilities in the valley that offered winemaking space (known as custom-crush) and barrel storage to consultant winemakers.

But there were limits to expansion. By the year 2000, Napa Valley was running out of plantable land, especially since environmental regulations, brought in to preserve water resources and combat erosion, made it increasingly difficult for entrepreneurs to buy land and plant vines. Other parts of California had land aplenty for would-be wine-label owners, but no other region had the prestige of Napa. The economic crisis of 2008 put the brakes on this kind of vanity operation; there was clearly a limit to the number of wines priced at more than $150 a bottle that a shrinking band of rich collectors and consumers was prepared to buy, especially since many of those wines had no track record, and the only proof of their quality was a score from one or more critics.

At the same time, there were signs of consolidation within the industry. Prestigious wineries—Mondavi, Ravenswood, Simi, Clos du Bois, Franciscan—were swallowed up by the mighty Constellation group. Beringer Blass (later owned by the Foster's Wine Group of Australia) owned Beringer, Meridian, Souverain, Chateau St. Jean, and other labels. This did not necessarily lead to a decline in quality, at least at the top levels. Jess Jackson, with more than 10,000 acres (4,000ha) of vineyards under his belt, created a range of "Family Estates," purchasing wineries but giving them considerable autonomy. These include Cambria, Arrowood, Stonestreet, Edmeades, Matanzas Creek, Hartford, and La Crema. Jackson created limited-production labels featuring certain styles of wine or wines from certain locations; among such labels are Vérité, Atalon, and Lokoya. In short, California had come to resemble most other mature wine industries, with small privately owned estates jostling for position alongside immense corporate entities, with a marketing muscle the smaller properties could not hope to match. But then the corporate entities had difficulty winning the kind of prestige for their products that a small but well-rated private estate with perfectionist ideals could obtain.

Surviving the crisis

Despite the economic crisis of 2008 and 2009, the California wine industry will survive. The domestic consumer base is very solid, and whole generations have now been raised on California wine. They know what they like, and they are prepared to pay for favorite labels and wines. One cannot dispute that, at the higher levels, the wines are very well made. Whether you consider that they offer good value or whether you like their style is a personal matter, but there is sufficient variety so that all kinds of consumer—from unassuming types partial to an off-dry Gewurztraminer, to followers of fashion keen on trying the latest hot Pinots, to the ultra-rich who want the right labels in their cellars, even if they rarely drink them—can find something. Even the denizens of bargain basements are quite well served; a recent tasting of Two Buck Chuck Chardonnay revealed an acceptable wine. The greatest wines of California are now international classics. No industry could ask for more.

JUSTIN
5½
MPH
A
Bray Vineyards

A Democracy of Wine

California is a democracy of wine. Wineries prosper at the whims of the market and decline for the same reason. This means that fashion can move more swiftly than a lumbering agricultural industry can respond to it. When the engaging but far from profound film *Sideways* put the Merlot variety out to pasture and gave top billing to Pinot Noir, this was bad luck for growers who still had thousands of acres of Merlot in the ground. (Fortunately, American wine law allows Pinot producers to blend in 15 percent of any other variety, including Merlot, so that can mop up some surplus production.) High scores from critics can propel previously obscure wineries to instant stardom, with a consequent effect on their sales and profitability, while the next hot winery can result in the slow descent to oblivion of the stars that twinkled so brightly a few years earlier.

Although this democratization of wine can lead to some unfortunate extremes, it is still a welcome feature. It makes it difficult for both producers and, indeed, regions to coast along on the basis of reputations that became tarnished long ago. Wineries cannot hide behind AOC or DOC labels or QmP authorizations. Either consumers like your wines, or they don't. In Europe, most wine producers, other than large négociant companies, are tied to estates, and that makes it very difficult for wineries to change gears or react swiftly to changes in market conditions. It can take years to alter the composition of your estate, and if you exist in a monovarietal region such as the Côte d'Or or the Rheingau, you simply have to weather any fads that decree your specialty will no longer do.

In California—and indeed, in other parts of the New World—the structure is very different. The estate winery is in a minority. Most wineries obtain grapes from outside sources. In the case of many quality-oriented wineries, this means contracts with leading growers. These, like any contract, are subject to renewal, but in many instances they are evergreen contracts that satisfy winery and grower alike, so long as the winery is happy with the quality of the grapes and the grower is happy with the price he obtains. Alternatively, or in addition, there is the spot market. Crush reports published each year make it very clear what the market price is for each grape variety in each region and give a basis for wineries to purchase fruit at various levels of the hierarchy of quality.

This gives wineries considerable flexibility. Shortfalls from one source can be replaced by supplies from another. An unexpected phone call from a grower eager to sell 100 tons of Sangiovese at a very advantageous price can lead to a new addition to the range. Similarly, the cancellation or loss of a contract can mean that the Bien Nacido Chardonnay, long a mainstay of your portfolio, is no longer available, and you must decide how to placate your customers. So, there is flexibility on the one hand and instability on the other. Fortunately, most consumers have fairly short memories—and anyway, few people can recall precisely which vineyard-designated wines were available the year before. Therefore, the surprise addition of new vineyard-designated wines need not offer a marketing problem, as long as the wine is as good as the wine it replaces.

Thoroughly domesticated

California also differs from other wine regions in the strength of its home market. In contrast, South Africa and Chile produce a great deal of wine, but domestic sales are limited. For such countries, export is essential to build recognition for the brand and to generate income. Wineries must be ready to spend considerable sums on export sales offices, participation in international wine fairs and competitions, and other forms of marketing. But this is not only a feature of New World wines.

Right: The freedom of the open road, here enjoyed by Mark Pisoni, is mirrored in the state's fast-moving wine culture

CALIFORNIA

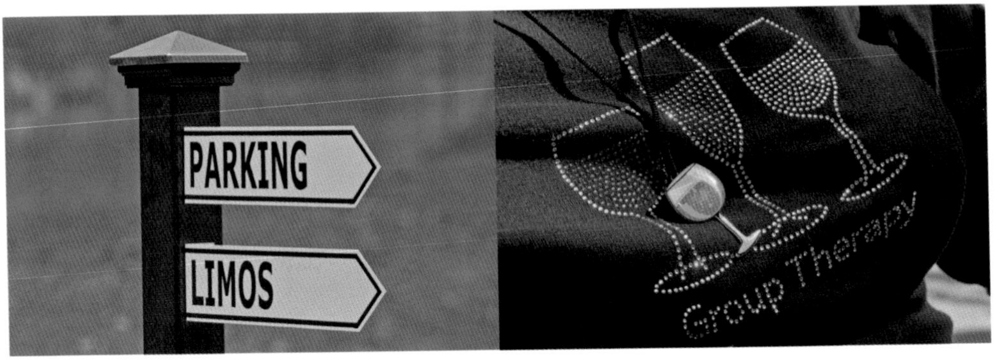

Above: At the state's many festivals and wineries, the boldly exclusive and communally festive happily coexist

Chablis would collapse were it not able to sell 90 percent of its production outside France.

In California, many wineries do make an effort to export, but it is not, except for very large companies, seen as essential. Domestic demand for prestigious wines such as Harlan Estate means that Mr. Harlan can save himself the trouble of finding importers and agents throughout the world. If a few dozen cases do slip into Moscow or London or Milan, that is more for the gratification of seeing the wine on top restaurant wine lists than because it makes any difference to the winery's bottom line.

Status symbols

Wine is associated with status in most parts of the world. At the top end, it has always been a luxury product. Successful businessmen yearn to become the owners of a classed growth in Bordeaux or a *fattoria* in Tuscany, and this is equally true of California. While it requires a huge outlay of cash to acquire a prestigious estate in France or Italy, such ambition can be achieved for a lesser cost in California, as has been explained in the previous chapter. There may be an international aristocracy of wine, but all you need to enter those circles is a fair amount of disposable income and a willingness to lose money—at least initially.

On the other hand, the consumer is regarded as all-important. In Bordeaux, a château owner need not worry much about nurturing the consumers of his wine, since it is all sold to merchants. Brand loyalty does exist, but it does not have to be assiduously cultivated. Not so in California. Wineries know consumers are fickle, blown this way and that by the latest gusts of wine scores, PR, word-of-mouth experiences, bloggers, and other forms of communication. With dozens of wineries competing for the same consumers, personal communication is highly rated. Tasting rooms, while expensive to operate, can be very lucrative. The costs can be substantial, since friendly and informed staff need to be hired, but the returns can be, too: tasting fees (usually refundable if a purchase is made), subsidiary sales of branded clothing and local foodstuffs, and the fact that all wines are sold at full price, since consumers, unlike distributors, do not demand discounts. It also opens a direct link between wineries and consumers that can be of immense importance. I have often noticed, as I lurk in winery tasting rooms, how many of those who arrive are repeat customers. For some wineries, sales generated in the tasting room contribute quite substantially to turnover. They also make a less measurable contribution to wine culture.

In 1998, I visited Matanzas Creek in Sonoma, then famous, or notorious, for releasing Journey at $75, making it America's highest-priced Merlot. I had tasted the Merlot Reserve, which was very good, and could find little difference between that $40 wine and Journey at almost twice the price. I asked the winemakers how this price difference could be justified, and other than some mumbling about barrel selection, the response was a shrug of the shoulders. Consumers, especially those not actually living in the California hothouse, are still mystified by the pricing of much California wine. Sometimes, it does indeed reflect quality. But it also has to do with market positioning, the wish of one proprietor to have his wine in the same bracket as those from some better-known neighbors. It may also have to do with scarcity, but often this scarcity is an artificial construct. Just because you have only 1 acre (2.47ha) of Cabernet Sauvignon doesn't seem a sufficient justification to price your wine outrageously on the grounds that there is little available. This is *garagisme*.

Often the most convincing explanation for the excessive price of some wines, especially but not solely from Napa Valley, is the high cost of land and vineyard development. Land is ferociously expensive in other parts of the world, such as Burgundy, but sales and acquisitions are relatively infrequent. When the deep-pocketed François Pinault, owner of Château Latour and much else, bought Domaine Engel in Vosne-Romanée for what was then considered an outlandish sum, concerns were raised about how this would affect land evaluation and inheritance taxes for his less prosperous neighbors. Even though there is little land left to buy or develop in Napa Valley, there are frequent transactions, especially when a grower cannot resist the checks being waved in his direction. The current price for prime Napa vineyard land is around $300,000 per acre. Mountain sites may cost less, but purchasers will need to spend a fortune on access roads, permits, and vineyard development.

Return on investment

Naturally, the owners of such expensive land will hope to recoup some or all of their costs. If they have constructed a winery rather than use leased space, those costs must be added to the investment. Sometimes, vanity or the sheer love of wine may be the motivation for acquiring such expensive property, but in most instances, investment is the guiding spirit. It is, of course, up to consumers to decide whether the very high prices demanded for many California bottles are justified, but a surprising number of American wine drinkers have been perfectly happy to pay prices equivalent to a Bordeaux super-second or even first growth for a wine with a rather scant track record. None of this is unique to California, but the scale is considerably magnified. Even the very finest wines of Australia or Chile (or Italy, for that matter) are not released at prices that many Napa wine fans consider normal.

Dreams of glory

Moreover, there are few equivalents in California to a German Gutsriesling or a modest Rosso di Montalcino or Montepulciano—a simple wine designed for everyday drinking. I have no doubt that everyone who buys or develops a vineyard in Napa Valley is convinced they will make a great wine; the notion that there could be second-rate land capable of producing only second-rate wines in Napa, Dry Creek Valley, or Santa Rita Hills is simply alien to most proprietors. As the wine editor of the *San Francisco Chronicle*, Jon Bonné, put it to me in a recent conversation, "All California wineries dream of glory. No one is content to make a vin de pays." To aspire to be the best is admirable; to fail to recognize that not all vineyards are equal—on the part of owners, as well as consumers—is an expensive mistake.

Defining California

The vineyards of California stretch all the way from Mendocino in the north down to San Diego, close to the Mexican border. There are considerable variations in climate, soil types, elevation, maritime influence, and other factors—all of which make nonsense of charts that pin down the quality of a vintage with a single number. A great year in Sonoma may be mediocre in Santa Barbara, and vice versa. Longitude is a significant factor, since the more one moves inland from the coast, the hotter it tends to be.

American Viticultural Areas

The major unit in defining regions is the county—as in Napa, Monterey, or Santa Barbara—and wines made from anywhere within a single county will carry the county appellation, unless the grapes are predominantly from a defined subregion such as Oakville in Napa or Carmel Valley in Monterey. These subregions are known as AVAs, or American Viticultural Areas, which first came into being in 1978. These are legally defined and can range from half a county in size (Sonoma Coast) to minuscule (Cole Ranch in Mendocino, with 60 acres [24ha] and no wineries). They are as much political as geographical entities and are created after a grower or group of growers successfully petitions the federal authorities. The motivation for so doing may be to increase the visibility or establish the identity of a particular area and its wines. Sometimes it is hard to discern what the motivation could possibly have been, so obscure is the AVA and so rarely is it glimpsed on a wine label.

How AVAs are made

The authorities need to be persuaded that there is a geographical or topographical cohesion to an area before a petition can succeed. Dossiers will be drawn up and expert opinion solicited from soil experts, historians, and meteorologists, plus lawyers are hired to make the case—a process that can take many years. Thus, the area now known as the Santa Rita Hills AVA in Santa Barbara was formerly part of the Santa Ynez Valley AVA, but the growers there argued, successfully, that the Santa Rita Hills were climatically distinct and deserved to be separated from the large Santa Ynez appellation. What the growers did not need to establish was that their wines were better. Quality is irrelevant. So long as a vineyard lies within the strictly defined boundaries of an AVA, its production can be labeled as coming from that AVA, however miserable the wine itself. In this respect, the American system differs radically from European systems such as the French AOC or the Italian DOC. The stated aim of the system is to "help consumers better identify the wines they may purchase, and [to] help winemakers distinguish their products from wines made in other areas." Vague? It is meant to be. It is not the role of an AVA to specify permitted grape varieties, crop levels, farming practices, or winemaking styles; it does no more than identify a geographical area.

Grounds for controversy

As AVAs proliferated, wineries that incorporated regional names without being based within those regions were faced with a dilemma. It was tempting for some wineries to name themselves after prestigious regions such as Napa or Rutherford, even if they used few or no grapes from that region. Before AVAs, it was hard to raise objections to the practice, but once AVAs had been defined, it was reasonable for consumers to assume that a winery called Rutherford Heights had a connection with the Rutherford AVA. On the other hand, long-established wineries were loath to change their brand names to fit in with legislation created long after the brands became established. This has been fertile ground for lawyers, who have agreed with the authorities a series of acceptable compromises.

Right: The legislation governing areas of production applies to the whole country, but the details are decided at state level

CALIFORNIA REPUBLIC

The petitioning process itself can be fraught with controversy. When discussions were taking place about the creation of the Stags Leap District AVA, there were angry debates about where the boundaries should be drawn. Because the new AVA, it was rightly assumed, would create what we would call "added value" for wines bearing its label, many estates wanted to be embraced within its boundaries. Were some valley-floor properties included, the specificity of the new AVA, and its prestige, would be diluted. On the other hand, valley-floor properties close to the proposed boundaries were bound to fight for inclusion. So the process is rarely without its *Sturm und Drang*.

If a wine is made from grapes from two AVAs—for example, a blend of Russian River Valley and Dry Creek Valley—the resulting wine can only be labeled as Sonoma County. If grapes are sourced from two counties, such as Mendocino and Sonoma, the wine must bear the California appellation.

Blurring the boundaries

What remains confusing, however, is that in some counties, AVAs are not discrete entities—thus, Green Valley is an AVA within the Russian River Valley AVA, and its growers may use either appellation on the label. However, Russian River Valley AVA is within the larger Northern Sonoma AVA, which carries less prestige than the Russian River appellation. Northern Sonoma is essentially an appellation used for blends from disparate regions within the northern part of the county, created at the behest of a very large winery because it gave the—possibly erroneous—impression of carrying more prestige than the widely used Sonoma County appellation. No consumer can be expected to memorize such complexities.

The principal AVAs are listed and discussed in the introductions to the regional chapters. The vast Central Valley that runs, roughly speaking, from Sacramento in the north to Bakersfield in the south is entitled to various AVAs, but these are so rarely used on labels (since the Central Valley is California's bulk-wine region) that there is no point listing and defining them in the context of this book.

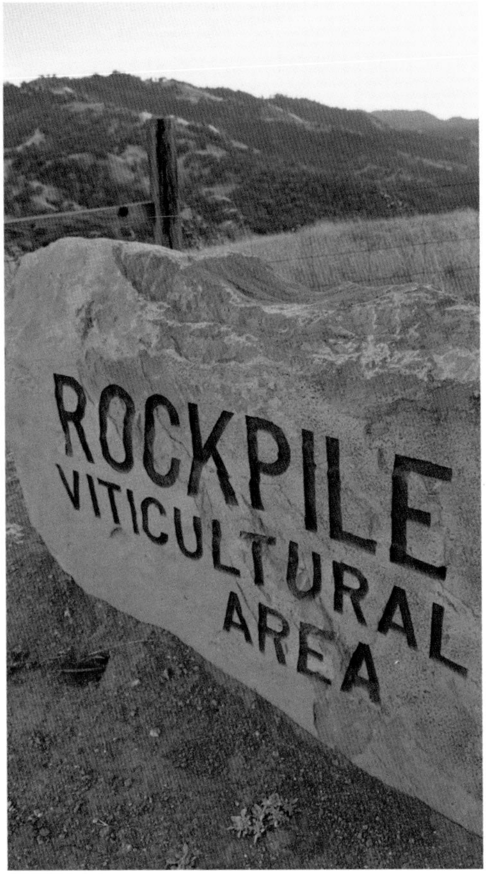

Above: AVAs are essentially geographical entities, but some, such as Rockpile (2002) are meaningful in wine terms, too

As AVAs become established, some do convey useful information to the curious wine lover. Thus, many aficionados of Napa Valley wines are aware that fruit grown at high elevations—from AVAs such as Mount Veeder, Diamond Mountain,

Howell Mountain, and Spring Mountain—do have a character distinct from valley-floor or benchland AVAs such as Oakville or Oak Knoll. This may aid consumers with defined stylistic preferences. Nonetheless, too many AVAs were too casually granted and, in the process, defined regions with no discernible typicity. In such cases, consumers are probably ill served by their mere existence.

Legal requirements

Other rules affecting wine production and marketing are as follows. If an AVA is identified on the label, then at least 85 percent of the grapes must come from that AVA. If the wine label merely cites a county appellation (such as Sonoma or Monterey County), then 75 percent of the grapes must come from that county. If a vineyard is "designated" on the label—for example, Ridge Monte Bello—then 95 percent of the grapes must be from that site. If a vintage is specified, then 95 percent of the wine must be from that vintage. If a variety is specified, then at least 75 percent of the grapes must be of that variety. If a wine is labeled as being "estate-bottled," all the grapes come from a single AVA from vineyards owned or controlled by the winery, and the wine has been bottled within that AVA. If a winery owns a vineyard outside the AVA in which it is based, then it must use a term such as "proprietor-grown" or "vintner-grown."

Although these rules are fairly lax, they used to be so broad as to be meaningless. Some decades ago, a "varietal" wine needed to contain just 50 percent of wine from that grape variety. Nonetheless, it is still perfectly legal for, to give an example, a Russian River winery to buy Syrah grapes from Paso Robles and blend them, up to 15 percent, into its Pinot Noir without disclosing the practice on the label. This is not a fanciful example.

American law is also cavalier when it comes to declaring the alcohol level in a wine. This is surprising given the American enthusiasm for health warnings on labels. If the wine has less than 14% ABV, the winery is allowed a range of 1.5%; if the wine has over 14%, the latitude is only 1%. Thus, many labels are entirely misleading when it comes to giving customers an indication of how much alcohol by volume there is in each wine.

What merit Meritage?

For some years, producers were unsure how to market Bordeaux blends. It became fashionable to follow the Bordelais model and use up to five of the traditional varieties—as in Cain Five—rather than produce varietal Cabernet Sauvignons. A winery could opt for a proprietary name, which allowed complete freedom in composing the blend. Or it could release the wine under the cumbersome name of Meritage, which signified a blend of two or more Bordelais varieties, with no one of them making up more than 90 percent of the blend. This also applied to white Graves-style blends. The concept of Meritage never really caught on, and most producers have preferred proprietary names such as Insignia (Phelps) or Optimus (L'Aventure).

Reserving judgment

Some common labeling practices have no legal definition. Reserve, as one would expect, implies a bottling of superior quality to a non-reserve. How that superiority is measured is entirely up to the winery. Consumers usually assume that a reserve wine will have been made from grapes cropped at lower yields, will have been aged in more, or at least better-quality, new oak, and could be a selection of the best barrels. And often this is the case. Northern California is rich in old vines, but again, the term is not legally defined. The consumer has a right to assume that, for example, an old-vine Zinfandel is made from vines at least 30 years old; often, indeed, the vines are much older. Producers have the option to include more specific information on back labels, should they choose to do so.

Allmand
Allmand

Growing the Vines

With very few exceptions, all the plantings of the 19th and early 20th centuries in California were of bush vines, or, to use the California term, head-pruned. Many of these vineyards still survive, even though some owners might have found them uneconomical, since they cannot be mechanized. In Mendocino, Sonoma, Napa, Paso Robles, and the Sierra Foothills, there are substantial pockets of old-vine Zinfandel and Petite Sirah, as well as the field blends that were often favored by early growers. By having more than one variety in the vineyard, there was a measure of insurance against natural setbacks such as poor flowering or disease. If the Carignane did poorly, at least the Alicante Bouschet and Zinfandel might have given generous and healthy crops.

Those early growers planted by instinct. Mostly immigrants, they had ancestral knowledge of which varieties would grow in which conditions. There was no such thing as soil analysis, let alone GPS mapping, but a few days on the site would convey a good deal of information about wind and rainfall patterns, diurnal range, and other factors. Tree size would tell them about the depth of the soils. Given that most of those old vineyards are still going strong, the original growers knew their stuff.

Post-Repeal mechanization

By the time Repeal had been enacted and the slump that followed had ended, new plantings were made on a very different basis. The model for viticulture was similar to that of other agricultural enterprises, which meant that vineyards needed to be easily accessible to tractors. Consequently, vine density, by modern standards, was low, with plants 8ft (2.5m) apart in rows spaced at 12ft (3.5m), giving around 475 vines per acre. Vines grew as steadily as trees, and canopies were full and lush. Crops could be huge, but often the grapes lacked flavor. Overhead sprinklers or drip irrigation, widely introduced in the 1970s, also encouraged growth and sugar accumulation, but again, flavor was often lacking.

Left: Much may still be done by hand, but modern ways, such as harvesting in the cool of night, have revolutionized viticulture

Quality control

In the 1980s, there was a growing realization that wide row spacing, low density, and jungly canopies weren't delivering the desired fruit quality. With European investment came experience of much tighter spacing. Marimar Torres was told by authorities at UC Davis that high-density planting was crazy, but she knew she could get better-quality fruit and smaller berries. Land use was also more economical, with more vines per acre; the number of clusters per vine was far lower than with the aforementioned 8-x-12ft plantings, but then there were far more vines in the ground. There were drawbacks, however, since American tractors were not designed for narrow rows.

Some of the early plantings at Opus One at the beginning of the 1990s mimicked Bordeaux-style density. Questions were immediately raised about whether such density was appropriate for the very different conditions of Napa Valley. The rich alluvial soils of Oakville are a far cry from the gravel *croupes* of Pauillac. Before too long, it was acknowledged that Bordelais density was too extreme, that the vines responded too vigorously to the soil conditions, resulting in bushy canopies and excessive shading, which in turn inhibited ripening and exposed bunches to risk of disease. Ted Lemon of Littorai comments: "If you wanted to invent a system designed to promote rot and mildew in California, it's French high-density planting." Moreover, planting costs were very high, so only a high bottle price could justify the expense. It became accepted that higher density gave better fruit than California's traditional John Deere spacing (named after the tractors that trundled between the vines), but the precise density needed to be adapted to the individual site.

Other trellising systems were tried to remedy the defects of close spacing. Dividing the canopy became popular, so as to allow more sunlight to penetrate the foliage and to increase the leaf surface to aid photosynthesis, and some vineyard managers opted for a lyre system. However, such attempts at beneficial canopy management, while generally successful, also resulted in higher costs. Moreover, some questioned whether aiding photosynthesis was such a great idea in California's steady warm sunshine, which always provided ripeness but sometimes left flavor on the sidelines.

Observing vineyards in different parts of California, it is very clear that spacing and density are now being related to site. Soils with very low vigor can accept high-density planting; other more fertile soils are simply unsuited to it.

Balancing yield and quality

Density also has an impact on yields, but whether yields have an impact on quality is still debated in California. There are arguments—as there are in Europe—about whether yield should be calculated in tons per acre (or hectoliters per hectare) or in bunch weight per vine. A handful of iconoclasts, such as Doug Meador in Monterey, insist that high yields are indeed compatible with quality, and Meador points to award-winning wines, such as his own Gewurztraminers, made from crops that most would regard as unacceptably high. Meador argued that the sole criterion that mattered was the ratio of bunch weight to exposed leaf surface, which he defined as the balance of the vine.

Much depends on the desired style of wine. A generic Sauvignon Blanc from an area where land is not expensive can be produced at high yields because consumer expectation of wine quality will be low. In contrast, a costly vineyard-designated Sonoma Coast Pinot Noir cannot be produced from overcropped vines, since critics, retailers, and consumers won't accept it's worthy of its price tag.

Any errors made in pruning or density can be corrected in the course of the growing season by measures such as shoot-thinning and green-harvesting. The latter practice also attracts criticism from those who argue it is a purely remedial measure that is only necessary if the pruning has been done poorly, or if there has been a wrong choice of rootstock and clone. It is far better, some argue, to control (and thus reduce) vigor by cutting down on fertilizers and following carefully regulated irrigation programs.

It is increasingly accepted that very low yields can often be an error. In vigorous soils, the vine will yearn to grow and produce, and by inhibiting that mechanism too severely, you can end up with vegetal wines. David Ramey, of Ramey Wine Cellars, observes that, in the fertile Alexander Valley, growers can obtain 12 tons per acre and still retain quality, whereas in the sparse Carneros soils, you would be better off aiming for 3 tons per acre.

Leaf-pulling is a more controversial method of accelerating the ripening of bunches than it is in Europe, simply because of the strength of the sunshine in California. Leaves are sugar factories, so to remove them at random could damage the photosynthesis. Advocates of leaf-pulling, which aerates the bunches but also exposes them more directly to sunlight, often argue that it is best done early in the growing season, so that the skins of the grapes can adapt more easily to sun exposure. Perform the operation during the height of summer, and you risk sunburned grapes.

Trellising systems

When I visited California vineyards 20 years ago, a wide range of trellising systems was employed. It was still common to see, even in prestigious Napa sites, high-trained vines at low density throwing enormous canopies that flopped this way and that. Here and there were Geneva double-curtain systems originally developed for New York State, but crops could be excessively high, so it is rarely seen nowadays. Systems such as Smart Dyson and Scott Henry trained shoots downward, as well as upward; some argued that crops were too high, and the main advantage was even spacing of well-exposed bunches that reduced harvesting costs. Again, these systems are still to be seen but are no longer very popular.

The trellising system that now seems most popular, at least in quality-oriented vineyards with moderate to high density, is VSP, or vertical shoot positioning, which trains shoots upward and exposes fruit to sunlight and aeration. It's most popular in cooler coastal areas, since the risk of disease is minimized. Respected growers such as Andy Beckstoffer are sure that the widespread adoption of VSP has led to higher quality overall.

The grower's hunch

There is no simple formula that growers can apply to ensure good fruit quality; rather, there is a series of hunches that can, if necessary, be corrected. Viticultural consultant Phillip Freese observes, "It's very tricky to plant a new vineyard to the required parameters of shoot development and other performance criteria. There's a lot of trial and error involved. High-tech methods allow us to map sites based on water and mineral content, and you can do soil analyses and measure water retention. We can accumulate more data than in the past, which should allow us to make better choices when deciding on rootstocks, irrigation, density, and so forth. But it's not an exact science."

One factor to which increasing attention is being paid is row orientation. The aim is to have optimal but not maximal sun exposure—and at the right time of day. Current thinking favors optimizing exposure to the morning sun, and minimizing exposure to the west, especially by retaining leaves, in order to avoid the power of the afternoon sun.

Vine diseases

Disease is far less prevalent in the vineyards of California than in much of Europe. Nonetheless, growers need to be very vigilant. As is well known, phylloxera returned to California in the late 1980s, affecting the thousands of acres planted on AxR-1 rootstocks, which, contrary to advice given by UC Davis, were not resistant to the louse. Most growers knew there was an element of risk in AxR-1, since French scientists at Montpellier had been issuing warnings for many years, but they were lulled into thinking that phylloxera was a distant threat, so the risk was worth taking, given the rootstock's other advantages. This would prove a costly mistake, especially since there was a gap between the first signs of phylloxera in 1983 and the first advice from Davis to stop planting AxR-1.

John Williams of Frog's Leap in Rutherford claims not to have been surprised by the outbreak. "The industry has been feeding young vines on a Coke-and-candy-bar diet of fertilizers and water. The roots stay up near the surface. If you irrigate, 80 percent of the roots are in the top 5ft [1.5m] of soil. Where does phylloxera live? You guessed it" (*Wine*, June 2000). Napa was worst hit, then Sonoma, and there were more sporadic outbreaks elsewhere.

By 1987, it was estimated that across the state some 35,000 acres (14,000ha) had been replanted. There were, as has already been noted, some positive consequences, since it gave growers an opportunity to replace antiquated trellising systems and unfashionable varieties with more up-to-date versions. Yet this was not all positive. In many instances, the varieties that were defined as "suitable" were, in fact, the varieties that were capable of attracting the highest prices.

The scourge of the sharpshooter

Diseases such as eutypiose (called eutypia in California) are also present in North America, but the one that causes growers most concern is Pierce's disease, caused by bacteria spread by blue-winged and glassy-winged sharpshooters, which thrive in riverbank vegetation. Thus it has been possible to control its spread by removing the habitats favored by these insects. It has been present in California since the 1880s, and there is no certain cure, though very cold winters can help. The worst-hit region has been Temecula in southern California.

Clonal selection

An important development has been the expanding selection of available clones. Larger wineries such as Mondavi have conducted their own trials to work out which of the newer clones work best in their conditions. Small estates have to rely on published reports and word of mouth to determine what will suit them best. It's a difficult issue, since it can take a decade or more before the character and quality of any one clone become evident—and of course it can vary from site to site.

There would appear to be two sets of good-quality clones: Dijon clones for Burgundian varieties, and Heritage clones. At first, it was assumed that the imported clones would be superior to the native ones, but in recent years there has been considerable discussion about this, which will be dealt with in more detail in the section on grape varieties. There has also been a vast improvement in the quality of the available clones of Rhône varieties. It is not that long ago that it was discovered that much California Roussanne was in fact Viognier—a muddle that seems to have occurred in a suitcase in which cuttings were being smuggled into the country.

A joint venture between wine importer Robert Haas and the Perrin family of Château de Beaucastel in Châteauneuf-du-Pape resulted in the creation of a nursery and vineyard in Paso Robles. It was a slow process, since the imported cuttings needed to go through quarantine before being planted, with the usual lapse of time between planting and vinification. But the venture proved successful, and today there is a reliable source of high-quality clonal material. The property, Tablas Creek, also produces its own exemplary Rhône-style wines.

Organic and biodynamic viticulture

Given California's mostly benign climate, it is surprising that its growers have been slow to adopt organic or biodynamic farming. By now, however, many top winemakers and growers have had direct exposure to the great biodynamic estates of Alsace and Burgundy and have been able to assess the pros and cons of these two systems of farming. It is difficult to know how widespread biodynamic farming, in particular, has become, since many wines made from biodynamic fruit are not identified as such on the label. It's impressive, though, that substantial vineyards such as Fetzer's Bonterra in Mendocino and Grgich Hills in Napa are now fully biodynamic, as are smaller estates such as Araujo, Benziger, and Beckmen. Moreover, many Russian River Valley vineyards are organic or biodynamic. All this activity simmers beneath the surface, since it is not sufficient for grapes to be organically or biodynamically grown in order for a wine to be labeled "organic." For that to be the case, the wine must be made without the use of sulfur dioxide, so only a very few properties are brave enough to produce "organic wines" as opposed to "wines from organically farmed grapes." Nor are "organic" wines much of a showcase for the method.

The influence of vine age

In Europe, it is always assumed that a vine must be of a certain age in order to produce good wine. A young vine in Burgundy or Bordeaux may be bearing fruit in its fourth year, but no conscientious producer would include such grapes in the grand vin. Indeed, there are many estates that routinely consign the wines from young vines to the second

Above: Growing environmental concerns are reflected in more sustainable viticultural and winemaking practices

label. Yet in California, I have tasted many terrific wines made from vines no more than three or four years old. No one seems able to explain this. John Alban in Paso Robles conjectures that young vines in California are irrigated and develop faster than European counterparts—but these days, most young European vineyards are also irrigated. David Ramey speculates that it may have to do with California's richer soils and benign climate, which encourages vines to develop and mature more rapidly. Even if there is still no single answer, California wines do seem to show great precocity.

Information overload

The major change in viticulture that has taken place over the past decade is the amount of data available to growers. Jim Young of Robert Young Vineyards in Alexander Valley notes, "We have more weather stations, more real-time data that allows us to decide well in time whether to take preemptive action against frost or other problems. We no longer have to rely on weather forecasts." Beckstoffer agrees: "We can monitor vines more efficiently and can speedily gather data on moisture levels, disease pressure, and other factors. We can adapt irrigation, for example, more effectively. The drawback is the growing temptation to farm from your office. The other major change is that the argument for sustainability has been won, and many growers, including ourselves, are now converting some vineyards to organic farming." One caveat from Phillip Freese: "The increase in data is entirely positive, but how do you translate that data into knowledge? That's why there has been an increase in viticultural consultants, who know how to interpret that data correctly." As for climate change, it appears to be of far less significance in California than in Europe—for now.

Hang-time

Finally, the great debate over the past decade has been about hang-time: when is the right time to pick the grapes? This is not so much a viticultural decision as a stylistic one. An experienced grower can chew on a grape and decide that it is ripe; his client, a winemaker, may chew on the same grape and decide the fruit is not yet ripe enough. The core of the argument is the balance between sugar accumulation (easy in California) and tannin ripeness (not quite so easy). Because this is really a stylistic issue, it is discussed under wine styles.

Cabernet to Zinfandel

This section does not contain details about every grape variety grown in California but, rather, explains the challenges presented to growers and winemakers by some of the more important varieties. Despite the widely held view that California produces only a handful of varieties, you can actually find wines from grapes as diverse as Aleatico, Negrette, Counoise, and Freisa—but often they bear little relation to their European precursors. In any event, such wines tend to be quirky specialties of obscure wineries.

Cabernet Franc

Just over 3,500 acres (1,400ha) of this variety are now grown in California (all statistics are from the 2008 vintage), and though its primary function is to serve as a blending variety, pure versions are quite common in Paso Robles and Santa Barbara. Savannah-Chanelle in the Santa Cruz Mountains area claims to have the state's oldest plantings, dating from 1923. By far the largest Cabernet Franc vineyards are farmed by the Kautz family in Lodi. Although pure varietal versions are rare on the North Coast, it plays an important part in wines such as Maya from Dalla Valle and Viader's proprietary red, both from Napa Valley.

Cabernet Sauvignon

The first documented plantings of Cabernet Sauvignon were in 1878 in Sonoma Valley, and by the end of the century it had become an important variety in quality-oriented vineyards. The degradation of California's vineyards after phylloxera and then Prohibition led to the virtual disappearance of Cabernet by the time of Repeal, when only 200 acres (80ha) were left. Plantings grew steadily. By 1961, there were still only 500 acres (200ha) planted, but by 1990 there were 33,000 acres (13,300ha) under vine, and by 2008, 75,000 acres (30,000ha). Napa remains the most important source of Cabernet Sauvignon, but there is substantial acreage in Sonoma, San Luis Obispo, and the Central Valley. Clonal selection is not a controversial issue, and top growers have good things to say about clones 4 (can be jammy), 6 (said to be an old Bordeaux selection), and 337 (a promising small-berried Bordeaux selection).

The well-drained benchlands so common in California's main wine regions are ideally suited to the variety, as are the poorer soils of mountain vineyards. Cabernet is a forgiving variety, adapting well to different conditions. Napa suits it perfectly, and there are excellent examples from Sonoma Valley and Alexander Valley, as well as from Santa Cruz Mountains, Carmel Valley, and Paso Robles. Consequently, the general standard of California Cabernet is high, though connoisseurs will happily argue about which are the supreme examples.

The style of California Cabernet has certainly changed over recent decades. In the 1970s and '80s, the grapes were picked at lower ripeness levels, giving wines with a Bordelais character. They could have a herbaceous edge, which often integrated into the wine after some bottle age, as it does in Bordeaux, but there were also too many wines that were simply green and that reeked of bell peppers. By the mid-1990s, it was becoming customary to pick at considerably higher ripeness levels, but these wines proved controversial in a different way. With their richer, jammier fruit and, structurally, high pH and high alcohol, they had immediate appeal and were to become the dominant style of modern California Cabernet. Critics argued they were fatiguing to drink and would not age well, but that has hardly dented their popularity. Old-school Napa winemakers, such as Bo Barrett at Montelena, Robert Travers at Mayacamas, and Randy Dunn at Dunn, continue to make wines in a more restrained and often tannic style, but there is no doubt that they need bottle age to show at their complex best.

Right: Although Cabernet Sauvignon was planted in California as early as 1878, few vines survived phylloxera and Prohibition

Charbono

This weird variety, of which only 88 acres (35.5ha) remain, is said to be related to Dolcetto or to Douce Noire of Savoie. It does not ripen easily, and it gives big, fleshy, tannic wines that can be stolid. Duxoup in Sonoma and Summers in Napa are the main producers, but even they would admit that Charbono is an acquired taste.

Chardonnay

So powerful is Chardonnay's domination of California's white-grape vineyards that it is difficult to recall that its popularity is recent. In the 1940s, UC Davis discouraged growers from planting it, saying it was difficult to grow. In 1961, there were only 300 acres (120ha); but in the 1970s, plantings accelerated. Even so, it was not until 1991 that plantings began to exceed those of the white blending variety French Colombard. The pioneers were Fred McCrae at Stony Hill, Wente in Livermore, Chalone, and Hanzell. Wente claims to have produced a varietally labeled Chardonnay in 1936, but it must have been a lonely wine. The significance of the Hanzell Chardonnay was that it was aged in French oak—a rarity in the 1950s.

One reason for Chardonnay's ascendancy is that it will grow just about anywhere. It is now recognized that some hotter areas, such as the floor of Napa Valley, are not well suited to the variety, and today the focus is on cool-climate sites such as Carneros, Russian River, Monterey, and Santa Barbara. But good examples can also be found in Mendocino and many other areas.

The early plantings at Wente provided source material for a clone—or, more accurately, a field selection—known as Old Wente, which may well be the primary source for all subsequent American selections other than the Mount Eden strain, which was derived from cuttings brought from Burgundy to California by Paul Masson in 1896. The so-called Martini clone seems to have been taken from cuttings from Stony Hill, which in turn had planted the Wente clone. Commercially available Wente clones include Clone 4, which is quite productive, and Clone 5. Burgundian clones became widely available in the 1990s, but some have reported that, in California's long growing season, these Dijon clones can lose acidity. Now Old Wente seems to be coming back into fashion.

Since unadorned Chardonnay is not a very expressive wine, it has always been good material for manipulative winemakers. Indeed, it demands manipulation, because choices need to be made: barrel-fermented or not; with or without malolactic fermentation; with or without lees stirring. Early Chardonnays from California—from Stony Hill, Mayacamas, Montelena, Forman, Far Niente, and others—did not go through malolactic fermentation, but critics often preferred the fleshier, more buttery, and richly textured wines that emerged after malolactic. It comes down to a matter of personal taste, and in practice a large number of California Chardonnays go through partial malolactic fermentation, since winemakers are more accustomed to assessing the nature of the fruit rather than applying a winemaking formula.

In the 1980s and '90s, and indeed earlier, many Chardonnays were grotesque, being overoaked and flabby—and often quite sweet, too. Doug Meador, a grower and winemaker in Monterey, once remarked, "Only a termite could love California Chardonnay." And Gary Eberle in Paso Robles may have coined the expression "Carmen Miranda syndrome" to characterize those heavy, sweet, fruit-salady wines. They remain crowd-pleasers. One of the state's bestselling Chardonnays, the Kendall-Jackson Vintner's Reserve, has always had a good dose of residual sugar, and consumers love it.

More recently, there has been a vogue, rather limited in extent, for unoaked Chardonnays, which can have a bright, refreshing character, though they still seem a long distance away from the

Chablis model that may be in the backs of winemakers' minds. Good examples include those from Melville, Iron Horse, and Marimar.

Unoaked Chardonnays are likely to remain a fringe interest, and in 2009, revered Chardonnay specialist Steve Kistler told me, "There is a growing consensus that the right way to go with Chardonnay is to use whole-cluster pressing and native yeasts, with less lees stirring than in the 1990s (because we don't need additional richness), full malo, less new oak than before, and no fining or filtration."

Chenin Blanc

This was a workhorse grape of the 1980s, when 40,000 acres (16,000ha) were planted, but Chenin's popularity has diminished, and today only 8,240 acres (3,330ha) remain, most used to refresh low-acid whites from the Central Valley. Many varietally labeled Chenins tend to be sweet and rather sickly, and sadly, the few remaining dry Chenins, such as those from Chalone, Chappellet, and Dry Creek Vineyards, seem to be an endangered species.

Gewurztraminer

Although ignored by most cognoscenti, Gewurztraminer has a popular following among those who enjoy its soft, gently sweet caresses. Plantings have remained steady for some years and now stand at 1,590 acres (640ha). Monterey and Mendocino are where it fares best.

Grenache

Although rarely identified on a label, Grenache is a workhorse grape of the Central Valley and a mainstay of inexpensive red blends. Nonetheless, acreage is slowly diminishing and now stands at 7,000 acres (2,800ha). Some good rosés are made from Grenache. When he was at Phelps, Craig Williams created Vin de Mistral, which took all the jug-wine grapes, especially Grenache, vinified them properly, packaged them smartly, and charged a moderate amount for a blend that, under a commercial label, would sell to the brown-bag market.

Marsanne

Marsanne has never caught on, and only 93 acres (37.5ha) are planted. There are good versions from Qupé and Tablas Creek.

Merlot

It is hard to imagine that a modest, gently amusing film set in California's wine country could deal a deadly blow to a major grape variety, but that is exactly what happened to Merlot after the success of the film *Sideways* (though Merlot's loss proved to be Pinot Noir's gain). In 1999, 47,600 acres (19,300ha) were planted, and by 2007 this had risen to 50,000 acres (20,200ha), only to fall back a year later to 47,200 acres (19,100ha).

Merlot, as a varietal wine, made an appearance in California only in the late 1960s, under the Martini and Sterling labels. At first, growers assumed that because Merlot grows best in the clay soils of Bordeaux, the same would be true in California. This proved to be a mistake, and Dan Duckhorn, one of the few Merlot specialists in Napa, argued that Merlot did better on drier, rockier soils that reduced the variety's natural vigor. Although serious producers such as Duckhorn, Matanzas Creek, Beringer, and Clos du Val made very good Merlots, the major plantings of the variety were in the Central Valley, where the results were usually insipid. Merlot is prone to irregular flowering, rot, and raisining and is by no means easy to grow. Forty years of experience suggests that, with a few specific exceptions, Merlot is best as a blending variety.

Mourvèdre

Often known in California as Mataro, Mourvèdre is a minor success story, with plantings rising from 202 acres (82ha) in 1900 to 852 acres (345ha) by 2008. Its reputation was made by the ancient vineyards in Contra Costa County owned by the Cline family. Cline, Ridge, and Rosenblum have all made splendid examples from these bush vines, which pre-date any surviving vines in Bandol, the variety's homeland.

Petite Sirah

Once regarded as no better than a source of robust jug wine, Petite Sirah is now in fashion. Its precise identity has been something of a mystery, though DNA tests have revealed some selections to be Durif and others to be Peloursin or Aubun, an obscure Rhône variety. Presumably, the name Petite Sirah was used as a catch-all for 19th-century plantings in field blends.

Its opaque color makes it a useful blending variety for those who revere depth of color in a wine, and its main drawback is very high tannin levels, which can make pure varietal versions extremely tough. It can also be an inert wine, in that age cannot wither it or even modify it greatly. Twenty-year-old Petite Sirah can resemble the same wine at two years old. However, winemakers are now learning how to moderate those chewy tannins and to highlight the dense, fruity quality of the grape. Plantings have almost tripled over the past decade and now stand at 7,320 acres (2,960ha). Despite this, prices have risen, and good Petite Sirah is no longer the bargain it once was.

Pinot Blanc

Chalone was the winery that made American drinkers aware of Pinot Blanc, but interest in the variety has dwindled. In 1990, there were 1,840 acres (745ha) under vine; today, no more than 450 acres (182ha). The revelation that much Pinot Blanc was in fact Melon from Muscadet hasn't helped. Nonetheless, a few attractive versions still emerge from Monterey and other regions.

Pinot Gris

This is a runaway success in California, as it has been elsewhere. Its virtues as a quaffable, undemanding white with vaguely chic Italian associations has made it popular. In 1999, there were 1,110 acres (450ha) under vine; today, almost 12,000 acres (4,860ha). Much of the wine is as undistinguished and inoffensive as the equivalents from the Veneto or Rheinhessen, but some producers are trying to make it in a more serious style akin to Oregon Pinot Gris—halfway between nondescript Pinot Grigio and heady Alsatian Pinot Gris.

Pinot Noir

Thanks to *Sideways*, Pinot Noir has soared into fashion. And why not? In California's cooler regions, it can produce beautiful and elegant wine. Plantings have doubled over the past decade and now stand at 33,000 acres (13,400ha). It was already producing fine wines in the 1940s from Beaulieu and Martin Ray, but by the 1970s it had retreated into obscurity. Winemakers who did try their hand at it tended to treat it as though it were Cabernet and ended up with tannic, volatile wines that did its reputation no favors.

Robert Mondavi and others took it seriously in the 1970s, and a handful of winemakers with direct Burgundian experience, such as Ted Lemon of Littorai, spread knowledge about winemaking techniques appropriate to the variety. It also became apparent that it had often been planted in areas that were far too hot. Sonoma's Russian River Valley became its most prized zone of production, but other cool areas, such as Mendocino's Anderson Valley, Monterey's Santa Lucia Highlands, and the cooler sections of Santa Maria Valley, all became the source of good Pinot Noir, as did Carneros, though Carneros Pinot could often lack personality. More recently, the highlands of the Sonoma Coast have proved outstanding, and more controversial wines, sometimes with uncomfortably high levels of extract and alcohol, are emerging from the Santa Rita Hills in Santa Barbara County.

Above: Especially for Pinot Noir, the most suitable Davis or Dijon clones and rootstocks are of fundamental importance

One could devote a treatise to discussing clonal issues, but broadly speaking there are the Davis clones, such as Martini, Pommard, and Swan, which fell from fashion once Dijon clones were introduced in the 1990s, and the Dijon clones, such as 115 and 828. Today, the former are being valued once again as it becomes apparent that the Dijon clones are not necessarily that well adapted to the California climate. However, superb wines have been produced from both sets of selections.

Most Pinot is now made along similar lines, with a cold soak of greater or lesser duration and manual punch-downs during fermentation. But there are considerable variations when it comes to whether or not to use whole clusters (and thus retain stems) and the length and nature of the oak aging. Once aged in heavy-toast barrels for up to two years, Pinot Noir today is more likely to be subtly oaked and for a shorter time.

Alcohol is the main issue, some winemakers arguing that California Pinot Noir will always have higher alcohol than Burgundy because of the climate and because of the high sugar-to-alcohol conversion rates of modern cultivated yeasts. Many wines need to be watered or subjected to spinning-cone or other technologies to bring the alcohol down to more comfortable levels.

Other winemakers argue that high alcohol is a consequence of poor farming: the wrong clone in the wrong spot, or the wrong decision on crop levels and harvesting dates. Joseph Davis of Arcadian, who farms the parcels he buys from, manages to release Pinots at under 14%, and Ross Cobb, with vineyards close to the Pacific in Russian River, tells me he can ripen fruit at under 13%.

To achieve the early ripening necessary for low-alcohol wines, crop levels must be kept low, which is expensive. Moreover, American palates are tuned to high alcohol and the sweetness it conveys; and for better or worse, raisiny Pinots with 15% often score far better in the wine press than more discreet, subtle examples at 13.5%. Davis admits that low-alcohol Pinots do take longer to develop complexity, whereas high-alcohol examples have an immediacy of fruit that can be appealing, even if fatiguing. But it's not surprising if the many new wineries focusing on Pinot Noir are taking as models the high-scoring, dark, powerful wines.

Riesling

Twenty years ago, there were 8,500 acres (3,400ha) of Riesling in California, and though the surface has shrunk to 3,000 acres (1,200ha), plantings remain steady. The German variety is not really suited to California—at least if one is seeking to make lean, racy, dry styles, at which both Washington and Oregon have been more successful. But it is possible to make good off-dry versions in cooler areas such as Monterey and, here and there, botrytized versions of great richness, though sometimes the vines are sprayed to induce noble rot. Navarro in Mendocino is probably the leading producer.

Sangiovese
This grape variety is a tough call in California, where growers struggle to control its vigor, bring its natural acidity down to acceptable levels, and retain its varietal character. Although 1,900 acres (770ha) are planted, the wines are not always recognizable as Sangiovese, often because they are overoaked.

Sauvignon Blanc
Producers have a difficult choice to make. US consumers are not fond of what is considered the grassy style of Sauvignon, with high acidity and a herbaceous character. Nor are heavier, more complex, oak-aged Graves-style Sauvignons much in favor. To make the latter style successfully costs as much as making a good Chardonnay, and the Chardonnay will fetch twice the price. The middle ground seems most successful: medium-bodied, delicately herbaceous, pear- or melon-scented wines produced in substantial volumes at a moderate price (and thus well below Chardonnay). Kenwood is the benchmark for this style. More and more Sauvignons are being produced in a zesty style for early consumption, and while they may find little favor from critics, they appeal to drinkers, especially when offered in tasting rooms, converting those who like to be refreshed rather than impressed. That may explain why plantings have risen (to 15,200 acres [6,150ha]) in recent years.

Syrah
The growth of this variety has been explosive. In 1990, there were just 344 acres (139ha) planted, and six years later only 2,000 acres (800ha). Today, there are close to 19,000 acres (7,700ha). Syrah has quite a long history in California. It was planted more than 70 years ago in Mendocino, in a vineyard now owned by McDowell Valley Vineyards, and a major planting took place in Paso Robles in 1974. At the same time, Phelps was producing a robust version. Initially, it was thought that Syrah needed a warm site, but the canniest winemakers soon saw that it gave its most characteristic wines in cooler regions.

However, Syrah has proved enormously adaptable, thriving in just about every part of the state, with outstanding versions from the Sierra Foothills, Sonoma, Napa, Paso Robles, and Santa Barbara. French and Australian clones are now supplementing those on which the major plantings were based. Syrah specialist Pax Mahle observes, "Syrah from young vines is usually better than from old vines planted in the wrong places."

Styles vary considerably, with blueberry, plum, anise, or black-pepper notes displayed in the wines to varying degrees, depending on where the grapes are planted and on the yields. Some growers opt for a jammy style with high alcohol; others, for a cooler, northern Rhône expression of the variety. Quality has been remarkably consistent, though some wines seem overpriced. However, Syrah has become a victim of its own success, and there is now too much wine chasing too few consumers.

Viognier
This is a tricky variety in California, since growers often don't know how to grow it, winemakers don't know how to keep its typicity, and consumers don't know how to pronounce it. High alcohol can require the use of spinning-cone technology to make the wine drinkable. Low yields mean that prices tend to be high, and so the wines meet consumer resistance. Nonetheless, there are many excellent examples from throughout the state, but consistency is undoubtedly a problem. Some 3,000 acres (1,200ha) are under vine.

Above: The quality and style range of Zinfandel is very wide, but its potential for fine wine is increasingly recognized

Zinfandel

Originally planted in Massachusetts as a table grape in the 1830s, Zinfandel, of Croatian origin and akin to Italy's Primitivo, came to California in the 1850s. Despite a tendency to ripen unevenly, it usually reaches maturity at high sugar levels, making it ideal material for jug wines. Its forthright love-me-or-leave-me character made it a favorite with home winemakers, too. Poor winemaking led to coarse and rustic versions, and the variety became underestimated by the general public. Had it not been for the invention of white (meaning pink and slightly sweet) Zinfandel in the 1980s, the variety might well have become marginal. Instead, the old vineyards mostly survived, and winemakers such as Paul Draper and Joel Peterson appreciated the extraordinary quality of the wine at its best.

Old vineyards survive throughout the North Coast, though those in Napa are an endangered species, since growers can obtain three times the price by planting Cabernet instead. It also does well in Paso Robles. Most would agree, however, that the finest expression of Zinfandel comes from Sonoma's Dry Creek Valley, where producers such as Ridge, Seghesio, and Nalle set a high standard. Russian River Valley also gives delicious Zinfandel, with a red-fruited, cool-climate character.

As with Pinot Noir and Syrah, high alcohol can be a problem, though the monstrous styles popularized by Turley and others in the 1990s are less common today. Zinfandel can swing from near-ripeness to overripeness in a couple of days, so the harvesting date is crucial. The more prestigious producers, who get good prices for their wines, can afford to invest in bunch-thinning and sorting tables, all with a view to minimizing uneven ripening and eliminating berries that are green or raisined.

In general, Zinfandel is best enjoyed young, when its primary fruit is to the fore, but the best examples will age for up to a decade and sometimes longer, though not always with interesting results. The variety is also versatile: as well as the despised but popular white Zinfandel, it can produce succulent late-harvest wines and some excellent Port-style wines.

Style Wars

Since the late 19th century, California wine producers have known that their state is capable of producing outstanding wines. After the long winter of phylloxera, Prohibition, and the postwar lull, a new generation of winemakers retained that consciousness. Martin Ray, Dick Graff, Robert Mondavi, and many others were determined to produce wines at a level equal to Europe's finest, while knowing that California, because of its climatic conditions and soil profiles, could never replicate the most renowned European styles.

It was natural for a showman such as Mondavi to line up his Cabernets with the best of Bordeaux and defy tasters to spot his wine. And it was an enormous boost to the industry as a whole when California wines triumphed over their European counterparts at Steven Spurrier's 1976 tasting in Paris, though it could be argued that the more austere French wines would inevitably suffer when tasted alongside California's sunnier, fruitier wines.

Nonetheless, there have been consistent shifts of style in California wines. When consumers, and winemakers, tired of big, rich reds, they switched to so-called food wines, less overtly ripe, gentler in alcohol, and supposedly more compatible with fine food. Then it was realized that many of these wines were simply mean and green, and there was a return to richer styles. Look at a lineup of Mondavi or Staglin Cabernets, and you can almost see the boundary, some time in the mid-1990s, when wines with 13.5% alcohol disappeared to be replaced by wines with 14.5% or more.

As a wine-consuming nation, the United States is still relatively young. The French or Italian teenager grows up with wine and is imbued with some notion of what it tastes like and its nuances on the palate. It's a kind of subliminal education in wine styles. In northern Europe, even though very little wine is produced, the knowledge of centuries has filtered down through the generations, leaving tiers of well-informed wine drinkers. In the United States, other than on the West Coast and some major cities, there is no such wine culture. Would-be wine connoisseurs must start from scratch.

The power of the press

The wine press has been an enormously powerful influence in establishing criteria for quality. The everyday drinker will probably be persuaded more by the special offers in the local Sunday newspapers than by the decrees of the dedicated wine press. But the more serious wine drinker will not know how to choose between a Landmark Chardonnay and a Cambria Chardonnay. The specialist wine press, and local newspaper wine columns, will score wines and give a very approximate idea of how they taste. In addition, interstate shipments are easier than in the past, enabling many more people to order wines that will suit their tastes and pockets.

That American consumers have easy access to information and guidance is entirely welcome, but the guidance comes from limited sources. James Laube of *Wine Spectator* and Robert Parker are the most esteemed reviewers of California wines, and their scores can make or break a vintage. Both men are experts at what they do, but they both favor bigger, richer styles. They are entitled to their tastes, but it comes as no surprise that winemakers, hoping to enter the elite of top-scoring wines and producers, mimic the styles that are rewarded with high numbers. (This is not the place to debate the pros and cons of a 100-point scale, but there is an inherent absurdity in scoring a product that, by its nature, is always changing.)

One would suppose that the end result of this dominance of the press by a handful of individuals would be increasing uniformity of wine styles. Yet this is less so than in the past. Zinfandels and Pinot

Right: Decisions from pressing onward have an effect on style
Over: Standards in making and maintaining barrels are high

Noirs now come in all shapes and sizes. Even if a critic such as Laube praises high-alcohol Pinots that, to a European palate, resemble Syrah more than Pinot Noir, not everyone follows in his wake. This is also a golden age for Zinfandel. Many are still hefty wines with a good whack of alcohol, but what matters is the inherent balance of the wine, and I find more well-balanced Zinfandels on the market than was the case ten years ago.

The god of phenolic ripeness

There is also a growing recognition that the once-mighty god of phenolic ripeness is flawed. Of course, tannins need to be ripe by the time a bunch is picked, but that does not necessarily entail prolonging the hang-time until grapes have turned into raisins. It is now being realized that it is not axiomatic that ripe tannins can only be attained alongside out-of-control sugar accumulation, and that farming can and should be adapted to ensure that tannins ripen before Brix numbers soar. As Ted Lemon of Littorai observed to me, "The problem with raisins is that one raisin tastes much like any other raisin." Fruit needs to be picked when its flavor is at its most acute, not when its sugars are most extreme.

So, while there are still many flagrantly overalcoholic California wines on the market, they are less common than they used to be. Winemakers are recognizing that there is no point in "vineyard designating" a wine if overripe flavors mean it is scarcely distinguishable from wine from any other vineyard. Wines from raisined fruit also have a high pH, exposing them to the risk of bacterial infections and Brettanomyces, and their longevity is in doubt—though since few wine drinkers cellar wines, this is scarcely a major issue. There is, however, a commercial drawback to more balanced wines: they can require more time in bottle before their true quality and character emerge. Mountain Cabernets from the likes of Mayacamas and Dunn are magnificent wines, but they demand the better part of a decade in bottle. Both properties have a loyal customer base that understands this, but larger wineries feeding major retailers and tasting-room visitors are reluctant to focus on this style of wine.

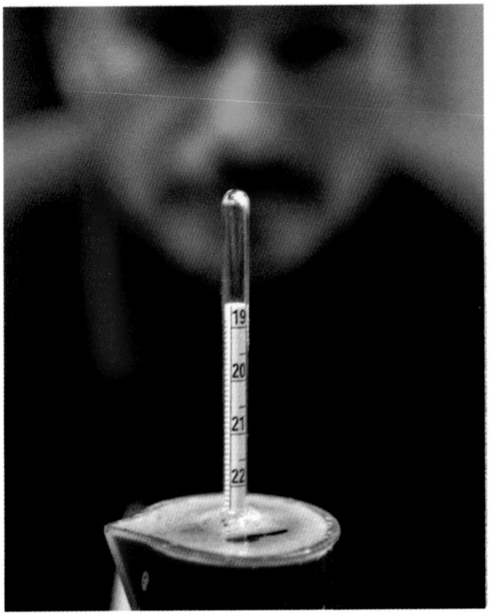

Above: Monitoring and occasionally reducing alcohol levels are both crucial activities in the ongoing style wars

Instant accessibility may be positive, given the nature of the market and the barely perceptible time gap between purchase and consumption among most consumers. But it may not be the best formula for fine and individual wines. It's a problem that wine producers worldwide have to face. In Bordeaux, too, young wines are more approachable than they used to be. Winemakers often argue that the key is balance, that a wine that is delicious young because of its perfect balance will also age well, and I see no reason to dispute this. As John Williams of Frog's Leap once remarked, "Ugly young, ugly old." And yet this is not always the case. While it is true that a wine that is clumsy or tough when young is never likely to blossom into something beautiful, there are certainly wines that are reticent and inexpressive in their youth and that need time in bottle to show at their best.

Access all areas

An admirable feature of the industry is the ease with which consumers can gain access not just to wines but to wineries, most of which have tasting rooms. A small fee is usually charged to taste a range of wines (typically refunded on purchase of a bottle), but visitors can gain an immediate impression of the style and quality of a winery's production, and tasting-room specials may allow them to try, and buy, older vintages or limited-production wines. It is probable that many tasting rooms make more money from selling T-shirts than they do from wine, but no matter. The consumer is regarded not as some distant and rarely glimpsed destination along the supply chain (which is the case in Bordeaux and some other regions) but as an individual to be engaged and persuaded, often through wine clubs that offer discounts and privileges.

Sometimes the tasting-room culture can be taken too far. Low-production wines, sold only from the tasting room, can be ridiculously limited, with some corner of some unknown vineyard being vinified separately and released with a very high price tag, justified, allegedly, by its scarcity and quality. Indeed, much vineyard designation has become virtually meaningless. The individual vineyards may exist, but they may not yet have achieved the individuality or the recognizability that justifies independent existence on a label. Often, vineyard designation is a way of gratifying the vanity of the grower and helping the winery cement a relationship with that grower.

The ultra-sophistication of an almost Burgundian vineyard designation (based more often on topography than terroir) seems a trifle odd, given that California is still unsure about what it does best. Varieties come and go: Merlot is all the rage one decade, a laughingstock the next. Viognier is chic and then all but abandoned. Randall Grahm has always maintained that it is odd that a very warm place such as California has taken as its model cool-climate wines such as Cabernet and Chardonnay. He would argue that the Mediterranean varieties—and that would include Rhône varieties—are better suited to California than the northern European classics. And those are precisely the wines that can be fashioned for early drinking. Syrah, in particular, fits the bill exactly.

Birth of a wine nation

Despite all the caveats, what remains indisputable to me is that California has, with remarkable speed, fashioned its own wine styles. Top Napa or Sonoma Cabernets are of stunning quality; coastal Pinot Noirs show increasing finesse and complexity; Syrah is a new star even if suffering now from overproduction; there are honorable stabs at wines from Petite Sirah, Sangiovese, and Barbera; and Zinfandel has established itself as the state's unique calling card, albeit with detractors as well as admirers. The skill of California's winemakers is remarkable, even if there is, in some quarters, an overreliance on such tricks of the trade as enzyme and tannin addition, watering, and high-tech alcohol reduction. Cooperage is of ever-finer quality, and that is especially true of the once-despised American oak. The roles of viticulturist and winemaker are no longer antagonistic, and the best winemakers pay more than lip service to the notion that great wine is made in the vineyard. California is a land blessed by nature and also by the richness of its human resources, allowing its wine industry to benefit from the best that money and good education can buy. Good California wine comes at a cost that may strike outsiders as excessive, but there are no longer any doubts as to the quality and personality of its best wines.

Mendocino

Mendocino is the most northerly of the California wine regions, beginning some 90 miles (145km) north of San Francisco and, until recently, better known for whitewater rafting, a dramatic coastline, logging, and marijuana cultivation than for viticulture. Maritime influence cools the more westerly appellations, but inland areas, separated from the ocean by chains of hills and mountains, can be decidedly warm. Vines were first planted here in the 1850s to supply wines for Gold Rush prospectors. The pioneers were mostly Italian immigrants, who planted on the lofty ridge tops, leaving the more fertile valley floor for vegetables and other food crops. Communications with other parts of the country were poor, given the mountainous terrain, so most grapes were shipped to wineries such as the celebrated Italian Swiss Colony in Asti. Any wine produced locally was usually consumed locally. When Prohibition came into effect in 1920, there was no national network to prop up wineries hoping to stay afloat, and the only company to keep going until repeal was Parducci. As recently as 1967, Parducci was the sole Mendocino winery, though Fetzer opened its doors a year later.

By the time of the wine boom of the 1960s, communications were no longer an issue, and more vineyards were planted—though it was not until the 1980s that the number of wineries began to expand. Most of the fruit grown in Mendocino was still shipped south to supply California's larger wineries, which eventually planted their own vineyards here. Mondavi, Beringer, and Gallo were particularly active. More recently, Napa wineries such as Cakebread and Duckhorn bought land in Anderson Valley with the aim of producing high-quality Pinot Noir.

One of the largest growers was the Fetzer family, and though they sold their wine-production

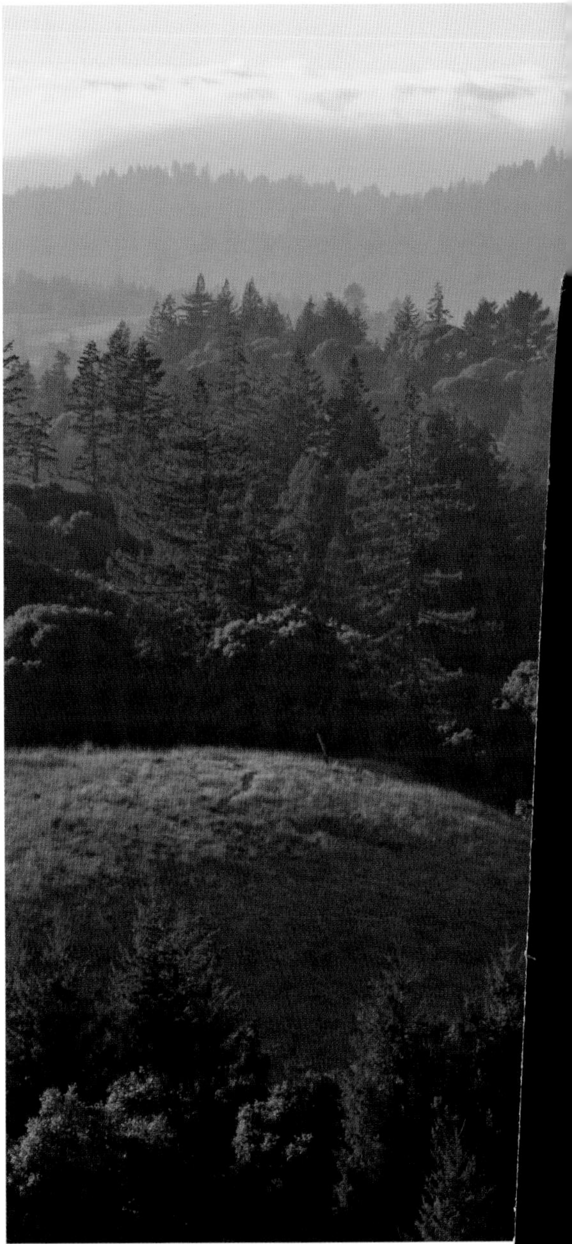

Right: Anderson Valley is one of Mendocino's coolest regions, but areas of the county farther inland are much warmer

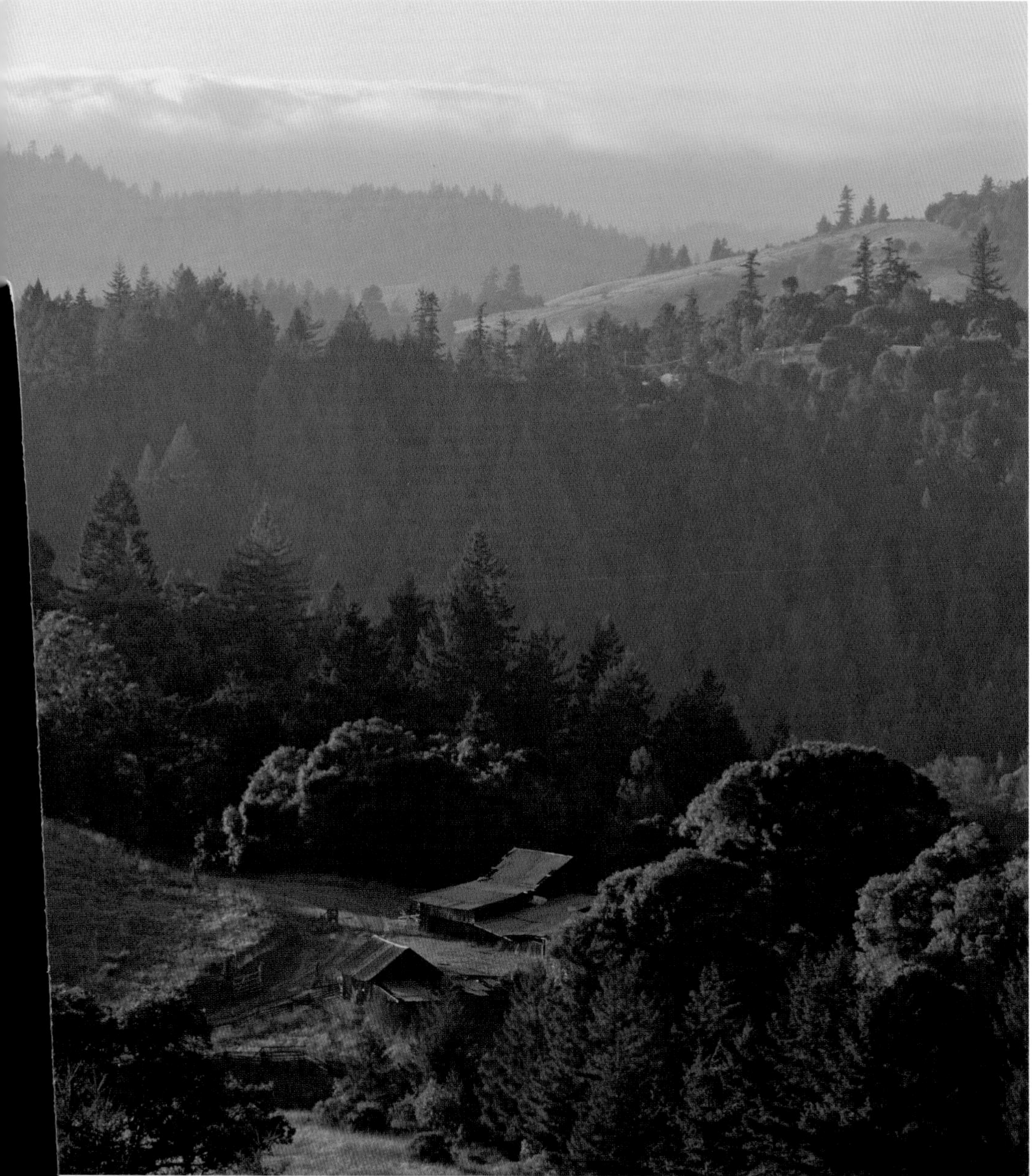

business to the Brown-Forman group many years ago, their influence remains profound. The Fetzers were keen on organic and biodynamic farming. Their senior winemakers—such as Paul Dolan and Phil Hurst, who subsequently left the company—carried that approach with them, and Mendocino remains a hotbed of organic farming, with about one-fifth of its vineyards certified.

Its climate and soils are so diverse that just about any grape variety can find a home somewhere in Mendocino's 17,000 acres (6,900ha) of vineyards. The traditional varieties of the region, as in Sonoma, were Zinfandel, Petite Sirah, and Carignane, and very old vineyards still survive in the Mendocino Ridges and elsewhere, the legacy of the original Italian settlers. In the cool Anderson Valley, maritime influence provides excellent conditions for Alsatian varieties, for Pinot Noir, and for sparkling-wine production. McDowell Valley is home to some of the earliest Syrah plantings in the United States. On the benchlands of the Redwood and Ukiah valleys, Chardonnay, Cabernet Sauvignon, and Merlot all do well. Growers such as Greg Graziano have carved out a niche for themselves in Italian-style wines, some of which are very good indeed.

Mendocino subregions

AVAs have proliferated in recent years, though some of them are so small as to seem pointless.

Anderson Valley This valley, which lies west of Ukiah, follows the Navarro River to the northwest for 25 miles (40km), where it opens on to the Pacific shore. Around 2,150 acres (870ha) are planted, almost half of that being Pinot Noir. The climate grows cooler as one moves northward. There used to be Cabernet and Merlot planted here, but the grapes struggled to ripen, and by the 1970s it was clear that the valley was better suited to cool-climate varieties. Husch was the first vineyard to plant Pinot Noir, in 1969, but vineyard expansion really got under way in the 1980s. A winemaker once dubbed Anderson Valley "Acid Valley," so thoroughly did the cold nights perform their task of acid retention. Although in some locations and some vintages this can be a drawback, in general it is the valley's trump card. The white wines never need acidification, and even in their simplest form they have a welcome crispness. Rot, however, can be a problem in some years, and rain can fall at awkward times in the growing season. In terms of wine production, the valley is versatile, excelling at sparkling wines, Burgundian varieties, and white varieties such as Gewurztraminer and Riesling.

Cole Ranch Located between Ukiah and Anderson Valley's capital of Boonville. Only 60 acres (24ha) are planted, and they are all owned by the Sterling family of Esterlina winery. The vineyards are high up, at over 1,000ft (300m), and hospitable to many varieties, including Riesling, Merlot, Cabernet Sauvignon (not ideal here), and Pinot Noir.

Covelo A paltry 2 acres (0.8ha) planted 45 miles (72km) north of Ukiah in a warm spot.

Dos Rios Another caricature of an AVA, with just 6 acres (2.5ha) planted in northern Mendocino on rocky soils.

McDowell Valley Lying east of Hopland, this is more benchland than a valley, with vineyards at 850–1,000ft (260–300m) on gravelly red and volcanic soil. It runs to about 600 acres (240ha), almost all grown and produced by McDowell Valley Winery, which has some ancient Syrah vines, as well as most other Rhône varieties.

Mendocino Ridge This formed part of Anderson Valley until 1997, when it won autonomy. The vineyards are planted at an elevation of at least

1,200ft (360m) on ridge tops between Anderson Valley and the Pacific. Thus, they lie above the fog line and benefit from more sunshine than chilly Anderson Valley. Zinfandel and Cabernet Sauvignon thrive here, but only 75 acres (30ha) are planted.

Potter Valley Some 12 miles (20km) northeast of Ukiah, Potter Valley lies at an elevation of 1,000–1,200ft (300–360m). There is little maritime influence, but the nights are cool, sometimes leading to frost, making this a good spot for Sauvignon Blanc, Chardonnay, and Riesling. About 1,000 acres (400ha) are planted, and much of the fruit is sold to wineries in Napa and elsewhere.

Redwood Valley A major growing region that follows the Russian River north of Ukiah. About two-thirds of the varieties are red, though Sauvignon Blanc and Chardonnay can be of good quality, too. Ocean breezes penetrate the valley, making it cooler than Ukiah. The soil is mostly red clay, with varying amounts of rock. As well as for Zinfandel and Cabernet Sauvignon, Redwood Valley is gaining a good reputation for its Sangiovese and Syrah.

Above: One of Mendocino's most interesting AVAs, the name reflecting the high altitude at which the vineyards are planted

Sanel Valley North of Hopland, this small region, 6 x 2 miles (10 x 3km), lies on the Russian River plain and is the warmest of the Mendocino appellations, with Cabernet Sauvignon and Merlot planted on well-drained gravelly soils.

Ukiah Valley A strung-out region following the main highway north of Sanel Valley. The Russian River plain is home to white varieties, whereas Cabernet Sauvignon and Zinfandel tend to be planted on benchlands. The valley is also proving to be a useful testing ground for Italian and Rhône varieties.

Yorkville Highlands An interesting region between Alexander Valley in Sonoma and Boonville. Because the valley along which it lies is frost-prone, all vineyards are planted at higher elevations. The days are warmer than in Anderson Valley, but the nights can be cold. Varieties such as Sauvignon Blanc, Pinot Noir, and Merlot do well here.

Navarro Vineyards

This beautiful property lies midway between Philo and Navarro and was part of a 910-acre (370ha) sheep ranch bought in 1973 by winemaker Ted Bennett and his wife Deborah Cahn. As well as planting Chardonnay and Pinot Noir, Bennett tested various German and Alsatian clones of varieties such as Riesling, Gewurztraminer, and Pinot Gris and, over the years, has made many adaptations in source material and planting patterns. In the 1990s, he planted Pinot Noir at Deep End, a vineyard with an elevation of 1,200ft (360m), and was pleased by the results. At higher elevations, he finds the daytime temperatures lower but the nights milder, giving a more temperate climate than on sites closer to the valley floor. Frost is a risk at certain times of the year, and overhead sprinklers are in place to offer protection when necessary.

Although not organic, Navarro is farmed with minimal use of herbicides and pesticides. One would have imagined that, in Anderson Valley, leaf-pulling would be standard practice, but Bennett avoids it, noting that daytime temperatures can be very hot, and leaf-pulling could expose the bunches to sunburn. He green harvests in August, however, to control crop levels, and the sheep reared to chew up the weeds and cover crop are also partial to leaves and suckers.

Bennett's devotion to Alsatian and German varieties is not restricted to the vineyard. He and his long-term winemaker Jim Klein choose to age the wines in French and German casks rather than barriques, though when it comes to Pinot Noir, he is more likely to turn to well-toasted French barrels.

Despite Navarro's reputation for Alsatian-style wines, the Chardonnays can be very good indeed, especially the Première Reserve, which is barrel-fermented and stirred. The grapes are a blend of a selection from the Robert Young vineyard in Alexander Valley, which was planted here 25 years ago, and more recently planted Dijon clones.

Above: Owners Ted Bennett and his wife Deborah Cahn, with the large casks ideally suited to Alsatian and German varieties

The most basic of the Alsatian-style wines is the Edelzwicker blend. In 2008, this was 42 percent Gewurztraminer, 32 percent Riesling, 26 percent Pinot Gris, and a drop of Muscat. With 16 grams of residual sugar per liter, this may be a touch sweet

No other West Coast winery, with the arguable exception of Chateau Ste. Michelle in Washington, produces such impeccably balanced sweet wines, with their blazing, refreshing acidity in perfect harmony with the lush, honeyed fruit

for some tastes, but allowances need to be made for the fact that this is an inexpensive quaffing wine and an admirable summer refresher. Moreover, the finish is remarkably dry.

Some of the Gewurztraminer vines are more than 30 years old, and it shows in the wines, which are aged in large, old, oval casks for eight months, as is the Pinot Gris. In California, winemakers are torn between those producing crowd-pleasing Pinot Grigio styles and a small group aiming for a more Alsatian style. Navarro's version is midway between the two, since it has more acidity and vigor than most Alsatian versions, without the nondescript character of the Italian imitations. The dry Riesling is not unlike a Mosel Kabinett, with residual sugar at around 10g/l, lower than its Mosel counterpart, but of course the grapes in Anderson Valley achieve higher ripeness levels.

As for the red wines, the Cabernet and most of the Syrah come from purchased fruit. The Mendocino bottlings come from neighboring vineyards, whereas the Cuvée à l'Ancienne and the Deep End cuvée are estate-grown. The latter, from the high-elevation vineyards, can be quite tannic in its youth and demands some bottle age. The Ancienne achieves an easier balance between structure and accessibility.

Navarro produces a large range of wines, but there is no doubt that the finest of them have always been the Cluster Select Riesling and Gewurztraminer, made from botrytized fruit. Bennett got the style right almost from the outset. The 1983 Late Harvest Riesling was stunning in its richness and intensity in 1986. Even in blind tastings in the United States, one sip is enough for tasters to murmur, "Navarro." No other West Coast winery, with the arguable exception of Chateau Ste. Michelle in Washington, produces such impeccably balanced sweet wines, with their blazing, refreshing acidity in perfect harmony with the lush, honeyed fruit. Although less sweet and intense, the Late Harvest Gewurztraminer is equally exquisite.

The enthusiasm generated within the Navarro tasting room is evidently infectious. Navarro is that rare thing: a winery perfectly in tune with its clientele

Wineries should not be judged on their tasting rooms, but stepping into Navarro's, it is easy to see why the winery has attracted such a fervent following, selling a substantial proportion of its very reasonably priced production directly to customers. The room is a bit cramped and boisterous. Many of the tasters are clearly regulars; there is no tasting fee (unusual at a winery of this caliber); water bowls are set out for visiting dogs; and the pourers are efficient, well informed, and friendly. Coming from Europe, where the reception at wineries can still be rather frosty, the enthusiasm generated within the Navarro tasting room is evidently infectious, judging by the number of customers wheeling cases of wine to their cars. Navarro is that rare thing: a winery perfectly in tune with its clientele.

FINEST WINES

(Tasted 2009–10)

Ancienne Pinot Noir 2008
Intense raspberry nose; charm and lift. Medium-bodied but ripe; sleek and fresh; purity and drive.

Dry Gewurztraminer 2007
Pretty, floral nose; litchis. Rich and firm, still tight, but vigorous and spicy and with a long, dry finish.

Dry Riesling 2008 [V]
Flowery, appley nose. Fairly rich and broad, yet there is marked acidity and a sweet-and-sour tone, with a peppery and distinctly dry finish, despite a dash of residual sugar.

Cluster Select Gewurztraminer 2006★ (197g/l RS)
Lush, tropical-fruit nose, with honeysuckle and marzipan. Fine attack, concentrated and tight, with terrific acidity for Gewurztraminer; brilliant length.

Cluster Select Riesling 2007★ (201g/l RS)
Heady, peachy, botrytis nose, with a light, honeyed tone. Very sweet, creamy and unctuous, with delightful acidity to keep it from being cloying. Stylish, piquant, and lively.

Navarro Vineyards
Area under vine: 90 acres (36.5ha)
Average production: 400,000 bottles
5601 Highway 128, Philo, CA 95466
Tel: (707) 895-3686
www.navarrowine.com

Roederer Estate

It took many years of exploration before Jean-Claude Rouzaud found the ideal spot in which to plant vines on the West Coast. With expansion within Champagne nearly impossible because of the cost of land, Roederer, like other Champagne houses, began looking elsewhere to create a satellite estate dedicated to sparkling wine. Moët & Chandon, Taittinger, and Mumm were already well established in California, so Rouzaud visited Carneros, from which the other houses were drawing much of their fruit, but decided it had too pronounced a typicity. He also looked at Oregon and was tempted by Sonoma's Green Valley but was unsure he could find sufficient land for his project. He finally decided on Anderson Valley, where Chardonnay, ripening at 11% ABV, could prove ideal for sparkling wine. The valley also has a long growing season, so it was not necessary to pick in August or early September, as was often the case in Napa.

Rouzaud decided on Anderson Valley, where Chardonnay could prove ideal for sparkling wine. These are clearly among the very best that North America has produced

Rouzaud bought land in the northern stretch of the valley, which is decidedly cool. The ranch was formerly used for sheep grazing and orchards. He began planting in 1982 and also bought a vineyard near Boonville, where the climate is slightly warmer than Philo; the existing vines were then grafted over. The Roederer vineyards have been gradually expanded, and phylloxera required some replanting. Today, there are some 350 acres (140ha) in production.

The initial winemaker was Dr. Michel Salgues, who had a doctorate in enology from Montpellier University and had trained at Roederer. He planted vineyards using lyre trellising, so as to give the bunches better exposure to air and sunlight. Yields are at 4–5 tons/acre, which is a good deal less than average crops in Champagne. Grapes were usually picked at ripeness levels of around 11% ABV, which was more than sufficient for sparkling-wine grapes. Salgues's method of production, not surprisingly, mirrored that at Reims. Only the first pressing, the cuvée, is retained; malolactic fermentation is the exception rather than the rule; and up to 20 percent of any vintage is set aside as reserve wines for subsequent blending with later crops. The wines are machine-riddled.

The basic wine is the Estate Brut, first made in 1988. The blend is approximately 70 percent Chardonnay, 30 percent Pinot Noir. The wine stays on the yeasts for around two-and-a-half years. The vintage wine is called L'Ermitage and was first made in 1989. The proportion of Pinot Noir is generally higher than in the Estate Brut, and the *dosage* is usually 11g/l. L'Ermitage spends between four and a half and five years on the yeast before disgorgement.

There are two rosés. The Non-Vintage is made from 60 percent Pinot Noir (of which about 5 percent is added as still wine) and 40 percent Chardonnay. The limited-production L'Ermitage Rosé, first made in 1999, is modeled on the regular L'Ermitage, with similar aging before disgorgement.

Dr. Salgues was succeeded by his assistant Arnaud Weyrich, who had experience in Reims, as well as in California. As was the case under Salgues, the blending panel includes top winemakers from Roederer in Reims. Weyrich has introduced some still wines, as have most other sparkling-wine houses in California. Although both the Chardonnay and the Pinot Noir are perfectly acceptable wines, they are not as interesting and characterful as the sparkling wines, which are clearly among the very best that North America has produced. Before he retired, Jean-Claude Rouzaud had experimented with Pinot Noir here but decided the wine was not up to standard, so the project was shelved before being revived more recently. No doubt commercial considerations play their part in the growing production of still wines.

Rouzaud always insisted that in coming to California he had no preconceptions about style. Nonetheless, the Roederer Estate wines are very close stylistically to Champagne and could easily be identified as such in a blind tasting. Most other California sparklers, with the possible exception of the top Schramsberg cuvées, have a more overt fruitiness and less grip.

FINEST WINES

(Tasted 2009)

Estate Brut★

Exemplary. The mousse is fine, the nose discreet and elegant, with a hint of yeast. The fruit is quite broad but laced with acidity, giving a citric lift to the wine, which is elegant and long.

L'Ermitage 2003

A biscuity nose, richer and broader than the 2000 vintage of the wine. The palate is also rich and full-bodied, and while nutty, it seems less tight and lemony than the 2000. The finish is long, with a touch of ginger.

Brut Rosé

Aromas of wild strawberries and some floral tones. Full-bodied and vinous, it nonetheless has a good attack and a long, nutty finish.

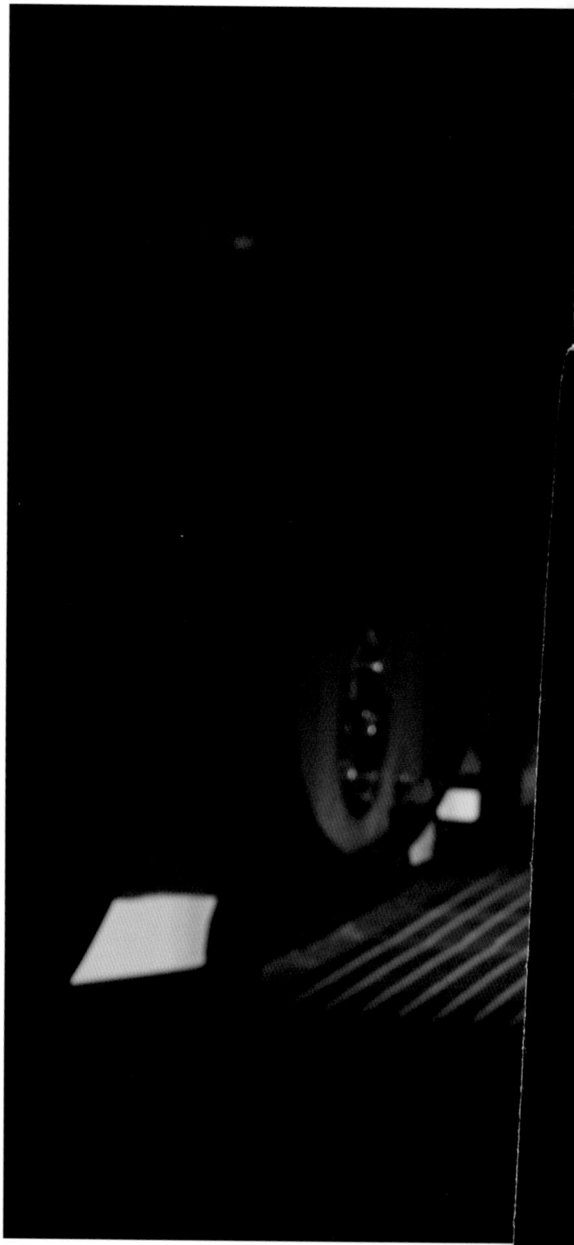

Right: Arnaud Weyrich, Roederer Estate's winemaker, who has added still wines to the company's range of superb sparklers

Roederer Estate
Area under vine: 350 acres (140ha)
Average production: 1 million bottles
4501 Highway 128, Philo, CA 95466
Tel: (707) 895-2288
www.roedererestate.com

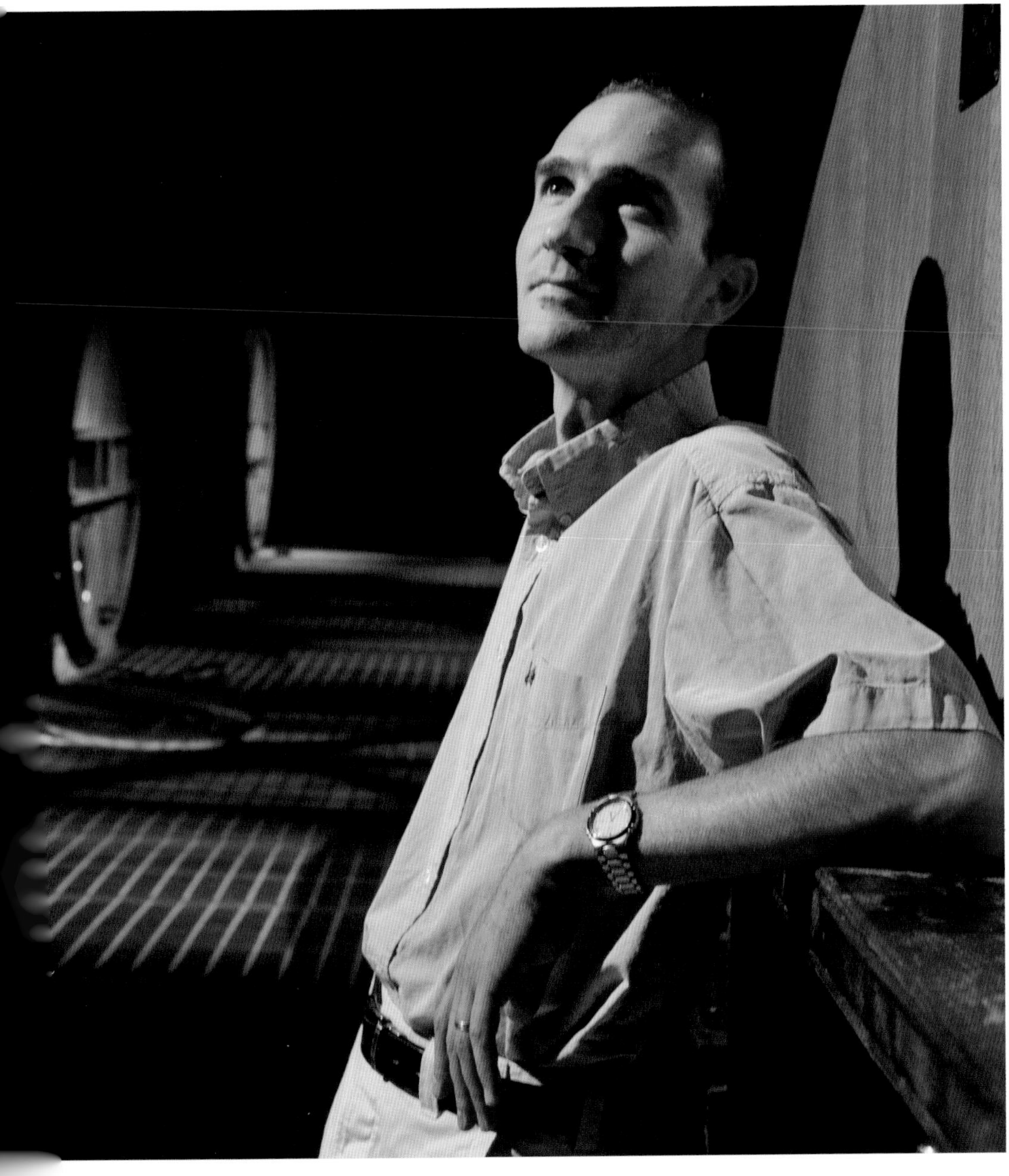

Napa Valley

For many lovers of California wine, that term is synonymous with Napa Valley, which takes its name from an American Indian word for "valley of plenty," appropriately enough. Indeed, the prestige of the region is such that almost every acre that can be planted with vines has been claimed. About 48,000 acres (19,400ha) are under vine, and the valley is home to around 400 wineries, though not all of them are physical structures. It is not uncommon for a grower to sell most of his production but reserve the best parcels for his own label, which may be vinified and cellared at a "custom-crush" facility. Thus, the label exists, but there is no winery dedicated to its production. No wonder it is so difficult to keep track of the valley's proliferating producers. This growth is fairly recent. In 1965, there were only some 25 wineries, and by 1987 that number had doubled. By the late 1980s, there were more than 200.

The explosive growth in Napa properties is, statistically, deceptive. Many produce no more than a few hundred cases of wine. These boutique wineries operate along similar lines: purchase or lease a small Cabernet vineyard in a promising location, hire a top vineyard manager to ensure fruit quality is outstanding, hire one of half a dozen top consultant winemakers both to make the wine and to ensure it will be reviewed by influential critics, guarantee sufficient scarcity to justify a very high price, and—finally—pray that it all works out. I have decided to exclude almost all such labels from this book, simply because the wines are almost impossible to find, since they are sold entirely to mailing lists of subscribers and on secondary markets at ridiculous prices. This is not an implied criticism of the quality of the wines. Screaming Eagle, to give just one example, is an excellent wine, but rarity as much as quality is the explanation for its cult status.

At first glance, the Napa Valley looks like a single entity, a fairly narrow valley running north to south for almost 30 miles (50km), hemmed in by steep hills; at its widest, the valley is 5 miles (8km) from side to side. Of course it is anything but uniform. Geologically, it is exceedingly complex, and it is climatically diverse. The valley itself is a former sea bed, now covered by sedimentary layers, but all around it are vestiges of volcanic activity. The valley, it is said, is home to no fewer than 100 soil variations, which I do not propose to enumerate. More importantly, there are two fundamental divisions: one based on latitude, the other on elevation. The southern part of the valley, where the Napa River flows into the San Pablo Bay, is too cool to grow varieties such as Cabernet Sauvignon; whereas the northern end, around Calistoga, can be torrid in summer. The valley floor, which slopes southward toward the bay, never rises above 250ft (75m), but on either side of the valley the mountains, and the vineyards scattered within them, can reach around 2,600ft (800m). Not surprisingly, this all leads to a plethora of growing conditions.

The heartland of Napa Valley, both historically and in terms of grape quality, lies on the valley floor. The central part of the valley, on either bank of the river, can be overfertile, but to the west is a series of alluvial fans of detritus washed down by creeks from the mountains. Geologically, these fans are composed of rocks and also of gravel and silt and other alluvial deposits that can vary in depth. These fans, also known as benchland, provide an ideal home for Cabernet Sauvignon in particular, and the valley's most famous vineyards—Napanook, To Kalon, Rubicon—are all located here. These benchlands provided the surface for the major 19th-century wineries—Beringer, Inglenook, Beaulieu, and others—to plant hundreds of acres. At the same time, artisanal growers, lacking the wealth and business acumen of men like Gustave Niebaum, climbed into the hills. For many of them,

Right: A vineyard on the floor of Napa Valley, the "valley of plenty," where almost every available acre has been planted

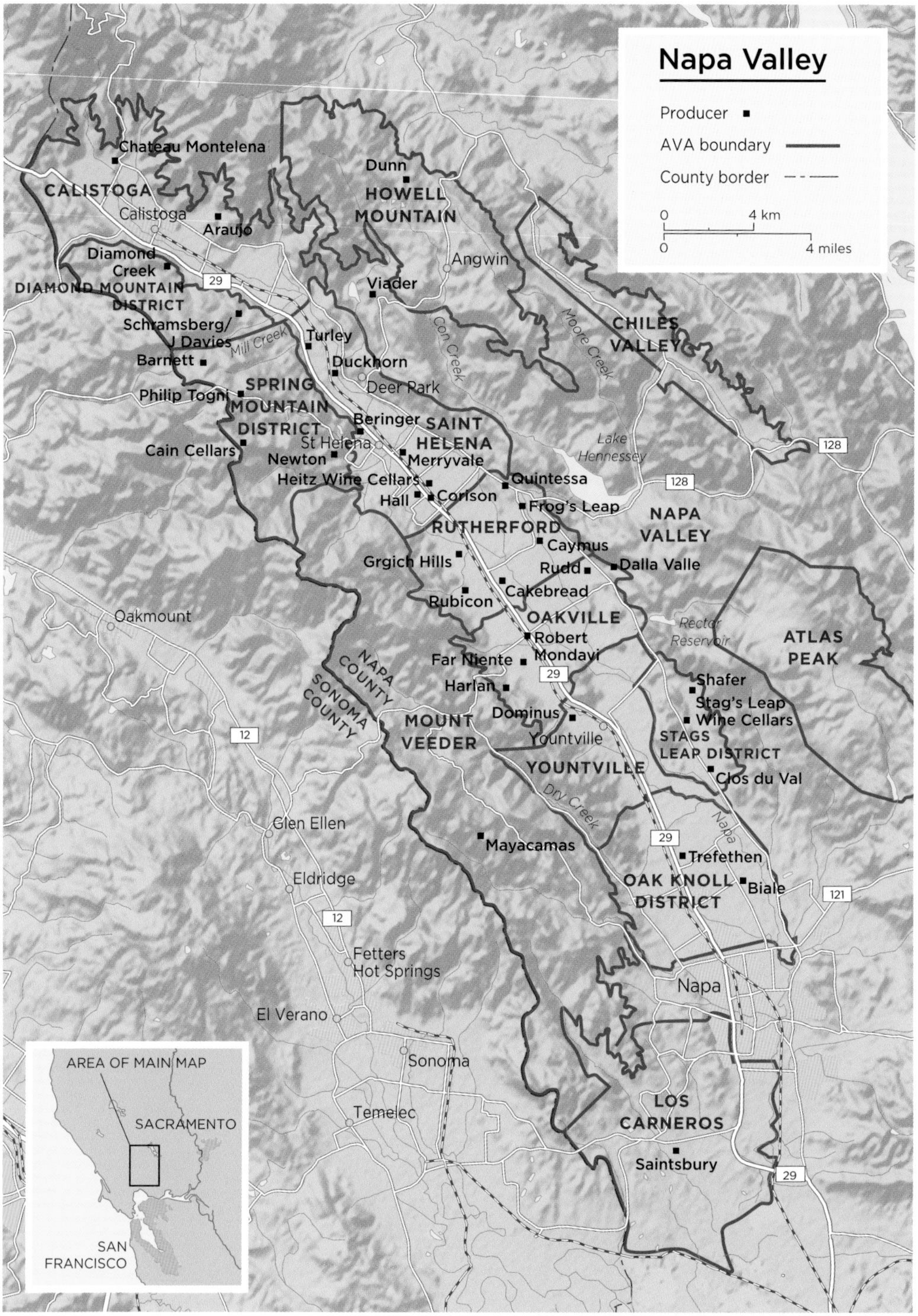
Napa Valley
Producer
AVA boundary
County border
0 4 km
0 4 miles
Chateau Montelena
CALISTOGA
Calistoga
Araujo
Dunn
HOWELL MOUNTAIN
Angwin
Diamond Creek
DIAMOND MOUNTAIN DISTRICT
29
Viader
Schramsberg/ J Davies
Mill Creek
Turley
Con Creek
Moore Creek
CHILES VALLEY
Barnett
Duckhorn
Philip Togni
SPRING MOUNTAIN DISTRICT
Deer Park
Beringer
SAINT HELENA
St Helena
Cain Cellars
Newton
Merryvale
Lake Hennessey
128
Heitz Wine Cellars
Quintessa
Hall
Corison
Frog's Leap
RUTHERFORD
NAPA VALLEY
Caymus
Grgich Hills
Rudd
Dalla Valle
Cakebread
Rubicon
OAKVILLE
Oakmount
Rector Reservoir
Robert Mondavi
ATLAS PEAK
Far Niente
NAPA COUNTY
SONOMA COUNTY
Harlan
Shafer
Stag's Leap Wine Cellars
Dominus
MOUNT VEEDER
12
Yountville
STAGS LEAP DISTRICT
YOUNTVILLE
Clos du Val
Dry Creek
Napa
Glen Ellen
Mayacamas
Trefethen
OAK KNOLL DISTRICT
Biale
121
Eldridge
Fetters Hot Springs
Napa
El Verano
Sonoma
AREA OF MAIN MAP
SACRAMENTO
Temelec
LOS CARNEROS
Saintsbury
SAN FRANCISCO

immigrants from Germany or Italy, it was natural to plant on steep slopes so as to benefit from good drainage and exposure to sunlight unhindered by the banks of fog that rolled into the valley on an almost daily basis.

To the west stand the Mayacamas Mountains, divided into different sectors: from south to north, Mount Veeder, Spring Mountain, and Diamond Mountain. To the east rises the Vaca range, divided into Atlas Peak in the south and Howell Mountain in the north. In general, the mountain vineyards experience far less maritime influence than the valley floor and the benches. Cool sea air, often fog-borne, enters the valley from San Pablo Bay to the south, and also through the Chalk Hill Gap that leads from Sonoma to the northwest into northern Napa, bringing some cooling effect to hot Calistoga. Elevation cools the mountain vineyards, giving markedly lower daytime temperatures; on the other hand, on vines planted well above the fog line, the grapes have longer exposure to sunlight and more uniform ripening. Cool nights help preserve acidity in the grapes. The mountain soils are generally far from fertile and can be rocky, whereas those down in the valley are far richer and more fertile. Mountain fruit often has smaller berries and less juice as a consequence of the low fertility, and this results in higher tannin levels.

Like the rest of the world, Napa Valley is exposed to climate change. A recent study by the Napa Valley Vintners, the leading growers' association, concludes that winter temperatures have risen by about 1°F (0.5°C); however, as the summer temperatures in California's Central Valley also increase, more fog and cool air than in the past may rush into Napa and Sonoma as that heat rises.

AVAs have proliferated, as each village claims typicity for its wines, but it would take an acute palate to differentiate in a blind tasting between wines from Oakville and Rutherford, or between Mount Veeder and Spring Mountain. Certainly there are distinguishing characteristics—the forested Mayacamas Mountains tend to be wetter than the more arid Vaca range—but quite how this plays into wine styles is less clear. As in other celebrated wine regions, too many other factors come into play: vintage character, crop levels, and the hand of the winemaker, of course.

Nonetheless, something needs to be said about each Napa subregion, moving from south to north.

American Canyon Not an AVA, but a cool breezy region across from the Carneros slopes. It has a growing reputation for Chardonnay.

Los Carneros (AVA from 1983) A cool area, close to San Pablo Bay, shared, as an AVA, with Sonoma County. The Napa side tends to be hillier. Originally planted with Chardonnay and Pinot Noir, it is now also sought after for its elegant cool-climate Merlot and Syrah. The region is an excellent source of grapes for sparkling wine, whose production has been holding up well, reflecting the suitability of Carneros for this style.

Mount Veeder (AVA from 1990) In the Mayacamas Mountains northwest of the town of Napa, with vineyard rising from 500 to 2,600ft (150–800m). The soils are thin, unfertile, and very varied, with sandstone, volcanic ash, and shale, as well as some clay. Planted mostly on frost-free, east-facing slopes, the most important varieties are Cabernet Sauvignon, Chardonnay, Zinfandel, and Merlot.

Oak Knoll District (AVA from 2004) The most southerly valley-floor subregion, by the town of Napa, with about 3,200 acres (1,300ha) planted. The soils are gravelly to the west, more silty and loamy on the flatlands near the river. Maritime influence is strong, and the wines are known for their acidity. Riesling does well here, and the Cabernet

Sauvignon has a cool-climate character. Trefethen and Monticello are the best-known wineries.

Yountville (AVA from 1999) Just north of Oak Knoll, with vines planted along the gravelly alluvial fans at the foot of the Mayacamas Mountains. Soils farther east have more silt and loam and can be distinctly vigorous. Like Oak Knoll, it enjoys strong maritime influence and a long growing season. Dominus and Domaine Chandon are the principal wineries.

Stags Leap District (AVA from 1989) On the eastern side of the valley, across from Yountville. One of the most distinctive of Napa's AVAs, though it took years of wrangling before the wineries could agree on its boundaries. Some wineries felt that the boundary was drawn too far to the north and west, allowing some less exceptional land to be included. As presently constituted, the Stags Leap District is bound to the east by the basalt Palisades in the foothills of Atlas Peak, to the west by the Napa River, to the south by flatlands close to the town of Napa, and to the north by the Yountville Cross Road.

The red loam soils seem to contribute to the supple tannins and velvety textures that are the hallmark of Stags Leap Cabernet. Elegant and approachable young, they nonetheless have the capacity to age well. Despite its relatively southerly location, Stags Leap can be quite warm, since the clifflike Palisades reflect heat back on to the vines, but afternoon breezes from San Pablo Bay help cool it down and preserve acidity. The best-known wineries here are Stag's Leap Wine Cellars, Shafer, Silverado, and Clos du Val, though many others, such as Robert Mondavi, have vineyards here.

Atlas Peak (AVA from 1992) This mountainous district northeast of Stags Leap has some 1,500 acres (600ha) planted. The terrain is volcanic and often rocky. Elevation ranges from 500 to 2,600ft (150–800m), and the upper stretches can be very cool, with a long growing season, giving considerable intensity of flavor to the wide range of grapes gown here. Tuscany's Antinori has developed vineyards here, but Bordeaux varieties seemed more successful than Sangiovese. All growers and winemakers have to struggle with rugged tannins and occasional herbaceousness.

Oakville (AVA from 1993) One of Napa's most prestigious regions, lying northwest of Yountville and Stags Leap. Soils vary from well-drained alluvial fans to the west, to heavier gravelly soil on the valley floor. The western side receives less afternoon sun. Ripening tends to be even, making Oakville wines instantly appealing, as well as discreetly structured. Wineries include Robert Mondavi, Opus One, Far Niente, Harlan, and Rudd.

Pritchard Hill Not an AVA, but a hilly area just northeast of Oakville and north of Atlas Peak. About 300 acres (120ha) are planted on rugged terrain. Wineries based here include Bryant, Chappellet, David Arthur, and Colgin—all properties that command high prices for their wines. Nonetheless, there is little pressure to create a new AVA here.

Rutherford (AVA from 1993) The heart of Napa, with 4,000 acres (1,620ha) of vines. Slightly warmer than Oakville to the south, but with a similar soil structure, the most prestigious land being the benches that spill down from the Mayacamas mountains. More fertile areas on the valley floor are equally entitled to the AVA. The benchland soils tend to be deep sandy loam with gravel; these soils are not especially fertile, but their balance of fine drainage and good water retention makes them ideal for Cabernet Sauvignon. These wines are said to exhibit a character known as "Rutherford dust," which seems elusive, but there is no doubt that the best wines from here show power, depth of flavor, good acidity, and considerable longevity.

Wineries include Rubicon, Staglin, Swanson, Grgich Hills, Caymus, Quintessa, and Frog's Leap, but vineyards such as Bella Oaks and Sycamore supply fruit to Heitz and Freemark Abbey.

Pope Valley Not yet an AVA, but a warm upland area that lies some 15 miles (24km) to the east. Purists maintain Pope Valley should not be included in the Napa Valley area, since it lies beyond the Napa watershed, but it seems probable that, with many large wineries owning vineyards here, inexorable pressure will lead to the eventual creation of an AVA. The principal attraction of the area seems to be the low price of land and thus grapes. St. Supéry, Flora Springs, Louis Martini, and Cosentino are among the wineries owning vineyards.

Chiles Valley (AVA from 1999) An obscure upland AVA, in the hills northeast of Rutherford and St. Helena. About 1,000 acres (400ha) are planted, mostly with red grapes, but few would make great claims for the quality of the fruit, because the valley enjoys a comparatively short growing season, which can hamper flavor development. Hardly any wineries are based here.

St. Helena (AVA from 1995) The narrow strip of land flanking Highway 29 is somewhat hotter than Rutherford and, especially, Oakville. The soils are sandy clay loams with good water retention that varies according to the amount of gravel. Cabernet from here can be outstanding, combining opulence with elegance. Many wineries are based here, but only a few, like Spottswoode, source their grapes from estate vineyards here.

Spring Mountain District (AVA from 1993) West of St. Helena. These steep and luxuriant hills, with mostly volcanic soils, house some surprisingly large estates, beautifully contoured over the dips and rises of the terrain. Soils vary greatly, especially in depth, but the region in general has more rainfall than the valley floor and ripens later. It is also quite warm, especially at night. Tannins tend to be forceful, but in the best wines they are balanced by formidable intensity of fruit. Wineries include Newton, Cain, Spring Mountain, Barnett, Pride Mountain, Stony Hill, and Togni.

Howell Mountain (AVA from 1984) This lofty region, already famous in the 19th century, lies northeast of St. Helena and is focused around the small town of Angwin, a Seventh-Day Adventist hotbed. Although only about 500 acres (200ha) are planted, it has a reputation for high-quality if robust Cabernet and Zinfandel. The vineyards benefit from constant sunshine but slightly lower temperatures above the fog line, and nights can be warm, too, as hot air rises from the valley floor. The soils are thin and volcanic, but well drained. Tannin management is the name of the game here, since the small-berried grapes can give high tannin levels. Only a few wineries are located here, such as Dunn and Ladera, but vineyards supply many wineries in various parts of the valley.

Diamond Mountain District (AVA from 2001) A small AVA north of Spring Mountain, with about 500 acres (200ha) under vine. Elevation ranges from 400 to 2,000ft (120–600m). Tannins can be formidable, as admirers of Diamond Creek are well aware, and the wines benefit from cellaring. Few wineries are here, but Diamond Mountain Ranch supplies Sterling with excellent fruit.

Calistoga (AVA from 2010) Although this is one of the hottest corners of the valley, nights can be quite chilly, and cooling winds arrive through Knights Valley. This is red-wine territory, with vineyards planted to Cabernet, Zinfandel, and Petite Sirah. Wineries include Chateau Montelena, Araujo, and Clos Pegase.

Robert Mondavi Winery

Visitors to Napa Valley are so used to the sight of the Spanish Colonial Robert Mondavi winery in Oakville that many must pass it without a thought. But when it was built in the mid-1960s, it must have made an extraordinary impression. Robert Mondavi was not a man of false modesty, so when he built the first major winery in the valley in many years, he did so with a flourish, so as to indicate this was no fly-by-night operation.

His father Cesare had begun his winemaking activities in 1921 in Lodi, not far from Sacramento, and thus well away from the prestigious vineyards of Napa Valley. In 1937 he created a winery in St. Helena called Sunny St. Helena—now Merryvale—but Robert persuaded him to buy the historic Charles Krug winery in 1943. His two sons, Peter and Robert (born 1913), were deeply involved, Peter on the winemaking side, while Robert was charged with sales and marketing. Robert's travels to European wine regions in the early 1960s made him realize how far California lagged behind in quality and technical skill, and he urged the family to aim for higher standards. But Charles Krug was doing well, so Peter saw no need to change. Tension between the two brothers increased until Robert was, essentially, forced out in 1965. He resolved to create his own winery and did so a year later, having first acquired some vineyards in Oakville. At the same time, he sued his brother for good measure. What is often forgotten is that at this time Robert was not a young upstart but was already in his early 50s.

Robert had little money and was dependent on other shareholders to finance his new venture and build the winery. Outside investment also allowed him to buy the historic, and very large, To Kalon Vineyard in Oakville. Only in the mid-1970s was the legal battle between the two brothers resolved. Robert was the victor, and Peter had to hand over millions of dollars in compensation, which allowed

Right: Bufano's statue of St. Francis and the mission-style Robert Mondavi winery catch the eye of every Napa visitor

When one considers the substantial volumes of wine that Mondavi produces, the standards maintained by the winemaking team have been remarkably high

Robert to buy out his investors. By 1978, he had full control of the Mondavi winery. The cost was high—some $20 million—but Robert clearly believed it was worth it. The winery was a family business, just like Charles Krug. His son Michael was the initial winemaker until 1974, though his skills lay more on the marketing side; then Michael's younger brother Tim took over the winemaking.

Anyone who met Bob Mondavi immediately recognized that he was a man driven by ambition—but an ambition inexorably linked to a passion for quality. He knew from long experience that Napa Valley was capable of producing truly great wines and that few wineries in the 1960s and 1970s were focused on quality. Mondavi was indefatigable in his pursuit of excellence, initiating costly and complex research programs at his winery and exploring different trellising systems in his vineyards. In 1993, the winery collaborated with NASA to develop aerial imaging systems that could provide and analyze information about vineyards.

He did more than import good-quality French oak to nurture his best wines; he tested endless combinations of country, cooper, forest, and toast in order to work out what would work best with Napa fruit. He was fearless in blind-tasting his own wines against the European competition, and that included the first growths of Bordeaux. When the Mondavi team believed it had reached important conclusions in its research programs, the results were shared with any other wineries that were interested. Mondavi recognized that if he alone raised his game, that would be rewarding; but if he could persuade others to follow his example, then the luster added to Napa's reputation and name could only benefit them all. In the early 2000s, Mondavi spent a fortune creating a new gravity-flow winery that was equipped with wooden fermentation vats for the top wines.

He was inventive, too, creating in 1966 what was for America a new wine style in his Fumé Blanc, which was loosely modeled on fine white Graves. In 1971 he made the first vintage of the celebrated Cabernet Sauvignon Reserve. He worked hard to improve the quality of varieties such as Pinot Noir, recognizing that to treat it like Cabernet or Petite Sirah was to rob it of all varietal character and finesse. He bought vineyards in Carneros and Stags Leap to augment his grape sources. He also expanded the company beyond recognition, by creating the Woodbridge winery in Lodi. An unashamedly commercial operation, it produced each year about 7 million cases of inexpensive but well-crafted wine. Quality was maintained by creating close relationships with local growers and rewarding them for the excellence of their grapes.

The expansion was relentless. New wines were introduced from the Central Coast, far from the Mondavis' usual viticultural stomping grounds. A collection of Italian varietals under the La Famiglia label was created, but it proved short-lived. The company bought up other wineries, such as Byron in Santa Barbara and Arrowood in Sonoma Valley. Joint ventures with the Frescobaldi family in Tuscany resulted in the creation of successful wines such as Luce, while similar ventures with Errázuriz in Chile led to the crafting of one of the country's icon wines: Seña. (After the takeover of Mondavi by Constellation in 2004, these joint ventures and vineyard acquisitions were sold off.)

But the most extraordinary undertaking, and the one that confirmed once and for all Robert Mondavi's stature, was the founding in 1979 of Opus One, the joint venture with Baron Philippe de Rothschild. It was an alliance of equals, as the label itself confirms, with its profiles of the two great men of wine. By the 1990s, Robert Mondavi was the grand old man of Napa Valley, universally respected if not perhaps liked by all. Contemptuous of neo-Prohibitionists, he (often accompanied by his equally energetic wife Margrit Biever) campaigned to spread the message that all readers of this book will intuitively accept:

Above: Another benign statue of St. Francis watches over the substantial volume of wine maturing in the Mondavi barrel cellar

that the moderate and informed consumption of good wine enhances rather than imperils our quality of life. Well into his 80s, he stumped his way across the world, attending events and spreading the word. He also helped found and finance COPIA, a complex that promoted wine, gastronomy, and the arts, located in downtown Napa. It closed in 2008, but was due to reopen in 2010 or 2011.

Despite the seeming success, there were problems with an increasingly complex business organization, and this was not helped by feuding among the family. Admittedly, Robert Mondavi could not have been an easy man to work for, especially if he was your demanding father. The winery became a public company in 1993, though the family maintained overall control. Then, in 2004, the corporation was restructured: the plan enriched the Mondavis but meant they no longer had a controlling interest in the company. The other shareholders came from the world of finance rather than wine and did not really understand the long-term nature of the business. A short while later, the board decided to sell the main winery and vineyards and focus on the high-volume Woodbridge winery. Michael Mondavi resigned, and Tim would follow a year later. In November 2004, the company was acquired by the giant Constellation corporation. That was the end of the family's association with the company that bore their name. Robert Mondavi died in May 2008, at the age of 94.

Outwardly, little has changed. Constellation, the Mondavi winemakers assure me, has no wish to damage a winning formula. Senior winemaker Genevieve Janssens, who has been at her post since the 1990s, remains in place, as do other winemakers who have been with the company for decades. The dedication to educating the public on the subtleties and benefits of wine, initiated by Robert Mondavi, remains unaltered, and the winery welcomes tens of thousands of visitors to its premises and tours, as well as to its culinary and cultural festivals.

Despite the worldwide renown of the company, I believe its accomplishments have been underestimated. Robert Mondavi, and also his winemaking son Tim, believed strongly that wine was to be consumed with food. That sounds like common sense to European readers, but in North America it is not necessarily the case. The acceptance of high-alcohol table wines is certainly related to the fact that such wines are often consumed as apéritifs. If you're used to a martini or a Manhattan at sunset, then a 15% Cabernet is not going to dismay you. But true to Italian tradition, the Mondavis believed the rightful place for serious wine was at the lunch or dinner table. As a consequence, Tim Mondavi in particular worked hard to produce wines that were moderate in alcohol and well suited to accompanying food.

This earned him some dismissive comments and reviews in the American wine press. James Laube wrote in *Wine Spectator* (July 2001), "At a time when California's best winemakers are aiming for riper, richer, more expressive wines, Mondavi appears headed in the opposite direction. [...] Tim seems to have overcorrected; the attempt to give his wines more nerve and backbone has come at the expense of body and texture." Such criticism damaged the company's reputation. It may have been that some individual wines, the Fumé Blanc in particular, were undernourished or unsatisfactory, but the great majority of the wines, especially the Cabernets, made in the 1980s and 1990s were beautifully balanced and stylish. Many of them are still delicious today. Robert Mondavi's very first bottling of Cabernet Sauvignon in 1966 was still remarkably fresh and stylish in 2009.

Considering the substantial volumes of wine that Mondavi produces, the standards maintained have been remarkably high. To produce a few hundred cases of outstanding wine from a small, well-placed vineyard is not so difficult. To produce around 40,000 cases of a very good wine, year in, year out, is a triumph, and I believe Mondavi, even today under corporate ownership, should be given credit for its achievement and consistency.

Above: Genevieve Janssens, Mondavi's senior winemaker for nearly two decades, has helped to maintain quality

FINEST WINES

The Chardonnay and Chardonnay Reserve are sound rather than exceptional, and it is arguable that the Sauvignon Blanc, in the form of its Fumé Blanc and Fumé Blanc Reserve, has more character. The basic Napa Valley Cabernet is of remarkable quality, given the substantial volumes that are produced; no doubt the winery's extensive vineyard holdings across the valley contribute to this excellence. There is also an Oakville Cabernet

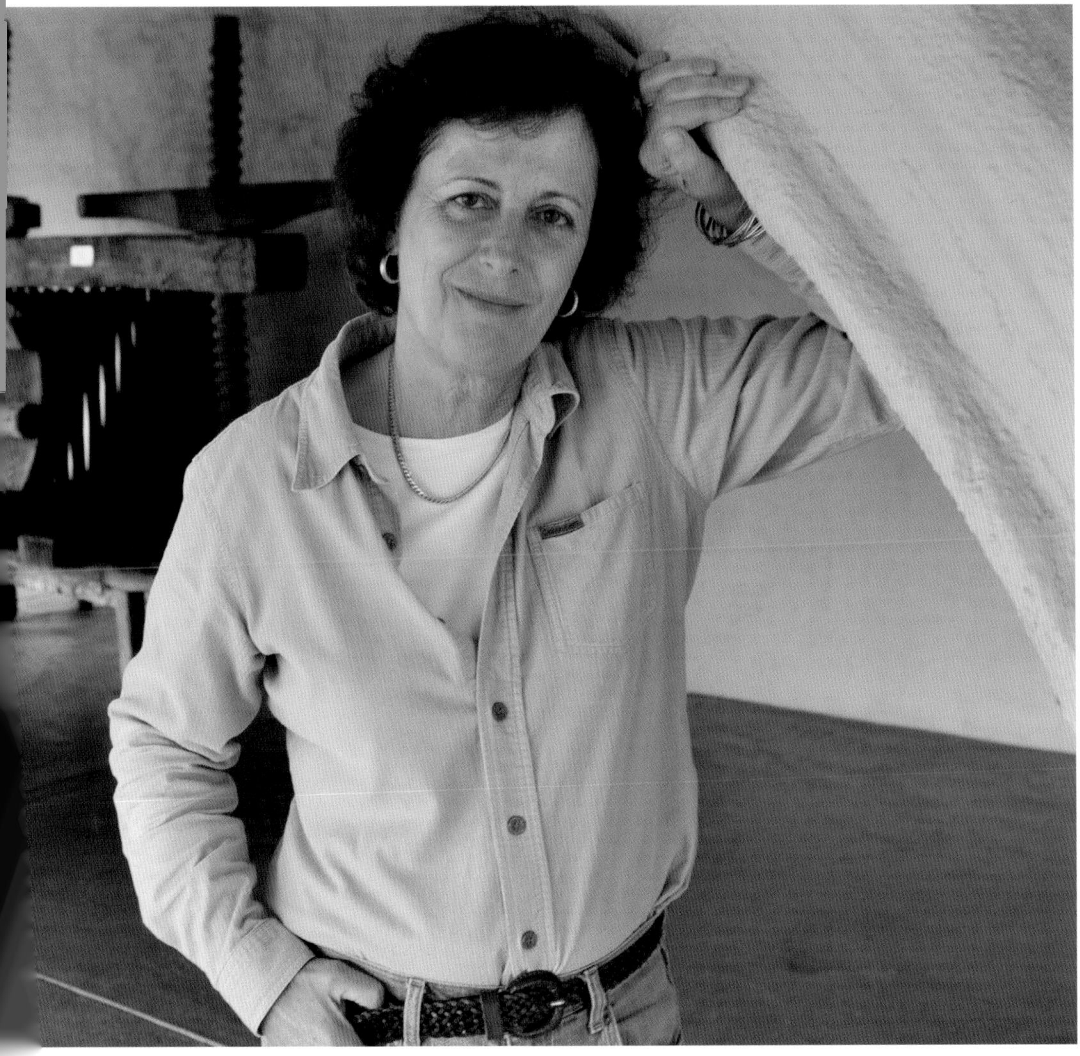

made mostly from To Kalon fruit, but the Stags Leap Cabernet appears to have been discontinued. The finest Cabernet is, of course, the Reserve—a remarkably consistent wine aged in new oak that is rarely perceptible. Although the wine is considerably higher in alcohol than it was in the 1980s, it remains balanced and elegant. In certain vintages, there are separate, small-volume vineyard-designated bottlings of both Fumé Blanc and Cabernet Sauvignon from the oldest vines in To Kalon. Of Cabernet Reserve vintages tasted recently, the most exciting were 1987, 1990, 1991, 1993, 1996, 1997, 1998, 1999, 2001, 2004, 2005, and 2006. No doubt others are equally fine.

Of the principal varieties, only Pinot Noir can sometimes disappoint, even though Mondavi was one of the pioneers of outstanding Pinot two decades ago. Some recent releases of the Pinot Reserve have been far too alcoholic, and the regular Carneros Pinot Noir has been preferable.

Robert Mondavi
Area under vine: 1,300 acres (525ha) in Napa and Carneros
Average production: 3.6 million bottles (Napa only)
7802 St. Helena Highway, Oakville, CA 94562
Tel: (707) 963-7777
www.robertmondaviwinery.com

Diamond Creek Vineyards

The late Al Brounstein, who created this estate on Diamond Mountain, used to delight in showing visitors around in his golf cart. Even though all too evidently afflicted with Parkinson's disease, he would whizz about at alarming speeds, pretending to have faulty brakes and admitting that he was trying to scare his passengers. The tour was worthwhile because of the beauty of the estate. The vineyards are planted on a variety of slopes and exposures, but some of the original vegetation has been retained, as well as man-made additions in the form of rose gardens, artificial lakes, and bridges. Even more remarkably, Brounstein devised an intricate series of waterfalls. Leaning out from his golf cart, he would flick a switch, and a torrent of water would come cascading out of the woods. At night, to gild the lily, they were floodlit.

If in those days nobody in California gave much thought to "terroir," Brounstein certainly did. He created three cuvées, each based on a different soil type

This may seem irrelevant to the quality of the wine, but it illustrates the extraordinary achievement of Brounstein and other mountain-vineyard proprietors. They took an inhospitable terrain that was strewn with boulders and other impediments and turned it into a viticultural paradise. Al Brounstein was one of the few producers who not only handled a bulldozer but turned the slopes of the Mayacamas Mountains into a landscape worthy of a Capability Brown or Humphrey Repton.

Brounstein became fascinated by wine while working as a sales representative for Sebastiani in the 1960s. He took wine-tasting courses in Los Angeles, further courses at the Sorbonne, and picked grapes at Ridge. By the late 1960s, he knew he wanted to make wine in Napa Valley. He had a few certainties in his mind: he wanted to make Cabernet, and from hillside vineyards. He talked to Louis Martini, Joe Heitz, and other established Napa winemakers. They gave conflicting advice, but Jack Davies at Schramsberg and André Tchelistcheff confirmed that this Diamond Mountain property had great potential. In 1967, Brounstein bought it.

He obtained budwood, he claimed, from some Bordeaux first growths. It was illegal to import such cuttings, but he had his own plane and was often flying back and forth to Tijuana with one girlfriend or another. The customs authorities just took him for a roué, though as Brounstein once told me, the flights were "strictly business." His cuttings made it successfully to Napa Valley and, fortunately, turned out to be disease-free.

Before planting them, he had to clear the land. He also had to sink a well in order to supply the property with water. He soon realized that the property included three distinct soil types. If in those days nobody in California gave much thought to "terroir" and microclimates, Brounstein certainly did. From the outset, he created three cuvées, each based on a different soil type: Volcanic Hill (8 acres [3.2ha]), Red Rock Terrace (7 acres [2.8ha]), and Gravelly Meadow (5 acres [2ha]). Later, he added a fourth called Lake (0.75 acres [0.3ha]), but it was only bottled separately when distinctive; in other vintages, it was blended with Gravelly Meadow. Jerry Luper was his first winemaker, and the first vintage was 1972.

The costs of developing Diamond Creek were enormous, and when, in 1976, Brounstein's bank manager urged him to buy grapes to make up for the shortfall caused by drought that year, he refused. He would make estate wine or nothing. The bank pulled the plug on his loan, and Brounstein had to dash around to find alternative financing. He once told me the property lost money for 15 years.

Right: Boots Brounstein, who continues to run Diamond Creek according to the principles of her late husband, Al Brounstein

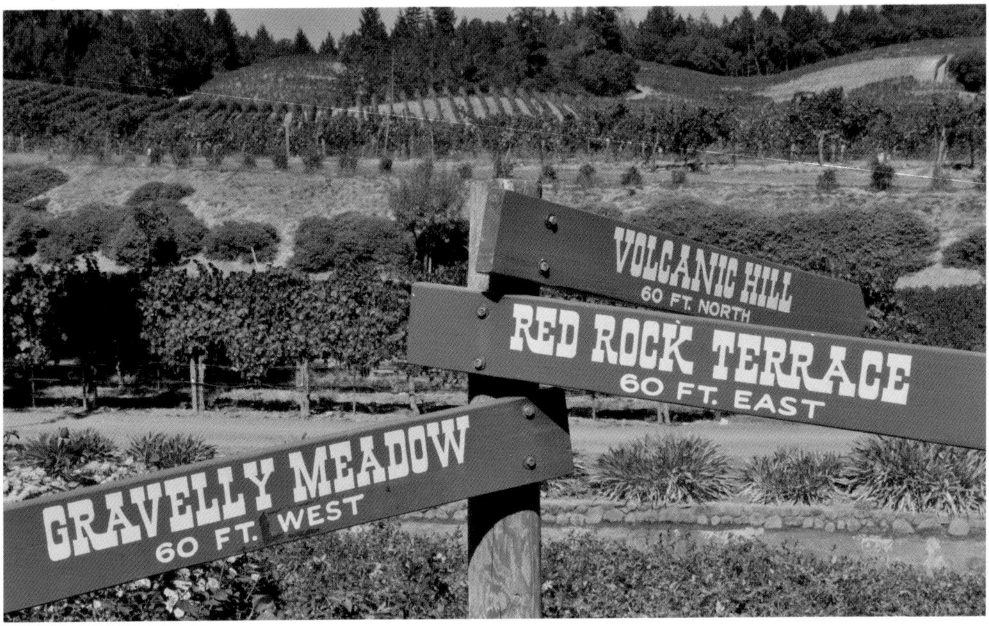

Above: Signs to the three original Diamond Creek vineyards, whose distinct soil types have always been its touchstone

The vineyards are no longer pure Cabernet Sauvignon; 6 percent is Merlot, and there is also a little Cabernet Franc and Petit Verdot. The oldest vines, on St. George rootstocks, are now more than 40 years old. Some replanting has been inevitable, but Al's widow Boots is determined to retain some of the original vines for as long as possible. So varied are the exposures and elevations—the highest spot is 800ft (245m)—that harvest can take eight weeks to complete. Within Volcanic Hill alone, there can be a difference of four weeks between picking the top of the slope and the bottom. Lake is often the last vineyard to be picked, in November, and it gives small berries that result in extremely intense wines. Yields are low, at around 2 tons per acre. Red Rock Terrace is steep and north-facing, and there is a good deal of iron in the soil; the wines are generally more forward and elegant than the other bottlings. Well-drained Volcanic Hill has ash in the soil, faces south, and gives wines that are dense and powerful. Gravelly Meadow faces east and has rockier soil and the lowest yields. Its wines can be very long-lived, and I often find them the most Bordelais.

Al Brounstein and his winemakers—Jerry Luper and then Phil Steinschriber—modeled the wines on Bordeaux. They were not afraid of powerful tannins. The Diamond Creek wines of its first decade could, however, be tough; in some vintages, such as 1974, the tannins did soften, and the wines were said to be magnificent, but not all vintages developed so successfully. Brounstein attributed the more user-friendly wines of the 1990s not to changes in winemaking but to the fact that the vines were older.

The winemaking is artisanal, with the must fermented in small, open wooden vats. Yeasts are inoculated and the cap punched down by hand. The four cuvées are made in much the same way and aged for up to 22 months in 50 percent new barriques, with varying toast levels. There is no fining or filtration. Brounstein said that he could keep the winemaking simple because Cabernet, unlike Pinot Noir, was a forgiving variety during vinification: "All you have to do is get out of the way," he once said.

The oldest vintage I have encountered is the 1991 Red Rock Terrace, so I cannot comment on the styles or ageability of wines from earlier decades.

Certainly the wines of the 1990s and early 2000s strike me as superb. They are true mountain wines, with firm tannins, an occasional earthiness, and a dense structure. But they have never been lacking in fruit or even opulence. They are very individual expressions of Napa Cabernet, with none of the blandness that can affect some Napa wines that reflect the hand of the winemaker more than any sense of place.

Al Brounstein, who died in 2006, is much missed, but he must have known he was leaving an extraordinary legacy, which is now cared for by his family. Behind his impish sense of humor, there must have been a will of steel, for wine properties such as this do not easily come into being. Nor, until his final days, did he view his illness as an impediment. In public, at any rate, he would always rise above it with a joke. When his arms trembled, he told visitors he always wanted to be an orchestral conductor—"but only fast numbers."

Many years ago, standing on the terrace of the winery overlooking the estate, Al Brounstein permitted himself a murmur of self-satisfaction: "Not bad for a poor boy from Minneapolis..." Not bad at all.

FINEST WINES

(Tasted 2007–09)

Red Rock Terrace

2006 Rich yet floral nose of black cherries and some red fruits, too. Medium-bodied, discreet, but intense; tannic, of course, but with fine acidity to give persistence. Long, delicate red-fruit finish.

2005★ Fine, spicy black-currant nose. Rich but not overblown, concentrated but not too massive, this has admirable intensity of fruit and a long, sweet, but not jammy finish. Excellent potential.

2004 Dense black-cherry nose, somber and impressive. Broad, opulent, and packed with fruit but, like many 2004s lacks some drive and energy.

2003 Rich juicy nose, ripe black currants. Very rich and concentrated, sumptuous fruit, sweet and pungent, yet with good acidity and length.

2002 Lush nose, with power, as well as richness, and a slight gaminess. Very rich and concentrated, spicy, tight, and forceful, with firm tannins and an abundance of black-fruit and licorice flavors. Very long.

1999 Still opaque red. Dense, flamboyant plummy nose. Dense, chocolaty, and highly concentrated; a huge powerful wine that is nonetheless balanced and long.

Gravelly Meadow

2006 Intense nose, raspberry coulis and a hint of beets. Supple, less grainy than Red Rock, with sweet, ripe fruit and integrated tannins. Concentrated without being too extracted, with plenty of lift on the long, elegant finish.

2003 Sumptuous, oaky black-currant nose. Full-bodied, dense, and a touch severe, with a certain rigidity on the mid-palate, but with sweet fruit on the elegant finish.

1999 Sleek, discreet black-currant nose, very stylish and enlivened with a touch of mint and chocolate. Very concentrated but elegant, thanks to a fine thread of acidity. Juicy, but has ample backbone and length.

Volcanic Hill

2006 Opulent but brooding blackberry nose. Suave and concentrated and more open than the nose, with grippy tannins—yet not too extracted or tough. Long, spicy finish, with good acidity.

2004★ Lush blackberry nose, explosively aromatic. Rich, with voluptuous black fruits, clearly structured but already accessible. Balanced and long.

2003 Spicy black-fruit-and-fruitcake nose, quite oaky. Dense and chewy, with hefty tannins balanced by sweet, tangy Cabernet fruit and lively acidity on the finish.

2002 Very rich brooding nose, with black-fruit and licorice aromas. Powerful black fruits on the highly concentrated palate make this something of a blockbuster. Pungent and dramatic, this still needs cellaring. Very long.

1999 Muted aromas of plums and black currants. Juicy and highly concentrated, with fine structure and acidity to give it finesse and length.

Diamond Creek Vineyards
Area under vine: 21 acres (8.5ha)
Average production: 35,000 bottles
1500 Diamond Mountain Road, Calistoga, CA 94515
Tel: (707) 942-6296
www.diamondcreekvineyards.com

Dominus Estate

Christian Moueix is best known as the astute and affable owner and manager of his family's négociant business in Libourne and properties in Pomerol and St-Emilion. But unlike most of France's great men of wine, he completed his studies at UC Davis. It seemed fitting for him, at some point, to acquire a property in California—not in order to replicate Pomerol in Napa, but, as he once remarked, to take up a personal challenge that would make him reconsider his French assumptions about winemaking.

He was lucky enough to acquire an historic property in Yountville. The Napanook Vineyard was established in 1836 and had been acquired by John Daniel of Inglenook and inherited by his daughters. In the past, it had been one of the sources, along with the estate's Rutherford vineyards, for the great Inglenook Cabernets. Moueix met the sisters and established a partnership with them in 1982, and in 1995 he became sole owner. (One of the daughters, Robin Lail, now produces excellent wine under her own label.) The Napanook Vineyard survived the outbreak of phylloxera in the 1980s, because it had been planted on St. George rootstock; nonetheless, much of the vineyard was replanted, at ever higher densities than previously, using both French and Californian plant material.

The first vintage was in 1983. The project was a genuine collaboration between Napa and Bordeaux, and Moueix's winemaker, the legendary Jean-Claude Berrouet, was heavily involved from the outset. The California-based winemaker from 1996 to 1998 was David Ramey, followed by Boris Champy until 2007, when Tod Mostero took over as technical director, after spending some years running Almaviva in Chile.

Christian Moueix is an art collector, but here at Dominus he commissioned an original work of

Right: The daringly original Herzog and de Meuron winery at Dominus is also natural, practical, and suitably self-effacing

Compared to some other classic Napa Cabernets, Dominus still has some Old World austerity, with quite marked tannins. But the past decade has produced wines of more opulence and greater polish

Above: Ted Mostero, technical director since 2007, who has continued the trend to greater opulence and refinement in the wines

art in the form of a dazzling winery by the Swiss architects Jacques Herzog and Pierre de Meuron. The main structure of steel and Plexiglas is surrounded by a cage of loose basalt rocks, which has numerous functions: it allows shaded natural light into the building, encourages air to circulate, and reduces the need for air conditioning, because the rocks absorb the heat. Somber from the outside, this large dark shed blends into the hillside behind it, and many people drive straight past the winery without even noticing that it's there. Moueix clearly finds this self-effacement pleasing, especially given the Napa inclination to veer in the opposite direction.

The vineyard is an alluvial fan, as is the case at many of the great Napa sites, so it lies on a gentle slope and has access to underground moisture, allowing the vineyard to be dry-farmed. The canopy is managed so as to provide parasols of vegetation that will shade the vines, because the main struggle here is to limit the dehydrating effect of autumn heat. Although the estate is not formally organic, since 2007 there has been an active biodiversity program, with the planting of trees and restoration of the creek to encourage flowering plants that harbor useful natural predators. A cover crop between the rows helps restrain the natural vigor of the site.

Moueix himself admits the first vintages here were unsatisfactory. Yields were rather high, too much press wine was retained, and there was too much Merlot in the blend, reflecting his Pomerol background. Moreover, the grapes were picked at 23° Brix, which may have been an ideal ripeness level in Bordeaux but was a shade ungenerous for Napa Valley, leading to some herbaceous tones and formidable tannins in certain vintages. Some of the earlier vintages were criticized, with some justification, for astringency and for forcing the wines into a Bordeaux mold.

It wasn't until the end of the 1980s that he completed the fine-tuning and was happy with the quality and style of the wine. In 1996, Moueix and Ramey created Napanook as the second wine, which also improved the overall quality of Dominus itself. Compared to some other classic Napa Cabernets, Dominus still has some Old World austerity, with quite marked tannins. But the past decade has produced wines of more opulence and greater polish. Following the Moueix style, the wine is fermented at moderate temperatures, only about one-third of the wine is aged in new oak, and the alcohol is kept in check at around 14%.

FINEST WINES

(Tasted from 2006)

2006 Opaque red. Lush black-currant and blackberry aromas, formidable and earthy. Suave and dense, ripe and fleshy, very tight in its grip now, but has beguiling sweetness of fruit and good length.

2005★ Very deep red. Juicy black-currant nose, with considerable finesse. Plump and full-bodied, with black-fruit flavors, fine-grained tannins, and exemplary elegance and length.

2004 Deep red. Sweet, rich smoky nose, ripe and oaky. Powerful and rather austere, this has richness, flesh, and weight, but it's massive for Dominus and lacks a little finesse. Still an imposing wine.

2002 Very deep red. Similar, aromatically, to 2006, but with surprising density. The palate is more accessible and graceful. There's a great deal of spice and vigor, yet the wine is curiously unevolved and will keep and improve for many years to come. Elegant and long.

2001 Very deep red. Opulent black-fruit nose. Splendid fruit on the palate, very concentrated but without harsh tannins, linear and with considerable grip; built to last. A great Dominus.

1994 Very deep red. Sweet and spicy nose, with aromas of licorice and cloves, ripe but not baked. Sleek and concentrated, with harmony and balance, sensuous yet backed by fine underlying tannins.

1991 Very deep red. Very rich nose, blackberries and licorice. Super-ripe, minty, and still showing good acidity; direct and long. Ready.

Dominus
Area under vine: 120 acres (48.5ha)
Average production: 145,000 bottles
2570 Napanook Road, Yountville, CA 94599
Tel: (707) 944-8954
www.dominusestate.com

Harlan Estate

Bill Harlan began professional life as a businessman, which he remains to this day. But he is a businessman who, from an early age, was determined to make Napa's equivalent of a first-growth wine. His ventures included spells as a successful poker player, a mortgage provider, and a real-estate tycoon. In 1979, he bought the Meadowood Country Club above the Silverado Trail in Napa and transformed it into the luxurious resort that it is today. Much earlier in his life, as a student in Berkeley, he had visited Napa regularly and dreamed of owning a vineyard. When, in 1966, Robert Mondavi opened the first new winery in the valley in decades, it made Harlan aware that the dream could, in principle, be realized.

Bill Harlan is a businessman who, from an early age, was determined to make Napa's equivalent of a first-growth wine

If only he had the money! His entrepreneurial gifts meant he was soon earning a good deal. His interest in wine was magnified after he spent some weeks touring France with Bob Mondavi in 1980, visiting Bordeaux and Beaune. In 1983, he founded Merryvale Vineyards, and was joined by Bob Levy, now the winemaker at Harlan Estate. Then, in 1985, Harlan found the land that he was sure would allow him to bring his dream to fruition.

The property was set in the hills just west of Oakville in a kind of horseshoe above Far Niente. Proximity to Oakville or Rutherford and a hillside location were two of the criteria Harlan had laid down for his ideal vineyard. But there was much to be done: trees to be cleared, roads constructed, and the land prepared for planting. The cost was enormous. Moreover, the first plantings succumbed to phylloxera. Bill Harlan was not deterred. The elevation—between 325 and 525ft (100–160m)—struck him as ideal, and he relished the multiple exposures of the slopes. He also paid great attention to aesthetic issues, retaining some woodland and burying cables and phone wires underground. The farming was essentially organic, and Harlan Estate was one of the first in Napa to use biodiesel.

Getting the vineyards right was the priority, and once that was accomplished, Harlan built a winery in 2002. It resembles a veranda-enclosed log cabin more than a conventional winery, and the building is mostly concealed within a grove of trees.

The harvest can take as long as four weeks, leaving Bob Levy with as many as 60 different lots to work with. Grape selection is fanatical, and any lots that Harlan and Levy are unhappy with are consigned to the second wine, The Maiden. Michel Rolland has been associated with Harlan since 1989, as much for his international influence as for his blending skills. Levy made wine here from 1987 onward but was unhappy with the first three vintages, which were never released—another sign of the Harlan perfectionism. The first commercial vintage was 1991, and even that wasn't released until 1996, 11 years after the founding of the estate.

Levy allows indigenous yeasts to ferment the wines and favors a prolonged maceration, with gentle punch-downs and pump-overs. Since 2001, some wooden vats (replaced every five years) have supplemented the winery's steels tanks. The wine is aged for at least 24 months in new French oak, but blending begins only after the first year. No press wine is used, and it is all sold off to other wineries that are not permitted to reveal the source.

Most of the wine is sold through a mailing list and usually sells out within a few days, by which time its price on the secondary market has usually doubled and may, in time, go considerably higher. It has devoted followers, including most of the

Right: Bill Harlan, who has realized his dream of producing a first-growth equivalent, albeit in a distinctive Napa guise

American wine press, and at a tasting of Napa Cabernets organized by the Institute of Masters of Wine in London, the 1994 was considered one of the stars of the event.

Harlan Estate has its detractors, too. André van Rensburg, an admittedly iconoclastic South African winemaker, believes the fruit is picked at excessive ripeness levels and that new oak has to supply the tannins that the grapes lack. American critic Matt Kramer applauds the smoothness of the wines but also finds them excessively oaky. Harlan Estate, whatever the aspirations of its owners to produce a first-growth wine, is not a Bordeaux replica. It is an intrinsically Napa wine: big and powerful, but also ripe and rich and oaky. It is polished and extremely well made, and those who doubt the wines' capacity to age are, in my limited experience, wrong.

Harlan and Levy have also created a parallel label called Bond, the name suggesting a relationship of trust between growers and the winery. It is essentially a négociant label, allowing Levy to work with fruit that is not estate-grown. At Merryvale, he and Harlan bought from some outstanding growers who had no ambition to make wine or create their own brand. They welcome the farming expertise of the Harlan team and a contract that gives them a share in the commercial success of their wine. Each Bond wine is released under a proprietary name, so that the names of the individual owners remain confidential. None of the five vineyards is larger than 9 acres (3.5ha), each has its own typicity and identity, and they are all sold at the same (high) price. The winemaking is essentially the same as for Harlan Estate, though Levy does allow himself some experimentation, such as barrel-fermentation for one of the wines. Production is limited to no more than 800 cases per vineyard, and the second label, Matriarch, uses declassified wine from all five sites. Despite the deliberate anonymity of the label, Bond has proved very successful, and the wines fetch high prices, though not nearly as high as those of Harlan itself.

Left: The artisanal feel created by natural materials belies the investment, passion, and perfectionism behind the winery

FINEST WINES

(Tasted from 2006)

2005 Muted nose: chocolate, plums, fruitcake. Not super-concentrated but has intensity of flavor and fine acidity. Fine-grained tannins, surprisingly elegant and long.

2004 Intense nose, savory and a touch tarry. Fresher and livelier than the nose suggests, very ripe but shows a light touch; has a light herbal tone but is fully ripe.

2003 Sumptuous black-fruit nose, with some minty lift; fruitcake. Very rich and highly concentrated; a bit leathery but has good acidity and remarkable length.

2002★ Opaque red. Ripe but very toasty nose. Rich, sumptuous, and minty; a huge wine, yet it has spiciness and vibrancy, too, and the power and tannins are balanced by fine acidity. Very long.

2001 Brawny, powerful, black-fruit nose, yet pure and without any tarry character. Lavish and very oaky, but the tannins are supple, and the fine acidity supports a long, majestic finish. Powerful but balanced.

2000 Less opulent nose than the 1999 but very elegant. Silky and seamless on the palate, and though not a wine of immense depth, it's harmonious and persistent and in no way forced.

1999 A perfumed and voluptuous nose of cherries and black currants and sweet new oak. Plump and super-ripe yet not jammy, with good acidity to keep it fresh. Complex and very long.

1998 (Pure Cabernet) Sumptuous and oaky nose, though with a slight herbaceous tone. Oaky and slightly aggressive, lacking a little flesh and body. Although very concentrated, it doesn't show much complexity, but the long finish is sweeter than the attack. A good result for the vintage.

Harlan Estate
Area under vine: 40 acres (16ha)
Average production: 30,000 bottles
PO Box 352, Oakville, CA 94562
Tel: (707) 944-1449
www.harlanestate.com
www.bondestates.com

Chateau Montelena Winery

One of Napa's historic wineries, Chateau Montelena is tucked into the hills just north of Calistoga. It was founded by rope manufacturer Alfred Tubbs, who in 1882 bought the 250-acre (100ha) estate and planted vineyards before building the grand chateau. Most of the cellars were underground, which was a rarity at that time. The initial winemaker, Jérôme Bardot, was a Frenchman. The venture prospered, and by 1896 Montelena was the seventh-largest winery in the valley. After Tubbs died in 1897, his son William inherited the property and had to cope with the numbing effects of phylloxera and Prohibition. Winemaking was abandoned during Prohibition, but William's son Chapin Tubbs revived the winery in 1933. In 1958, the family put the property on the market.

The new owners were the Frank family, who bought the property as no more than a retirement home. They spent their years landscaping the grounds and putting in a lake, which has subsequently become a wildlife sanctuary. Montelena changed hands again in 1968, when Lee Paschich became the owner, but he brought in some partners, including a lawyer named James Barrett, with the aim of replanting the vineyards and restoring the old winery.

The first Montelena vintage was 1972, but that was made from purchased fruit. The 100 acres (40ha) of existing vineyards had been planted with varieties such as Alicante and Carignane, which were of no interest to the new owners, who replaced them with mostly Cabernet Sauvignon. But it would take a few years for the new vines to deliver a usable crop. In 1973, the Barretts hired a Croatian winemaker, Mike Grgich, who had worked under Tchelistcheff at Beaulieu Vineyard and then at Mondavi. It was he who made the famous 1973 Chardonnay that triumphed at the Judgment

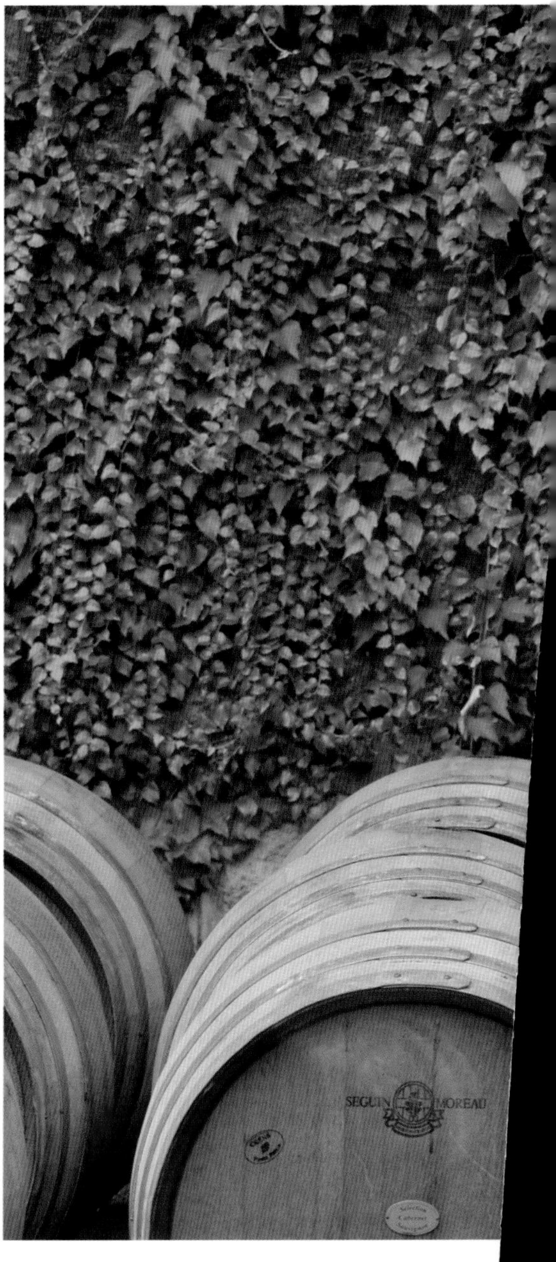

Right: Bo Barrett, Montelena's general manager since 1981, who has maintained standards at this historic Napa property

The wine is made in a classic, even old-fashioned style, with a fairly low pH and alcohol that rarely exceeds 14%. Barrett wants the wine to reflect the vineyard, and not show the hand of the winemaker

of Paris tasting in 1976. The fruit came from three different vineyards; none of it was estate-grown.

Grgich left in 1975 and founded his own winery, Grgich Hills, in 1977. His replacement was Jerry Luper, who had made his reputation at Freemark Abbey. It was he who made the first Estate Cabernet in 1978. He stayed until 1981, when James Barrett's son Bo took over. In those days, when I first met him, Bo Barrett looked as though he would be happier surfing or skiing than doing pump-overs in a winery, and somehow the atmosphere of the beach party managed to invade the tasting room whenever he was there. Yet he was no dilettante, and he and his team maintained his predecessors' high standards. He recalled his mixed emotions when the 1973 Chardonnay had outgunned the best white wines of France. "Beating the French is like beating your dad at tennis: it's a bittersweet experience." Bo went on to become the general manager of the winery but always longed for the day when he could retire, giving up such chores as buying dental insurance for the employees and returning to driving a tractor around the vineyards.

The well-drained estate vineyards are on two types of soil: alluvial and volcanic. The former, in Bo Barrett's view, gave blackberry and chocolate characteristics, while the volcanic soils gave a more cedary character. Because all the blocks are picked separately, Montelena is able to juggle the various lots to come up with a final blend each year.

There used to be two Chardonnays, but the one from Alexander Valley was phased out long ago. The grapes for the Napa Chardonnay are now sourced from a leased vineyard in Oak Knoll, which was one of the sources for the 1973 wine. They are hand-picked at night, partly pressed without skin contact, and partly whole-cluster pressed and fermented in steel tanks. There is no malolactic fermentation. The wine is aged for some ten months in French oak, but only about 10 percent of the barrels are new. Barrett is looking to produce a mouthwatering rather than voluptuous style, "because the first job of a white wine is to get you in the mood for a red wine."

When the vineyards were replanted in the 1970s, the Barretts had the sense or luck to plant on St. George rootstock, which proved resistant to phylloxera. So the Cabernet vines from 1972 and 1974 are still in production and provide the backbone of the estate Cabernet. Most of the vineyards are dry-farmed, so berries are small and yields are very low. In January, the lots are tasted, and those not good enough for, or not suited to, the Estate wine go into the Napa Cabernet. The Estate wine is aged for up to 30 months in 25 percent new barriques, and a little Merlot and Cabernet Franc are blended in; the Cabernet Franc's role, according to Barrett, is to open up the wine on the palate and to give it some approachability when it's young. The wine is filtered but not fined. Overall, the wine is made in a classic, even old-fashioned style, with a fairly low pH and alcohol that rarely exceeds 14%. Barrett wants the wine to reflect the vineyard and not show the flavors developed by an overripe and much-manipulated bottle that shows the hand of the winemaker more than the site.

In the 1990s, some neighboring growers in Calistoga had developed a small local cooperative, but it went bust in 1997. Barrett knew many of the vines were old and exceptional, so he arranged to buy the fruit for a wine called Calistoga Cuvée, which was first produced in 1993. It was a way to give visitors to the tasting room who could not afford the expensive Estate Cabernet a more economical experience of a Cabernet that was, nonetheless, purely from Calistoga fruit. In 2000, a few other vineyards were allowed into the blend, so to speak, so the wine was renamed the Napa Cabernet. Less structured than the Estate wine, it was aged in oak for up to 16 months.

There are a few other wines, but they rarely have much distribution beyond the tasting room: a Riesling, which comes from Potter Valley in Mendocino, and some old estate-grown Zinfandel.

There were some difficult moments over the past decade, notably a TCA or cork taint problem that affects a few vintages—in particular, the 2001 Estate Cabernet. As so often happens when TCA rears its ugly head in a winery, those who work in it are the last to recognize that there is a problem. But by 2004, Montelena admitted that it had had TCA but had also worked hard to eliminate it. Indeed, recent vintages show no trace of it.

By the late 2000s, Bo Barrett was looking wistfully at that tractor and contemplating how he could escape his manager's office for good. There had been some offers from would-be purchasers of Montelena, but none of them seemed to strike the right note, and the Barretts had turned them down. There was no compelling reason for the family to sell up, but Bo's numerous siblings were co-owners who would need to be bought out if he were to keep Montelena in the hands of his descendants. However, when Michel Reybier, the owner of Château Cos d'Estournel in St-Estèphe, expressed an interest, Barrett was tempted. Reybier and the estate's manager, Jean-Guillaume Prats, came to visit Montelena, and all parties thought they could work together. Bo Barrett might stay on for a while, but Reybier's wealth would allow for some costly but necessary improvements to be made. The property, in Bo's words, "could be put into dry dock and given a proper overhaul."

The deal was announced in the fall of 2008, but a few months later Reybier pulled out. No one is quite sure why, but the worsening economic situation may have persuaded him that this was not the moment to expand his business.

Although the Chardonnay is an appealing wine, Montelena's enduring reputation rests on its often magnificent Estate Cabernet. It has all the richness and warmth one would expect from a Calistoga wine. As well as a wealth of black fruits, it can show pronounced secondary flavors such as black olives and chocolate. It is also exceptionally long-lived.

FINEST WINES

(Tasted 2007–10)

Estate Cabernet

2006 Opulent black-currant nose, bright and pure. Full-bodied and chunky, with considerable weight of fruit as well as spice, lively and exuberant with suave tannins. Long.

2005 Sweet, pure black-currant nose, very stylish. Powerful, spicy, and concentrated, with some vigor and good length. Still needs time to open up on the palate.

2003 Dense, brambly nose. Voluptuous, highly concentrated, and spicy, this has a good deal of drive, with earthy but not tough tannins to give grip and persistence.

2000 Rich black-currant nose, lean and tight. Sumptuous, but has a lot of spice and vigor, as well as good acidity and length.

Chateau Montelena Winery
Area under vine: 121 acres (49ha)
Average production: 500,000 bottles
1429 Tubbs Lane, Calistoga, CA 94558
Tel: (707) 942-5105
www.montelena.com

Opus One

Now that 30 years have gone by since the first vintage of this famous wine, it is hard to recall how daring it was to set up the project in the first place. It began as a partnership between Baron Philippe de Rothschild of Mouton Rothschild and Robert Mondavi, and after Mondavi winery was bought by Constellation, that large corporation acquired its share of Opus One. The baron had approached Mondavi in 1970, which shows great foresight, given that Mondavi's own winery had been founded only four years earlier. Both men realized they were not yet ready to form a partnership on this ambitious scale, and it was not until 1978 that the deal was made. It was an extraordinary expression of confidence by one of Bordeaux's grandees in the ability of Napa Valley to produce a world-class wine that could be spoken of in the same breath as a Médocain first growth. It was a unique collaboration of mavericks.

It was not an easy matter to divide the various responsibilities between the two very different owners and their companies. Rothschild, it appears, sent their vineyard manager to lay out the high-density vines (some of the first to be planted in California), while Mondavi supplied most of the grapes until the Opus vineyards were mature. The Mondavi team would make the wine, but the Mouton winemakers would visit regularly to contribute their views. Over the long term, the costs of the winery would be shared, as would any profits.

Both the winery, which was completed only in 1991, and the vineyards would cause considerable difficulties from the outset. The winery design, by Scott Johnson of Los Angeles, placed the structure atop a mound, with the barrel cellars deep underground. Higher-than-expected soil temperatures on the site posed a problem, solved by costly insulation. There are sumptuous public areas furnished with 18th-century antiques and Miró paintings, but the working areas of the winery are modern and functional, while the showpiece

Above: The striking Opus One winery, atop a small mound, with the large circular barrel room and winery well below ground

of the structure is the superb circular barrel room, which allows a thousand barrels to be stored on a single level. Opus sets out to impress; even the paper towels in the restrooms are stamped with its logo.

Early vintages were made from Mondavi's To Kalon vineyard, which was much the same source as for Mondavi's own Cabernet Reserve. In 1984, the Opus vines went into the ground, but many were replanted in 1989. The original arrangement was that Tim Mondavi and Mouton's Lucien Sionneau

Today Opus One seems to find its harmony and balance with enviable ease. Recent vintages have been consistently superb, and so they should be, for this is one of Napa's most expensive wines

(followed in 1985 by Patrick Léon) would taste all potential lots for Opus together. The Mouton winemaker could choose whatever he felt was most suitable for the Opus style, but if Mondavi wanted it for his Reserve, the wine would be split between them, though in practice this rarely happened. Nowadays, of course, Opus has its own vineyards, those around the winery, a parcel across the other side of Highway 29 next to Martha's Vineyard, and 50 acres (20ha) of To Kalon that were ceded to Opus by Constellation. At first, the Opus vineyards were tightly spaced, and vines planted in 2009 are at an even higher density (3,320 vines per acre, or 8,200 vines per hectare), the aim being to increase the leaf area, have fewer clusters per vine, and achieve full maturity at moderate sugar accumulation.

Joint ventures have their difficulties, however amicable the relations between the two parties. Thus: who is making the wine? Inevitably, it smacked of committee work at first, with both parties making their contribution. However, in 2001, Michael Silacci—who had degrees from UC Davis and the University of Bordeaux and had been the winemaker at Stag's Leap Wine Cellars

Above: Michael Silacci, who, with degrees from Bordeaux and UC Davis, is ideally qualified to oversee Opus One's winemaking

for some years—came on board. As skilled in the vineyard as in the winery, Silacci would prove an excellent choice. He instituted major mapping of the soils, with a view to improving the drainage and making modifications that would allow him to convert them to dry-farming. He also introduced night-harvesting.

Although Silacci takes advice from Philippe Dhalluin, technical director of the Mouton group, and from long-term Mondavi winemaker Rich Arnold, he makes the final decisions. He is aided by the fact that the Mouton winemaker, Eric Tourbier, was a classmate at Bordeaux University, so he knows he can trust his judgment. But it's a position that requires tact, since there is no single owner he can turn to should the need arise. The sale of Mondavi has also affected the promotion of the wine. In the past, big hitters such as Philippine de Rothschild and Tim Mondavi would travel the world presenting vertical tastings and other events. Baroness Philippine is still able and willing, in theory, but then Constellation would want one of its figureheads to share the duties with her, which might make for a less charismatic presentation.

Silacci sees his role as producing a wine that faithfully reflects the site and the vintage. He only gets one shot at it. There is no proper second wine at Opus, and although he can presumably sell off unsatisfactory lots, there are limits to how much wine he can get rid of in any vintage. The actual winemaking is classic: sorting after the harvest, destemming, the use of gravity to shift grapes into the tanks, a cold soak, the use of both native and cultured yeasts, very gentle handling of the young wine without pumps and hoses, and sufficient richness and body in the final wine to justify the use of solely new French oak.

As for house style, Silacci does not want to leave too strong a personal imprint on the wine. Even though the model for Opus One has always been the first growths of Bordeaux, he knows he cannot, and should not, make replicas of those great wines. Nor does he want to produce a big, jammy Napa Cabernet that will appeal to many American palates, since a third of the wine is exported around the world. His goal is balance and what he calls natural winemaking, which is to say no added acidity, no watering of the must, and no dealcoholizing.

Opus One has had its critics, and inevitably some vintages have been weaker than others. Over the years, there have been changes to the blend, such as the introduction of Malbec in 1994, and variations in the oak regimen. The early vintages had shorter macerations than would be the case today and had long barrel aging. There are fewer rackings than in the past, and no fining since 2004. More importantly, there have been changes in the vineyards and fruit sources. But Opus One has achieved a kind of stability of style and quality, even though Silacci and his team are constantly fine-tuning.

In general, quality is higher today than in the distant past, when Opus was still finding its way. Early vintages showed an austerity and angularity that are no longer evident in the wine. Opus One now seems to find its harmony and balance with enviable ease. Recent vintages have been consistently superb, and so they should be for one of Napa's most expensive wines.

FINEST WINES

(Tasted 2009)

2007 (shortly before bottling) Dumb black-fruit nose, somewhat stalky. Quite different on the palate: sumptuous and full-bodied, generous and succulent, with rich blackberry fruit and fine acidity and length.

2006 Rich, heady, bold nose, with strong black-fruit character. Full-bodied and burly, and lacking the usual Opus finesse. But this is a vintage for the long haul. Very concentrated and structured; spicy and complex and long.

2005 Resplendent nose, with bright cherry and black-currant fruit and some mint. Medium-bodied, with mouthwatering fruit, thanks to lovely acidity. A slender but very stylish wine, concentrated but not to excess, and at present quite tannic on the finish.

2004★ Intense and refined black-fruit nose, quite oaky, with a whiff of eucalyptus. Silky, concentrated, less brash than many 2004s, but still quite tannic, with a core of sweet fruit and fine acidity to give elegance and length. Outstanding.

2001 Nose still marked by new oak, but has finesse and purity, with blackberry and black-currant fruit. Certainly ripe, but medium-bodied, with fine-grained tannins. Perhaps a touch jammy, but there is a firm tannic backbone to balance it. Long.

Opus One
Area under vine: 170 acres (69ha)
Average production: 320,000 bottles
7900 St. Helena Highway, Oakville, CA 94562
Tel: (707) 944-9442
www.opusonewinery.com

Rubicon Estate

Rubicon is the modern incarnation of the celebrated Inglenook estate in Rutherford, which has had a long and rather complex history. Gustave Niebaum is usually described as a Finnish sea captain, but he was more than that. He was a fur trader and businessman, and when he came to Napa Valley in 1879, he brought a large fortune with him, some of which he spent on the 1,000 acres (400ha) he acquired from WC Watson, who had originally named the Inglenook estate. Niebaum took his new property seriously and modeled it on the top estates of Europe. He planted excellent varieties, as well as some that were more commonplace but suited to large-volume wine production. But few other estates at the time could match Inglenook for its championing of such varieties as Sauvignon Blanc, Riesling, the Bordeaux red varieties, and Pinot Noir.

The winery, which still dominates the property today, was built in 1886 to designs by Hamden McIntyre. At a time when most wines were sold to and bottled by brokers in San Francisco, Inglenook was unusual in commercializing its wine as estate-bottled. Niebaum died in 1908, and his widow Suzanne handed its management to her niece's husband, John Daniel. Inglenook lost some of its renown in the first decades of the 20th century, and Prohibition dealt a further blow. After Repeal, the winery reopened. John Daniel Jr. revived the property after inheriting it from his father; working alongside him from 1935 to 1964 was the winemaker George Deuer from Germany. Deuer was rather too fond of the bottle, but no one disputed that he made great Cabernets, some of which are still drinking well today. The fruit came from Rutherford and from the family's other vineyard, Napanook in Yountville, now Dominus.

Deuer introduced rudimentary temperature control in the form of tubes of cold water that hugged some of the fermentation tanks. The wines were usually aged in large German casks. Inglenook produced Charbono and Pinot Noir but was best known for its Cabernet Sauvignon. Quality control was strict: the regular bottling was known first as Estate, then as Classic Claret, and in outstanding vintages single-cask bottlings were made and labeled as such. Wines that did not make the grade were sold under a different label. Total production was no more than 5,000 cases.

In 1964, Daniel sold the winery. The purchaser was United Vintners, which was part of the Allied Grape Growers cooperative, but two years later the estate was sold on to Heublein for $12 million. Undertakings were given to the Daniel family that quality would be maintained, and while some of the top Cabernet wines remained of sound quality, what the Daniels did not realize was that Heublein planned to expand the range and transform the brand beyond recognition. John Daniel stayed on as a consultant but retired in 1966. Winemaking was moved to more modern facilities at St. Helena; the Niebaum winery was used primarily for storage. By the 1970s, Heublein was releasing 4 million cases a year, mostly vinified from Central Valley grapes, as Inglenook, so trashing one of Napa's great names.

Heublein had a change of heart in 1979 and replanted the Rutherford vineyard. It also restored the historic winery and introduced a wine called Reunion made from Rutherford grapes. But by this time, the brand was in decline, and in 1993 the winery was put up for sale. Film director Francis Ford Coppola was already installed on the property, having bought the Niebaum homestead in 1975, as well as some of the vineyards. In 1994, he was able to buy the winery as well. Coppola had been making wine here under the Niebaum-Coppola label since 1978. He was fortunate in being able to retain the services of Rafael Rodriguez, who had been the vineyard manager under Daniel since 1952. Rodriguez had resigned in 1972 when Heublein

Right: The historic 1886 winery on the Inglenook estate, now Rubicon, restored to its former glory by Francis Ford Coppola

started using pesticides on the vineyard, but Coppola enticed him back in 1976, and he remains a valued member of the Rubicon team. He knows the 125-acre (50ha) vineyard like the back of his hand and can advise on massal selections and other farming matters. The block owned by Coppola lay between the winery and the Mayacamas foothills, with well-drained gravel soils. Shaded from the fierce afternoon sun by their location, the vines ripened slowly and evenly.

When Coppola bought the winery in 1994, he also bought another 60-acre (24ha) parcel of the historic vineyard. Then, in 2003, he bought a further 55 acres (22ha) from the Cohn family for what was then a record price for a Napa vineyard. However, he had succeeded in reuniting most of the property. The Cohn vineyard was poorly drained, and the decision was made to replant and restore the whole sector, which must have added further to the cost. A rare Cabernet clone, known as Clone 29, was identified in 2002 and is believed to have come from Bordeaux in the 1880s. It was chosen for the Cohn blocks, and these replanted blocks came into production in 2006.

The restored winery is now a tourist destination, since it incorporates a museum devoted both to the wines and to Coppola's film career. It also serves as the winery for the top wine Rubicon. In 2005, new wine caves were completed in the foothills behind the winery. Niebaum himself had originally wanted to construct caves in which to age his wines, but he had to abandon the idea after it became clear that the tunnels would be unsafe. Today, experience and technology allow such caves to be dug in safety.

Coppola produces a great deal of wine under a fluctuating range of labels, such as Diamond Collection, Pennino, Coppola Presents, and Director's Cut. The top wine, Rubicon, tended to get lost among this roster of less expensive wines mostly made from purchased grapes. Such wines offered visitors to the estate affordable souvenirs, since Rubicon was always very expensive. In 2007, Coppola bought the former Chateau Souverain winery in Sonoma's Alexander Valley, now renamed Francis Ford Coppola Winery, which has become a second tourist destination, complete with more of Coppola's movie memorabilia. In the past, there was not always a clear distinction between the estate wines and the other ranges; today, with two wineries in different counties and both open to the public, that distinction is more transparent.

The Bordeaux blend Rubicon remains the flagship wine, with its second wine, Cask Cabernet, in its wake. The Rutherford vineyards also produce a white Rhône-style blend under the rather clumsy name of Blancaneaux, and very limited releases of Estate Cabernet Franc, Merlot, and Syrah. Although Rubicon has always been the main focus of the winery, it was never a wine that was easy to love. It was made in quite an extracted style and aged for about two years in mostly new French oak; early vintages received additional aging in large casks. The tannins could be alarmingly grippy when the wine was young, so Rubicon was often not released until about eight years after the vintage. Even then, it could be tough. Since 2002, the wine has been aged for 20–24 months in entirely new barriques.

The Cask Cabernet, which was introduced in 1995, is made mostly from younger vines in a more accessible style than Rubicon. It is aged for 28 months in 500-liter American oak barrels, coopered from wood that has been air-dried for three years. Compared to Rubicon, it lacks structure and is clearly not intended for long cellaring.

The other major estate wine, Blancaneaux, was first made in 1999 and initially contained a good deal of Chardonnay, as well as the Rhône varieties. By 2004, Chardonnay had been eliminated from the blend, which became Roussanne-dominated. The first vintages were aged in new oak, but since 2005, Blancaneaux has been aged in steel on its fine lees, giving a more austere but also more elegant wine.

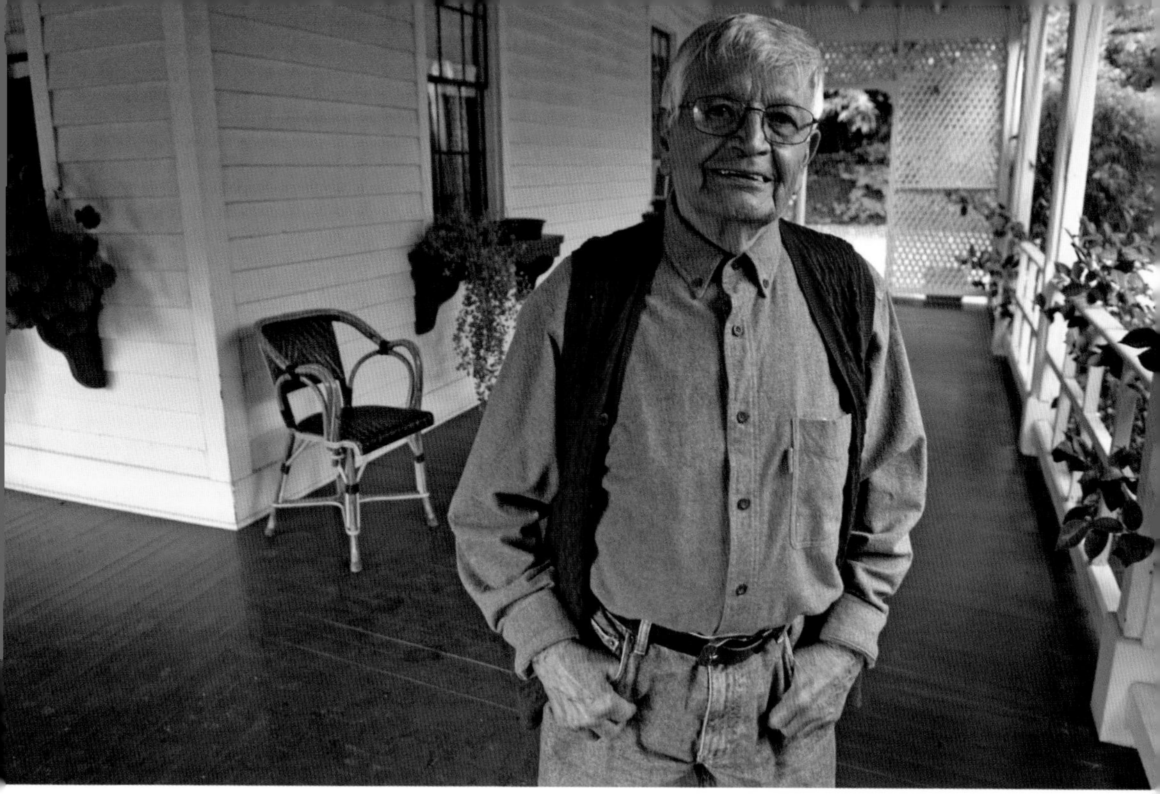

Above: Rafael Rodriguez, Rubicon's vineyard manager for more than 50 years, whose experience and expertise are vital

Larry Stone, one of America's top sommeliers, was general manager from 2006 to 2010. Part of his role was to act as a kind of brand ambassador, touring the world and conducting tastings of the Coppola wines. One of his exciting innovations was the appointment in 2008 of Stéphane Derenoncourt as consultant. This was an astute idea, since the estate wines, for all their quality, still need a lighter touch. Rubicon can be great, but like Léoville-Las-Cases, it's a very earnest wine. Although the estate has one of California's greatest vineyards, more could still be done with it.

FINEST WINES

(Tasted since 2006)

Rubicon

2005 Dense, spicy, savory dark-chocolate nose. Immensely concentrated, powerful, and with considerable drive, yet it also has a voluptuous texture and good depth of flavor. But it's a bit heavy and dogged and could use a bit more acidity and freshness on the finish.

2004★ Smoky, jammy nose, immensely rich. Opulent, spicy, very concentrated, but surprising freshness and balance on the finish for the vintage.

2003 Delicate black-currant nose. Concentrated and lush, not especially extracted; ripe black fruits, well balanced and stylish. Good length.

2002 Dense, complex nose, with aromas of black cherries, meat, leather, ink, and oak. Sumptuous, full-bodied, and vigorous, with refined tannins, excellent balance, and a very long, elegant finish.

2000 Discreet nose of cherries and red fruits, with pronounced new oak. Somewhat lean and herbaceous, with a rather hard texture. The acidity gives some elegance, but this is atypical.

1996 Sweet, intense cherry nose, with mint and cedar tones. Medium-bodied yet concentrated, surprisingly unevolved, still tight, bright, and long.

1992 Dumb nose, with a light floral tone and some black fruits and mint. Sleek and compact, and still showing considerable tannin, though it is well integrated. Not a lush style but has sweet fruit and a sleek texture, if not much excitement.

Rubicon Estate
Area under vine: 235 acres (95ha)
Average production: 300,000 bottles
1991 St. Helena Highway, Rutherford, CA 94573
Tel: (707) 963-9099
www.rubiconestate.com

Stag's Leap Wine Cellars

In the mid-1960s, a young political-science lecturer and occasional hobby winemaker from Chicago named Warren Winiarski loaded his family, including two very small children, into a car and headed for Napa Valley. He had already had some contact with the winemakers of the time, such as Martin Ray, and gained the confidence to start a new life by applying for a job as a cellar rat at Sonoma County's Souverain Cellars. Subsequently, he worked for two years at the recently founded Robert Mondavi Winery. Over the next few years he gained a lot of experience, but he yearned to own his own vineyard and, in 1970, was able to buy 45 acres (18ha) in what became Stags Leap District. He planted the site, which he named Stag's Leap Vineyard (SLV), with Cabernet Sauvignon and Merlot, and the first vintage was 1972.

The following year, he made his wine again: 1,800 cases of wine that he aged in new but lightly toasted French oak for 21 months. This time he had the benefit of advice from the great winemaker André Tchelistcheff, who had only recently left Beaulieu Vineyard. Winiarski probably attached little significance to it at the time, but his 1973 Cabernet was one of the California wines that Steven Spurrier chose for what became known as the Judgment of Paris tasting in 1976. The Stag's Leap wine, made from three-year-old vines, received the highest number of points, outscoring Mouton Rothschild and Haut-Brion. Nobody took the event terribly seriously until George Taber's report on the tasting was printed in *Time* magazine—and the rest is history.

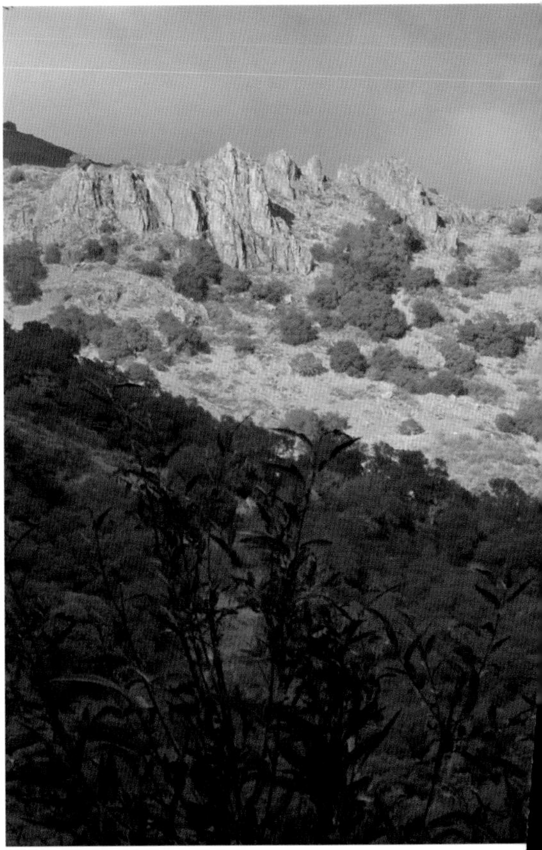

Above: The dramatic backdrop for the vineyard that Warren Winiarski bought in 1970 and dubbed Stag's Leap Vineyard

Winiarski admired the wines from an adjoining site, the Fay Vineyard, and was able to buy it in 1986; the first vintage was in 1990. He had tasted some wine made by Nathan Fay and knew that he could make something remarkable from this site. Whereas SLV has some Merlot in the field, Fay is almost all Cabernet, except for some rows of Petit Verdot. Although the winery produces other wines, notably some Chardonnays, the heart of the property is the two Cabernet vineyards, for this part of Stags Leap District is surely one of the finest spots in California in which to grow Cabernet.

The structure of these two dry-farmed vineyards is fairly similar: volcanic soils toward the slopes of the Palisades, and alluvial soils on the flatter land that lies between those slopes and the knoll to the west, on which the winery is located. Wines from the lower, alluvial sector have more softness and

Although the winery produces other wines, the heart of the property is the two Cabernet vineyards, for this part of Stags Leap District is surely one of the finest spots in California in which to grow Cabernet

flesh, while those from higher up the slope, where the soil is different, have greater concentration. Each vintage, Winiarski sought to bring these two elements into harmony in his wines. Being of a philosophical bent, Winiarski likes to describe the process as taking the fire of the volcanic soils and wrapping it in the softer glove of the alluvial soils. Certainly there is an alliance in the Stag's Leap wine between grip and succulence.

Despite the similarity of their soil structure, Winiarski finds the two vineyards have a different personality: the 60-acre (24ha) Fay is more perfumed and delicate, more supple in its texture, whereas the 36-acre (14.5ha) SLV is more robust and structured, since the proportion of volcanic soil is higher. Each of the many blocks within each vineyard is picked and vinified separately, giving the winemaking team many building blocks to work with.

There is a third Cabernet called Artemis, which has replaced the Napa Valley bottling. This wine is a blend of about one-third estate fruit with two-thirds purchased fruit.

In the great 1974 vintage, Warren Winiarski found one batch of wine he liked so much that he

Above: Nikki Pruss, chief winemaker since 1998, has helped ensure continuity since Warren Winiarski's sale of the company in 2007

bottled it separately, calling it Cask 23. Thereafter it became a policy, in outstanding years, to produce a blend that reflected the best of the vintage, while leaving enough wine to produce Fay and SLV bottlings with their own typicity. This blend continues to be known as Cask 23, and between 1,000 and 2,000 cases are produced in suitable years. I once asked Winiarski whether there had been any vintages when he had come to prefer one of the single-vineyard wines over the prestigious blend, and he admitted that it had happened.

Although he claims not to make wine with a view to long cellaring, it is clear that the best wines do age very well, thanks to their exemplary balance. The legendary 1973 Cabernet, retasted blind during the 2006 rerun of the Judgment of Paris tasting, still showed very well.

In 2007, Winiarski—by then almost 80 years old, though still perfectly vigorous—decided to sell the company, and found ideal purchasers: a partnership between the Tuscan Antinori and Chateau Ste. Michelle in Washington State. (The two wineries had already joined forces to produce a wine called Col Solare in Washington.) Winiarski still lives on the property and takes an active part in promoting the wines. Indeed, it has been some years since he has been the dominant winemaker at Stag's Leap, and since 1998 that role has been filled by Nikki Pruss, who was preceded by Michael Silacci, now the winemaker at Opus One. Nonetheless, Winiarski liked to participate in assembling the final blends.

Savoring a glass of mature old Cask 23, Warren Winiarski looked up and mused, "People like to say that wine is a living thing. That's wrong. From the moment you pick the grapes and crush them, wine is a dying thing. But the great thing is that as it goes into chemical decline, the better it gets!"

FINEST WINES

(Tasted 2006–09)

Fay Vineyard

There are times when this Cabernet does not show particularly well in its youth. Its discreet structure leads it to be overlooked in comparative tastings. But some recent vintages have been impressive.

2005 Toasty nose, a touch tarry, but has spice and vigor. Voluptuous, with considerable complexity, assertive acidity, and depth. Still tight and long.

2003 Plums and mocha on the nose. Broad but graceful; the acidity is moderate yet persistent, the tannins barely perceptible, the finish discreet.

2001 Lean, oaky nose; very fragrant and stylish cherry fruit. Medium-bodied and quite tight, with fine-grained tannins and a lively lifted finish.

1998 Dense nose yet quite floral. Full-bodied and spicy, with a hint of dried fruits and lively acidity; a touch hollow but juicy, forthright, and long.

Stag's Leap Vineyard

Despite its allegedly more robust character, it is not easy in blind tastings to tell Fay and SLV apart, at least when they are young. For SLV at its best is not lacking in finesse, nor is Fay lacking in structure.

2005 A ripe, seductive nose, with discreet oakiness wrapping the blackberry fruit. Medium-bodied and svelte, with good acidity; no blockbuster but elegant; seems to lack only a little weight of fruit.

2003 Muted nose: plums and coffee. Plump, juicy, and concentrated, with more overt tannins than Fay; well structured and long.

2002 An opulent nose, with a good deal of oak. Voluptuous, with firm but not harsh tannins; powerful yet elegant; complex and long.

2001 A reserved nose, with black cherries and black currants. Firm, tannic, and dense; quite powerful and unusually chewy. Less refined than Fay, but it has weight and persistence.

2000 A gorgeous nose, with sumptuous cherry fruit. Full-bodied, with a slight earthiness; complex and balanced. May lack a little acidity, but a hugely appealing mouthful. Long.

1992 Delicate, smoky nose, with a trace of oxidation. Supple, concentrated, and spicy, with quite high acidity balancing the sweet fruit. Linear, with light tannins on the finish and good length. Ready.

Cask 23

The crème de la crème, yet despite its premium, not always finer than the single-vineyard bottlings.

2005★ Vigorous, oaky blackberry-and-licorice nose. Suave, luminous, and concentrated, with rather chalky tannins and moderate acidity, but spicy and tight and still in its infancy.

2004 Slightly jammy, toasty nose. Rich and rounded, with huge tannins, but lacks some vigor and freshness. Medium length.

2001 Smoky, leathery, cedary nose that shows some evolution. Silky, concentrated, quite oaky, but has fine acidity to lift the palate; not super-rich but spicy, complex, and long.

1999 Evolved nose with complex notes of coffee and tobacco—but lifted, too. Discreet, with more intensity than power, fine-grained tannins, and zesty acidity; a delicate, red-fruit style.

1997 Discreet savory nose, poised and elegant. Ample body, weight, and tannin, as well as lively acidity to give a persistent finish, but a little warm.

1995 Subdued cigar-box nose, a touch herbaceous but perfumed. Medium-bodied, quite soft, delicate, with a dash of acidity on the finish. Drinking now.

1994 A cedary nose, very elegant and poised. Concentrated and silky, firm tannins supporting the fruit; exemplary balance and a long, stylish finish.

1992 Muted nose: tobacco, leather, cloves. A discreet style, with delicate cherry fruit, intense and textured, with acidity giving fine length.

1991 Ripe cherry nose, with smoke and mocha tones; very complex. Medium-bodied but has assertive acidity; brisk, slightly chewy; youthful and tangy if not especially complex.

1985★ Sweet, meaty, savory nose. Soft, sweet, and intense, with fine-grained tannins, seamless and harmonious. Has balance and persistence, with mocha on the finish.

1984 Slightly baked nose. Still rich and firm, with marked tannins; a muscular style, with rough vigor.

1977 Rich plump nose: plums, as well as black currant and blackberry. Full-bodied; has volume and concentrated light coffee tone; masses of sweet fruit but without jamminess. Long, vibrant finish.

1974★ Lush, generous, charming nose, abundant black fruits. Supple and juicy, but still bright and fleshy. No blockbuster but has freshness and verve. Excellent balance, irresistible fruit.

Stag's Leap Wine Cellars
Area under vine: 141 acres (57ha)
Average production: 850,000 bottles
5766 Silverado Trail, Napa, CA 94558
Tel: (707) 944-2020
www.cask23.com

Araujo Estate Wines

Nobody, it seemed, knew very much about this vineyard until it was bought by former house-builder Bart Araujo and his wife Daphne in 1990. Eisele was certainly an ancient site, and there are records of Zinfandel and Riesling having been planted there in the 19th century. The previous owners, Milt and Barbara Eisele, had bought the property in 1969, and before that the grapes had been sold to the local cooperative, ending up in Gallo's jug wines. In 1972 and 1973, Mondavi bought some of the fruit, but the wine was blended into their own Cabernets. In 1974, Conn Creek was the purchaser and apparently made an outstanding wine that year. So Eisele certainly had a good track record.

At first, Araujo intended to continue the work of the previous owners, growing the grapes and selling them. But he was soon persuaded to produce his own wine from the vineyard, so the contract with Joseph Phelps came to an end. Araujo was eager to maintain the high standards Phelps had set, and hired the best in the business to help him achieve this goal. Vineyard consultant David Abreu was taken on to supervise the replanting of much of the vineyard. Consultant winemaker Tony Soter, formerly of Spottswoode, came on board (he was later replaced by Michel Rolland), and the initial in-house winemaker was Françoise Peschon, a Frenchwoman who had previous experience at Stag's Leap Wine Cellars and Etude. Art Burtleson, Napa's foremost wine-cave engineer, was commissioned in 1994 to create the tunnels where the wines would be aged.

In 1997, the Araujos were able to buy a neighboring 5-acre (2ha) parcel that had once been planted with Cabernet until new owners took out the vines and turned the land into a horse paddock. They replanted vines, extending their holdings. The oldest vines at the former Eisele Vineyard dated from 1964, but the Araujos were unable to keep them in production, and in the late 1990s they were grubbed up and replanted. At Soter's suggestion, the Araujos added Cabernet Franc and Petit Verdot to the vineyard, and once Rolland had begun his consultancy, some Merlot was added.

The Araujos wanted to produce more than Cabernet Sauvignon, though that would always be the core of the enterprise. Soter was an enthusiast for Sauvignon Blanc, so both Sauvignon and Viognier were planted. They found some Syrah vines on the property that had been planted in 1978 and added more, using a variety of clones. The Araujos tried their hand at Sangiovese, with unhappy results, so they grafted those vines over to Grenache. Attempts to improve quality have been relentless: in 2007, numerous pits were dug in the vineyard so the team could undertake detailed soil analyses. And since 2000, the whole property has been farmed biodynamically.

The site lies close to cliffs that resemble the Palisades in Stags Leap, some miles to the south. It's a volcanic alluvial fan and exceptionally rocky, ensuring excellent drainage. Flash floods from the creek that traverses the vineyard have, over the centuries, removed much of the topsoil from its lower sections. Calistoga is said to be the hottest spot in Napa Valley, but current winemaker Matt Taylor notes that in summer the vineyard is considerably cooler than properties half a mile (800m) away on the Silverado Trail, thanks to breezes flowing in from Knights Valley, and in winter it is considerably warmer. Thus, Araujo does have a distinctive microclimate.

Michel Rolland also introduced some fine-tuning. The grapes are now picked at night and sorted before and after destemming. Some parcels are fermented in new small concrete tanks. As many as 20 lots are aged separately, since Rolland likes to blend as late as possible. About one-third of the wine is usually declassified—not because it

Right: Daphne and Bart Araujo, whose attention to detail and top vineyards have earned them an enviable reputation

is of poor quality, but because its texture or tannic structure would unbalance the blend. (A second label, Altagracia, was created in 1999.) The wines spend about 22 months in French oak barrels, of which about 80 percent are new. Bart Araujo insists that they work hard to avoid overripeness in the vineyard, and thus in the wine; the aim is elegance, though this can be hard to achieve in the warm conditions of Napa Valley.

The Sauvignon Blanc is planted on north-facing slopes where Cabernet wouldn't ripen and is mostly the Musqué clone, which gives some exotic aromas and flavors. Tony Soter always liked to age Sauvignon in steel drums, to preserve freshness, as well as a small proportion of barriques (new at Araujo). There is no malolactic fermentation, and usually a small amount of Viognier is blended in, which adds another exotic component. The wine is usually lush and creamy, with some tropical fruit flavors, but can, in some vintages, be a touch heavy. There is also a varietal Viognier.

The Syrah, vinified in open-top fermenters with punch-downs, is exceptional, too, but it lacks the finesse of the Cabernet. Instead, it can show more meaty, tarry aromas and more overt tannins and alcohol. It's at the wilder end of the Syrah spectrum but is none the worse for that.

Not surprisingly, the great wine here is the Cabernet Sauvignon. It's a very expensive wine, but the vineyard has demonstrated its quality for decades. The attention to detail here is total, and the result is a wine that is complex in its aromas and flavors of black fruits, black olives, and chocolate, as well as being highly polished in its structure. It fully deserves all the accolades.

FINEST WINES

(Tasted 2010)

2009 Sauvignon Blanc
Limpid, grassy nose, touch of gooseberry. Silky, concentrated, and stylish, with richness balanced by fine acidity and length.

Cabernet Sauvignon
2007 Dense nose with unusual power. Fleshy and weighty, with sweetness of fruit and considerable structure; sumptuous but still elegant and long.
2006★ Muted, oaky black-currant nose, hint of gumdrops. Supple yet has intensity and drive, concentrated but not heavy despite firm tannins on the long finish.
2005 Dense, brooding black-currant nose. Medium-bodied and discreet, supple, with sweetness on the mid-palate and fresh acidity on the finish. Poised and claretty.

2007 Syrah
Oaky nose, blueberries and violets. Opulent but not showy, juicy and forward, with less zest and complexity than the 2005 and 2006.

Araujo Estate Wines
Area under vine: 38 acres (15.5ha)
Average production: 50,000 bottles
2155 Pickett Road, Calistoga, CA 94515
Tel: (707) 942-6061
www.araujoestatewines.com

Beringer Vineyards

It's impossible to drive through the Napa Valley on Highway 29 without noticing the imposing Rhine House, built from stone and redwood in 1884 just north of St. Helena. The Beringer vineyards had been planted in 1875 by German immigrant brothers Frederick and Jacob, and almost a decade later they built a gravity-operated winery on this gently wooded slope. Teams of Chinese laborers hacked their way into the rocky slope behind the winery to create the tunnels, still used today, in which the wines were aged. This is the oldest continuously operating winery in the valley, because it kept functioning through Prohibition by producing sacramental wines. On the same property stands the Beringer family home, which was occupied by members of the family until 1971.

This is the oldest continuously operating winery in the valley, because it kept functioning through Prohibition by producing sacramental wines

Despite its pedigree, the quality of the Beringer wines in the 1960s left much to be desired. Then, in 1971, the business was bought by Nestlé, which was the owner until 1995. Veteran winemaker Myron Nightingale was hired by Nestlé to clean up the old winery and improve its wines. Being of an older generation, Nightingale was not really up to speed with the latest developments, and his far younger assistant Ed Sbragia became the driving force in creating the more sophisticated Private Reserve ranges. Nightingale had an adventurous side, producing botrytized wines, mostly from Semillon, by leaving fruit in a humidified cold chamber and spraying it with botrytis spores. The results were quite impressive, and Beringer occasionally still produces wines in this style. In 1984, Nightingale retired, and Sbragia took over as chief winemaker.

In 1995, Beringer was bought by Silverado Partners, a consortium headed by a former president of Beringer, Michael Moone. Five years later, it became part of the Australian Mildara Blass group, which was renamed Beringer Blass; this group was in turn absorbed by Australian brewers Foster's and now forms part of its Treasury Wine Estates. Though Beringer itself had extensive vineyards, including 1,800 acres (730ha) in Napa Valley, 600 acres (240ha) in Knights Valley in Sonoma County, and 120 acres (48.5ha) in Carneros, it now had access to fruit from other wineries in the group, such as Meridian in Paso Robles. The winery found itself in some trouble when it created an inexpensive range of wine called Napa Ridge, from grapes grown anywhere but Napa. There was outrage at the exploitation of the valley's famous name, especially by one of its leading wineries, and in 2000 Beringer sold the brand to Bronco Wine Company.

Beringer produces about 8 million cases of wine. Much of this consists of fairly basic ranges bearing the California appellation; vast quantities of Blush Zinfandel are also produced. It is hard to keep up with the constantly evolving less expensive ranges such as Stone Cellars and Appellation Collection, and they do not concern us here. Of greater interest are the Napa Valley and Knights Valley wines, such as the Sauvignon Blanc and Zinfandel, which are well made and excellent value.

Beringer's inclusion in this book is justified by the Private Reserve wines that Ed Sbragia created. Although he handed over the chief winemaker's role to Laurie Hook in 2007 and retreated to his native Dry Creek Valley to set up his own winery, he still luxuriates in the title of emeritus winemaker and keeps an eye on Beringer's top wines. Laurie Hook was trained at Davis and first arrived at Beringer as an enologist in 1986. Sbragia would be the first to admit that the credit for the quality of the Private Reserves should be shared with Bob Steinhauer, the vineyard manager for decades, now retired.

The Private Reserve Chardonnay usually comes from six Napa vineyards; the fruit is mostly barrique-fermented and stirred for 14 weeks; the wine goes through full malolactic fermentation, and the portion of new oak is around 70 percent. The style is almost stereotypical Napa Chardonnay: very ripe, massive, buttery, oaky. Although many winemakers on the North Coast are now striving to make more elegant Chardonnays with less overt oak influence, this has never been the Beringer style. Sbragia developed a wine that some find heavy-handed, but it has an eager following.

The Private Reserve Cabernet Sauvignon, first made in 1977, is at the weighty end of the Cabernet spectrum but stylistically consistent and generally of very high quality. Sbragia used grapes from the top Napa Cabernets within Beringer's portfolio: the State Lane vineyard in Yountville, the Home Ranch on the lower slopes of Spring Mountain, Chabot on the eastern side of St. Helena, and Bancroft Ranch on Howell Mountain. The blend contains at least 90 percent Cabernet. Vintages from the late 1970s and early 1980s could be overly tannic, but since the mid-1990s, when 100 percent medium-toast new oak came into use for aging the wine, this Private Reserve has been better balanced. Sbragia admits that the ripest years are not always the vintages best adapted to long cellaring but says he was always surprised by how well this strapping wine could age.

Equally successful is the Private Reserve Merlot, which comes entirely from the Bancroft Ranch on Howell Mountain and can claim to be one of California's top Merlots, with all the backbone and grip that mountain fruit can give to a variety better known for its flesh than for its structure.

Far less celebrated but still of considerable interest is a wine called Alluvium Blanc, which comes from the vineyards in Knights Valley. There have been many previous attempts to make a Graves-style white, but few have survived. The problem is that the cost of production is high, but consumers are unwilling to pay Chardonnay prices for a Sauvignon-dominated blend. Alluvium is composed of more or less equal measures of barrel-fermented Sauvignon and Semillon, with a dash of Chardonnay and Viognier to give a little exoticism to the blend.

Left: Laurie Hook, the UC Davis graduate who first came to Beringer in 1986 and took over as chief winemaker in 2007

FINEST WINES

(Tasted 2009)

Private Reserve Chardonnay 2007
Rich tropical-fruit nose, especially pineapple. Full-bodied and concentrated, but also a touch sweet. There is some acidity, but overall this is quite caramelly, with a fairly blunt finish.

Private Reserve Cabernet Sauvignon 2005
Sweet ripe nose, quite shy and delicate, giving a pure expression of cherry and black-currant fruit. Although not super-concentrated on the palate, this has elegance and some freshness, though it's unusually forward and accessible, with light tannins. Long, but lacks a little grandeur.

Private Reserve Bancroft Vineyard Merlot 2004★
Mellow smoky nose, with aromas of plums and coffee. Very rich, with a plumpness and fullness on the palate, and great concentration and power. Yet the tannins are under control, and the secondary flavors of licorice and cloves contribute complexity and persistence.

Nightingale 2006
(70% Semillon, 30% SB) Gold. Light caramel-and-butterscotch nose. Sleek and medium-bodied, concentrated and reasonably fresh, with an amalgam of apricot and peach fruit, with some butterscotch tones. Less sweet than its 120g/l RS would lead one to expect. Quite long, but still far from complex.

Beringer Vineyards
Area under vine: 10,000 acres (4,050ha)
Average production: 95 million bottles
2000 Main Street, St. Helena, CA 94574
Tel: (707) 963-4812
www.beringer.com

Cain Vineyard & Winery

When you stand 2,000ft (600m) up on Spring Mountain and gaze at the beautifully contoured vineyards all around you, you wonder how such a civilized landscape was carved out of such rough slopes. Across the valley, on Howell Mountain and Atlas Peak, are plateau areas where planting vineyards is not especially hard. But Spring Mountain is steep. It is difficult and costly to plant here. Indeed, that may be why electronics tycoon Jerry Cain and his wife Joyce, the main force behind the creation of the Cain estate in 1980, sold their share in the estate in 1991 to their partners Jim and Nancy Meadlock, who remain the sole owners to this day.

There has been continuity of ownership here for 20 years, and the same is true of the winemaker, Chris Howell, who has been running Cain since 1990 and still lives on the property. Although a hands-on winemaker, he has an intellectual side, and an evening spent in his company is always rewarding for exposing the breadth of his interests. He studied enology at the University of Montpellier in southern France and gained work experience at Mouton Rothschild. He then worked for various wineries in Napa and Sonoma, before landing the job at Cain.

Between 1981 and 1990, 84 acres (34ha) were planted at what had been the 550-acre (220ha) McCormick Ranch, high on Spring Mountain. The vineyards are terraced around a kind of amphitheater, but the soils are more sedimentary than volcanic, with much sandstone and shale and enough clay to give good water retention. Because the exposures vary so much on this mountain site, Howell finds that Cabernet expresses itself very differently in terms of both maturation and flavor according to where it is planted. The goal was always to focus on producing a blend of the five Bordeaux varieties, but a little Sauvignon Blanc and Syrah

Right: The intellectual and well-traveled Chris Howell, who has been running Cain Vineyard & Winery since 1990

Now that the replanted vineyards are beginning to reach maturity, the welcome reemergence of Cain Five as an estate wine will allow Howell and his team to express the complexity and grandeur of this remarkable site to the fullest degree

were also planted. The vineyard was replanted after 1996 on phylloxera-resistant rootstocks.

The principal wine, Cain Five, was first made in 1985. Earlier vintages with the Cain label had been made from purchased fruit, and there have been lengthy periods when the estate production was blended with fruit from the valley floor. At other times, notably 1991–94, it has been purely an estate wine, and this has been the case since 2007. Howell picks relatively early, though the harvest can last for six weeks, and each variety is vinified separately with the indigenous yeasts. The length of the maceration and other winemaking decisions are made by taste. Blending begins after the wines have been in barrel for about three months. The wine is aged for 22 months in about 75 percent new French oak and is usually egg-white fined but, more often than not, unfiltered. The percentages of the five varieties vary from vintage to vintage, but Cabernet Sauvignon is rarely as dominant as in most Napa Valley Bordeaux blends. In 2005, the proportions were 60 percent Cabernet Sauvignon, 16 percent Cabernet Franc, 14 percent Petit Verdot, 8 percent Merlot, and 2 percent Malbec.

In 1993, a second wine, Cain Cuvée, was introduced, but it did not consist solely of declassified lots and included a good deal of fruit from other Napa appellations. Before long, it had turned into an unusual blend of two vintages, since Howell felt this gave the wine greater complexity. The aim is a more accessible, less extracted, less oaky wine than Cain Five; it is produced in larger volumes and sold at a lower price.

Then a third wine emerged: Cain Concept. This wine seems to have been conceived after prolonged thought, since it employs all the winemaking techniques applied to Cain Five but applies them to fruit of entirely different character. Most of the grapes for Cain Concept come from valley-floor benchland vineyards in Oakville and Rutherford. This is high-quality fruit, yet the wine is offered at about half the price of Cain Five, which makes it something of a bargain. In the past, Cain also had a good reputation for its lush, hedonistic Sauvignon, Cain Musqué, but Howell stopped producing it in the early 2000s, because it seemed too remote from the winery's core interests.

Some of the shifts in Cain's winemaking strategy may have been confusing, especially since the names of the various blends are so similar, but the quality of the wines has certainly remained very high. Now that the replanted vineyards are beginning to reach maturity, the welcome reemergence of Cain Five as an estate wine will allow Howell and his team to express the complexity and grandeur of this remarkable site to the fullest degree.

FINEST WINES

(Tasted 2009)

Cain Five

1999 Made from 65 percent estate fruit, as well as grapes from York Creek Vineyard on Spring Mountain and To Kalon in Oakville. Very deep, but showing some slight maturity. The nose is ripe, charming, and fleshy, and the mushroomy tone that marked the wine a year earlier seems to have vanished. Medium-bodied, with a structure closer to claret than Napa Cabernet. Though there is ample grip, the tannins are supple, and this is no blockbuster. Firm, mineral, and long.

2005★ A rich, smoky, tobacco nose, quite savory. Medium-bodied and still tight, this is quite mineral and severe and far from being a fruit-forward style. It has grip, persistence, spiciness, and underlying vigor; clearly still very young.

Cain Concept

2005 A lush, oaky, blackberry nose. Dense and muscular on the attack but has flesh and vigor and a fine thread of acidity. The finish is stern in a positive way and undeniably long.

Cain Vineyard & Winery
Area under vine: 84 acres (34ha)
Average production: 250,000 bottles
3800 Langtry Road, St. Helena, CA 94574
Tel: (707) 963-1616
www.cainfive.com

Cakebread Cellars

Let them eat Cakebread! It's a foolish cry, but it escapes every time I drive past the handsome wooden winery in southern Rutherford. Cake and bread also feature prominently in the winery's self-presentation, because the family has created various culinary enterprises, such as cooking classes and food-and-wine pairing sessions, and in effect run a private restaurant under their resident chef. At the tasting room, one can buy vegetables from the winery garden, as well as wines.

Jack Cakebread ran an auto-repair business in Oakland before buying 20 acres (8ha) of land in Rutherford in 1971. Two years later, he built a winery, planting Zinfandel and Sauvignon Blanc in 1976. The winery's first release was a 1973 Chardonnay, its first Cabernet Sauvignon following a year later. It was another 15 years before Cakebread felt ready to relinquish his Oakland business and focus on his vineyards and winery. Today, the property is run by his sons Bruce and Dennis—Bruce on the winemaking side, Dennis in charge of sales. Bruce Cakebread, who trained at UC Davis, retreated from daily winemaking responsibilities in 2002 to become president. The full-time winemaker here is Julianne Laks, who used to be his assistant.

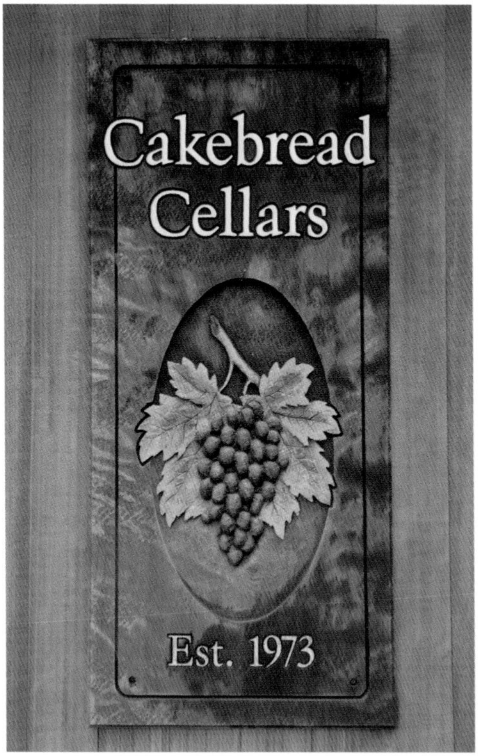

The vineyard that Jack bought lies on the boundary between Oakville and Rutherford. Since those early days, holdings have been considerably expanded, since the family profited from the retirement of growers in various parts of the valley. As well as over 60 acres (24ha) around the winery, there are 164 acres (66ha) in Carneros, 27 acres (11ha) on Howell Mountain, and, a more recent acquisition, 45 acres (18ha) of Chardonnay and Pinot Noir in Mendocino's Anderson Valley. Most Cakebread vineyards were affected by phylloxera and were replanted from 1994 onward. Their own holdings are supplemented by purchased grapes.

As well as Cabernet Sauvignon, Cakebread has, for decades, enjoyed a good reputation for Sauvignon Blanc, most grown around the winery. The wine is fermented both in older barrels and in tanks, with about 15 percent remaining in stainless steel. The style is fairly rich, with pronounced melony aromas and moderate acidity but no herbaceousness. The regular Chardonnay, which is based on fruit from southern Napa and Carneros, also has an unoaked element, while the Reserve is barrel-fermented in mostly new oak.

Inevitably, the main focus is on Cabernet Sauvignon. The standard bottling is not especially complex, but it's a classic expression of the Napa style. There are also limited-production releases that highlight the typicity of various Napa subregions. The Vine Hill bottling comes from a well-regarded Yountville vineyard on benchland

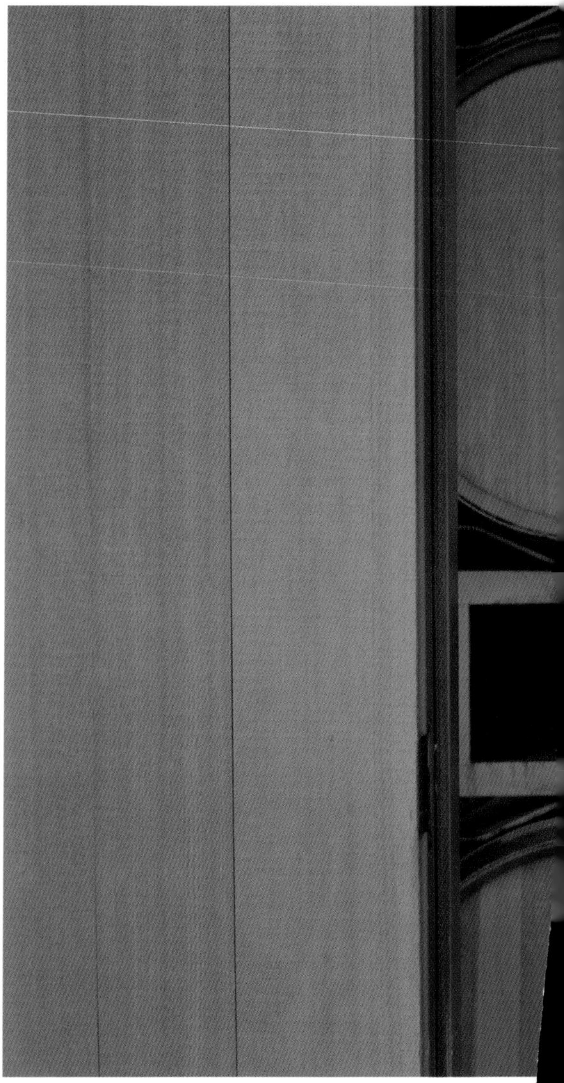

to the west of the village. It's a structured wine that is aged for almost two years in about two-thirds new oak. (Cakebread uses only French oak for its barrel-aged wines.) There is some Vine Hill fruit in the Benchland Select bottling, too, but the main components are from the Rutherford benches. For the first year, the wine is aged in mostly new oak and then racked into one-third new oak. In 2002, Cakebread introduced a new cuvée called Dancing Bear Ranch, made entirely from Howell Mountain fruit; this stays in a slightly lower proportion of new oak than the other top Cabernets.

As for the Burgundian varieties, the top Chardonnay is clearly the Carneros Reserve bottling, though the Anderson Valley wine shows great promise. On the other hand, the sleek, smoky Anderson Valley Pinot Noir shows more complexity than the easygoing Carneros Pinot Noir.

Although they do not show it, the Cabernets do have high alcohol, at around 15.5%. Bruce Cakebread is well aware of this and is working with Julianne Laks to see if they can alter their farming so as to have lower sugars at the time of harvest. They have made changes to the trellising and altered the irrigation program to prevent the vines from shutting down during the hottest spells, the idea being to ensure more even maturation. But Bruce admits they are still a long way from their goal.

With its emphasis on structured tastings for visitors and on food-and-wine matching and other culinary activities, Cakebread is among the more sophisticated of the valley-floor wineries. If the Napa premium attached to the standard varietal wines means that they can seem rather expensive for what they are, the Reserves and special bottlings are often outstanding. Given the size of the winery, overall quality is high. But Cakebread is not resting on its laurels. Bruce and his team are always looking for ways to expand the range, as well as to improve quality even further.

FINEST WINES

(Tasted 2009)

(Cabernet Sauvignon)

Napa 2005

Rich, spicy black-currant nose, with some eucalyptus tones. Fairly rich and concentrated, but braced by acidity that keeps the palate lively. Sumptuous black-cherry fruit marks the finish, which is long if not especially complex.

Vine Hill 2005

Dense, chocolaty nose, with a savory edge. Svelte

and very concentrated, this nonetheless has some freshness and vigor—and despite the tannins, it's spicy and far from heavy-handed. Good length.

Benchland Select 2005★
A splendid, voluptuous, exuberant black-cherry-and-plum nose. The palate is full-bodied, with ample, juicy fruit, the firm tannins balanced by the overall freshness and harmony of the wine. Good length.

Dancing Bear Howell Mountain 2005
Rich, plummy nose, more dramatic than the other cuvées, with depth and power. Rich, suave, and not too concentrated, this has firm tannins but no hint of toughness. A slight jamminess on the palate is balanced by a lively pepperiness on the finish.

Above: Jack Cakebread, having handed the company over to his children, is now free to pursue another of his passions

Cakebread Cellars
Area under vine: 440 acres (180ha)
Average production: 1.8 million bottles
8300 St. Helena Highway, Rutherford, CA 94573
Tel: (707) 963-5221
www.cakebread.com

Dalla Valle Vineyards

The Italian-born Gustav Dalla Valle, whose family had been wine producers for generations, made his fortune producing scuba-diving equipment and bought a small 5-acre (2ha) property in Oakville in 1982. There were some vines on the property, which he grafted over to Bordeaux varieties. A winery was constructed in 1986, and there is a whiff of Tuscany about the buildings and vegetation. The site lies on red, rocky, volcanic soil at 400ft (120m) just north of the Stags Leap District, on the east side of the Silverado Trail. Facing west, the vines benefit from afternoon sunshine and ripen relatively early. Moreover, the vines are often just above the fog line, which means that, overall, the vineyard is warmer than those just below on the valley floor; on the other hand, there are some maritime breezes that help preserve acidity. The terroir is clearly exceptional here, but the drawback is that yields are extremely low.

There is a slightly austere character to the wines, but to European palates that is far preferable to the sugar coating that characterizes so many Napa Cabernets

The first wine produced here, in 1986, was a Cabernet Sauvignon, and two years later they made the wine for which the estate is best known: Maya, which comes from a 6-acre (2.5ha) parcel with a good deal of Cabernet Franc. The initial consultant winemaker was Heidi Peterson Barrett, but after the death of Gustav Dalla Valle, his widow Naoko replaced her with Mia Klein. Klein stayed ten years, and in 2006 Andrew Erickson was taken on in her place. In the same year, Naoko Dalla Valle added Michel Rolland to her team of consultants. Naoko was born in Kobe, Japan, where her ancestors were sake producers, requiring a slight shift of gears on her part to adapt to wine production. She is very much in charge of the property and has had to make some difficult decisions over the years.

Dalla Valle has been through some rough times. The vineyards have suffered badly from leafroll virus, and replanting became imperative. In the 1990s, the estate had produced a rather good Sangiovese called Pietre Rosse, but by 2001 it had been phased out. By the mid-2000s, production had dropped to a mere 400 cases, and there was no Maya at all. The replanting program was completed by 2007, and one advantage of the costly process was that the team could choose more appropriate rootstocks and alter the spacing and row orientation. At the same time, with the arrival of Michel Rolland, there was some fine-tuning in the winemaking: a sorting table was introduced, and the pre-fermentation cold soak was prolonged.

The Cabernet Sauvignon, which can have up to 15 percent Cabernet Franc in the blend, is aged in 60 percent new barriques and bottled without filtration. Maya is very different, with close to 45 percent Cabernet Franc and a higher proportion of new French oak, at about 75 percent. The nature of the site from which it is made limits the production to no more than 500 cases. Certainly the Cabernet Franc gives some lift and freshness to the wine, because the Cabernet Sauvignon has been criticized for being too monolithic and excessively tannic. That may well have been true of some of the earlier vintages, but my experience of the wine, which began in 1994, reveals that it is in balance. There is definitely a slightly austere character to the wines, but to European palates that is far preferable to the sugar coating that characterizes so many Napa Cabernets.

The wines can be hard to find, since one-third is sold to a mailing list that has been closed for some years. But Naoko Dalla Valle does make a point of selling to a range of retailers, too, so consumers who know where to look can still snap up new vintages as soon as they are released.

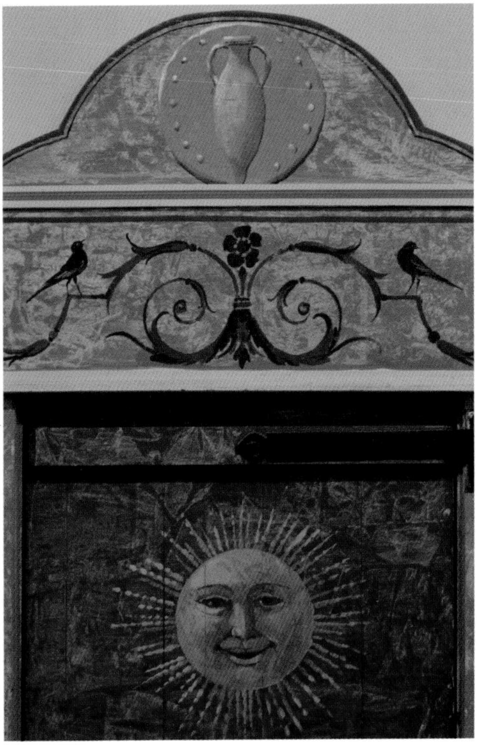

Previous page: Naoko Dalla Valle, who came from a family of sake producers but has mastered her Oakville winery

Above: The decor recalls the Italian origin of Gustav Dalla Valle, whose family had been vintners for three generations

FINEST WINES

(Tasted in 2007)

Cabernet Sauvignon

2005 Tasted just before bottling, the nose was closed and smoky, with black-currant aromas. Very intense attack, with fine acidity, yet it has flesh and fine-grained tannins. There's great purity of black-currant fruit, always a hallmark of Dalla Valle, as well as a light coffee tone from the oak; very long and very stylish.

1999 Still opaque in color. Very rich smoky nose, with super-ripe aromas of black cherries and plums, but there is no jamminess and even a slight savory tone. On the palate, this is lush and luxurious, with black fruits; tannic and concentrated, yet finely balanced with a sweet (but not confected), complex, stylish finish.

Maya

2005★ Tasted just before bottling, the aromas were subdued. Very rich and concentrated, but fresh and spicy and vigorous, with substantial but ripe tannins. It has flesh and weight but not at the expense of freshness. Excellent balance and length.

1999 Opaque red. Dense, savory tone, with an underlying sweetness of fruit and a touch of mint. Dense and chewy, with powerful tannins; more chocolaty than the Cabernet Sauvignon but still quite austere. Long.

Dalla Valle Vineyards
Area under vine: 21 acres (8.5ha)
Average production: 35,000 bottles
7776 Silverado Trail, Oakville, CA 94562
Tel: (707) 944-2676
www.dallavallevineyards.com

Duckhorn Vineyards

The genial Dan Duckhorn came to wine from a managerial background and was involved in a vineyard management company in the 1970s. In 1976, he became a consultant for Heublein, which in those days was a major player in Napa Valley, being deeply involved in the expansion of the historic Beaulieu winery. Dan Duckhorn and his wife Margaret bought their first small property in 1976 and assembled a consortium with other families to bring more financial backing to the venture. The first vintage was in 1978.

Until 1994, the Duckhorns bought most of their grapes from growers, but they then began acquiring vineyards. By 1999 they owned 278 acres (113ha), mostly in Napa in seven locations, but also in Anderson Valley in Mendocino. Although at first Duckhorn took a fairly eclectic approach to its product ranges, by the late 1990s those ranges had become diversified. Rather than yoke them together under one managerial roof, the Duckhorns created separate wineries for their enterprises. The mother ship was near the Silverado Trail in St. Helena. Their proprietary red blend, Paraduxx, was given its own winery and winemaker, and the same became true of their Anderson Valley project, called Goldeneye and devoted to Pinot Noir.

The divorce of the Duckhorns and a complex setup of shareholders led to the sale of a controlling share of the company in 2006 to GI Partners, a private-equity investment firm. The Duckhorns, however, remain as nominal heads of the company, even if the day-to-day winemaking and management are now in the hands of others.

The winery's principal calling card has long been Merlot. Dan Duckhorn visited St-Emilion and Pomerol in 1977, sparking his interest. Rather than buying Merlot from fertile clay soils, which one might have expected after a foray to Bordeaux's Right Bank, Duckhorn opted instead for grapes from rocky alluvial soils that gave wines of more personality. The first vintage of Merlot was in 1978. It was not easy to find sources in those days, because the variety was not that popular. Duckhorn's early vintages came from the Beatty Ranch on Howell Mountain, from the Steltzner vineyard in Stags Leap District, and from the Three Palms Vineyard that the winery would soon make famous as a vineyard-designated bottling. Dan Duckhorn admits there was no commercial motivation for focusing on Merlot—it was simply that he liked the wines.

Today, under winemaker Bill Nancarrow, a New Zealander, Duckhorn produces three Merlots. The Napa Merlot is the basic bottling. The Estate Merlot, launched in 1995, is made from vineyards in St. Helena and Calistoga and is aged in new barriques for 20 months. Duckhorn's most famous wine, the Three Palms, comes from vines planted on a rocky, well-drained alluvial fan on the northeast side of the valley. It, too, is aged in new oak for 20 months. In the past, there were occasional bottlings from the Vine Hill vineyard in Oakville and from Howell Mountain, but these seem no longer to be produced.

The winery's reputation for Merlot has obscured the fact that it also makes first-rate Cabernet, especially the Estate Cabernet and the single-vineyard Patzimaro Vineyard Cabernet from an excellent site just west of the town of St. Helena. However, within a few years both the Estate Merlot and Cabernet will be phased out. Nancarrow is working on a new Bordeaux blend to be called Discussion, which will, presumably, fuse the merits of the two wines. There is also a very reliable Sauvignon Blanc, of which 20 percent is barrel-fermented in new oak, while the rest stays in tanks.

Duckhorn created an individual red blend called Paraduxx in 1994. It has evolved into a blend of mostly Zinfandel, with Cabernet making up the balance, with sometimes a dash of Merlot, too. Both French and American oak barrels are used, with about half those barrels being new. The well-packaged wine has proved a great success as an accessible, fruit-forward wine that is easy to

enjoy. Now that Paraduxx has its own winery and winemaker (David Marchesi), it has developed a few special bottlings under the Postmark label. In 2004, Duckhorn also created a new wine called Canvasback (the supply of duck images seems endless), a Rhône-style blend from Howell Mountain fruit, but only 400 cases are produced.

Most Napa wineries with a yearning to produce Pinot Noir look to Carneros for their grapes, but not Duckhorn. Instead, the company astutely bought land in Anderson Valley in 1996. This was the former Obester estate. There were sound existing vines, but Duckhorn embarked on plantings of its own and, by 2001, had a substantial estate with 150 acres (60ha) spread over five sites, comprising 19 clones and 11 rootstocks of Pinot Noir. The first vintage, a small one, was in 1997. Selection has been severe from the outset, with declassified wines consigned to a second label, Migration. Then, in 2004, some other wines were added: Confluence, The Narrows, and Gowan Creek, all from individual sites, and Ten Degrees, a blend of the ten best barrels. The wines, made by Zach Rasmuson, are serious and expensive and have met with critical acclaim. Just as Paraduxx took on a life of its own, so Migration has evolved as a second label that has been given its independence, and its own winemaker, Neil Bernardi, as of 2009.

All this means that Duckhorn is no longer a single winery but a cluster of wineries with different focuses. The duplication of wineries, winemakers, and presumably sales and marketing organizations may seem needlessly complicated, but no doubt the Duckhorn executives have thought this through. And it seems to work. The wines are very good, although as with many long-established Napa wineries, they tend to be underestimated. This is a dynamic company, skilled at marketing, as well as wine production, yet there is no dumbing down. Paraduxx suggests a certain frivolity (and why not?), but it is a joy to drink. Moreover, Nancarrow and his team do not rest on their laurels, and the company is constantly evolving—and in ways that are not easily predictable. This is a strength, not a weakness.

Left: Dan Duckhorn, who remains, with his former wife Margaret, the nominal head of their expanded company

FINEST WINES

(Tasted 2009–10)

Duckhorn

2005 Estate Cabernet Sauvignon★

This has a stylish black-currant-and-black-olive nose. Concentrated and sumptuous but not flabby, with good acidity and a long, black-fruit finish.

2005 Patzimaro Vineyard Cabernet Sauvignon

Smoky black-currant nose, with charred oak. Very concentrated but suave, with integrated tannins and ample lift and drive. Long.

2007 Three Palms Vineyard Merlot

Fleshy, oaky nose, with blackberry and mint. Very ripe but not overblown, with integrated tannins, reasonable freshness, and a long, chocolaty finish.

2006 Paraduxx

Bright, fresh cherry-and-raspberry nose, with vanilla tones. Fresh, silky, fruit-forward, and juicy, lively and bright; not complex but enjoyable.

Goldeneye

2004 The Narrows Pinot Noir

Sweet, intense, oaky nose: raspberries and beets. Intense and high-toned; a touch high in alcohol, but it has ample sweetness and zest.

2005 Gowan Creek Pinot Noir

Heady, savory nose, with cherry fruit and considerable oak. Intense, ripe, a bit fiery; lean and assertive, with marked red-fruit flavors.

2006 Pinot Noir

Lean, stylish, cherry nose. Medium-bodied but silky and concentrated, with ripe tannins; precise and elegant and persistent.

Duckhorn Vineyards

Area under vine: 278 acres (113ha) in Napa, 150 acres (60ha) in Mendocino
Average production: 2.4 million bottles (Napa), 240,000 bottles (Mendocino)
1000 Lodi Lane, St. Helena, CA 94574
Tel: (866) 367-9945
www.duckhornvineyards.com

Dunn Vineyards

With his straggly mustache, a twang in his voice, and a battered straw hat on his now-white-haired head, Randy Dunn looks more like a stereotyped farmer in a television sitcom than one of California's most respected winemakers. After graduating from UC Davis in 1975, he cut his teeth at Caymus from the mid-1970s to early 1980s, and while still there he started up his own winery. He remains a man without pretension but with a deep commitment to the traditions of Napa Valley, which leads him to be quite scornful of modern conventional wisdom.

His own winery, and home, are in Angwin, on Howell Mountain, where he has teetotal Seventh-Day Adventists for neighbors. He began with just 14 acres (5.5ha) of vines, which allowed him to release 500 cases of Cabernet in 1979, but

Randy Dunn is in no doubt that the elevation and the red volcanic soil of Howell Mountain bring a special quality to his wine

his winery was not bonded until 1982. Over the years, he has continued to work as a consultant winemaker for other wineries such as Pahlmeyer. To expand his property, he gradually bought other parcels, including the Park Muscatine Vineyard that used to be leased by Ridge. Today, he owns or controls 30 acres (12ha), of which 24 acres (10ha) are Cabernet Sauvignon, at an elevation of 2,100ft (640m). These grapes form the basis of his Howell Mountain Cabernet, while he uses some purchased fruit to make his Napa Valley Cabernet. Dunn remains flexible on his fruit sources, selling some of his own production, as well as buying in grapes that seem of outstanding quality. The Napa Cabernet is not a valley-floor wine, because it contains a growing proportion of Howell Mountain fruit, and recent vintages have included as much as 85 percent. That means that, in practice, the Napa Cabernet is more or less the winery's second label, though it can be very close in quality to the more prestigious Howell Mountain bottling.

Randy Dunn is in no doubt that the elevation and the red volcanic soil of Howell Mountain bring a special quality to his wine. Because the vineyards are well above the fog, the nights tend to be warmer than on the valley floor, but budbreak is later; yet Cabernet ripens earlier than down below. Overall, the climate is cooler and windier, so canopy development lags behind that of valley-floor vineyards. The breeze can be an advantage when there has been rain, and it is imperative that the bunches dry out as rapidly as possible. Rot is rarely a problem here. Dunn would like to see yields of 4 tons per acre but does not usually obtain more than 2.5 tons per acre. Shoots are thinned in May, and he may green-harvest during the summer if he thinks it necessary. Harvesting is selective, since different parcels will ripen at different times. One advantage of the early ripening is that there is less sugar accumulation and thus moderate levels of alcohol.

The winery is little more than an unkempt shack, but it serves its purpose. This is not a high-tech operation, and it is run by Randy Dunn, his wife Lori, and their children Kristina and Mike, with very little hired labor. However, Dunn has invested in a costly wine tunnel, which he had built 20 years ago so that his wines can age in tranquillity at a constant temperature and humidity level. The winemaking is straightforward. The grapes are destemmed and crushed and fermented with cultivated yeasts; there is no cold soak and no extended maceration, both because Dunn believes it's a practice that softens a wine that he wants to be long-lived, and because it would

Right: The straight-talking Randy Dunn, skeptical of modern conventional wisdom but deeply committed to Napa tradition

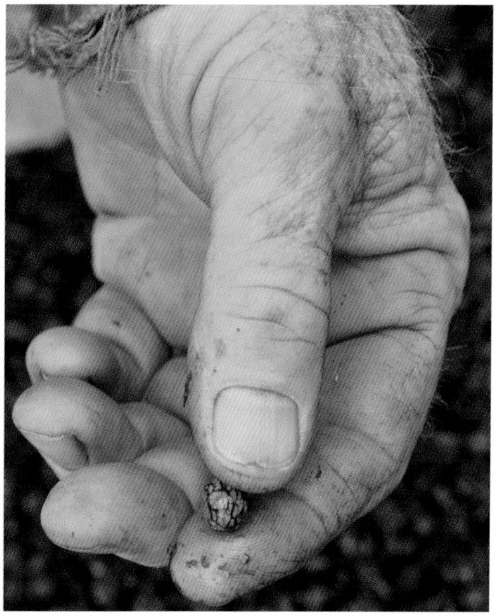

Above: A small berry typical of the high-altitude, low-yielding Howell Mountain fruit that defines the reserved Dunn style

require him to buy many more tanks in which to store the wine after the primary fermentation. Only French oak is used, and the proportion of new oak has fluctuated from 40 to 75 percent, depending on the character of the fruit in each vintage. The wine spends some 30 months in oak and is filtered but not fined before bottling.

Like Cabernets from Mayacamas Vineyards, those from Dunn are not intended to be drunk young, and they can be at their most complex and enjoyable at about 20 years old. Dunn is against the fashionable trend toward overripeness and succinctly told me that he believed the reluctance of some winemakers to pick grapes until the seeds were brown was "bullshit." As a result, his wines are, by California standards, moderate in alcohol—between 13.3 and 14%—and austere when young. This is the style he wants, and his customers know that these are wines to be cellared.

Production has remained steady for many years, and Dunn has no wish to expand. He likes being able to control all aspects of production and doesn't want the winery to turn into a business that would result in his spending most of his time in the office or on the road on sales trips. He seems content to do one thing—make Cabernet Sauvignon—but it is one thing he does supremely well.

FINEST WINES

(Tasted 2007–09)

Howell Mountain

2004 Reserved nose, with a touch of mint and licorice. Rich, full-bodied. Mouth-filling, with ripe but not especially chewy tannins; harmonious, with a sweet, firm finish and good length.

2003 Reserved, dense, plummy nose. Very rich and full-bodied, tannic but not tough, mouth-filling and opulent. Unusually accessible, but less persistent than some other vintages.

1999★ Lovely nose, sweet and ripe black-currant fruit, with both purity and intensity. Very concentrated, with very ripe tannins and a supple texture, with unusual sweetness of fruit for Dunn. Good acidity gives fine length.

1993 Discreet black-currant nose. Fine attack, very concentrated but still tight and youthful; has purity and fine acidity and excellent length.

1988 The color is lightening up and showing some evolution. Complex nose, leathery and herbal, but with no lack of fruit. Lush, full-bodied, still quite youthful; coats the mouth with flavor, with a good deal of spice on the finish. Very long.

Napa

1999 Sweet, ripe black-currant nose; not especially oaky, so the fruit shines through. Quite rich blackberry fruit on the palate, with fresh acidity and ripe tannin, fine texture, and excellent balance and length.

Dunn Vineyards
Area under vine: 30 acres (12ha)
Average production: 50,000 bottles
805 White Cottage Road, Angwin, CA 94508
Tel: (707) 965-3642
www.dunnvineyards.com

Far Niente

Hidden away on the hillier part of the Oakville benchlands, this showcase Napa winery sails like a galleon across a 13-acre (5ha) sea of azaleas and flowering dogwood. This slate-roofed, stone winery was built in 1885, then abandoned at Prohibition. A businessman from Oklahoma, Gil Nickel, bought the property in 1979 and spent a fortune restoring it. He found the words "Far Niente" ("Without a Care") carved into the walls and realized he had a name for his winery.

Nickel brought in Larry Maguire as general manager of the property and, in 1983, Dirk Hampson as winemaker. They devised the strategy for Far Niente, and it has changed little. They produce just three wines: a Chardonnay, a Cabernet Sauvignon, and a sweet wine, Dolce, modeled on Sauternes. Hampson had studied at UC Davis and had wide winemaking experience at Schloss Vollrads in the Rheingau, at Mouton Rothschild, and at the Burgundy négociant Labouré-Roi.

Nickel, who had started his career as a nurseryman and expanded his fortune by going into the oil-and-gas industry, never stinted when it came to investing in Far Niente. He built extensive wine tunnels in the 1980s, long before it became de rigueur in the valley, and created entertainment facilities on a grand scale. The caves are used not just to store barrels, but function as an extension of the fermentation facilities. The tanks on display in the stone building are just part of the winery, which despite its traditional appearance, is gravity-fed and solar-powered. Far Niente was intended from the start to be a luxury brand, expensive and unswerving in its style and focus. There is no second label, so any wine not up to snuff is sold off.

Much of the fruit comes from the Nickels' 100-acre (40ha) Stelling Vineyard nearby on the Oakville bench, and there are additional vineyards in southern Napa that supply much of the Chardonnay. Some other sites are leased and farmed by Far Niente, but no grapes are purchased from growers.

Hampson wants a Chardonnay that is rich and oaky but also multilayered and capable of aging. The ideal window for consumption, in his view, is between three and six years after the vintage. Fermentation begins in steel tanks but finishes in 50 percent new Burgundian barrels. Then the wine stays on its lees for ten months, with some stirring. Because he does not want an immediately accessible buttery style, Hampson (now director of winemaking) and current winemaker Nicole Marchesi block the malolactic fermentation. The penalty, says Hampson, is that the wine is reticent on release and so does not get those all-important high scores from wine critics. But the wine blossoms and gains complexity with bottle age.

Early vintages of the Cabernet were very tannic, but today Hampson aims for a softer style. The grapes are sorted at the winery, destemmed, fermented with pump-overs and an extended maceration, then blended, before being aged in mostly new oak for about 16 months. Hampson's inspiration was Mouton—that blend of opulence and elegance—but he admits that the early Cabernets were rather too massive for their own good. Today, the wine is riper, sweeter, and more textured. The blend once contained Merlot, but Hampson found it contributed little and has dropped the variety, though he retains about 10 percent of Cabernet Franc and Petit Verdot.

Far Niente is particularly proud of Dolce, and there are certainly few other wines being produced in this style in California. It is not made every year, because it is dependent on the arrival of botrytis of good quality. Like Sauternes, the blend is dominated by Semillon, with Sauvignon Blanc making up the balance. The Semillon comes from a spot in Coombsville, east of the town of Napa. Being a cool site, it does not develop botrytis until late in the growing season, but the damp, foggy conditions most mornings mean that noble rot turns up more often than not. The process is

encouraged by allowing huge canopies—a rarity now in California—that impede aeration and allow rot to spread. Unfortunately, this also inhibits the ripening process, which explains why the harvest tends to be very late. As in Sauternes, the grapes are picked by selective harvesting. Wasp damage is common, so they pick whole clusters of botrytized fruit and then cut out any damaged portions. Ripeness can vary from 28 to 40° Brix, giving an average of around 34. The Sauvignon comes from 1.5 acres [0.6ha] of contracted vines, and these grapes rarely attain ripeness higher than 25° Brix.

The wine is barrel-fermented and aged 32 months in new barriques. Evidently, Yquem was the original model for the wine, even though Hampson admits the sunnier climate of California gives a very different kind of sweet wine. Production varies from 300 to 3,000 cases. Since 1989, Dolce has had its own bonded winery within the Far Niente winery, making it a distinct brand. It also has its own winemaker, Greg Allen, whose former career was as a medical researcher at MIT.

Dolce is very expensive to produce and carries a high price tag that does not always seem justified by the quality of the wine. It can be marked by new oak and can suffer from a certain heaviness and lack of zest—no doubt a consequence of that sunny Napa climate that Hampson readily acknowledges.

Gil Nickel died in 2003, but his family continues to run the wine businesses, which include two other ventures. Nickel & Nickel is a high-quality winery focusing on single-vineyard wines from its own modest estate and from sites it regularly buys from. There are now about 18 separate bottlings. The Nickels have also created a winery in Russian River Valley called En Route, its first release a 2007 Pinot Noir. So, the Nickels do not lack dynamism, even if Far Niente itself seems content to stick to its own tested formula.

Left: Dirk Hampson, winemaker since 1983 and now director of winemaking, with the confidence that comes from experience

FINEST WINES

Chardonnay

When I first tasted the 1988 vintage, I noted that the wine had "a reined-in opulence." That still seems quite an accurate definition of the Far Niente style. Some vintages have been lean, others very oaky, others trying too hard for a kind of Burgundian grand cru grandeur. But vintages in the 2000s have been more consistent and more impressive. The 2007 has complex aromas of banana and apple, and the oak is delicate and stylish. The palate is medium-bodied and quite toasty, with spiced-apple flavors rather than any coarse butteriness, and it finishes with considerable verve and limpidity.

Cabernet Sauvignon

Throughout the 1980s and early 1990s, the wine was marked by its tough tannins, though there were better-balanced vintages such as 1985. But from the mid-1990s, there was a distinct improvement, with the wines showing both more opulence and more finesse. And there has been no let-up in the present decade; vintages such as 2002, 2003, 2004, and 2005 have received enthusiastic comments from me in blind tastings. The current vintage, the 2006, is equally fine, with intense black-currant and blackberry aromas, a medium-bodied palate that shows both flesh and concentration, and a certain muscularity that is typical of the year.

Dolce

In 2009, I was able to taste a number of vintages at the winery. The 1998 has some vegetal aromas; while the palate is still fresh and sleek, the wine seems understated, though there is some vigor on the finish. The 1999 is more honeyed and voluptuous on the nose, though there is also a touch of caramel; the palate is rich, velvety, and burnished, but it's also quite heavy and oaky and lacks some freshness on the finish. The 2005 has discreet apricot aromas that are still delicate; stone-fruit flavors dominate the palate, which shows a good deal of ripeness but not much unctuousness or lift.

Far Niente
Area under vine: 250 acres (100ha)
Average production: 420,000 bottles
1350 Acacia Drive, Oakville, CA 94562
Tel: (707) 944-2861
www.farniente.com

Frog's Leap

In the 19th century, a commercial frog farm flourished just north of St. Helena. It is honored in the name of the winery created in 1975 by Larry Turley and John Williams. Turley had bought the property in 1974, and not long after, the young John Williams, touring Napa on his motorcycle, pitched his tent on the land so as to avoid the overnight fee charged by the state park nearby. He had a bottle of wine with him, which he used to appease Larry Turley when he discovered his uninvited guest. The two men realized they shared an aspiration, as well as an attachment to motorcycles, so they eventually teamed up, sold their bikes, and set up their fledgling winery. To earn money in the meantime, Williams worked for Warren Winiarski, helped found the Glenora estate in New York State, and became winemaker at Spring Mountain. They planted some vineyards, but most of the fruit for Frog's Leap came from local growers.

Initial vintages were, to say the least, artisanal, and legend has it that Larry Turley made his 1980 Cabernet in his hot tub. The first commercial vintage was 1981: 700 cases of Sauvignon Blanc and Zinfandel. Chardonnay and Cabernet would follow in 1985. From the start, it would seem, the partners were determined to have fun. A simple but highly effective label portrayed the elegant leaping frog, which bore a passing resemblance to the better-known Kermit. The corks were stamped with the word "Ribbit," and winery literature asserted that its motto was, "Time's fun when you're having flies." I first encountered the partners when I went to the winery to taste a 1986 late-harvest Sauvignon Blanc called, of course, Late Leap. (Its stylish label was cheekily modeled on Yquem's, with a coronet over the frog's head.)

But by 1994, the enterprise had outgrown the rustic premises at the frog farm. At the same time, the partners were wanting to move in different directions, so they split the company. Their personal tastes were certainly diverging, with Turley showing a preference for big, powerful wines, while Williams was eager to make lighter but more elegant styles. Larry Turley stayed put and founded Turley Wine Cellars. John Williams bought a property in Rutherford and kept the Frog's Leap label. On the property was a magnificent red barn in which walnuts and plums had been stored in the 1940s; Williams gradually restored the structure to its original glory. He was able to acquire more vineyards in the 1990s and also converted them to organic viticulture. Indeed, many of the farming practices are now biodynamic, though the estate is not certified. Williams has also been keen to give up on irrigation, at least for established vines, and by 2009 he was able to dry-farm everything, which would ensure that the roots would dig deep for nutrients and water.

The winemaking is straightforward, and only native yeasts are used for fermentation. Very little new oak is used—thus, only 80 percent of the Chardonnay is barrel-fermented, and only 10 percent new oak is used. For the Cabernet, too, the wine spends about 16 months in mostly neutral oak, though the top Rutherford cuvée sees about 25 percent new oak. This latter wine is a bargain when one considers that most of the grapes for it come from the Rutherford bench. What is most striking about the Frog's Leap wines is that their alcohol never exceeds 14%, since Williams is able to pick at between 23 and 24° Brix. As a consequence, the reds in particular don't have the sheer richness and weight of more stereotypical Napa reds, but they are balanced and age well. He also makes a lot of Merlot, though he once remarked to me, "The Merlot is nice, but the Cabernet is wine," and I am inclined to agree. There is also a delightfully fresh Zinfandel and a small quantity of good Petite Sirah.

Frog's Leap wines are not fashionable, but they are just the kind of Napa wines that customers

Right: The current Frog's Leap winery is no longer at the original frog farm but has retained the name and symbolism

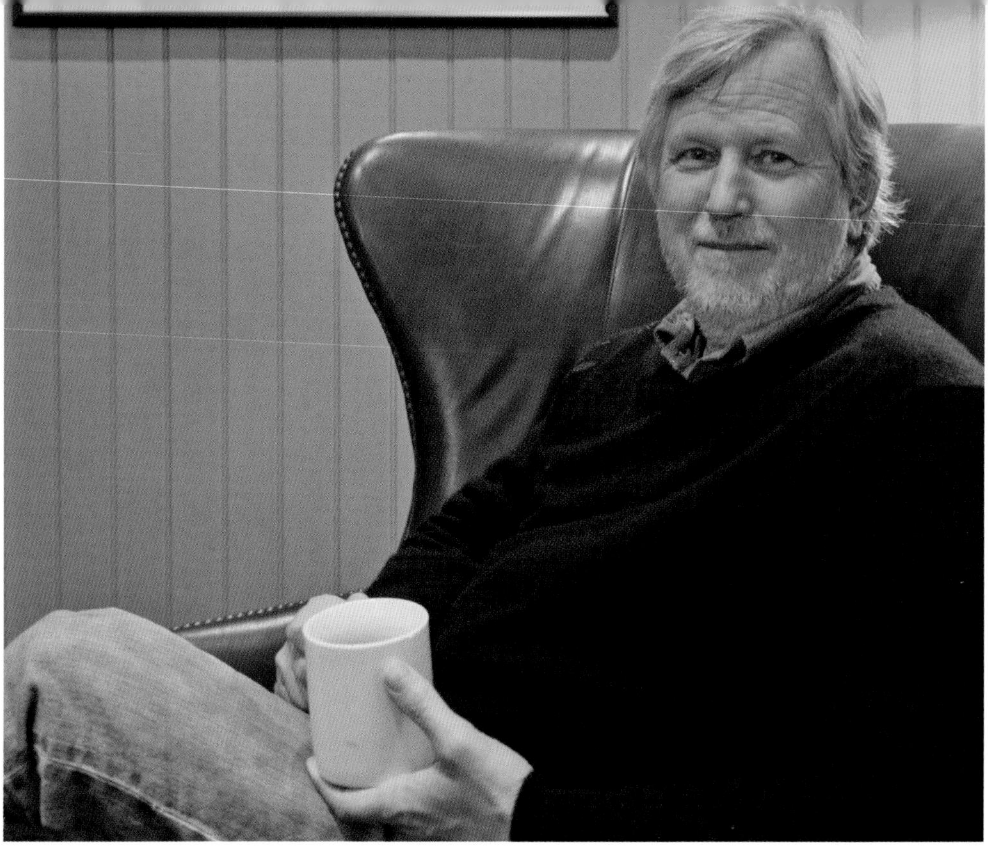

fall upon in restaurants: they are well made, harmonious, balanced, and reasonably priced. If some of them show a touch of herbaceousness, this is part of the personality of the wines, and they are never raw or green. Although Williams is satisfied with the range he has developed over the years, he hasn't lost his willingness to experiment with a few zany wines. Leapfrögmilch was a low-alcohol Chenin Blanc, discontinued after three years. More recently he has produced a TBA-style Riesling called Frögenbeerenauslese; it is made from botrytized fruit from Rutherford, and the most surprising thing about it is that Williams is still growing 70-year-old Riesling in this grandest of Napa appellations.

FINEST WINES

2008 Sauvignon Blanc [V]
Lean melon, citrus, and white-peach nose. Bright, fresh, and lightly herbaceous, with excellent acidity and vibrancy. Long citric finish.

Above: John Williams has retained his sense of fun but produces naturally expressive wines in an elegant style

2007 Zinfandel
Subdued cherry-and-cranberry nose. Fresh but concentrated, with light tannins. Some white pepper. Has delicacy and charm rather than complexity.

2006 Cabernet Sauvignon★
Lightly herbaceous black-curranty nose; has finesse. Fairly rich, not too extracted, but with underlying tannins and good acidity to keep it fresh. Elegant rather than profound, but balanced and long.

2005 Rutherford Cabernet Sauvignon
Sweet, intense, oaky nose, quite minty, with a hint of herbaceousness. Suave—and fine acidity gives it drive. There's a slight earthiness, as well as grip; this is elegant, poised, and long.

Frog's Leap Winery
Area under vine: 140 acres (56.5ha)
Average production: 700,000 bottles
8815 Conn Creek Road, Rutherford, CA 94573
Tel: (707) 963-4704
www.frogsleap.com

Grgich Hills Estate

Miljenko Grgić (or Mike Grgich) was born in Croatia in 1923, the last of 11 children. His family were peasants who cultivated vines as well as other crops, so he was familiar with wine from his infancy. After World War II, he had to think about a career and chose to study viticulture in Zagreb. Uncomfortable with the restrictions of life in Yugoslavia under Communism, he applied for a program in West Germany to pursue agricultural studies. While there, he became determined to make his way to North America and, in 1958, managed to get to California via Canada. There he applied for a job as a winemaker and ended up working for the respected Lee Stewart at Souverain Cellars. At last, he had his foot in the door.

Grgich did not get along well with Stewart, so he looked for other opportunities: he went to work for the Christian Brothers winery and then moved on to Beaulieu, where André Tchelistcheff was in charge. He was the most respected enologist of his day, and Grgich learned a great deal from him. In 1968, he went to work for Robert Mondavi, and he moved on to Chateau Montelena in 1972.

Here he had a great stroke of luck. He made the 1973 Chardonnay that triumphed at the Judgment of Paris tasting in 1976. His career was now taking off, and in 1976 he was able to buy 20 acres (8ha) of land in Rutherford but was unable to afford to build a winery. Fortunately, he was able to team up with Austin Hills, whose family were well-known coffee producers. In 1977, Grgich and Hills created, on a 50/50 basis, the new winery. Many visitors assume that Grgich Hills is a bucolic fantasy name, but in fact it is no more than a fusing of the founders' surnames. The first vintage was in 1977.

In the 1980s, Grgich followed the standard California pattern for making wine, sourcing grapes from various vineyards, as well as developing his own sites. He liked old-vine Zinfandel, which he sourced from the Sausal vineyards near Healdsburg in Sonoma County. Sauvignon Blanc came from Pope Valley and was made in a high-acidity style that could be quite assertive. Cabernet Sauvignon was introduced only in 1980, and ten years later Grgich began to produce his Yountville Selection Cabernet from 50-year-old dry-farmed vines. There are also bottlings of Petite Sirah and Zinfandel that come from his own vineyards.

Chardonnay, inevitably, was the wine with which Grgich was most closely associated, and it was regularly acclaimed as one of Napa's finest. He tended to block malolactic fermentation, and in the 1980s the wines were mostly aged in Limousin oak, which was also the case at Heitz. In the 1990s, he added a more complex Carneros Selection Chardonnay to the range, a wine made from the Wente clone. Occasionally he makes sweet wines: one called Violetta (after his daughter Violet), which was a rather strange blend of Riesling, Sauvignon Blanc, and Gewurztraminer; and, more recently, an Essence from Sauvignon Blanc.

In the 1990s, Grgich Hills seemed to be on autopilot. The wines were good—and possibly better than in the 1980s—but the winery was generating little excitement. All this would change with the arrival of Grgich's great-nephew Ivo Jeramaz. Born in 1959, he had studied engineering in Zagreb and emigrated to California in 1986. He came to work at the winery, learning the ropes—from the most menial tasks, to helping with the winemaking. As Mike Grgich was getting on in years, Ivo took on more and more responsibility.

In 2003, Jeramaz heard the high priest of biodynamism, Nicolas Joly from France's Loire Valley, give a lecture at Benziger. He found the whole concept exciting and discussed it with his great-uncle. Mike Grgich was sympathetic to the idea of farming as naturally as possible, since that was how grapes had been grown in Croatia when

GRGICH
HILLS

he was growing up. He told Ivo to go ahead, and by 2006 the estate was fully biodynamic.

This was a remarkable undertaking, given the size of the property. Moreover, since 2003, all Grgich wines had been estate-grown, so the winery could no longer rely on outside sources if their own grapes underperformed. The estate consists of five different sites. There are 20 acres (8ha) of Chardonnay in Yountville; 25 acres (10ha) of Chardonnay and 42 acres (17ha) of Cabernet Sauvignon next door to Dominus in Yountville, and now the source of all their Cabernet; Olive Hills, planted with Chardonnay, Riesling, and Sauvignon Blanc; and over 100 acres (40ha) in Carneros, planted with Chardonnay. Finally there is a relatively new vineyard, first planted in 1996, in southern Napa in the town of American Canyon, a cool, windy site of over 160 acres (65ha) of Sauvignon Blanc, Chardonnay, and Merlot.

All this activity has given Grgich Hills a new lease on life. Jeramaz has moved away from barriques, though all oak used is French. He has introduced *foudres* (large casks) in which to age some of the red wines, and some of the casks, equipped with temperature control, are used to ferment the Sauvignon Blanc. Zinfandel, too, is no longer aged in small oak but in 600-liter barrels. Jeramaz has also installed Oxoline racks, widely seen in Bordeaux, enabling barrels to be rolled; this allows the lees to be stirred without exposing the wine to air and the risk of oxidation. And since 2006, the whole winery has been solar-powered.

The full control of vineyards and the fine-tuning within the winery itself suggest that Grgich is all set to revive its reputation in the years ahead. And Grgich himself has not opted for an easy retirement: back in his native Croatia, he has founded Grgić Vina, a 3,000-case winery specializing in Plavac Mali.

Left: Energetic Mike Grgich, whose faith in his grand-nephew Ivo Jeramaz has given his Rutherford winery new impetus

FINEST WINES

(Tasted 2009–10)

2007 Fumé Blanc

Rich, floral nose, with tropical fruit. Plump, rounded, and full-bodied; this is a touch heavy, though there is some refreshing acidity on the finish.

2006 Carneros Selection Chardonnay

Ripe, stylish, appley nose. Creamy and full-bodied, some evident oak gives plenty of spice, and the finish is long and fresh.

2006 Zinfandel

Slightly raisiny, cherry nose. Medium-bodied but concentrated, quite peppery, with a dried-fruit character. Fresh rather than succulent. Quite long on the finish.

2005 Miljenko's Vineyard Petite Sirah

Muted, plummy nose. Rich, forthright, and spicy on the palate; ripe yet somewhat rigid tannins; vigorous and long.

Cabernet Sauvignon

2006 Sweet, gently oaky nose, showing cool red fruits. Firm and tannic, with some austerity and chewiness that still needs time to soften and open. But it has grip, concentration, and good length on the finish.

2004 Sweet, intense, black-currant nose; perfumed and shows charm and finesse. Ripe, with good concentration and firm tannins, with ample spice and acidity, and more freshness than many 2004s. Well balanced and long.

Yountville Selection Cabernet Sauvignon

2005★ Ripe, hefty, black-currant nose. Suave, juicy, and polished on the palate, with admirable concentration; stylish but peppery and with ample grip on the persistent finish.

2004 Dumb nose. Intense, minty, and peppery; rather closed but has piercing fruit. Clearly needs time. Good length.

Grgich Hills Estate

Area under vine: 370 acres (150ha)
Average production: 800,000 bottles
1829 St. Helena Highway, Rutherford, CA 94573
Tel: (707) 963-2784
www.grgich.com

Newton Vineyards

There are many beautiful vineyards following the contours of Spring Mountain, but few can surpass those of Newton. They follow the twists and turns of the landscape, interspersed with native vegetation, giving many different blocks with different soil types—from rocky loam to volcanic—and expositions. The elevation ranges from 500 to 1,600ft (150–500m). A red-lacquer Chinese gate frames one of the vineyards, and Chinese stone lanterns here and there are reminders that one of the founders of the property, Dr. Su-Hua Newton, was born and raised in China.

Her late husband, Peter Newton, had been one of the partners who established Sterling in Calistoga, and after Coca-Cola bought Sterling in 1977, he used some of the proceeds to buy the 560-acre (225ha) Spring Mountain ranch. The new estate's calling card in the 1970s was Merlot, and it is still a variety that Newton handles well, though less of it is produced than in the past. The Newtons were also eager to produce a Graves-style white wine and did so in the early 1980s. But in 1987, the wine was abandoned. As a barrel-fermented Sauvignon/Semillon blend, it was expensive to produce but could not be sold at a profit, because American consumers didn't understand why a Sauvignon Blanc should be as expensive as a Chardonnay.

Over the years, the range of wines became refined down to Chardonnay, Merlot, and Cabernet Sauvignon, plus a Bordeaux blend called The Puzzle. For a while, there was a Cabernet blend called Cabernets, but that was phased out. Today, there is a range of second wines called Red Label.

Part of the problem at Newton was a lack of clear direction. The winery employed excellent winemakers, but they tended to be kept in the background, with Su-Hua Newton very much in the foreground. The initial winemaker was Ric Forman, who had been at Sterling, but he quarreled with

Right: Dr. Su-Hua Newton, who has always played a major role, continues to promote the wines following the sale to LVMH

There are many beautiful vineyards following the contours of Spring Mountain, but few can surpass those of Newton. They follow the twists and turns of the landscape, giving many different blocks with different soil types and expositions

the Newtons and left to set up his own eponymous winery. In 1983, John Kongsgaard became the winemaker; he, too, now has his own labels. In the 1990s, Michel Rolland was taken on as the consultant winemaker. Luc Morlet followed until 2001, and the present winemaker is Chris Millard. As winemakers came and went, so did specific bottlings and cuvées, making it difficult to keep track of the Newton style. The major change took place in 2001, when the French luxury-goods giant LVMH took a controlling interest in the company. For some years, the Newtons continued to run the property, but Peter Newton's health declined; after his death in 2008, LVMH took full control of the estate, though Su-Hua continues to play a role in the promotion of the wines.

There is considerable use of native yeasts, and the Newtons were proud of the fact that their top wines were all bottled without filtration

The red grapes are mostly grown on the estate, but all Chardonnay is bought from growers in Carneros. Burrowed into the hillside, the winery is divided into seven temperature-controlled chambers, so that, for example, one chamber can be heated to provoke malolactic fermentation, while its neighbor can be cooled to keep the wines stored there stable. There is considerable use of native yeasts, and the Newtons were proud of the fact that their top wines were all bottled without filtration, as the label confirms, though the practice is far less novel nowadays than it was 15 years ago. The chilly cellars allow the red wines and the Unfiltered Chardonnay to be kept in barrels for almost two years before bottling.

In recent years, the wines seem to be going through a clumsy stage, and there is a lack of purity overall. But now that the ownership of the property has been sorted out and a new winemaker is in place, quality and consistency should both improve.

FINEST WINES

(Tasted 2008–09)

Chardonnay

The 2006 Unfiltered has a lush tropical fruit that is quite oaky. The palate is rich, broad, and creamy but has fair acidity and some spiciness. It's sleek, stylish, and quite long. The 2005 is more buttery and sweet and higher in alcohol; unlikely to age well.

Merlot

The 2005 Unfiltered has a heady savory nose, with black-cherry fruit and some coffee and nutmeg tones. The palate is suave, concentrated, and spicy, with some pungency and persistence, even if the sour-cherry finish seems somewhat atypical of the variety. The 2002 shows traces of Brettanomyces.

Cabernet Sauvignon

The 2005 has a tarry black-fruit nose. It's rich, full-bodied, and lush, and although quite tannic, it has good balancing acidity. Perhaps it lacks some vigor and personality, though.

The Puzzle

In 2005, the blend was 46% Cabernet Sauvignon, 29% Merlot, 21% Cabernet Franc, and 4% Petit Verdot. The nose is dense, lush, and meaty and has weight at the expense of purity. The palate is very rich and full-bodied and highly concentrated, making this a tannic and structured wine, built to last. The voluptuousness of the fruit and the massive structure effectively disguise the distinctly high alcohol. However, the 2002 is less well balanced, with milk-chocolate tones, an excessive fruit sweetness, and a hot finish. The Red Label version, called Claret, also has a savory meaty tone but shows a lighter touch than its bigger, far more expensive brother.

Newton Vineyards
Area under vine: 120 acres (50ha)
Average production: 480,000 bottles
2555 Madrona Avenue, St. Helena, CA 94574
Tel: (707) 963-9000
www.newtonvineyards.com

Shafer Vineyards

In 1972, John Shafer was a successful textbook executive in Illinois, but he decided to move with his family to California to grow grapes. In those days, he was not a connoisseur of wine, and the move was essentially a business venture. But he had good instincts and knew he wanted to plant his vines on a hillside site. Luckily, he found a suitable property in Stags Leap that had been on the market for three years. It was already planted with vines, but the varieties were the likes of Zinfandel and Carignane, which had been sold to Gallo, who used the fruit as components in their Hearty Burgundy. Shafer thought he could do better and replanted the vineyard, favoring Cabernet Sauvignon.

John Shafer had good instincts and knew he wanted to plant his vines on a hillside site. Luckily, he found a suitable property in Stags Leap

His first vintage was 1978, and this Cabernet was still drinking nicely in 2007. More than 50 acres (20ha) of Cabernet and Merlot are planted on southwest-facing terraces over thin volcanic soil. It's a hot spot, but fortunately nights can be cool, which prevents the fruit from becoming cooked. Other vineyards are planted near Chimney Rock winery on heavier soil that can be quite vigorous, and there are 60 acres (24ha) in Oak Knoll and 68 acres (27.5ha) more in Carneros. Since 1990, the vineyards have been managed sustainably by employing cover crops, relying on natural predators rather than pesticides, and using solar power.

John Shafer, now in his early 80s, is still very much present, but the daily management of the property is in the hands of his son Doug. Doug Shafer recalls that they often had to improvise at harvest. "In 1983, which was my first vintage here, we custom-crushed the grapes, took them to the Markham winery in St. Helena for fermentation, then barrel-aged the wines in American oak somewhere in Calistoga that didn't have proper temperature control. We had to induce the malolactic by wrapping barrels in electric blankets. But you know what? The wine still turned out okay."

There is something restless about the Shafer project as father and son try to establish what works best in their vineyards. In the mid-1980s, they were unhappy with their Zinfandel and grafted it over to Merlot. In 1980, they began producing Chardonnay from their Stags Leap vineyards, but John Shafer never liked it. Winemaker Elias Fernandez, who has been at the estate since 1984 and is treated as one of the family, said he could produce a worthy Chardonnay if they planted the variety in Carneros. The Shafers took his advice, and that was the beginning of the Red Shoulder Ranch Chardonnay, which was first produced in 1994.

The Shafers were fans of Antinori's Tignanello so tried their hand at Sangiovese. The result was Firebreak, a blend of Sangiovese and Cabernet Sauvignon, using fruit from Stags Leap and Oak Knoll. It was first made in 1991. Firebreak was one of Napa's better attempts at Sangiovese, but Doug decided to phase it out after the 2003 vintage. No doubt it occurred to him that the winery could earn more money from Cabernet, at which it excelled, than from a Sangiovese with a limited following.

In 1999, the winery introduced a Syrah called Relentless. The name was apt: it has always been a rather massive wine. The grapes are grown in Oak Knoll on shallow rocky soil, and some Petite Sirah is blended in. The wine is aged for 28 months in mostly new French oak. The result is plummy, sumptuous, and concentrated and a touch too high in alcohol.

But the wine that has made Shafer's reputation is its Hillside Select Cabernet, which was first produced in 1983. The wine is composed from various blocks on its hillside vineyards and from the various clones that are planted there. These

blocks receive a good deal of exposure to the hot afternoon sun, resulting in a big and sturdy wine. It is also aged for 32 months in new French oak, which is a long period, even in California. The wine has critics, as well as admirers, and some argue that so much new oak and power mask what should be the typicity of a top Stags Leap vineyard. That makes sense in theory, but the wine, for all its power and richness, usually comes across as balanced if somewhat monolithic.

The regular Cabernet used to be the Stags Leap Cabernet, but it became the Napa Cabernet when the fruit sources were expanded. In 2004, Doug Shafer decided to start from scratch and produced a new Cabernet blend from two of their Stags Leap estate vineyards. It is overwhelmingly Cabernet Sauvignon, with just a dribble of Petit Verdot. Unlike the Hillside Select, the new wine, called One Point Five, is half aged in American oak. There is also a Merlot, among the best from Napa Valley.

Despite the occasional swerves in direction and style, Shafer remains a consistently good and reliable winery. In the past, the Red Shoulder Carneros Chardonnay could be disappointing, with an excess of tropical fruit, buttery textures, and alcohol, though many rate it highly. Since the early 2000s, Doug Shafer and Elias Fernandez have fermented 20 percent of the wine in steel tanks, so as to give the wine more freshness and verve. This, to my palate, has resulted in a more enjoyable and vigorous wine.

FINEST WINES

(Tasted 2008–09)

Hillside Select Cabernet Sauvignon

2005 Burly nose, with plums, as well as black-currant and blackberry fruit. Very concentrated but supple on the palate, textured and generously oaky, but perhaps lacking a little finesse and finishing rather hot and peppery.

Left: John Shafer and his son Doug, who have worked hard to establish one of Napa's best and most consistent wineries

2004 Lush, minty, oaky nose, with black-currant fruit. Very ripe and concentrated, assertive, dramatic and spicy, yet slightly marred by some evident alcohol on the finish.

2003 Flamboyant and voluptuous black-currant-and-new-oak nose. Very concentrated, but the alcohol is held in check, and the finish is very persistent, even if the wine overall is far from elegant.

2002★ An opulent and oaky black-fruit nose. Sumptuous, highly concentrated, with massive tannins, but smoky and complex, with terrific drive but no jamminess. Very long.

2001 Sweet, sensuous, black-currant nose, with coffee tones. Rich if somewhat soft; super-ripe and somewhat flat on the finish, but not overblown. Good length.

1999 Still opaque red in color. Restrained but rich black-currant nose, with vanilla notes. Very concentrated, lush, and spicy black fruits; moderate acidity but still tastes youthful.

1994 Lively, oaky, minty nose. Ripe and concentrated, though medium-bodied. Lacks a little persistence but far from tiring.

Shafer Vineyards
Area under vine: 200 acres (80ha)
Average production: 385,000 bottles
6154 Silverado Trail, Napa, CA 94558
Tel: (707) 944-2877
www.shafervineyards.com

Spottswoode Estate Vineyard & Winery

A few blocks from the busy main road that traverses St. Helena, there's a rather grand mansion, settled plumply into its lush gardens, that could be mistaken for an old inn. That's because, in the 1880s, German immigrant George Schonewald modeled the house he built here on a luxurious hotel in Monterey. After his death, it passed through various hands, including those of a Mrs. Albert Spotts, until it was bought by Dr. Jack Novak, who thought this would be the perfect spot to raise his family. The property included a vineyard, which he replanted in 1973, replacing varieties like Napa Gamay and French Colombard with Sauvignon Blanc and Cabernet Sauvignon. (In 1990, phylloxera attacked, and most of the vineyard had to be replanted yet again.)

The aim at Spottswoode has always been to produce a ripe, supple wine, without excessive tannins or extraction. Balanced and sensuous, the Cabernet can age for up to 15 years

At first, the grapes were sold to other wineries, including Duckhorn and Shafer, until both Dan Duckhorn and John Shafer suggested to the Novaks that they produce their own wine.

Jack Novak died in 1977 at the age of 44, which must have devastated his young family. But his widow Mary forged ahead, hiring Tony Soter (later a celebrated consultant, before departing for his native Oregon to establish his own vineyard and winery) to make the wines. The first vintage was 1982, and three years later the entire property became organic. Today, Mary's daughter Beth Novak Milliken runs Spottswoode with energy and pride. Although there is no feminist manifesto here, all the winemakers since Tony Soter's departure have been female: Pam Starr, Rosemary Cakebread, and, since 2006, Jennifer Williams.

Spottswoode produces only three wines: a Sauvignon Blanc and two Cabernets. The Cabernet is grown entirely on the estate, as is some of the Sauvignon, though other batches of Sauvignon and Semillon are bought in from vineyards in Carneros and Calistoga. The estate vineyard lies behind the house in a single block on gravelly loam and clay soils. The major tool used to control growth, yields, and sugar accumulation is careful irrigation. There have been refinements over the years. Since 2005, the harvest is conducted at night to prevent the grapes from heating up. And a second wine, Lyndenhurst, has been launched, allowing the Estate Cabernet to be made with even more rigorous grape selection.

The Cabernet Sauvignon is vinified conventionally in stainless-steel tanks, goes through its malolactic fermentation in barrels, and is usually blended with a small portion of Cabernet Franc. It is aged for 20 months in up to 70 percent new oak, though it rarely comes across as an oaky wine. The aim at Spottswoode has always been to produce a ripe, supple wine, without excessive tannins or extraction. "We think the terroir here is some of the finest for Cabernet in California," opines Beth Milliken. "We want to honor the vineyard, and that means not aiming for a super-concentrated, overblown style." Balanced and sensuous, the Spottswoode Cabernet can age for up to 15 years, sometimes longer, but its exquisite fruit seems to be most expressive when the wine is about ten years old.

The Sauvignon Blanc, a favorite wine of Mary Novak, is taken seriously here and aged in a judicious mix of steel drums, oak barrels, and small egg-shaped cement amphorae. It has been very consistent over the years, with melony aromas and flavors, good weight of fruit, fine acidity, and an overall delicacy and refinement.

Right: Beth Novak Milliken, who runs Spottswoode with pride, prioritizing the vineyard and producing balanced, elegant wines

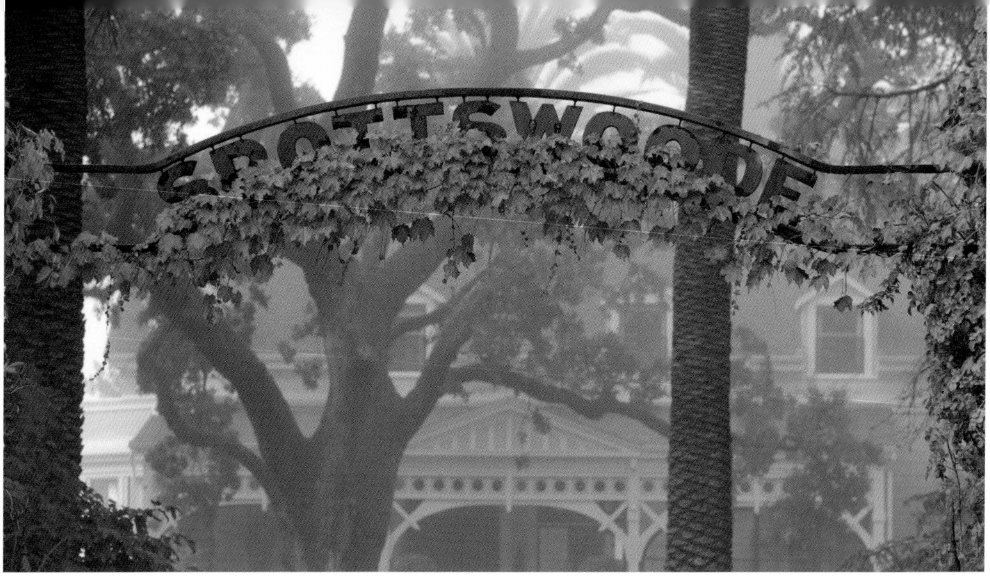

In an industry increasingly dominated by corporations and super-rich but often absentee proprietors, the happy family enterprise that is Spottswoode seems particularly appealing. On a recent visit, I was warmly greeted by Mary and Beth, ushered into the kitchen for a tasting, and urged to stay for a garden party. I saw some of Napa's great and good arriving in their flowery shorts and flip-flops, and admired the car of Beth's sister Lindy, the estate's marketing manager; never had I seen so many anti-Hummer stickers on a single bumper. It's fanciful, of course, to associate the warmth of a family with the character of their wine, but it crossed my mind that the harmony and finesse of the Spottswoode wine just might be infused with the atmosphere in which it is created.

FINEST WINES

(Tasted 2007–09)

Estate Cabernet Sauvignon

2006 A minty, zesty nose. Medium-bodied but concentrated and silky, with bright acidity and considerable delicacy, despite pronounced, youthful tannins. Great potential.

2005 Muted black-cherry and mint aromas. Suave, velvety, and concentrated, with fine-grained tannins and moderate acidity. This has gorgeous fruit, with a slight savory character, and impeccable length.

2004★ Fresh, vibrant black-currant nose. Rich and full-bodied, very concentrated, with unusual weight and grandeur. Firm tannins but not too extracted, and some lead-pencil tones on the long finish.

Above: The stylish 1880s mansion, modeled on a luxurious hotel in Monterey, remains at the heart of the family winery

2003 Dense plummy nose, not very expressive. Juicy, succulent, and full-bodied, with black-fruit flavors; concentrated, but lacks some grip and length.

2002 Rich, oaky nose: blackberries and black cherries. Super-ripe, concentrated, with sweetish fruit that's lush and a touch one-dimensional but supported by a firm tannic backbone. Long.

1999 Dense, brambly nose, with some tobacco tones. Sweet and intense, with splendid fruit, drive, and precision, fine acidity, and a silky texture. Very complete and long.

1997★ Dense but stylish, savory nose. Suave, concentrated, and delicious, with good acidity and excellent balance. Drinks well now but has ripe tannins and will evolve further.

1994 Slightly reserved black-cherry-and-plum nose. Concentrated, juicy, and succulent, and still fresh, ripe tannins and outstanding balance. While ready to drink, it will surely age further. Very long.

1987 The nose is still dense and rich but distinctly savory. Dense on the palate, too, but lively, with plenty of sweet fruit and a fine texture. Fresh for a wine of its age; very attractive and still going strong.

1982 Deep brick red, quite evolved, with a trace of tar. Medium-bodied, supple, a touch hollow, and now developing some astringency. It's beginning to lose fruit and develop some soy tones, but it's still silky and intense.

Spottswoode Estate Vineyard & Winery
Area under vine: 40 acres (16ha)
Average production: 60,000 bottles
1902 Madrona Avenue, St. Helena, CA 94558
Tel: (707) 963-0134
www.spottswoode.com

Viader Vineyards & Winery

Delia Viader, a petite and very pretty woman who scarcely seems to have aged since she came to Napa Valley in the mid-1980s, is, despite appearances, no Napa trophy wife. She came to the valley from Argentina via UC Davis and is armed with a doctorate in philosophy and business degrees from Berkeley and MIT. At Berkeley she became intrigued by the possibility of producing wine in Napa Valley. The fact that her father had bought a property there with the idea of building a retirement home on it gave her a springboard from which to leap into the industry.

Aided financially by her father, she began planting her vineyard at around 1,000ft (300m) on the slopes below Howell Mountain in 1986. The venture, which cost a small fortune, attracted considerable criticism from environmentalists. Today, such a complex project of clearing and planting the hillside scrub would probably be prohibited for fear that it could encourage erosion. Though a permit to develop the land was eventually granted, Dr. Viader first had to overcome opposition from the local political body, the Napa Board of Supervisors, which initially argued that the plan was not feasible. Whatever the politics of the matter, the 30-acre (12ha) Viader vineyard is an impressive sight, swooping down the thin, impeccably drained, rocky volcanic soils. Instead of planting on terraces, Delia Viader opted for vertical plantings, which were highly unusual in Napa Valley at the time. As in Portugal's Douro Valley, this method is more effective at countering erosion than planting on terraces.

Viader remains an extremely robust wine, with sumptuous fruit but less of the obvious fleshiness of more conventional Bordeaux blends from the valley floor and the benches

Farming on such a steep site was inevitably tricky, and yields are low, at around 2 tons per acre. These high-density vineyards, already organic, were being converted to biodynamism until 2008, when Delia Viader's son Alan, the property's director of operations, halted the program, which he found excessively labor-intensive.

Dr. Viader's first vintage was in 1989, when she produced 1,200 cases. From the beginning, she was an enthusiast for Cabernet Franc, a reflection of her particular passion for Cheval Blanc, which also has a considerable proportion of Cabernet Franc in its blend. Tony Soter was the original winemaker here, but today Alan Viader runs the vineyards and winery, with Michel Rolland acting as a consultant. The top wines are aged in specially constructed caves for two years, in a high proportion of new barriques.

The wine that has made Viader famous is simply called Viader and usually contains at least 40 percent Cabernet Franc. Apart from the act of homage to Cheval Blanc, the inclusion of so much Cabernet Franc is intended to temper the rugged character of Cabernet Sauvignon grown on volcanic soil. Nonetheless, Viader remains an extremely robust wine, with sumptuous fruit but less of the obvious fleshiness of more conventional Bordeaux blends from the valley floor and the benches. This is a wine with backbone, a touch of welcome severity, and a good deal of spice.

The Viaders also produce other wines from the estate, albeit in lesser quantities. A Syrah was first made in 2000, from both French and Australian clones. Alan Viader separates the vinification of the two sources, adapting the winemaking to the fruit quality, and only blends them later. It is aged for almost two years in 600-liter barrels. The result is a super-ripe, broad-framed wine, arguably more Australian in style than French, with power rather than finesse to the fore. It has to be remembered that this is a mountain-grown Syrah that certainly reflects its volcanic origins. Another intriguing wine is called V, with 50–70 percent Petit Verdot, the balance being Cabernet Sauvignon and Cabernet Franc. This is aged in new oak. It's a forceful wine, sometimes a bit overbearing, but it certainly has personality. No more than 500 cases are produced of each of these wines.

Alan Viader has introduced a second line of wines called, with a pun on half the family name, Dare. These are varietal wines made from purchased fruit, allowing the winemaking team to experiment and enjoy themselves. At present the range consists of a Cabernet Franc, a Cabernet Sauvignon, a Tempranillo, and a rosé made from Cabernet Sauvignon. Considerably less expensive than the estate wines, the Dare range offers a more affordable taste of the forthright Viader style.

The Viader estate seems admirably equipped to meet the future. The reputation of the Viader wine itself is secure, and the secondary estate wines also have a firm following. At the same time, although Delia Viader is still very much present at the property, Alan Viader appears to have a free hand to develop other projects and shape the estate and its wines as he sees fit.

FINEST WINES

(Tasted 2008–09)

Viader

In its youth, the wine can be tannic and even austere. There is power, but no coarseness, and an energy that carries the wine through to a long finish. It does seem to reflect vintage character more than most Napa wines. Thus, the 2006 is distinctly burly and chewy, but the extraction is not excessive, and the wine should evolve well. The 2005, which has less Cabernet Franc than most vintages, marries opulence and structure, and the aromas—of dark cherries steeped in chocolate—are particularly beguiling. The 2004 has an extremely ripe yet perfumed nose and surprising delicacy for a vintage that delivered many massive and overripe wines. The 2003 is less successful, but the 2002, 2001, 2000, 1999, and 1996 are all first-rate.

Syrah

The volcanic Viader vineyards deliver power, so this Syrah is far from being a retiring or discreet wine. From the outset, the wine was persuasive: both the 2000 and 2001 were super-ripe, slightly gamey, and had splendid fruit, without tipping over into jamminess or excessive tannins. The 2006 has a particularly vibrant nose, with aromas of plums, cherries, and pepper; the palate seems supple initially, but then the tannins make their presence felt, leading to a rather blunt finish. The 2005 has more complexity, with its plummy, baconlike aromas and a plump fleshiness on the palate that is allied to a powerful structure.

Above: Delia Viader and son Alan, in the winery above their Howell Mountain vineyard, which produces powerful wines

V

The wine suggests why Petit Verdot is favored more as a blending grape than for varietal wines. There are certainly a bluntness and density to V that make it, at least in its youth, less beguiling than the other estate wines. It has black-cherry aromas, allied in vintages such as 2002 to red-fruit aromas reminiscent of raspberry coulis, but on the palate, for all its concentration and intensity, there is a somewhat one-dimensional quality. The most recently tasted vintage, the 2006, also has a somewhat charred finish. The Viaders value it highly, pricing it higher than the other two estate wines, and it may well be that, like Viader, it simply needs time to develop more complexity and finesse.

Viader Vineyards & Winery
Area under vine: 30 acres (12ha)
Average production: 85,000 bottles
1120 Deer Park Road, Deer Park, CA 94576
Tel: (707) 963-3816
www.viader.com

Robert Biale Vineyards

The story of the Biale family replicates the experience of so many grape-farming families in California. Pietro Biale was an immigrant from Genoa who settled outside the town of Napa, where he engaged in mixed farming, raising chickens, walnuts, and plums, as well as grapes—"anything to make a living," says Pietro's grandson, Robert. Pietro also looked after vineyards owned by others and planted his own parcel of vines in 1937, naming it Aldo's Vineyard after his son. Pietro died in an industrial accident in 1942, leaving his widow, who spoke no English, and their 13-year-old son. They managed to hang on to their property and eventually bought more plots of land, some of which were planted with vines. Aldo, and then his son Robert, kept their land and, by the late 1980s, found themselves owners of some mature vineyards that became surrounded by housing as the town expanded.

Winemaking standards are consistently high at Biale, allowing the terroir of each site to sing out. There is no Portiness and no alcoholic burn

The grapes were sold to large producers, such as Gallo. In the 1970s, Gallo asked them to dig up their Zinfandel vines and replace them with other varieties, but the Biales refused. In 1991, they decided to start bottling their own wines. Robert Biale, who trained as a missionary, recruited two other partners, one of whom was winemaker Al Perry, who remained at his post until 2008. All the partners kept their day jobs until 1999; Perry was a winemaker at Beringer. Robert Biale thought they could put the business on a firmer footing and, in 2001, planned a new winery, which was completed in 2005. In 2008, Stephen Hall joined the company as the new winemaker; previously the winemaker at Jarvis, he had been a long-term fan of the Biale wines.

About 90 percent of production is from Zinfandel. In 1999, they made eight Zinfandels, as well as some other wines, and in 2007 the range expanded to a dozen. The partners always had their ears to the ground for word of Zinfandel vineyards that might be open to a contract with Biale. "Growers in Napa Valley who still have Zinfandel planted know they could make more money by replanting with Cabernet," Robert told me when I visited the estate. "The fact that they haven't done so tells us that these growers have a love for these vines, most of which are very old. So, when we offered to buy their grapes and thus help preserve the vineyards, they were usually happy to agree, especially now that we have a good track record with Zinfandel."

The 8-acre (3.2ha) Aldo's Vineyard within the Oak Knoll AVA is still in production. Biale also sources fruit from vineyards including Monte Rosso, Old Crane Ranch, Falleri, and Valsecchi, and he collects parcels of old vines, such as 80-year-old Barbera from Calistoga, and some Petite Sirah. Some growers have agreed to plant additional Zinfandel that will eventually go to Biale, though Robert admits it will probably take ten years before the vines start to give interesting wine.

Hall admires the transparency of Zinfandel as a variety. "Zinfandel peers into each site, and it amazes us how different the fruit expression is from each of them, whereas Cabernet Sauvignon would taste fairly similar. But old Zin has deep roots that soak up the flavor. So, we're still picking up new contracts. Some growers tire of dealing with corporations and very large wineries. They'd rather deal with us, because we care about their vines." Indeed, in some cases, the Biale team becomes closely involved with the farming of such parcels.

The wines are made as if they were Pinot Noir, because the skins can be fragile. Vinification

Above: The late Aldo Biale (center), with his son Robert (right) and partner Dave Pramuk, at their original, modest Napa winery

takes place in open-top fermenters, with regular punch-downs of the cap. Both indigenous and selected yeasts are used. The wines are aged for 10–14 months in mostly Burgundian oak, of which about one-fifth is new; some Hungarian barrels are also used. Winemaking standards are consistently high at Biale, allowing the terroir of each site to sing out. There is no Portiness and no alcoholic burn, despite alcohol levels that range from 15 to 15.5%, though sometimes, as in 2008, there may be a slight raisiny character that is derived from the vintage.

FINEST WINES

(Tasted 2009)

Zinfandel

Aldo's 2007 Subtle cherry fruit on the nose, with some red-fruit lift and a trace of bonbons. Medium-bodied, surprisingly delicate, though concentrated; an elegant and subdued style rather than explosive, and with moderate length.

Old Crane 2007 Cherry nose, quite dusty and earthy. Medium-bodied, concentrated, but shows no overextraction; elegant but lacks a little persistence.

Varozza 2007 Very ripe and pure: red-fruit-and-cherry nose. Suave and concentrated, with a fine texture. There's lovely sweetness of fruit but no jamminess. Refined and balanced and long.

Monte Rosso 2007★ Rich, stern nose, with great depth of fruit and considerable power. Ripe cherry fruit, direct and intense, with great energy; power, swagger, and spiciness—exuberant and long. A superb expression of this great Sonoma vineyard.

Robert Biale Vineyards
Area under vine: 8 acres (3.2ha)
Average production: 120,000 bottles
4038 Big Ranch Road, Napa, CA 94558
Tel: (707) 257-7555
www.robertbialevineyards.com

Caymus Vineyards

The Caymus property once typified old-style Napa. The Wagners were immigrants from Alsace. Carl Wagner began farming in Napa in 1906 and built a bulk winery in 1915. His son Charlie bought more land in Rutherford in 1941, though it was not planted with vines until the 1960s. The varieties of choice were Riesling, Pinot Noir, and Cabernet Sauvignon (from cuttings taken from the Fay Vineyard, which now forms part of Stag's Leap Wine Cellars). The first vintage of the Caymus estate was 1972. I was cordially received by Charlie Wagner in the mid-1980s and tasted an eclectic range, including Zinfandel, Pinot Noir, and late-harvest wines from Semillon and Riesling. Charlie's son Chuck was the winemaker by then (and still is), though Charlie lived on until 2002.

George Deuer of Inglenook was the initial winemaker, but Caymus began to attract attention when Randy Dunn took over in the mid-1970s, staying in place until 1986. It was Dunn who, in effect, created the wine for which Caymus is most famous: the Special Selection Cabernet Sauvignon. In 1975, this was a parcel selection from 14 acres (5.5ha) in Rutherford, given longer barrel aging of around four years in a mixture of new and old oak. Since the late 1990s, the Special Selection is aged for no more than 18 months in about 90 percent new oak, because Wagner finds the wines come around faster than the vintages of earlier decades.

The purely varietal Special Selection is a controversial wine. The wines are considerably higher in alcohol than in the past, acidity tends to be low, and some vintages give an impression of sweetness on the finish, though it is hard to say whether this is due to residual sugar or alcohol. The wine is certainly styled to be drinkable on release, though it can age well. About 1,000 cases are made, but not every year. It clearly has an avid following, as well as its critics.

Since the early 2000s, the range has been pared down, and the Caymus brand now focuses only on Special Selection and the Napa Cabernet, which is made mostly from purchased fruit, as well as about 15 percent estate fruit. As is common at many California wineries, part of the estate fruit is sold off. Chuck Wagner has no interest in retaining wines that he finds either herbaceous or light in color, since these are alien to the Caymus style. The Napa Cabernet is made from fruit picked at a lower Brix level than the grapes for Special Selection, because Wagner wants the wines to be clearly differentiated. It is aged in around 30 percent new oak—mostly French, with a few American barrels thrown in—for around 20 months.

Wagner can afford to jettison the wines that used to feature in the Caymus portfolio because he has very cleverly created other brands from outside Napa. In Napa, he farms about 150 acres (60ha) but owns considerably more acreage in Santa Lucia Highlands in Monterey County. This is the source of his Mer Soleil Chardonnay, a hugely popular wine that has purists wrinkling their noses. The style is unashamedly crowd-pleasing, with vivid tropical-fruit flavors, ample oak, and a dollop of residual sugar. The vineyards were planted in 1988, and the first vintage was 1994. The vineyard also contains white Rhône varietals. Ever responsive to changes in the market, Chuck and Charlie (the Mer Soleil winemaker) have introduced Silver, an unoaked Chardonnay, and small quantities of a late-harvest Viognier simply called Late, which can be distinctly syrupy.

Mer Soleil is also one of the sources for another of Wagner's hit wines, Conundrum, a bizarre blend of Sauvignon Blanc, Chardonnay, Viognier, and Muscat Canelli. As the blend suggests, the goal is an exotic, perfumed, slightly sweet wine designed to satisfy the numerous American palates that do not enjoy dry white wines. It bears the California appellation, since grapes from many parts of the state are blended in. Jon Bolta is the winemaker, and production is around 100,000 cases.

Above: Chuck Wagner, who produces a broad range of wines but is best known for his iconic Special Selection Cabernet

But the Wagner enterprise does not stop there. The winery has launched Belle Glos, a small range of Pinot Noirs named after Chuck Wagner's late mother. The first vintage was in 2001 and was made from Santa Maria Valley fruit from Santa Barbara. The range has since expanded to include Pinots from the Sonoma Coast and Santa Lucia Highlands. There is also an entry-level cuvée, Meiomi, which can be a blend from all three regions.

It is, however, the Napa wines that earn Caymus inclusion in this book. Despite its controversial style, the Special Selection has become a Napa Valley icon—a wine that, for many drinkers, epitomizes all that is best and richest about Napa Cabernet. It is not a wine with much finesse; nor is that its stylistic goal. I have tasted more than a dozen vintages of Special Selection, and although some of them strike me as overripe, they are fairly consistent in style. And some vintages, such as the excellent 1994, have aged very well. It has been Chuck Wagner's goal to give Special Selection the same kind of historic brand status as top Bordeaux, without in any sense trying to replicate the French style. In the eyes of many, he has succeeded.

FINEST WINES

(Tasted 2009)

Special Selection Cabernet Sauvignon

2004 Super-ripe nose of plums and black cherries, with a great deal of oak influence. Rich and highly concentrated, this is sumptuous and toasted, but the high alcohol is pronounced, and the finish, although long, is quite raisiny.

2006★ Rich if reticent black-currant-and-vanilla nose, with a touch of chocolate. Suave and velvety, this still has marked tannins and some overripe flavors. Low acidity deprives the wine of some complexity and nuance, but it doesn't lack length.

Napa Cabernet

This shows little vintage variation and is stylistically consistent. The nose is richly fruity, with blackberry, cherry, and black-currant aromas. The palate is plump and slightly sweet but less overtly alcoholic than the Special Selection. It is drinkable on release, but in top vintages such as 2004 the wine also has boldness of flavor and considerable length.

Caymus Vineyards
Area under vine (Napa): 150 acres (60ha)
Average production: 350,000 bottles (Napa); total 2.4 million bottles
8700 Conn Creek Road, Rutherford, CA 94573
Tel: (707) 963-4204
www.caymus.com
www.mersoleilvineyard.com

Clos du Val

Since its founding in 1972, Clos du Val has been a remarkable partnership between proprietor John Goelet and winemaker Bernard Portet. Both have their roots in Bordeaux: Goelet comes from a family of négociants, while Portet's father was *régisseur* at Château Lafite, where Bernard grew up alongside his brother Dominique, who would become the winemaker at another of Goelet's New World properties, Taltarni in Victoria.

Bernard Portet had a hunch that Stags Leap District would be a good place to grow Cabernet, even though, in 1972, there were very few vineyards to support that view. He, like his brother Dominique, wanted to make European-style wines. That did not mean wines with an identical fruit profile to the celebrated growths of Bordeaux, but wines that were designed to be drunk with food. This entailed firm tannins and moderate levels of alcohol. Nearly 40 years later, Clos du Val remains true to those aims.

Harmoniousness and balance are the defining features of Clos du Val wines, which remain self-effacing and, as a consequence, are often overlooked

The winery has evolved significantly since those early days. Its vineyard holdings have expanded, with more than half the surface being Chardonnay and Pinot Noir in Carneros. Many of the early plantings succumbed to phylloxera and were replanted in the late 1980s, which means they are now fully mature. Since 1999, the winemaker has been John Clews, a soft-spoken native of the former Rhodesia, who had already acquired considerable experience in California.

Clos du Val is one of the few wineries in California to take Semillon seriously. It is not an easy variety to cultivate here, since it tends to produce very large bunches that give wines that can lack character. Portet began making Semillon here in 1983, and in 1997 it was replaced by a blend called Ariadne, which is three-quarters Semillon grown in Stags Leap District and one-quarter Sauvignon Blanc. The wine is aged for ten months in about 20 percent new French oak. Such Graves-style blends are a rarity now in California, and this is one of the most successful.

There is nothing at all flashy about Clos du Val wines. They are all about restraint. Most varieties are picked at no more than 24° Brix, because Clews finds that the relatively cool microclimate in Stags Leap makes it feasible to attain ripeness at moderate sugar levels. Nor is there an inordinate use of new oak. Varieties such as Pinot Noir and Cabernet Sauvignon are aged in 25–35 percent new oak, though Reserve bottlings and the top-of-the-line Stags Leap District Cabernet could see as much as 50 percent. Reserve bottlings are made only in exceptional years, and even then, sales are often restricted to the tasting room.

It was always the intention of Goelet and Portet that the wines should be capable of aging in bottle. The 1972 Cabernet (which featured in the Judgment of Paris tasting in 1976) was certainly losing some fruit at the 2006 version of that tasting and showing some astringency. But other vintages, such as the 1978, have indeed aged very well. And they weren't simply Médoc lookalikes. In their ripeness, supple texture, and overall stylishness, they were very much Napa expressions of Cabernet—but Napa before it succumbed to the cult of overripeness. Harmoniousness and balance are the defining features of Clos du Val wines, which remain self-effacing and, as a consequence, are all too often overlooked when it comes to compiling hierarchies of the best Napa wines.

Above: John Clews, the soft-spoken Clos du Val winemaker since 1999, in a winery that reflects its Old World inspiration

FINEST WINES

(Tasted 2009–10)

2006 Merlot

Lush nose of blackberries and coffee. Fleshy and supple, this has a hint of tobacco, as well as black fruits. Structured with moderate tannins and acidity, this has good length and, while drinking well young, should also age well over the medium term.

2006 Cabernet Sauvignon

Muted, black-cherry nose, with a light but far-from-disagreeable herbaceous tone. Concentrated and moderately rich, with firm tannins and quite good acidity. Full-bodied but restrained by grainy tannins that suggest the wine needs further bottle age.

2005 Stags Leap District Cabernet Sauvignon★

Although aged for two years in oak, the wine has sufficient richness and power to absorb that oak effortlessly. Black fruits and chocolate characterize the nose, but there is no tarriness. Suave and luxurious in texture, this is concentrated and vigorous and has supple tannins and a charming lightness of touch, without any lack of structure or length. The 2004 is as fine if rather more showy and opulent.

2007 Carneros Chardonnay

Muted oaky nose, with aromas of melon and apricot. Fairly rich and creamy, but good underlying acidity and a fresh, lively aftertaste. Balanced and long.

2007 Ariadne

Ripe melony nose, perfumed and fresh. Medium-bodied, this has fine acidity and a beguiling tanginess, with persistent flavors of melons and ripe lemons that linger on the finish.

Clos du Val
Area under vine: 330 acres (133.5ha)
Average production: 800,000 bottles
5330 Silverado Trail, Napa, CA 94558
Tel: (707) 261-5200
www.closduval.com

Corison Winery

With her granny glasses and cropped hair, Cathy Corison looks more like a New England schoolteacher than a Napa winemaker. She has a purist approach to her winemaking, but that is what makes her so greatly admired by critics and consumers alike. In an age when points and profits seem to depend on making wines on a massive scale, Corison has stuck to her guns by making the kinds of wine that she likes to drink. She has immense experience, having worked at Freemark Abbey, Chappellet, and Staglin while setting up her own label in the late 1980s. For some years, it was a business she ran alongside her winemaking and consulting activities, and she made the wine in rented facilities. It was not until 1999 that her husband designed the barnlike winery that now stands in St. Helena along Highway 29.

Cathy Corison has a purist approach to her winemaking, but that is what makes her so greatly admired by critics and consumers alike

Apart from a small quantity of Anderson Valley Gewurztraminer, she makes just two wines, both Cabernet Sauvignon. The first is a blend from the benchlands along the western side of the valley, drawing on fruit from three neighboring vineyards that she has farmed for more than 20 years, on agreements based on no more than handshakes with the owners. She invariably buys more fruit than she uses after making her barrel selection, and so she sells some wine in bulk each year. Corison admits she picks the grapes relatively early, because she farms the vineyards with a view to attaining ripeness at moderate sugar levels, so that the wines never exceed 14% ABV. Once the grapes are safely gathered in, she inoculates with cultured yeasts to get the fermentation off to a good start, and then she allows the native yeasts to take over and complete the process. The wine is then aged for almost two years in 50 percent new barriques. She never adds acidity.

In 1995, she bought the 8-acre (3.2ha) Kronos Vineyard, which lies behind the winery on gravelly loam soils. Her first Kronos vintage was in 1996. Before she bought the vineyard, the fruit had been sold to Mondavi for its Cabernet Reserve. She was told that the vines had been planted on phylloxera-prone rootstock, but she knew this was not so and, as a consequence, was able to buy the site for an affordable price. It's an old-fashioned vineyard, planted to wide spacing on St. George rootstocks. Originally planted as bush vines, the vineyard is now trellised, but visually it looks more or less untouched. She farms Kronos organically, and vine age and uneven fruit-set mean the yields are very low, at no more than 1.5 tons per acre. Individual vines are now beginning to die; these are replaced by Corison and watered by hand to ensure they become established. Drip irrigation has been installed here, but she only makes use of it if a heat spike is imminent. Only 400 cases are produced, so the Kronos Cabernet is far scarcer than the standard Cabernet bottling.

In 2007, a tasting of the regular Cabernet from 2004 to 1989 demonstrated that a well-balanced wine, even with moderate extraction and alcohol levels, can age extremely well, though it is since 1994 that quality has really soared. To be sure, the Kronos Cabernet has more depth and density, but the regular wine shows a gracefulness and freshness that are admirable.

FINEST WINES

(Tasted 2009)

Cabernet Sauvignon

2006 Rich, black-cherry nose. Supple and juicy, this is surprisingly fruit-forward and less tannic than many 2006s from Napa. The finish is stylish, delicate, and long, with a light coffee tone.

2005★ Rich nose, quite savory, with a hint of dill. Medium-bodied and zesty, with little savory or herbal character. The oak and tannins are balanced by the sweetness of cherry fruit, and the finish is piquant and long.
2004 Lush black-fruit nose. Rich and solid but lacks the flair and freshness of some other vintages, since there is, or appears to be, lower acidity than usual. Moderate length.

Kronos Cabernet Sauvignon
2004 Bright, oaky nose, with red fruits and mint. Full-bodied, silky, and juicy, with fine underlying acidity that gives freshness. The finish is clean and precise, with black- rather than red-fruit flavors.
1998 Firm, savory black-fruit nose, with a touch of licorice. Medium-bodied but concentrated, with keen acidity, fine texture, freshness, and precision, as well as a long, delicate finish.
1997★ Intense, lifted, savory nose, with blackberry fruit. Rich and concentrated, but keen, tangy acidity gives lift and freshness and a long, lively finish.
1996 Rich, oaky nose, if a touch stalky. Medium-bodied, juicy and fresh, with purity and lift. It is delicate and precise yet packed with flavor and admirable in its length.

Above: The principled, highly respected Cathy Corison, who continues to produce the style of wine she enjoys drinking

Corison Winery
Area under vine: 8 acres (3.2ha)
Average production: 30,000 bottles
987 St. Helena Highway, St. Helena, CA 94574
Tel: (707) 963-0826
www.corison.com

Heitz Wine Cellars

The late Joe Heitz was a man of his times. He was a classic California winemaker, in the sense that he saw his job as transforming grapes into wine. After serving in the Air Force during World War II, he studied at UC Davis, and he worked for Gallo and Beaulieu in the 1950s before founding his own winery in 1961. He had to borrow $5,000 to purchase a vineyard planted with Grignolino, of all things. In 1964, he bought a ranch on Taplin Road, on the eastern side of the valley, which came with an old stone winery from 1898.

Although he believed it was the role of the grower to farm grapes and that of the winemaker to make wine, he was always prepared to pay top dollar for good-quality fruit. He soon established long-term relationships with two vineyards that he would make famous: Bella Oaks in Rutherford, and Martha's Vineyard in Oakville.

Bella Oaks, with 17 acres (7ha) of Cabernet Sauvignon, was owned by Bernard (Barney) and Belle Rhodes. The site was planted in 1971, and Heitz first made wine from here in 1976. It was assumed by many people then that the Rhodeses were shareholders in Heitz, or vice versa, but this was not so. The Bella Oaks wine is lighter than Martha's Vineyard, more claretty, leaner, with higher acidity.

The 35-acre (14ha) Martha's Vineyard was planted in the early 1960s by the Rhodeses, but in 1963 they sold it to Tom and Martha May. Heitz was quick to spot the potential of the site, located on a rocky, gravelly bench along the western foothills of the valley. The vineyard is not particularly well exposed to constant sunlight, but this has the advantage of extending its growing season. After phylloxera, it was replanted with a massal selection that gives small berries and loose bunches. For the past ten years, Martha's Vineyard has been organically farmed. The wine has its own famous hallmark: an aroma of eucalyptus that many believe is directly related to the presence of eucalyptus trees along its boundaries. Heitz himself discounted the theory, pointing out that other vineyards lined with eucalyptus trees did not have that character. His own view was that the aroma was linked to the selection planted.

When he started out, Heitz made mostly Chardonnay and Pinot Noir. He first bought Cabernet from Martha's Vineyard in 1965, but it was blended into his Napa Cabernet. From 1966, the wine was vineyard-designated. The vintages of the late 1960s (1968 in particular) and early 1970s were spectacular and made Heitz's reputation. By the 1980s, enthusiastic wine lovers would line up for hours outside the Heitz tasting room on the day when the new vintage of Martha's was due to be released. By the late 1980s, however, it was clear to many that there was a problem at Heitz. Many of the wines were tainted with TCA, and it took several years for the Heitzes to acknowledge the problem and deal with it. (In this, they were not alone; wineries the world over would be slow to recognize the TCA taint that infused their cellars and wines.)

In 1989, Heitz added a third single-vineyard Cabernet to the range: Trailside, from their own 100-acre (40ha) vineyard along the Silverado Trail. The vines are farmed organically, and the wine is aged in new oak. In terms of price, it is between Bella Oaks and the expensive Martha's Vineyard.

Joe Heitz was not a man to move with the times. He tank-fermented his Chardonnay and blocked malolactic fermentation. He stayed loyal to the Grignolino rosé he had made as a young man, and he even made a Port-style wine from the variety. He aged his Cabernet, and some of the Chardonnay, in Limousin oak—a practice that is continued to this day. He bought Limousin barrels because he disliked American oak, and the range of French oak in the 1960s was limited. I once asked Heitz why he had stuck to a wood that most winemakers disliked, and he replied, "In the beginning, we used what we had, and it worked.

Why should we change just because other people are sheep?" Joe Heitz was no diplomat.

Heitz had a major stroke in 1996, and he died at the age of 81 in 2000. The property, which has now expanded to 375 acres (150ha) of vines (much of the fruit is sold off), is still in family hands, with his son David making the wine and his daughter Kathleen Heitz Myers the president of the company. Although David, unlike his father, has shunned the limelight, he was assisting Joe as long ago as 1974. During that celebrated vintage, Joe put his back out and ended up in the hospital during the harvest, so the winemaking was mostly undertaken by David, who at the end of each day would take samples to his father's hospital bed for his approval.

Although Heitz still suffers from the slide in its reputation in the 1980s, the wines have fully recovered. Despite the family's conservatism, the Cabernets today seem more fruit-forward, more modern in style than the wines of the 1970s. But the property is not stuck in a rut. David introduced an unoaked Sauvignon Blanc as recently as 2007. Kathleen Heitz is unrepentant: "I know we're considered rather old-fashioned, but we believe in sticking to what we do best. Sometimes it seems that Napa wines are becoming standardized, so if we're somewhat apart from most other wineries, that may be no bad thing."

FINEST WINES

(Tasted 2009)

Martha's Vineyard Cabernet Sauvignon

2004 Very deep red. Rich brambly nose, with clove, coffee, and eucalyptus tones. Full-bodied and voluptuous, with a firm tannic backbone that gives considerable grip and length.

2002★ Opaque red. Dense, lush, smoky nose: plums and mint. Broad and spicy, with sumptuous fruit; highly concentrated, without being heavy. Well focused, balanced, and long. A superb wine.

1999 Very deep red. Sumptuous blackberry-and-black-currant nose, with a piercing mintiness that gives it vibrancy. Fine sweet attack on the palate, with a svelte texture, quite assertive in its tannins yet with abundant fruitiness on the long finish.

1997 Very deep red. Muted blackberry nose. Opulent and very ripe, but still distinctly tannic and lacking in flesh in the mid-palate. But it has great intensity and an almost gawky youthfulness.

1992 Very deep red; some evolution. Rather singed and smoky nose, leathery and quite evolved. Sweet and gentle, ripe and concentrated, with ample tannic grip and a peppery aftertaste. A vigorous wine, but it lacks some complexity and finesse.

1974★ Deep brick red. Intense smoky nose, with lift and freshness. Medium-bodied but fresh and limpid; intense and highly concentrated, with purity and drive and some residual tannins to firm up the finish. Mature but still going strong.

1970 Dense deep red, with a little browning. Rather Porty nose, with secondary aromas of leather shimmering over the ripe fruit. Dense, tannic, and imposing, with robust yet sweet tannins, this is still a wine of considerable power and energy. It may not be subtle or elegant, but it remains a mighty Napa Cabernet that is far from tiring.

Heitz Wine Cellars
Area under vine: 375 acres (150ha)
Average production: 500,000 bottles
500 Taplin Road, St. Helena, CA 94574
Tel: (707) 963-3542
www.heitzcellar.com

Mayacamas Vineyards

Many of the smaller estates established in Napa Valley in the 19th century were located up in the mountains, leaving the valley floor to the large-scale growers and wineries. Few of the historic wineries have had such a continuous history as Mayacamas. Its old stone winery was built by the Fischer family in 1889; the date is on the lintel. Being immigrants from Germany, the Fischers were presumably accustomed to planting on very steep slopes. Although the property changed hands many times, it somehow managed to keep going through Prohibition and, in 1941, was bought by an Englishman, Jack Taylor, who sold the grapes until 1946, when he reopened the winery and named it Mayacamas after the mountain range that separates Napa and Sonoma counties. The Taylors tried their hands at everything—from sparkling rosé to vermouth. Philip Togni was the winemaker in the late 1950s.

Travers sells his wines to private clients and to restaurants, which means he doesn't need to worry unduly about conforming to modern expectations of Napa Cabernet

The Taylors sold up, says Togni, because they had no successors and had not proved adept at marketing their wines. In 1968, a San Francisco financial broker called Robert Travers bought the property, which by then was run down and partly abandoned. He appointed winemaker Bob Sessions, who stayed for four years before going to Hanzell, where he would remain for three decades.

These beautiful vineyards, close to the county line, traverse volcanic soil at elevations that range from 1,700 to 2,400ft (520–730m), where Sauvignon Blanc is planted. The vines right in front of the winery and house are in an extinct crater. The vineyards are dry-farmed and very low-yielding, with the crop rarely exceeding 1.5 tons per acre. Travers likes to pick at no more than 24° Brix, and sometimes even lower, giving his wines a youthful austerity that has led many to underestimate their quality. The soil is rocky and sparse, which Travers believes accounts for the longevity of his vines, whereas on the vigorous valley floor the same varieties would survive for only half as long. The oldest Chardonnay vines date from 1950; the oldest Cabernet, from the 1960s. In the past, Travers bought a good deal of fruit, such as the Zinfandel, from his neighbors, but today all wines are grown on the estate.

The winemaking is idiosyncratic—some might even say eccentric. All wines, Chardonnay included, are fermented in open epoxy-lined cement vats. The Sauvignon Blanc is aged in old American oak vats; there is neither malolactic fermentation nor lees aging, so as to preserve the purity and steeliness of the fruit. The Chardonnay is made along much the same lines, except that it receives further aging in small barrels, of which 25 percent are new. The Cabernet Sauvignon, which also contains about 15 percent Merlot and Cabernet Franc, is aged for 18 months in large casks and then for a further year in French oak barrels, of which no more than 20 percent are new. The wine is lightly filtered and then given considerable bottle age before release.

Travers sells his wines to private clients and to restaurants, which means he doesn't need to worry unduly about conforming to modern expectations of Napa Cabernet. He cheerfully admits that he likes to make his Cabernet in a claret-like style, with no trace of overripeness and a persuasive elegance. Although he wants his wines to be accessible on release, he also wants them to be capable of further age, and when we lunched together a few years ago, he served a Cabernet over 25 years old—just the age at which he enjoys them.

Of course, there are bound to be misses as well as hits. Some vintages show astringency, others will eventually dry out. I suspect Bob Travers is not too fazed by this, since the same would be true of much classic Bordeaux. Although Mayacamas, with the next generation now taking charge, remains true to the style Travers created nearly four decades ago, it is worth remembering that he was always ready to experiment. In the 1970s, he tried his hand at Pinot Noir rosé (not a success, at least not in 1977), as well as some extraordinary Late Harvest Zinfandel, which was last made in 1984. It was a wine he first made by accident in 1968, when a lack of tank space meant he had to ask a grower to delay picking for over a week. The result was a massive, mouth-filling, Porty wine that won the admiration of Michael Broadbent MW, among others.

But the reputation of Mayacamas rests on its Sauvignon, Chardonnay, and Cabernet Sauvignon. The Merlot, when bottled separately, can be a delightfully fresh and pungent wine, but quantities tend to be very limited. Bob Travers now spends half his time in southern California, and his son Chris runs the property on a day-to-day basis. He shows no signs of wishing to wrench this classic mountain estate into the new century.

FINEST WINES

(Tasted 2006–09)

Cabernet Sauvignon

2003 Deep red. Slightly herbaceous, minty nose. Medium-bodied, with firm tannins countering an intense sweetness of fruit; vivid, bright, and long.

2000 Very deep red. Rich, blackberry nose. Very concentrated, with high acidity that should guarantee a long life but makes the wine quite hard to enjoy now. An intense and minty finish, with remarkable length.

1999 Fairly deep red. Dumb nose. Fine attack, bright and concentrated; assertive but lean and still adolescent. Very long.

1996 Deep red. Ripe, succulent nose: earthy and cedary. Dense and still tannic but has impressive weight of flavor; vigorous and complex, with a long, peppery finish. The palate is far less evolved than the nose, and this still needs time.

1994 Fairly deep red. Austere nose, with just a touch of oak. Robust and full-bodied but not heavy; dense and powerful, but discreet overall, and very long.

1992 Deep red, slightly evolved. Lean and elegant nose, with aromas of cedar and mocha. Medium-bodied, with pronounced acidity, but mineral and tangy and stylish. Reaching its prime.

1991 Very deep red. Exquisite blackberry nose, and little sign of age. Firm, rather severe, tight, with high acidity; little evolution, but it is assertive. Lacks some flesh and shows a slight greenness on the finish.

1979 Opaque red, with only slight evolution. Dense, leathery nose. Rich, sweet, and intense, and still backed by some bracing tannins; slightly earthy, but not dour or tiring, and very long. At its peak, but no rush to drink. Classic Mayacamas.

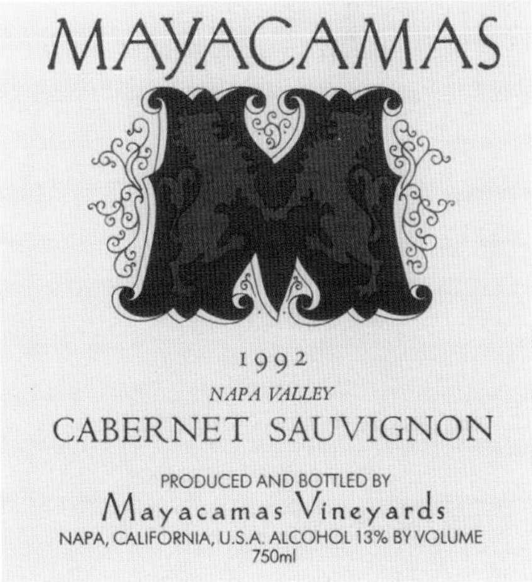

Mayacamas Vineyards
Area under vine: 52 acres (21ha)
Average production: 60,000 bottles
1155 Lokoya Road, Napa, CA 94558
Tel: (707) 224-4030
www.mayacamas.com

Merryvale Vineyards

Merryvale began as Sunny St. Helena, the first winery built in Napa Valley after Repeal. In 1937, it was bought by Cesare Mondavi—the father of Peter and Robert, who had begun his winemaking career in Lodi—but he sold it six years later. The winery went through a dim period in the 1960s, when it became the headquarters of a cooperative; and in the 1970s, the Christian Brothers, who at that time ran a major winery in Napa Valley, used its spacious buildings for storage. In the mid-1980s, Bill Harlan and some partners bought the property, and once again it became a working winery, with Bob Levy running the cellars. In the early 1990s, the Swiss Schlatter family bought a 50 percent interest in Merryvale, taking full control of the business in 1996. Bob Levy, who by then was making the wine for Harlan Estate, left Merryvale for good in 1998, handing over to Steve Test, who had previously worked for Jess Jackson as winemaker at Stonestreet.

This long tale of shifting owners and personalities is all too typical of the California wine industry, but at present the winemaker is Sean Foster, who began working at Merryvale in 1995 as assistant winemaker. Craig Williams, former winemaker at Phelps, acts as a consultant (a role filled in the 1990s by Michel Rolland). Merryvale seems to switch consultants with rather alarming frequency, and Williams's predecessor was the gifted Australian winemaker Larry Cherubino.

With so many changes, it is difficult for a winery such as Merryvale to maintain its identity, but it earns its place here for its consistently high quality and, by Napa standards, sensible prices. Even the second range, Starmont, is extremely dependable. Indeed, in terms of volume, Starmont dominates production, since only about 12 percent of bottles bear the Merryvale label.

Merryvale owns 50 acres (20ha) in Carneros, on the historic Stanly Ranch, also the site of its Starmont winery, which is operated by solar power. It owns 25 acres (10ha) just east of St. Helena, too, and shares the production from 100 acres (40ha) at the Juliana Vineyard in Pope Valley. Merryvale also buys fruit from prestigious vineyards such as Hyde and Stagecoach and, until very recently, bought Cabernet Sauvignon from Andy Beckstoffer's first-rate vineyards in Oakville and Rutherford, but that contract came to an end in 2006.

Located along the main road through St. Helena, the winery attracts many visitors and treats them well. Visitors to the tasting room usually wander into the adjoining Cask Room, a lofty hall lined with two rows of 7,570-liter (2,000-gallon) German casks that's more reminiscent of the Rheingau than Napa Valley. These cellars are no longer in use, and the wines are made in more functional buildings behind the historic winery, as well as at the Starmont winery. For the top wines, the harvesting practices are meticulous. Fruit is hand-picked early in the morning, stored in refrigerated conditions until ready to be sorted on vibrating tables, then fed by gravity into the fermentation tanks. White wines are whole-cluster pressed.

The range of Merryvale wines used to be eclectic, with some wines made from Sonoma fruit and a number of Reserve wines. Steve Test added Pinot Noir in 2001, and some excellent Syrahs from Napa and Dry Creek were made at about the same time. Today, the range has been simplified. With Starmont providing good-value wines at a modest price, Merryvale has, in effect, become the reserve range, so the Reserve category has been phased out. So, Merryvale now offers standard varietals, as well as small lots of purely estate-grown wines, such as a Cabernet Sauvignon and Petit Verdot, and some winemaker's indulgences such as a late-harvest Riesling from Russian River Valley.

The top red wine is a Bordeaux blend, dominated by Cabernet Sauvignon, called Profile, aged for 18 months in mostly new barriques. It's a very reliable and polished wine, even though it is made in quite substantial quantities (about 5,000 cases). Merryvale's finest Chardonnay is called

Above: Sean Foster, who began working at Merryvale in 1995 and now presides over the company's broad range of wines

Silhouette. Made mostly from Carneros fruit, it is barrel-fermented with indigenous yeasts, goes through full malolactic, is aged in two-thirds new barriques, and is bottled without filtration.

Now that the range has been rationalized, one can hope that Merryvale will pursue a steady course, not just maintaining quality but offering a coherent list of wines related, at least at the top level, to its mostly excellent vineyard holdings.

FINEST WINES

(Tasted 2009–10)

2007 Carneros Chardonnay
Toasty nose, with pear aromas. Medium-bodied and fresh, concentrated and spicy, with a deft light touch, leading to a long, acidity-refreshed finish.

Silhouette Chardonnay
2007 Spicy buttery nose, very oaky and overt. Full-bodied, weighty, and showing more power than finesse. A somewhat manufactured Chardonnay of the old school but imposing, spicy, and long.
2005 Powerful, toasty nose. Full-throttle on the palate, concentrated, structured, and mineral, with apricot and apple-compote flavors.

2006 St. Helena Estate Cabernet Sauvignon★
Very deep red. Discreet, black-cherry, black-olive, and black-currant nose, with considerable purity. Sumptuous and full-bodied, with very ripe tannins, and both power and freshness on the finish.

Merlot
2006 Fleshy, oaky blackberry nose. Full-bodied and robust, a firm Merlot with rigor and length.
2005 Smoky, savory nose but a more restrained palate, with rich, juicy fruit and a slightly dry finish.

Profile
2006 Powerful and sumptuous on the nose, with black fruit aromas and a pronounced, savory tone. A full-throttle Bordeaux blend, powerful and chunky, with masses of fruit but moderate acidity and finesse. Yet impressive and long.
2004 Aromatically complex, with black cherries, eucalyptus, and leather. No blockbuster, but a spicy, concentrated wine that has elegance, despite a slight earthiness and a savory finish.

Merryvale Vineyards
Area under vine: 75 acres (30ha)
Average production: 1.3 million bottles
1000 Main Street, St. Helena, CA 94574
Tel: (707) 963-7777
www.merryvale.com

Quintessa

What is most puzzling about Quintessa is how such a prime piece of land in Rutherford could remain vine-free for so many decades. The explanation is that the property, a former cattle ranch, used to be owned by George Mardikian, a San Francisco restaurateur who had a vague intention of planting the land but somehow never got around to it. He died in the early 1980s. Agustin Huneeus, the Chilean wine entrepreneur and owner of Franciscan winery in Rutherford, came to hear about the estate and, in 1989, sent his wife Valeria to San Francisco to negotiate. Other winery owners had their eye on the virgin property, too, but the deal with Huneeus was eventually made, and planting began in 1990. The first vintage of this large property along the Silverado Trail was in 1994. The concept was not dissimilar to that at Opus One: a single Cabernet-based wine.

The vines are contoured around five low hills, giving different expositions and explaining the winery's name. Since 2000, the wine has been first-rate

As at Opus One, some years would go by before the winery was completed. Its beautiful structure, designed by architects Walker Warner in San Francisco, comprises a wide arc of mottled yellow stone facing Silverado Trail from the west, with ramps on either side leading to the offices and the grape-reception area. Since the grapes arrive at the highest point, the winery itself operates by gravity.

Until 1999, Quintessa was partly owned by Franciscan as well as Huneeus, but after the sale of Franciscan in 1999, he retained Quintessa as his personal property. He retired in 2009 but still contributes occasional advice, usually in the form of: "You decide what you think is best."

The first winemaker was Alan Tenscher, succeeded by Sarah Gott, Aaron Pott, and, from 2007, Charles Thomas, who had been the winemaker at Mondavi, Rudd, and elsewhere. There have inevitably been changes over the years. Some blocks were replanted in the 2000s to a higher density, and since 2005 the property has been cultivated biodynamically. The vines are contoured around five low hills, giving different expositions and explaining the winery's name. The soils are varied, too: they are mostly alluvial, but there is also volcanic ash, volcanic red soil, loam, and gravel. Cabernet Sauvignon is by far the most important variety, followed by Merlot, and as well as the other Bordeaux varieties, there are 4 acres (1.6ha) of Carmenère—a small Chilean imprint on the property—and some Sauvignon Blanc. Yields are generally about 3 tons per acre. The harvest can take four weeks because of the differences between parcels, giving the winemakers about 50 lots of different wines to work with.

The winery is ultra-modern, as one would expect. Fermentation takes place in a blend of vats: wooden and concrete, as well as steel, and Thomas favors the use of native yeasts, though it is not a dogma. There are new hydraulic presses, and wine caves are tunneled into the hillsides. Quintessa is aged for about 18 months in 80 percent new, medium-toast barriques.

In recent years, the range has been diversified, which is hardly surprising, given the difficulties of selling yet another high-priced Napa Cabernet made in substantial quantities. Huneeus devised a second wine called Faust—not a dumping ground for declassified lots, but a wine made from purchased fruit from outstanding vineyards, such as Beckstoffer, Pahlmeyer, and Stagecoach. This is aged in one-third new barriques.

There is also a Sauvignon Blanc. Although there are Sauvignon vines on the property, most of the fruit is purchased. The wine is fermented and aged in a combination of steel tanks and concrete "eggs"—a small type of fermenter much favored by biodynamic properties. Just over half the wine is aged in neutral oak, while the remainder stays in steel or concrete.

There were disappointing vintages of Quintessa during the mid- to late 1990s, when the vines were young and the winery was still finding its way. Since 2000, however, the wine has been first-rate and a welcome reflection of the vintage.

FINEST WINES

(Tasted 2008–10)

2008 Sauvignon Blanc Illumination
Fresh, aromatic nose: apples and ripe citrus. Quite rich but has Sauvignon typicity; ripe but fresh, with vibrancy and persistence.

2006 Faust Cabernet Sauvignon
Rich, elegant nose, with cherries and red fruits. Supple and medium-bodied, and despite some firm tannins, quite a gentle style, with a sweet but not jammy finish. The 2005 was more weighty and lacked freshness.

Quintessa
2007 Very toasty nose, with opulent black-currant fruit. Very rich and dense, with sweet yet not jammy fruit; supported by powerful and chewy tannins, yet has polish, complexity, and length.
2006 Rich, firm nose: black currants and cherries. Suave, very concentrated, with dense tannins and impressive weight of fruit. The acidity is a little low, but the finish is long and shows a light touch.
2005★ Elegant black-currant nose; a hint of red fruits, too. Supple, elegant, and medium-bodied; a cool style, with good acidity and lift. Needs some time to fill out, but long and stylish.

Right: Charles Thomas, Quintessa's winemaker since 2007, who favors natural techniques in both vineyard and winery

Quintessa
Area under vine: 170 acres (69ha)
Average production: 300,000 bottles
1601 Silverado Trail, Rutherford, CA 94574
Tel: (707) 967-1601
www.quintessa.com

Rudd

American foodies know that Dean & DeLuca is synonymous with fine groceries and wines, and the chain's emporium in St. Helena is packed with wonderful products, if at alarming prices. In the mid-1990s, the founders sold a controlling interest to Leslie Rudd, the owner of a large wine distributorship and a chain of steakhouses who also happened to be passionate about wine. In 1996, Rudd bought the former Girard winery along Silverado Trail in Oakville, rebuilt most of the structures, and hollowed out underground wine caves in the cellars. He hired David Ramey as his winemaker. Ramey was hugely impressed by the vineyard around the winery, some 45 well-drained acres (18ha) of red potato-sized stones, more reminiscent of Châteauneuf-du-Pape than Napa Valley. He was sure it was capable of making great red wine. He also made elegant Chardonnays from Carneros and Russian River Valley fruit and a Bordeaux blend from Jericho Canyon, a terraced vineyard north of Calistoga. In 2000, an Estate Cabernet was added to the range.

Ramey left in 2001 and was succeeded by Charles Thomas, who in turn left in 2007 to take up a similar position at Quintessa. The current winemaker is Patrick Sullivan, who had worked here alongside Ramey in the 1990s. Rudd wants his wine to be first-class and has hired some expensive consultants: David Abreu to manage the vineyards and, from 2008, Michel Rolland to advise on the winemaking and blends. Charles Thomas favored small berries with great fruit concentration, but Abreu aims for a slightly higher crop, with a more developed root system, which should give the wine a stronger personality. One consequence is that the vines will have a longer hang-time, without excessive sugar accumulation.

The estate vineyard was replanted with the five Bordeaux varieties from 1997 onward, to much higher density than previously. New parcels of vines were acquired: 8 acres (3.2ha) just south of the winery, 16 acres (6.5ha) on Mount Veeder, and a fascinating property just south of St. Helena called Edge Hill. This had been the Louis Martini homestead. When Rudd bought it, there were no longer any vines on the property, but there were records of an old field blend that had been planted on this spot in the 19th century. With advice from Paul Draper of Ridge, cuttings were selected and the old plantings replicated.

The range has changed considerably since Ramey's day. The top wine is the Oakville Estate Proprietary Red, and the Crossroads Oakville Cabernet is effectively the second wine. The Jericho Canyon wine is no longer made, and although some Chardonnay is still purchased from Russian River, it is likely to be phased out. There is also a Sauvignon Blanc, barrel-fermented and aged in older barrels, steel drums, and concrete "eggs." There is no malolactic fermentation.

The winemaking is fairly standard, though only native yeasts are used. Sullivan will occasionally acidify to avoid a higher pH than he considers acceptable. The red wines are aged in at least 80 percent new barriques for 20 months and are bottled unfiltered. When he was the winemaker here, David Ramey told me that Leslie Rudd wanted to release only the very best wine possible, so he faced no objections when he decided to declassify or sell off anything not of the highest standard. Eight years later, Patrick Sullivan told me the same thing, adding that half the wine never makes it into bottle.

FINEST WINES

(Tasted 2009)

2007 Sauvignon Blanc

Rich, ripe melony nose. Broad, plump, and solid—a touch heavy for Sauvignon.

Estate Red

2007 (from cask) Dense nose: black fruits and licorice. Rich, hefty, and tannic, with its power and fruit sweetness not yet in harmony. Long.

Above: Patrick Sullivan, Rudd's winemaker, with the relaxed stance of somebody who can afford to bottle only the very best

2005★ Majestic nose, with considerable power; black fruits but no tarriness. Highly concentrated and dense, with ripe tannins; structured and powerful, but not without freshness and persistence. This is a mighty wine.

Crossroads Cabernet Sauvignon
2006 Sumptuous black-fruit nose, just a hint of tar and coffee. Spicy, vibrant, with good acidity and vigor, and a long if slightly dry finish.

2004 Sweet, oaky black-currant nose. Juicy, opulent, and concentrated, with moderate acidity and no hard edges.

Rudd
Area under vine: 74 acres (30ha)
Average production: 42,000 bottles
500 Oakville Crossroad, Oakville, CA 94562
Tel: (707) 944-8577
www.ruddwines.com

Saintsbury

This Carneros winery was founded in 1981 by Richard Ward and David Graves, both scientists by training who were wooed away from their professions by the allure of wine. They met at UC Davis. They named their project after the British wine connoisseur George Saintsbury, who might not have approved of the partners' whimsical naming of their rosé as Vincent Vin Gris.

Their first two vintages were made at other wineries, and they moved to their present premises in 1983. They expanded the buildings in 1988, because production grew more quickly than anticipated. From 2007, the winery has been solar-powered. Thirteen acres (5ha) were planted in 1986, and in 1990 the partners also bought the nearby Brown Ranch, a slightly warmer site that they planted two years later to a high density with Dijon clones. The Saintsbury vineyards are not extensive enough to supply the winery's needs, so much fruit is purchased, from 24 other Carneros properties. Many now-eminent winemakers have worked here over the years, and since 2005 the winemaker has been Jerome Chery, who worked for seven years as Ted Lemon's assistant at Littorai, which sounds like a perfect qualification for the post.

Ward and Graves have devoted many years to studying clonal variations and other variables. The result is a quarter-century of highly consistent wines

For many years, the range was simple enough: a Chardonnay and Reserve Chardonnay, and three tiers of Pinot Noir—the light, fruit-forward Garnet, the Carneros bottling, and the Reserve. In 2004, Saintsbury replaced the Reserve with vineyard-designated wines from Stanly Ranch and Toyon Farm. A year later, they added non-Carneros Pinot: Cerise Vineyard from Anderson Valley. There are also Brown Ranch bottlings of both Chardonnay (replacing the Reserve Chardonnay since 2002) and Pinot Noir, which are the most complex expressions of the Saintsbury style.

The Carneros Chardonnay comes mainly from purchased fruit, though some estate fruit is used. The wine is barrel-fermented and aged for eight months in about one-third new oak, with regular stirring of the lees. Since 1993, the wine has been bottled without filtration. The Brown Ranch Chardonnay comes from an 8-acre (3.2ha) parcel and only receives a little more barrel aging than the Carneros; but then it is given further aging for six months in steel tanks.

Garnet is essentially a selection of the lightest wines, made in the spring following the vintage. They are taken out of barrel fairly early and bottled in the summer. This has always been a wine of charm and has never pretended to be complex. The remaining barrels are given longer aging and are bottled as the Carneros Pinot Noir. Here the goal is a balanced wine of considerable richness but without the effortful, jammy style of some North Coast Pinots. Twenty years ago, another Carneros winery, Acacia, was specializing in single-vineyard Pinots, and over the past decade Saintsbury has adopted a similar view, persuaded that Carneros is not as uniform in its terroir as many suppose.

There are other new additions to the range in the form of two cool-climate Syrahs—one from Carneros (though bottled under the Sonoma Coast appellation) and the other from Sonoma Valley. But it is Pinot Noir that most grips Ward and Graves, and they have devoted many years to studying clonal variations and other variables introduced by modifications to winemaking. The result is a quarter-century of highly consistent wines. Now that so many other fine Pinot producers are on the California scene, Saintsbury has lost some of its preeminence, which it is seeking to reclaim with its vineyard-designated wines.

FINEST WINES

(Tasted 2007 and 2009)

2007 Chardonnay [V]
Fresh lime nose. Good attack, leading to a fresh medium-bodied wine, with a light but attractive phenolic tone. Good acidity and length, with lime on the finish.

2007 Carneros Pinot Noir
Bright cherry nose, very ripe and fragrant. Fairly rich and vibrant, with light tannins and quite good acidity; has drive and freshness. Excellent balance and poise.

2007 Stanly Ranch Pinot Noir
Lush yet perfumed red-fruit nose. Firm and full-bodied but not heavy or extracted. Spicy and vigorous, with light tannins on the finish, which is quite long.

2007 Toyon Farm Pinot Noir★
Fragrant, oaky nose: cherries. Bright, fresh, high acidity gives intensity; concentrated but lively. Has a light touch and admirable length.

2005 Brown Ranch Pinot Noir
Lean, spicy, oaky nose. Juicy, concentrated, quite tannic and peppery, with good acidity and length.

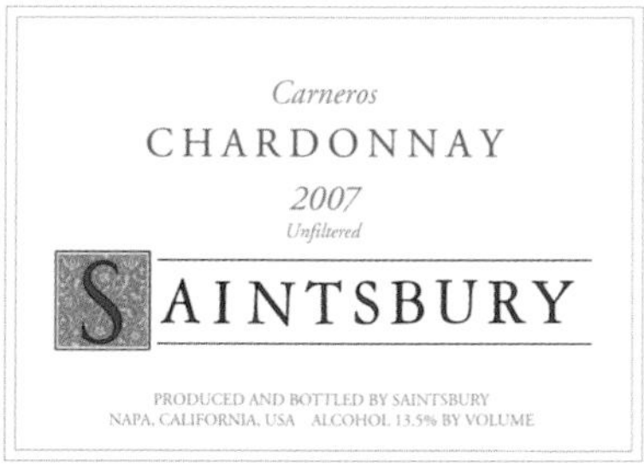

Right: Richard Ward, Saintsbury's co-founder, who is aiming to restore its preeminence with single-vineyard wines

Saintsbury
Area under vine: 54 acres (22ha)
Average production: 720,000 bottles
1500 Los Carneros Avenue, Napa, CA 94559
Tel: (707) 252-0592
www.saintsbury.com

Schramsberg Vineyards

In the Schramsberg tasting room, there is a photograph of founder Jacob Schram, paunchy and white-bearded, reclining in a wooden chair on the porch of his house, which still stands on the slope next to the winery. He is either napping or resting after a copious lunch, and he has good reason to look pleased with life. In 1862, he had bought land south of Calistoga on the slopes of Diamond Mountain. Here he created one of its earliest wineries, hiring Chinese laborers, facing unemployment after working on the railroad, to build caves in which he could age and store his wines. The winery prospered, and its Rieslings and "Burgundy" were shipped far and wide.

After Schram's death in 1905, the estate was sold and then passed through many owners, none of whom made a success of the property. In 1965, the derelict property was bought by Jack and Jamie Davies, who had been shareholders in the Martin Ray winery decades earlier. Their vision was to create a property dedicated to *méthode Champenoise* wine production. There were quite a few other sparkling-wine houses in California, especially in Sonoma, but their wines were aimed at the mass market. The Davieses wanted to produce wines of the same caliber as good Champagne. They bought grapes from various sources, as well as using their own vineyards, until it became clear that northern Napa Valley was just too warm a spot to give good sparkling wines. In 1998, the vineyards around the property were replanted with Bordeaux varieties, and fruit for the sparkling wines would eventually be sourced from 90 different vineyards, mostly in Carneros, but also in Sonoma, Anderson Valley, and Marin County.

Schramsberg faltered after Jack Davies died in 1998. There were bitter family disputes that marred the next ten years, until Jamie's death in 2008. Thereafter, their youngest son, Hugh, was firmly in control. The winery pursued two very different directions: the high-quality vintage sparkling wines for which it had always been known; and a Bordeaux blend under the J Davies label. Sean Thompson is the winemaker for the latter, while Keith Hock is in charge of the sparkling wines, though Hugh Davies is also closely involved.

About half the base wines are barrel-fermented, and all the vintage wines spend at least four years on the yeasts. The *dosage* of the Brut wines is 11–12 grams per liter. The top cuvées are hand-riddled, and the cellars hold a stock of 2.7 million bottles.

The range is extensive. The Blanc de Blancs used to have some Pinot Blanc in the blend but is now pure Chardonnay. The Blanc de Noirs is made mostly from Sonoma and Anderson Valley fruit and contains about 10 percent Chardonnay. The Brut Rosé used to include some Gamay, but today it is about 40 percent Pinot Noir, the remainder being Chardonnay. Mirabelle is the Non-Vintage wine, with about 20 percent of reserve wines in the blend, and is aged for two years; there is also a rosé version.

The top wines are the Reserve and J Schram. The Reserve was first made in 1974 and is around 70–75 percent Pinot Noir, the rest Chardonnay. About 40 percent of the wine is barrel-fermented, and the wine spends six years on the yeasts. J Schram is a more recent product, first made in 1987. Like the Reserve, almost half the wine is barrel-fermented, but the fruit sources tend to be in Carneros. The 2001 J Schram was a blend of 78 percent Chardonnay and 22 percent Pinot Noir, aged for six years before disgorgement. There are also small quantities of J Schram Rosé, which thus far has been made only in 2000 and 2004.

These sparkling wines are well made in a fairly solid style, but there is a gap in quality between the regular cuvées and the prestige cuvées, the latter being highly impressive—and expensive.

It's hard to think of a more contrasting style from these sparkling wines than a complex Bordeaux red, but since the first vintage in 2001, the J Davies has been very impressive. The soils around the

winery are volcanic, and this keeps yields low, at around 2.5 tons per acre. Cabernet takes up about 80 percent of the blend, the rest being Malbec, Petit Verdot, and Merlot. The wine is aged for 22 months in 80 percent new oak, which is effortlessly absorbed by the density of the blend.

FINEST WINES

(Tasted 2009)

2006 Blanc de Noirs
Earthy, appley nose, with considerable weight of fruit. Rich, creamy, and full-bodied; weighty, with only modest acidity. Has typicity but lacks some zest and persistence.

2005 Blanc de Blancs
Rich, bready nose, a bit earthy. Hefty, full of fruit; broad, but lacks some precision.

2005 Brut Rosé
Pale peach-red. Delicate, strawberry nose. Full-bodied, quite broad; has weight, grip, and a light toastiness. Robust for rosé, but quite good length.

Above: Hugh Davies, Schramsberg's president and CEO, in charge of a broad range, topped by the Reserve and J Schram

2001 J Schram★
Rich, appley nose, broad and toasty. Precise attack, lean and concentrated, with fine acidity that gives some raciness. Long, with a sherbetty finish.

2001 Reserve
Nutty, yeasty nose, rich and quite powerful. Plump, but has backbone and concentration, grip and persistence. Quite long, with grilled nuts on the end.

2005 J Davies Cabernet Sauvignon★
Super-ripe black-currant-and-blackberry nose, oaky and dense, with licorice and nutmeg. Supple, rounded, very concentrated, with oaky bite and a lick of vanilla. Voluptuous but not heavy. Very long.

Schramsberg Vineyards
Area under vine: 42 acres (17ha)
Average production: 880,000 bottles
1400 Schramsberg Road, Calistoga, CA 94515
Tel: (707) 942-2434
www.schramsberg.com

Philip Togni Vineyard

Few California winemakers can match the depth of experience enjoyed by Philip Togni. Today an alert if somewhat grizzled figure, with a dry sense of humor and an absence of false modesty, Togni studied with Emile Peynaud at the University of Bordeaux and began his winemaking career at Château Lascombes in Margaux in 1956. Two years later, he was in California, making the wines at Mayacamas, Chalone, and Chappellet. At Mayacamas and Chalone, in particular, Togni grew used to making wine in highly adverse conditions, but his admiration for mountain vineyards was born there, so it was not surprising that when, in 1975, he decided to buy his own property, he opted for a site 2,000ft (600m) up on Spring Mountain.

He began planting vines in 1981 but chose the AxR-1 rootstock, with the consequence that most of the vines succumbed to phylloxera and had to be replanted. Togni was also unlucky in having Pierce's disease on the property, but he has managed to curb, though not eliminate it. About 80 percent of the surface is planted with Cabernet Sauvignon; the rest with Merlot, Cabernet Franc, and, since 1999, Petit Verdot. There is also a small parcel of Black Hamburgh of the Muscat family. Back in the 1980s, Togni grew and produced a few hundred cases of unoaked Sauvignon Blanc, mostly to provide himself with a wine with which to accompany oysters, since this style of wine was virtually unknown in California at the time. The last vintage was 1994, and red Bordeaux varieties have replaced the Sauvignon plants.

The soils here are clay over a volcanic base, and the result is a fiercely structured Bordeaux blend. With just a small vineyard at his disposal, Togni can consider with each harvest whether or not to co-ferment some of the varieties, and by the time he blends, he can have as many as 20 different lots to work with. The press wine is kept apart, and only at the final moment, after 20 months of barrel aging, does he decide how much to blend in. Togni favors two coopers, Nadalié and Taransaud, and the proportion of new wood is around 40 percent. He is not afraid of good natural acidity and works hard to keep the alcohol below 14%. The wines are bottled without fining or filtration. Any lots with which he is not satisfied are released under the Tanbark Hill label, but the aging of the two wines is identical, because he blends late.

Togni's first vintages were massively tannic, but by 1990 he had gotten to grips with the vineyard and the wines it was likely to produce. Although the wines remain very tannic, there is no lack of opulence or complexity in vintages from the 1990s and the present century. Togni recognizes that these are wines that demand cellaring, so he rereleases a ten-year-old wine to his mailing list each year.

The Black Hamburgh, released under the Ca' Togni label, is a real curiosity, and Togni believes it is the only example of the black-berried variety produced in Napa Valley. Only tiny quantities are produced, because the vines have proved particularly susceptible to Pierce's disease. The grapes are picked very late, at sugar levels of 32–35° Brix, but the high sugars derive from shriveling, not botrytis. By the time harvest takes place in November, wasps and birds have supped on some of the grapes, thus reducing an already small crop even further. The must is fermented in old barrels and aged for a year, and then a little brandy is added before bottling. Togni gives the wine about five years' aging before it is released at a high price. The 2003 had a fair amount of alcohol, at 14.5%, plus 230 grams of residual sugar per liter.

Philip Togni is still active, but he is increasingly aided by his Swedish wife Birgitta and their daughter Lisa, who has an MBA degree under her belt but has also worked harvests at properties such as Léoville Barton in St-Julien. So the succession is assured, and it is unlikely that Lisa Togni will make radical changes to the approach established decades ago by her father.

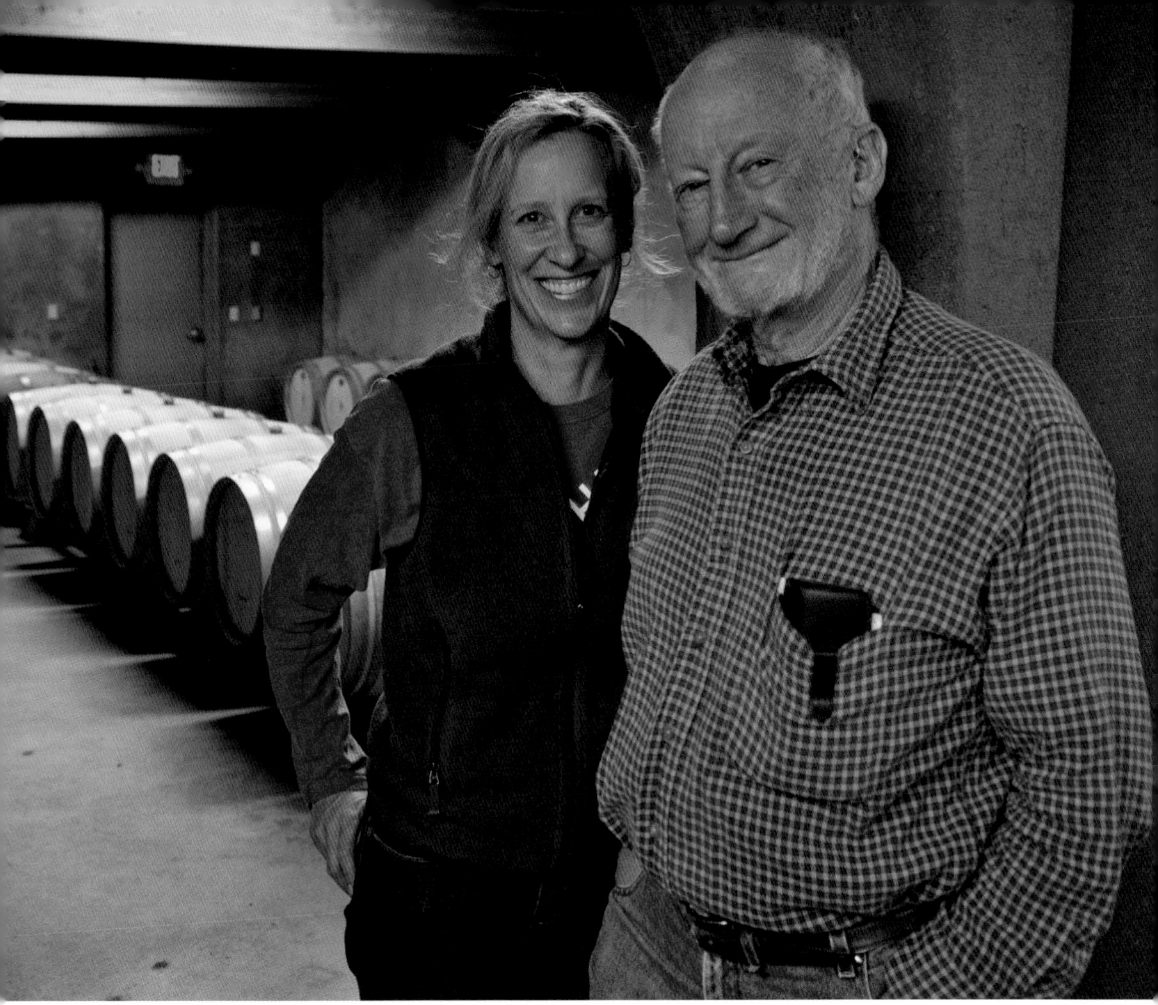

Above: Philip Togni with his daughter Lisa, whose experiences in Bordeaux have shaped their powerful Spring Mountain wines

FINEST WINES

(Tasted 2009–10)

Cabernet Sauvignon

2006 Deep in color, with a brooding blackberry-and-black-currant nose and a whiff of chocolate. A classic Togni wine, rich, full-bodied, and voluptuous, with admirable concentration and assertive but ripe tannins and a very long, chocolaty finish.

2005 Sweet, intense black-curranty nose, showing a good deal of oak. Rich and intense, spicy and peppery; vigorous, despite a slight raisiny tone. The finish is broad and supple, yet persistent.

2001 Stern black fruits and chocolate nose, still quite austere. Very concentrated, rich, and bold, with an earthy mineral tone, grainy tannins, and ample grip. This is still adolescent but shows spice and complexity and admirable length.

1991 Tasted in 1998, this was a terrific wine with damsony, minty aromas and great concentration and length. Retasted 11 years later, it hadn't changed that much, though the aromas were more delicate and herbaceous, and the palate, still packed with flavor, had developed a silkiness and refinement that were most appealing. This is in its prime.

Ca' Togni

2003 Rich, heady, floral nose, with unmistakable Muscat perfume. Very sweet, plump, and luxurious, with a velvety texture and enough acidity to give some freshness to the finish. Long and satisfying.

Philip Togni Vineyard
Area under vine: 11 acres (4.5ha)
Average production: 24,000 bottles
3780 Spring Mountain Road, St. Helena, CA 94574
Tel: (707) 963-3731
www.philiptognivineyard.com

Trefethen Family Vineyards

The Trefethen vineyard occupies a large tract of land just east of Highway 29 between Yountville and Napa. Its first incarnation was in the 1880s, when it was known as the Eshcol Ranch and was owned by bankers James and George Goodman, who only sold wines in bulk. This policy continued after a change in ownership in 1904, and after J. Clark Fawyer died in 1940, the vineyards were leased to Beringer. In 1968, the property was bought by rich industrialist Eugene Trefethen Jr., who turned over the running of the estate to his son John and daughter-in-law Janet. Janet Trefethen remains very much at the helm, though now assisted by her son Loren and daughter Hailey. The Trefethens replanted the vineyard in the late 1960s, and their first vintage was in 1973. Unfortunately, the vineyard succumbed to phylloxera in the late 1980s and had to be replanted again in 1990.

The Trefethen wines are restrained, relatively high in natural acidity, and far from super-concentrated. Those weary of blockbuster wines will find much to admire and enjoy

The main vineyard consists of a single 440-acre (180ha) block surrounding an impressive wooden structure that was the original Eshcol gravity-flow winery and has been restored by the Trefethens. Another block, known as Hillspring, is, at 35 acres (14ha), much smaller; it is located about 3 miles (5km) to the north in the foothills of the Mayacamas Mountains. Both parcels are in the Oak Knoll District AVA. Trefethen can supply all its needs from these two vineyards, and surplus grapes are sold off to other wineries. Hillspring was always part of the property, since it had natural springs that supplied the main ranch with water. Lying above the valley floor, Hillspring has very different soils of sandstone and shale on an alluvial fan, whereas the main ranch lies over loam, sand, and silt. Hillspring is planted with red Bordeaux varieties and gives wines with more heft than those from the valley floor. The farming here has always been "sustainable"—a term too broad to have much precise meaning, but the Trefethens were already recycling their water back in 1973 and have since installed solar power. They also reuse the pomace after vinification for compost.

Lying toward the southern end of the valley, Trefethen is cool enough to grow excellent Riesling, as well as the Cabernets and Merlot. The red wines from the main ranch are very distinctive: in the 1970s, many vintages were herbaceous, but today they are perfectly balanced, with a freshness, delicacy, and lift not often encountered in more highly regarded Cabernet zones such as Oakville and Rutherford. The delicate nature of the fruit encourages the Trefethens to avoid heavy use of new oak because they seek to retain varietal purity. Thus, only half the Chardonnay is aged in oak, and very few of the barrels are new.

It takes a large team to run a property of this size. David Whitehouse, now styled as winemaster, has been here since 1975, and another winemaker, Peter Luthi, arrived in 1985 and retired in 2009 to be replaced by Zeke Neeley. A more recent member is the highly qualified viticulturist Jon Ruel. The indefatigable Janet Trefethen oversees everything. A born communicator, she is the highly visible public face of the winery.

The range of wines is quite extensive. As well as the regular Chardonnay, there is a single-block reserve-style version called Harmony from Dijon clones. The Riesling is fresh and floral, and in certain years there is a fine late-harvest version, too. Viognier was added to the white-wine range in 2001. This being Napa, Cabernet Sauvignon takes precedence, and as well as the standard bottling, aged in French and American oak, there is a more powerful Reserve that receives much longer barrel aging of about 30 months. The top Cabernet, however, is called HaLo (a fusion of the younger Trefethens' names) and comes exclusively from the Hillspring vineyard, whereas the Reserve sources grapes from both sites.

There are small-volume bottlings of Cabernet Franc and Pinot Noir, and a light and unpretentious Bordeaux blend called Double T. A new addition to the red-wine range is called Dragon's Tooth. Also made from Hillspring grapes, this is dominated by Malbec, planted on a gravelly parcel in 2000, and topped off with Cabernet Sauvignon and Petit Verdot. The first vintage was 2007. It's a dramatic wine, quite different in character from the usual well-manicured Trefethen style. Indeed, because the Trefethen wines are restrained, relatively high in natural acidity, and far from super-concentrated, they are often underestimated. When very young, they can seem undemonstrative, and these are wines that do benefit from some bottle age. They don't match the stereotype of Napa Cabernet as exceedingly rich and oaky; the Oak Knoll microclimate just won't deliver that style of wine, though the Reserve often heads in that direction. This makes them admirable wines with food. They don't draw too much attention to themselves but sit back, as it were, and effortlessly blend into the background. Lunching at Trefethen on prosciutto and the family's own organic vegetables, it was tempting to keep reaching for another refreshing glass of Riesling, Chardonnay, or even Cabernet. Those weary of blockbuster wines will find much to admire and enjoy at Trefethen.

FINEST WINES

(Tasted 2009–10)

Cabernet Sauvignon

2006 Muted blackberry nose. Medium-bodied but sleek and refined on the palate. Quite tannic, but in balance, thanks to ample fruit concentration. Brooding and tight, with a welcome freshness and good length.

2005 A discreet nose: black cherries and chocolate, mildly herbaceous. Concentrated but graceful, with ample tannins but not too extracted. Balanced and long on the finish.

2005 Reserve★ Very rich, savory nose, leathery and smoky. Very concentrated, dense, and chewy, with fairly raw tannins and a muscular structure. But it's also vigorous and has a fresh finish. Long, but it needs a few years to harmonize.

2007 Dragon's Tooth

Dense, brooding black-fruit nose. Rich and concentrated, spicy and jazzy, with a Rhône-like *sauvage* character. Plenty of weight and grip, but also fresh and long.

2008 Riesling [V]

Assertive aromas of citrus and pears. Quite rich, but has clean, crisp acidity and tastes fully dry, despite a small quantity of residual sugar. Long.

2007 Chardonnay

Delicate, understated nose, showing lime and apricot fruit. A fairly lean style, with bright acidity. A silky texture, brisk rather than profound, but refreshing, zesty, and long.

2007 Late Harvest Riesling

Honey and lime on the nose. Medium-bodied but silky, with fine acidity to balance the sweetness; plump yet persistent. This should gain depth with more bottle age.

Trefethen Family Vineyards
Area under vine: 475 acres (190ha)
Average production: 700,000 bottles
1160 Oak Knoll Avenue, Napa, CA 94558
Tel: (866) 895-7696
www.trefethen.com

Turley Wine Cellars

Larry Turley was, for many years, John Williams's partner at Frog's Leap. But in 1993, the partnership was dissolved. Williams eventually moved to new premises in Rutherford, while Turley remained at the former frog farm north of St. Helena. He took his own winery in a very different direction from the fruit-forward but refined wines for which Frog's Leap was, and is, renowned. Turley clearly had a penchant for sturdy reds from old-vine Zinfandel and Petite Sirah. In the 1990s, it was not that difficult to find grapes from these old vineyards on which, by definition, the Cabernet spotlight did not shine. Turley's sister Helen, arguably America's most celebrated winemaker thanks to the adoring palates of Robert Parker and others, introduced her brother to a young winemaker, Ehren Jordan, who had worked with her, and he soon came on board at the new winery.

Turley began with a single acre of Sauvignon Blanc, which hardly fitted his new program, but as well as negotiating contracts with growers he esteemed, he gradually purchased sites that interested him, such as Rattlesnake Ridge on Howell Mountain and the 50-acre (20ha) Pesenti estate in Paso Robles. The Turley team sent in their own vineyard crew to manage some of the vineyards they bought from, to ensure they had maximum control over the quality of the fruit. They also favored organically farmed sites.

From the start, the wines were, to say the least, controversial. The style Turley and Jordan were aiming for was maximum ripeness, and if that meant the wines that emerged were very high in alcohol and, in some instances, carrying some residual sugar, that was a price they were willing to pay in order to achieve the highest conceivable ripeness levels. The critical acclaim for the wines was widespread but far from universal. When I first visited the winery in 1998 and tasted a fairly complete collection of the numerous single-vineyard wines that were being produced, I was dismayed. With few exceptions, the wines were raisiny and hot and sometimes quite sweet as well. Late-harvest Zinfandel is a perfectly legitimate California style—Ridge, Mayacamas, and others had been making it since the 1960s—but the wines needed to be in balance, and the Turley wines seemed indifferent to the very concept.

They were also impossible at the dinner table. While dining with journalists at the valley's top restaurant, The French Laundry, in 1998, our hosts generously ordered a bottle (the wines have never been cheap), but most of us took a single sip and thereafter left the glass alone. Ehren Jordan himself was aware that the wines were made in a strapping style that not everyone found irresistible, and he used to joke, "If you can't finish the bottle, you can always paint your house with it." There were also a few white wines, such as a Roussanne sourced from John Alban that was bottled unfiltered and as cloudy as a glass of milk but a good deal less appealing.

Ten years on, Jordan was still in charge, but the wines were far better, and the excesses of the 1990s were few and far between. The alcohol level can still be bewilderingly high, at around 16.5% in some wines, but is far less perceptible than it used to be. Ehren Jordan has his own vineyard, Fialla, high in the Sonoma Coast, where he has been producing delectable Pinot Noir and other wines, so he was clearly perfectly capable of making balanced and succulent wines if he chose to do so. By the late 2000s, the range had altered. Some of the Napa contracts were no longer in existence, but in their place Turley was producing excellent Zinfandels from other areas such as Paso Robles, where a second winery has been built on the old Pesenti property. There were also relatively inexpensive blends, such as the California Juvenile and the California Old Vines, that give less well-heeled enthusiasts a taste of the Turley style.

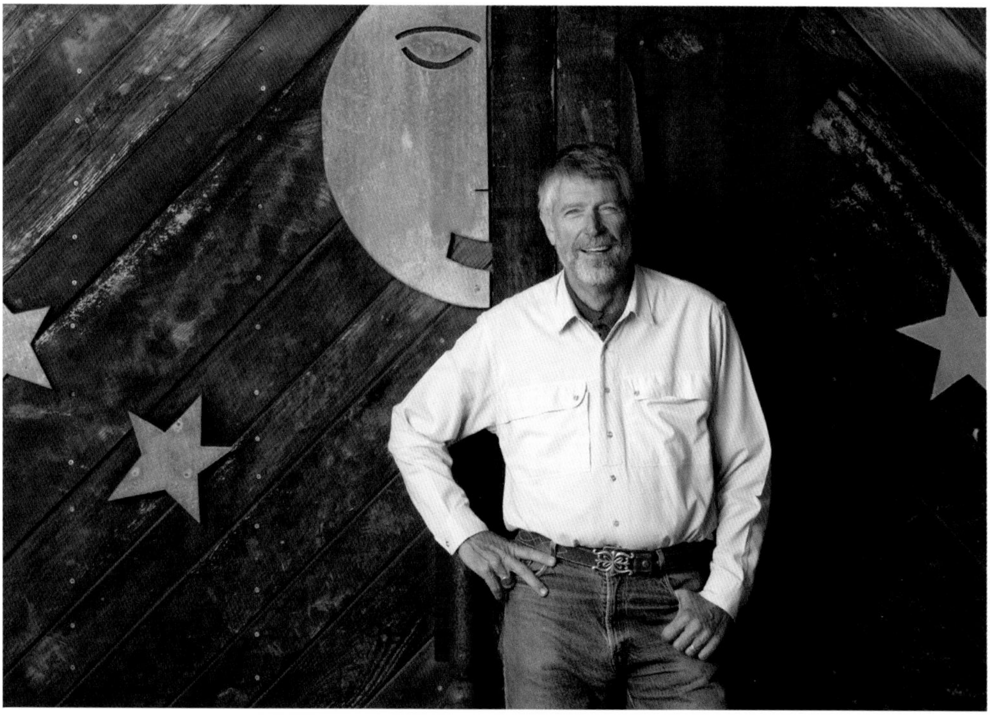

Above: Larry Turley, whose broad range of wines is rounded off with naturally made, potent, mainly single-vineyard Zinfandels

Today, the wines are made to a high standard, using uncrushed berries and native yeasts, and no acidity is added. There is a sparing use of new oak, and the wines are bottled without fining or filtration. Because one of the raisons d'être of Turley is to highlight vineyards of exceptional interest, bottlings are numerous, so the notes that follow represent only a small selection of the production.

FINEST WINES

(Tasted 2009)

2007 California Old Vines [V]
Not especially deep in color. There are rich, ripe, juicy cherry and blackberry aromas on the nose, with a touch of mint. On the palate, there are no raisiny or Porty tones, the tannins are discreet, and the fruit is bright and delicious.

2007 Duarte Vineyard Contra Costa County Zinfandel★
Slightly jammy nose but not overdone. Ripe, juicy, and concentrated, with upfront fruit and a good deal of spice. The lush palate is balanced by light tannins and an almost racy acidity that gives length and even some finesse.

2007 Mead Ranch Atlas Peak Zinfandel
Rich, succulent nose, with bright cherry fruit. Concentrated and lively, ripe and juicy; has vigor and weight balanced by light tannins. Quite long, with a peppery finish.

2006 Hayne Vineyard Napa Zinfandel
Rich and jammy nose, with red-fruit aromas. These vines, planted in 1903, yield a wine that's plump and concentrated but has no harsh tannins, showing a light touch and good length.

Turley Wine Cellars
Area under vine: 175 acres (70ha)
Average production: 180,000 bottles
3358 St. Helena Highway North, St. Helena, Napa, CA 94574
Tel: (707) 963-0940
Tasting room: 2900 Vineyard Drive, Templeton, CA 93465
Tel: (805) 434-1030
www.turleywinecellars.com

Barnett Vineyards

Estates are springing up, as it were, all along Spring Mountain Road, and indeed these slopes do produce some of the most beguiling wines of Napa Valley. Many of these are newcomers, but Hal and Fiona Barnett have been here for longer. In the early 1980s, Hal Barnett was a housing developer in San Francisco and his British-born wife Fiona an accountant, but they were increasingly drawn to Napa Valley. In 1983, they were shown this property, which consisted of 40 acres (16ha) of woodland. They cleared the land and planted grapes but only with the intention of selling their Cabernet Sauvignon, Cabernet Franc, and Merlot to wineries. Since their careers were still making great demands on their time, they had to flit between San Francisco and Spring Mountain for nine years. By 1989, the Barnetts were ready to switch course and produce their own wines, and local winemaker Kent Rasmussen came on board to produce their first vintage—a mere 300 cases.

The business slowly took off, and in 1991 the winery was built. At the same time, the Barnetts expanded production by interplanting between the rows. Wine caves were added in 2008, providing perfect conditions for barrel aging their wines.

The vineyard, at 1,700ft (520m), lies on volcanic soil, and like others on steep sites on Spring Mountain, it needs to be terraced to counter erosion. Yields, unsurprisingly, are low, rarely exceeding 2 tons per acre and giving fruit of great intensity. The finest sector lies on a rocky knoll, the source of Barnett's most celebrated wine, the Rattlesnake Hill Cabernet, though in good vintages the regular Spring Mountain Cabernet, which includes fruit from neighboring vineyards, seems almost or just as good. Another Cabernet, called Cyrus Ryan, is made from a nearby vineyard of which they are co-owners. What is remarkable about all these wines is that they show no excessive density, let alone rusticity. They are among the most polished of Napa's mountain wines yet have sufficient structure to absorb effortlessly the high proportion of new French oak in which they are aged.

Barnett winemaker David Tate, who worked for five years at Ridge as assistant winemaker, also has a fondness for Pinot Noir and is happy to continue producing a range of wines from other parts of California. These now account for almost half the production. They include Chardonnay and Pinot Noir from the Savoy Vineyard in Mendocino's Anderson Valley, as well as a Pinot Noir from Tina Marie Vineyard in Green Valley. Of these, the elegant Savoy Chardonnay and perfumed Savoy Pinot, with flavors of crystallized fruit, seem the most successful. But the reputation of Barnett will always rest on the quality of its superb Cabernets.

FINEST WINES

(Tasted 2009–10)

2006 Spring Mountain Cabernet Sauvignon
Fleshy black-fruit nose, quite tarry and savory, but with clear black-currant fruit. Suave, voluptuous, and creamy, yet there's ample grip and structure behind the fruit, which is spicy, lifted, and piquant. Stylish and persistent, with dark chocolate on the finish. The 2007 shows even greater potential.

2006 Cyrus Ryan Cabernet Sauvignon
Opulent and luxurious on the nose, with a complex bouquet of black fruits, chocolate, and black olives. Richly concentrated, tannic, and oaky, yet the texture is supple, and the fine acidity gives lift, freshness, and admirable length.

2006 Rattlesnake Hill Cabernet Sauvignon★
Toasty black-olive nose, with savory tones. Very concentrated, but the tannins are refined, and the texture is plump and suave; toasty and savory tones give spice and complexity, but the final impression is of an assertive fruitiness and remarkable length.

Barnett Vineyards
Area under vine: 15 acres (6ha)
Average production: 70,000 bottles
4070 Spring Mountain Road, St. Helena, CA 94574
Tel: (707) 963-7075
www.barnettvineyards.com

Hall

Craig and Kathryn Hall are a power couple who made their careers and their fortunes in Texas. Craig Hall, born in 1950, is a financier, property developer, art collector, and philanthropist. His wife Kathryn is a lawyer by training and an activist in social causes such as mental health; she served as ambassador to Austria from 1997 to 2001. Her family are grape farmers in Mendocino, so she is no newcomer to wine production. The Halls own substantial vineyards in Napa, built their winery in 2005, and have commissioned Frank Gehry to design a new one.

All this suggests the Halls are typical Napa Valley incomers, throwing money around and enjoying the status that comes from their new calling.

There is no doubt that the Hall wines are very good indeed. In large part, this must be due to the fact that they own some excellent vineyards

That they have named one of their wine ranges Exzellenz (with its ambassadorial resonances) is far from reassuring, as is the fact that they have seemed to go through winemakers with bewildering rapidity. The incumbent is Steve Leveque, who spent many years at Mondavi and at Chalk Hill Estate in Sonoma County. The consultant winemaker is David Ramey.

What counts, however, is the wine, and there is no doubt that the Hall wines are very good indeed. In large part, this must be due to the fact that they own some excellent vineyards: Sacrashe in the Rutherford Hills, Bergfeld on the valley floor in St. Helena, Napa River Ranch north of Napa itself, and the T Bar T Ranch in Alexander Valley. Most of these are now farmed organically, though the property is not certified, and most of the fruit is actually sold to other wineries. Moreover, despite this substantial portfolio, the Halls also still buy fruit from other growers.

Hall produces a number of varietal wines from Sauvignon Blanc (one, unoaked, from Napa; another from T Bar T Ranch), Merlot, Malbec, and Cabernet Franc, a Syrah/Cabernet blend called Darwin, and Bordeaux-style reds from a range of sources. The main range is the Napa Valley Collection, but of greater interest is the Artisan Collection, which consists of limited-production wines made to a very high standard. The winemaking is thoroughly up to date, with sorting tables, destemming, cold-soaking, a mixture of native and cultured yeasts, and the exclusive use of French oak, with quite a high proportion of new barrels.

FINEST WINES

(Cabernets tasted 2009–10)

The standard 2006 Napa bottling certainly has Napa typicity, with its sumptuous but piercing black-currant nose and a palate that has opulent, hedonistic fruit, fleshy and chocolaty, spicy and complex, and with good length. The 2005 Kathryn Hall Cabernet, which contains 18 percent Merlot and Malbec, is equally ripe and sumptuous on the nose but has floral tones and tremendous lift. As well as black-currant fruit on the palate, there are some red-fruit tones. It has power, opulence, and fine acidity, adding up to a very well-balanced wine. The 2005 Bergfeld Vineyard is super-ripe, so the texture is velvety, but there are lively and well-integrated tannins, too; this is suave and long. The 2007 Diamond Mountain, from purchased fruit, is pure Cabernet that shows its mountain origins; the nose is dense, brambly, and brooding, with black-currant fruit and more than a touch of mint. It's powerful and full-bodied, bold and intense, with hefty tannins and fine length.

Hall
Area under vine: 550 acres (220ha)
Average production: 480,000 bottles
401 St. Helena Highway South, St. Helena, CA 94574
Tel: (707) 967-2626
www.hallwines.com

Sonoma

In terms of its soils and microclimates, Sonoma County is as diverse as any of California's wine regions. To the east, it hugs the western slopes of the Mayacamas Mountains; to the south, it shares the cool Carneros district with Napa; to the north are valleys that tend to be dry and hot; and to the west are chillier regions mostly planted with Burgundian varieties. In recent years, vineyards have been planted just a few miles from the Pacific shore; prone to fog incursions and chilly temperatures, they can be marginal. About 65,000 acres (26,000ha) are under vine, some 1,300 growers farm the vineyards, and there are at least 250 wineries. This makes Sonoma a serious player in terms of volume, as well as quality.

The precise origins of viticulture in Sonoma are unclear. Some historians argue that grapes were first planted in 1855, after the Hungarian Agoston Haraszthy imported cuttings that were widely planted. Others believe that Russian settlers at Fort Ross, along the coast, had already planted vines in the 1820s. Certainly by the end of the 19th century, grape farming had become an important business, and by 1891 there were 4,000 acres (1,600ha) under vine. German immigrants had been a major force in the development of Napa Valley, but it was Italians who created Sonoma's vineyards. Moreover, many of the sites they planted at the end of the 19th century and the beginning of the 20th are still in existence, providing a fabulous resource of ancient Zinfandel and Petite Sirah that are among the many glories of Sonoma. To this day, some of the wineries founded generations ago—Pedroncelli and Foppiano being well-known examples—are still thriving.

By the late 2000s, Chardonnay had become the most prolific variety in the county, with Cabernet Sauvignon not far behind. Pinot Noir is almost as widely planted as Cabernet, with some 11,000 acres (4,500ha) under vine, while there are nearly 6,000 acres (2,400ha) of Zinfandel. There is sufficient diversity in the county to support a gamut of varieties. This may rob Sonoma as a whole of regional identity, but it also means that excellent examples of just about anything can be—and are being—produced in the region.

Above: In the west of Sonoma, some of the best Chardonnay and Pinot Noir is now planted within sight of the Pacific Ocean

Napa Valley is clear cut in its appellations, but Sonoma is annoyingly complicated, simply because so many AVAs overlap. Thus, Green Valley is an enclave within Russian River Valley, which itself forms just part of the vast Sonoma Coast appellation. It is not surprising that many people are quite confused about the distinctions between them, not to mention between Sonoma Valley, Sonoma Mountain, and the catch-all Sonoma County. The latter allows wineries to blend grapes from various AVAs, but other appellations—such as Sonoma Coast and Northern Sonoma—are so large as to be meaningless, even though excellent wines are made bearing those AVAs.

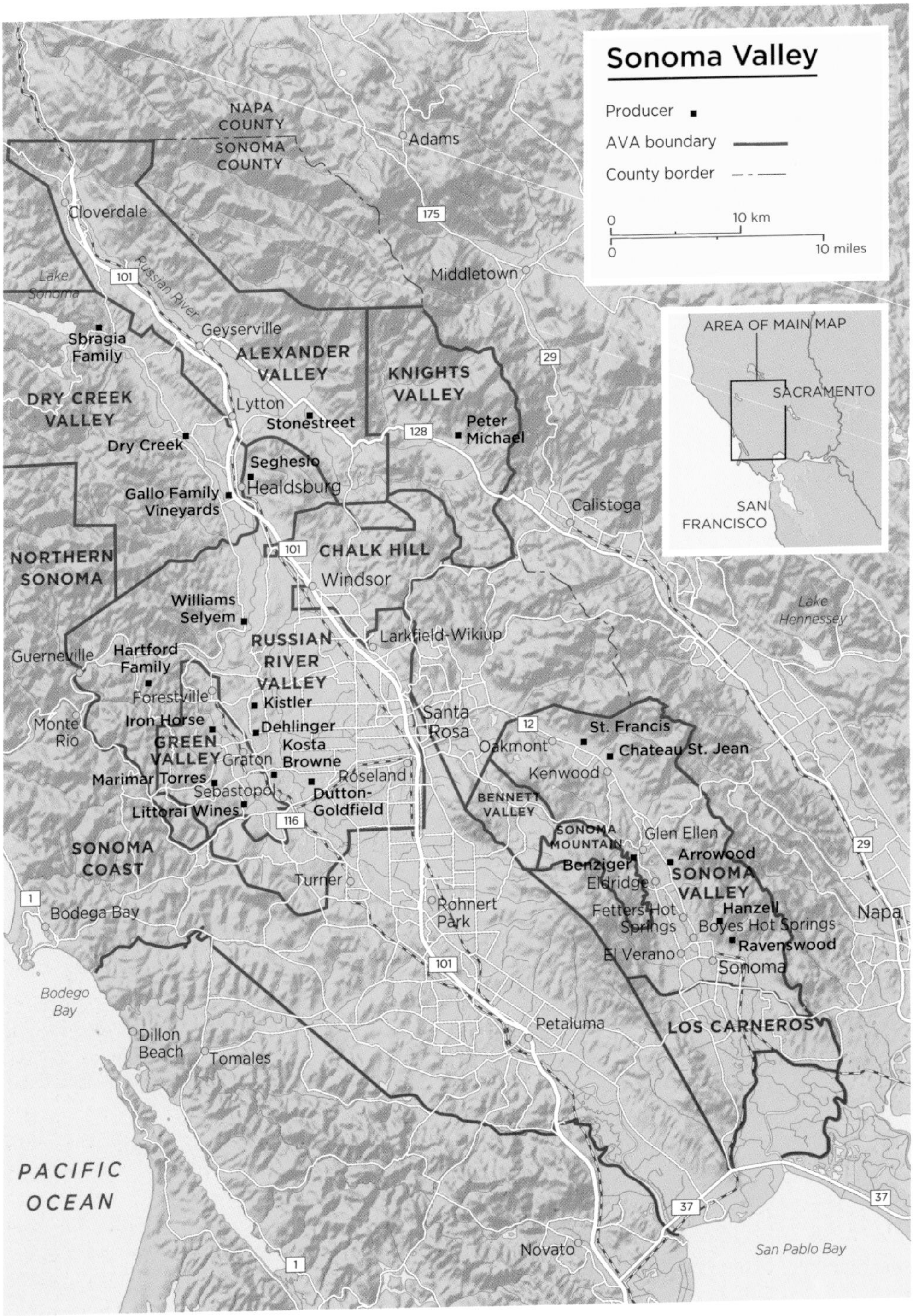
Sonoma Valley
Producer
AVA boundary
County border
0
10 km
0
10 miles
AREA OF MAIN MAP
SACRAMENTO
SAN FRANCISCO
NAPA COUNTY
SONOMA COUNTY
Adams
Cloverdale
175
Lake Sonoma
101
Russian River
Middletown
Geyserville
Sbragia Family
ALEXANDER VALLEY
KNIGHTS VALLEY
29
DRY CREEK VALLEY
Lytton
Stonestreet
128
Peter Michael
Dry Creek
Seghesio
Healdsburg
Gallo Family Vineyards
Calistoga
NORTHERN SONOMA
CHALK HILL
Windsor
Williams Selyem
Lake Hennessey
RUSSIAN RIVER VALLEY
Larkfield-Wikiup
Guerneville
Hartford Family
Forestville
Kistler
Monte Rio
Iron Horse
Dehlinger
Santa Rosa
12
St. Francis
GREEN VALLEY
Graton
Kosta Browne
Oakmont
Chateau St. Jean
Roseland
Kenwood
Marimar Torres
Sebastopol
Dutton-Goldfield
BENNETT VALLEY
Littorai Wines
116
SONOMA COAST
SONOMA MOUNTAIN
Glen Ellen
Arrowood
Benziger
Eldridge
SONOMA VALLEY
Turner
Rohnert Park
Fetters Hot Springs
Hanzell
Boyes Hot Springs
Napa
Bodega Bay
Ravenswood
El Verano
Sonoma
Bodego Bay
Dillon Beach
Tomales
Petaluma
LOS CARNEROS
PACIFIC OCEAN
37
Novato
San Pablo Bay
1

These are the current AVAs, in alphabetical order.

Alexander Valley (AVA from 1990) The valley, with about 15,000 acres (6,000ha) of vines, follows the Russian River from north of Cloverdale until Healdsburg. It varies in width from 2 to 7 miles (3 to 11km), and although most of the vineyards are planted on low-lying land, some on the eastern side of the region rise up to 2,400ft (730m).

Chardonnay and Cabernet Sauvignon are the most widely planted varieties. The Chardonnays can be big and lush, whereas the Cabernets vary greatly in quality and style. The soils on the valley floor are sandy loam with gravel in some sectors, and their vigor, which can give rise to excessive shading, used to result in rather weedy, herbaceous Cabernets. Raisining can also be a problem, encouraging growers to pick grapes before they are fully ripe. However, in recent years, canopy management and other techniques, especially yield reduction, have led to better-balanced vines and fairly soft, forward wines. Cabernet grown at higher elevations has a more rugged quality: Stonestreet and Ferrari-Carano are the main wineries with high-altitude Cabernet vineyards.

The northern part of the valley, around Cloverdale, can be very hot, and Zinfandel feels at home here. This area's best-known version is probably Ridge's Geyserville bottling.

Alexander Valley is home to many medium to large wineries such as Clos du Bois, Simi, Silver Oak, and Jordan. There are 42 wineries in all.

Bennett Valley (AVA from 2003) This is a small region in the northwestern part of the Sonoma Valley AVA. Bennett Valley begins just southeast of the city of Santa Rosa and runs for some 5 miles (8km) to the southeast. Some 650 acres (260ha) are planted, and the main winery is Matanzas Creek, which petitioned for the creation of the AVA. Merlot ripens more easily here than Cabernet Sauvignon.

Carneros (AVA from 1987) Some 7,500 acres (3,000ha) of this shared AVA fall within Sonoma County. Like the Napa sector, this part of Carneros enjoys strong maritime influence from San Pablo Bay, and strong winds can inhibit ripening. Overall, the Sonoma sector is slightly cooler, and Merlot and Syrah, which are planted on the Napa side, would struggle to ripen here. Burgundian varieties fare best, for both still and sparkling wines.

Chalk Hill (AVA from 1988) Chalk Hill actually forms part of the Russian River Valley and nestles into one of its corners, just east of the town of Windsor. The only important winery within its borders is, unsurprisingly, the Chalk Hill winery, though Rodney Strong has bought fruit from here for many years. Chardonnay and Merlot are the principal varieties. Despite its name, there is little chalk in the soil, and the misnomer derives from the substantial presence of volcanic ash in a soil otherwise based on sandy and silty loam.

Dry Creek Valley (AVA from 1983) The valley runs in a northwesterly direction from near Healdsburg up to Lake Sonoma and Geyserville. Vines were first planted here in 1870. It's a narrow valley, never more than 2 miles (3km) wide, and about 70 percent of all the plantings are on the valley floor, with the remainder mostly on benchlands on either side. Soils are varied, with alluvial deposits on the valley floor and rockier reddish soils on the benches. The subsoils retain water well, so dry-farming is possible.

The area under vine is 9,300 acres (3,760ha) and there are about 150 growers. As in Napa, the north of the valley is warmer than the south, mostly because of overnight fog, while the east is warmer than the west. Although many varieties are planted here, the star is undoubtedly Zinfandel, and many fanciers of the grape believe that Dry Creek Zinfandel is the finest in California. However, in terms of acreage, Cabernet Sauvignon is more important, and Rhône varieties can also give good results. Among the white varieties, Sauvignon Blanc is particularly successful.

Green Valley (AVA from 1983) This is a subregion within Russian River Valley, located at the cooler southwestern end of the zone some 10 miles (16km) from the ocean. The soil is primarily sandy loam. Plantings have now reached 3,600 acres (1,450ha), though not all producers use the Green Valley AVA on their labels. One well known winery here is Iron Horse, renowned for its sparkling wines. Marimar Torres, sister of Spanish wine grandee Miguel Torres, also chose Green Valley for her principal vineyard, planted with Chardonnay and Pinot Noir. Wineries such as Hartford and Dutton-Goldfield source some of their grapes from Green Valley vineyards. Cool, even cold, nights preserve the acidity so essential for sparkling wines, and even the still wines tend to have a bracing quality to them.

Knights Valley (AVA from 1983) Providing a connecting route between Alexander Valley and northern Napa, Knights Valley is profusely planted with 2,000 acres (800ha) of grapes, many of them owned by Beringer. Most of the vines are on the valley floor, which can be a very hot spot. One of the few wineries here, Peter Michael, has also planted on higher slopes, which can give Chardonnay and Cabernet Sauvignon of excellent quality. Beringer uses the AVA on some of its wines; otherwise, it languishes in obscurity.

Northern Sonoma (AVA from 1990) Since the Northern Sonoma encompasses Knights Valley, Alexander Valley, Dry Creek Valley, Russian River Valley, and much of the Sonoma Coast, it is, as an AVA, all but useless. But Gallo has found it handy, allowing the producer to blend wines from various regions under this umbrella of an AVA.

Rockpile (AVA from 2002) Rockpile lies just north of Dry Creek Valley. Fog incursions are minimal here, especially at elevations that range from 800 to 2,000ft (240–600m), and the fruit tends to ripen earlier than in Dry Creek. There are only 400 acres (160ha) of vineyards, and although the Bordeaux varieties and other grapes such as Tannat have been planted here, it has gained the best reputation for its vivid and structured Zinfandels. Mauritson and Seghesio are the best-known producers.

Russian River Valley (AVA from 1983) A large region, with 15,000 acres (6,000ha) under vine. To the eye, this is not really a valley at all, but a gently undulating flood plain that lies east of the Sonoma coastal range. It includes the western part of the Chalk Hill AVA and all of the Green Valley AVA. Soils are varied, with alluvial deposits, sand, gravel, degraded sandstone, and some clay. The most widely encountered soil type, however, is Goldridge sandy loam, which is quite powdery but drains well. There is maritime influence here, with fog entering the valley through the Petaluma Gap and moving northward into the main part of the flood plain.

More than 20 years ago, Russian River won its reputation for some of California's finest Pinot Noir, grown mostly on gravelly benchland quite close to the river in the northern part of the AVA. Rochioli was the name to conjure with but has now been joined by many others. Now, plantings have spread throughout the region, especially into cooler areas close to the coastal range around Sebastopol, Forestville, and Guerneville. But some more easterly areas are warm enough for Zinfandel, and some very old vineyards survive. Chardonnay and Sauvignon Blanc also flourish here. Pinot Noir is of course the main attraction, and both quality and style can vary considerably depending on elevation, exposure, clonal selection, and other factors. It would be hard to disagree with those who maintain that California's finest Pinots come from here.

Sonoma Coast (AVA from 1987) A meaningless appellation of 480,000 acres (190,000ha) that stretches from the border with Marin County in the south all the way up to Mendocino in the north. It was created after petitioning by Sonoma-Cutrer, which wished to include all its vineyards within the new appellation. What is especially confusing is that Sonoma Coast also refers to the coastal ranges that lie between the Russian River Valley and the Pacific shore. These elevated vineyards, generally well above the fog line, have been producing some of the state's most exquisite Chardonnay and Pinot Noir for a decade or more. There are moves to create a new AVA, possibly named Fort Ross, that would be restricted to these coastal vineyards, but this has not yet been approved.

These coastal vineyards lie at an elevation of over 1,000ft (300m) and have won an enormous reputation. Some of the best-known sites are Flowers' Camp Meeting Ridge, Martinelli's Charles Ranch, Marcassin, and Hirsch, as well as recent plantings by Pahlmeyer, Peter Michael, and other wineries based outside the region. Its very size, running from Annapolis in the north to Freestone in the south, makes it difficult to generalize about the vineyards, especially since the difficult mountainous terrain has inhibited extensive plantings. It is sometimes said that the coastal ridges are especially cool, but this is not necessarily so: elevation ensures direct sun exposure, and high alcoholic degrees are by no means unusual. Nonetheless, maritime influence does moderate the climate and explains why the Burgundian varieties deliver such good results. Impoverished soils and low yields usually result in fairly muscular wines with, in some vintages, high acidity.

Also within the appellation are the vineyards to the south around Petaluma, which are lower but very cool, though frost-free. Here the soils are sedimentary and have more clay. Vineyards such as Keller are based here.

Sonoma Mountain (AVA from 1985) This is a subregion of Sonoma Valley, just west of the village of Glen Ellen and abutting Bennett Valley to the north. Although the highest areas are at 1,600ft (500m), not all the vineyards are that high, and there are some east-facing sites as low as 400ft (120m). Nonetheless, most of the AVA is above the fog line and thus warmer than most of Sonoma Valley. The area under vine is 800 acres (320ha), much of it on volcanic soils, and the most widely planted varieties are Cabernet Sauvignon and Zinfandel. Very few wineries are based here, the best known being Benziger and Laurel Glen.

Sonoma Valley (AVA from 1982) The valley, well settled yet richly agricultural, begins in the southern suburbs of Santa Rosa and stretches in a southeasterly direction to the town of Sonoma, flanked on its eastern side by the Mayacamas Mountains. Vines were extensively planted here in the 19th century. Vines are planted both on the valley floor, which is quite narrow, and on the slopes on either side. One of the most important growers, Kunde, has vineyards at elevations that range from 200 to 1,400ft (60–430m), giving them immense flexibility. Some 200 growers cultivate 14,000 acres (5,700ha). The region is warm, with the coolest spots around Sonoma and the hottest near Glen Ellen, which is known as the "banana belt." There is some maritime influence, but fog entering the valley from both the north and south usually burns off by mid-morning, and afternoon temperatures can be high. Nonetheless, the region as a whole is less hot than the Dry Creek or Alexander valleys. A huge range of grape varieties are grown here, and Merlot, Cabernet Sauvignon, Cabernet Franc, and Zinfandel are widely planted reds (with Pinot Noir restricted to the southern end and to higher elevations). Chardonnay tends to be the best of the white varieties, though Viognier and Sauvignon Blanc can do well, too.

Benziger Family Winery

Many wineries start small and expand. Benziger followed that course but then, unusually, shrank itself down again. Once Prohibition was repealed, the Benziger family set up a liquor-importing business in suburban New York. Bruno Benziger's son Michael graduated from college in Boston in 1973 and, for want of anything better to do, drove across country with his girlfriend. The money ran out in San Francisco, so Mike found a job in a wine store. It was limited to shifting cartons around, because he was still only 20 years old. A few weeks later, he turned 21 and was legally allowed to sell wine. He grew more and more fascinated by wine and, by the late 1970s, was gaining experience as a cellar rat.

What makes Benziger of exceptional interest is not just the fact they are making biodynamically farmed wines of fine quality. They have transformed the property

Eager to acquire their own property, he and his wife Mary would spend weekends visiting potential sites and eventually heard about a place on Sonoma Mountain. They visited it and were entranced, even though there were only a few patches of vines and the whole place was run down. Bruno Benziger, skeptical despite Mike's enthusiasm, came to inspect the property and was equally fascinated. It lies in a kind of amphitheater, on rocky loam soils with some clay. In 1980, Bruno sold his share of the business and moved to Glen Ellen. By 1981, the whole Benziger clan had migrated west, including Mike's five siblings.

After cleaning up the place, the Benzigers bought some grapes and made some white wines in former milk trucks. Despite the amateurish start, friends suggested they enter the wines into the Sonoma Harvest Fair. To their amazement, the Sauvignon Blanc and the Chardonnay won the two top places. The newly hatched Benziger winery was on the map. In 1982, they bought more fruit and made wines rather grandly labeled Proprietor's Reserve. Bruno Benziger was a born salesman and soon sold the lot, so they started buying all the bulk wine they could get their hands on. By 1989, Benziger was selling a million cases. Four years later, sales had expanded to 4 million cases, and the company employed 650 people.

In 1994, the Benzigers sold the Glen Ellen brand to Heublein. They were left with 100 acres (40ha) of vineyards and a pile of cash. Bruno Benziger had died in 1989, and Mike had become increasingly frustrated with the direction the business was taking. Wine had become a mere commodity, and the family had become salesmen in an increasingly corporate environment. After the sale, Mike Benziger was free of these constraints but unsure what to do with the property. In 1995, he read about biodynamism and started talking to Mendocino grower Jim Fetzer, who was flirting with the methods of biodynamic theorist Rudolf Steiner. Mike was impressed by what he saw in Mendocino and launched a trial in his own vineyards, with advice from biodynamic consultant Alan York.

Mike liked the results and decided to convert the whole property to biodynamism. The rest of the family was uneasy about heading into uncharted waters, so Mike took them all to France to meet growers such as Anne-Claude Leflaive in Puligny-Montrachet and Michel Chapoutier in Tain-l'Hermitage, so they could all learn more about how the arcane system actually worked. Everyone became convinced and backed Mike's plans; by 2000, the property was certified, and the first biodynamic wine was made in 2001.

Alan York tells how they were on the point of tearing up their Sauvignon vines on Sonoma Mountain, because the barrique-aged wine was so miserable. After converting it to biodynamism,

Above: Mike Benziger, who was happy to sell the family's mass-market brand Glen Ellen and begin the conversion to biodynamism

the transformation was rapid. Not only was the viticulture different, but York and Benziger "went naked," as they put it, with the winemaking, reverting to natural yeasts and dispensing with enzyme additions, acid adjustments, and oak aging. By 2005, the result was arguably California's best Sauvignon Blanc. The estate red, a Bordeaux blend called Tribute, which is aged for 20 months in one-third new French oak, is also of exceptional quality. In the early 2000s, Benziger supplemented their biodynamic estate-grown range with a new line called Signaterra—a series of vineyard-designated wines either from their own grapes or from top organic sites.

The vineyards owned by the family today consist of the exceptionally beautiful 42-acre (17ha) Sonoma Mountain property, a Pinot Noir site called De Coelo in Freestone, and a property high up in Alexander Valley. Another vineyard, Bella Luna, is being developed near Occidental in Russian River Valley. But most of the wines produced by Benziger are made from grapes purchased from growers who between them have roughly 1,000 acres (400ha) under vine. These are released as Sonoma County wines and are, for the most part, of sound but not exceptional quality. With these wines, too, Mike Benziger wants to eliminate what he perceives to be bad farming practices, so he has encouraged many of his growers to switch to either organic or biodynamic farming. By 2007, this process was complete, and almost all the Benziger growers were certified as organic.

Mike Benziger himself acted as the estate's winemaker until 2005. As the property grew in complexity, a new winemaker was hired: Rodrigo Soto, who had made superb wines at Matetic, a biodynamic property in Chile. Alan York insists that at Benziger there is no real distinction between the roles of viticulturist and winemaker. In demand as a biodynamic consultant worldwide, York spends only about one week per month at Benziger, but it's clear that he, Mike Benziger (aging with distinction, with flowing gray locks and a small goatee), and Soto are an admirable and efficient team.

What makes Benziger of exceptional interest and importance is not just the fact they are making biodynamically farmed wines of fine quality. Benziger and York have transformed the undulating Sonoma Mountain property into a closed ecosystem. Their own cows and sheep provide the manure from which the compost is made and, when the time is right, supply the meat for winery dinners. All the plants required for biodynamic preparations are grown on the property. Water is recycled by being pumped into a pond and oxygenated, then undergoing a natural filtration through wetlands before arriving by gravity in a second pond, where it can be stored until reused.

When I first visited Benziger in 1995, before all these changes had taken place, the family was already keen on educating its visitors, and this aspect of the property has been developed brilliantly. Tram tours take visitors around the estate, so they can see biodynamism in practice and understand the complete ecosystem that has been created here. Visitors also have the option of renting an iPod and using it on a self-guided tour at their own pace.

"We have to explain how acting responsibly in terms of the environment is related to producing better wine," says Mike Benziger. "If you care for the land, it cares for you. The tours allow us to point to things, not just give a dumb-ass PowerPoint presentation. I believe natural beauty has an impact on us and on animals and plants, too.

"Biodynamism isn't just about burying horns," Benziger continues. "It means going beyond all that to issues of health and quality. Biodynamism is a dating service for all the components of nature. People can feel this intuitively, how it all comes together. It's not just an intellectual system. We want to connect thought with emotion."

FINEST WINES

(Tasted 2009)

White

2008 Signaterra Shone Farm Russian River Valley Sauvignon Blanc Vibrant and pungent grassy nose. Fine attack, followed by a creamy texture; concentrated, weighty, and intensely fruity, this exudes ripe citrus fruit and has exceptional length.

2006 Estate Sauvignon Blanc★ Ripe lime and pears on the nose. An explosion of flavor on the palate, lively and spicy, showing great concentration, impact, and vigor, and superb length.

Red

2006 De Coelo Terra Neuma Pinot Noir A lively, perfumed nose, with aromas of violets and raspberries. Sleek, stylish, and pure, with fine acidity on the palate; not super-concentrated, but lively and fresh, with good length.

2006 Tribute Estate Red★ (77% CS, plus CF, M, and PV) Opaque in color. Dense black fruits, menthol, and licorice on the nose. A good attack, tight and tannic, with remarkable lift and persistence; deep and complex and almost bitter in its youthful grip on the palate.

2007 Signaterra Bella Luna Russian River Valley Pinot Noir Rich and slightly tarry nose, with black-fruit aromas. Medium-bodied but creamy and concentrated, with formidable weight and excellent texture. Perhaps lacking some Pinot typicity, but spicy and long.

Benziger Family Winery
Area under vine: 165 acres (67ha)
Average production: 2 million bottles
1883 London Ranch Road, Glen Ellen, CA 95442
Tel: (707) 935-3000
www.benziger.com

Dry Creek Vineyard

Founded in 1972, this was the first winery to be established in Dry Creek Valley since Prohibition. David Stare, a graduate of MIT, had been a marketing man in Boston; he moved to California in the late 1960s, went to UC Davis, and, his studies completed, bought land in Dry Creek, because he was looking for a fairly cool area in which to grow Sauvignon Blanc and Chenin Blanc. He found that the valley was a more versatile growing region than he had supposed, so he added Chardonnay and the principal Bordeaux varieties to his vineyards. At one time, he also planted Petite Sirah, Gewurztraminer, and Riesling, but they were subsequently discontinued. Production is substantial, and the estate vineyards supply only about two-thirds of the winery's requirements.

Quality and style have remained remarkably consistent at Dry Creek Vineyard over the years. These have never been wines that strive to impress

For almost two decades, the winemaker was Larry Levin, and he was succeeded at the end of the 1990s by Jeff McBride, who in 2002 handed over his role to Bill Knuttel, who had been the winemaker at Chalk Hill. In 2006, David Stare retired and handed the business to his daughter Kim and her husband Don Wallace.

Quality and style have remained remarkably consistent at Dry Creek Vineyard over the years. These have never been wines that strive to impress. Made in quite large quantities, they offer immense drinkability, and prices have always been modest. David Stare was never a fan of heavy oaking and used a fair amount of American oak for some of his wines, though in recent years the winery has used more French oak and left some of the red wines in barrels for a longer period than in the past.

Stare was always keen on Sauvignon Blanc, which he preferred to label as Fumé Blanc. It was modeled on Sancerre and made in a dry, crisp style that could be slightly grassy (in an attractive way) and bracing. There is also an estate-grown version, entirely unoaked, called DCV3, and sometimes a wine from the Sauvignon Musqué clone, also unoaked, from Taylor's Vineyard. Chardonnay used to be a blend from various Sonoma regions, but today the only version is a barrel-fermented wine from Russian River Valley fruit..

Chenin Blanc has for many years been sourced from Clarksburg near Sacramento. Chenin has lost ground in the United States, because many versions had been made in a rather sickly, off-dry or blatantly sweet style. Dry Creek's version has always been dry, at least in flavor. With its freshness and acidity, it remains a bargain—inexpensive but refreshing and balanced.

Dry Creek Valley is known for its Zinfandels, and this is a variety that the winery has never ignored. The two most consistent bottlings are the Old Vines (a term, incidentally, that the winery claims to have been the first to use on a label) and the Heritage. The oldest plants in the former date from 1892, and the wine is blended with about 20 percent Petite Sirah. The Heritage vineyard was developed from 1982 onward, when cuttings from some of the county's most impressive pre-phylloxera vines were brought here and propagated. It was only in 1997 that the vines had developed enough character to permit a special cuvée to be inaugurated, allying the vigor of fairly young vines to the DNA, as it were, of old vines. There are also two single-vineyard Zinfandels and an occasional late-harvest bottling.

The Cabernet Sauvignon has improved greatly over the decades; once-ungainly tannins have been polished up to give a more fleshy and appealing wine. There used to be a Reserve bottling, but this has been discontinued in favor of three other

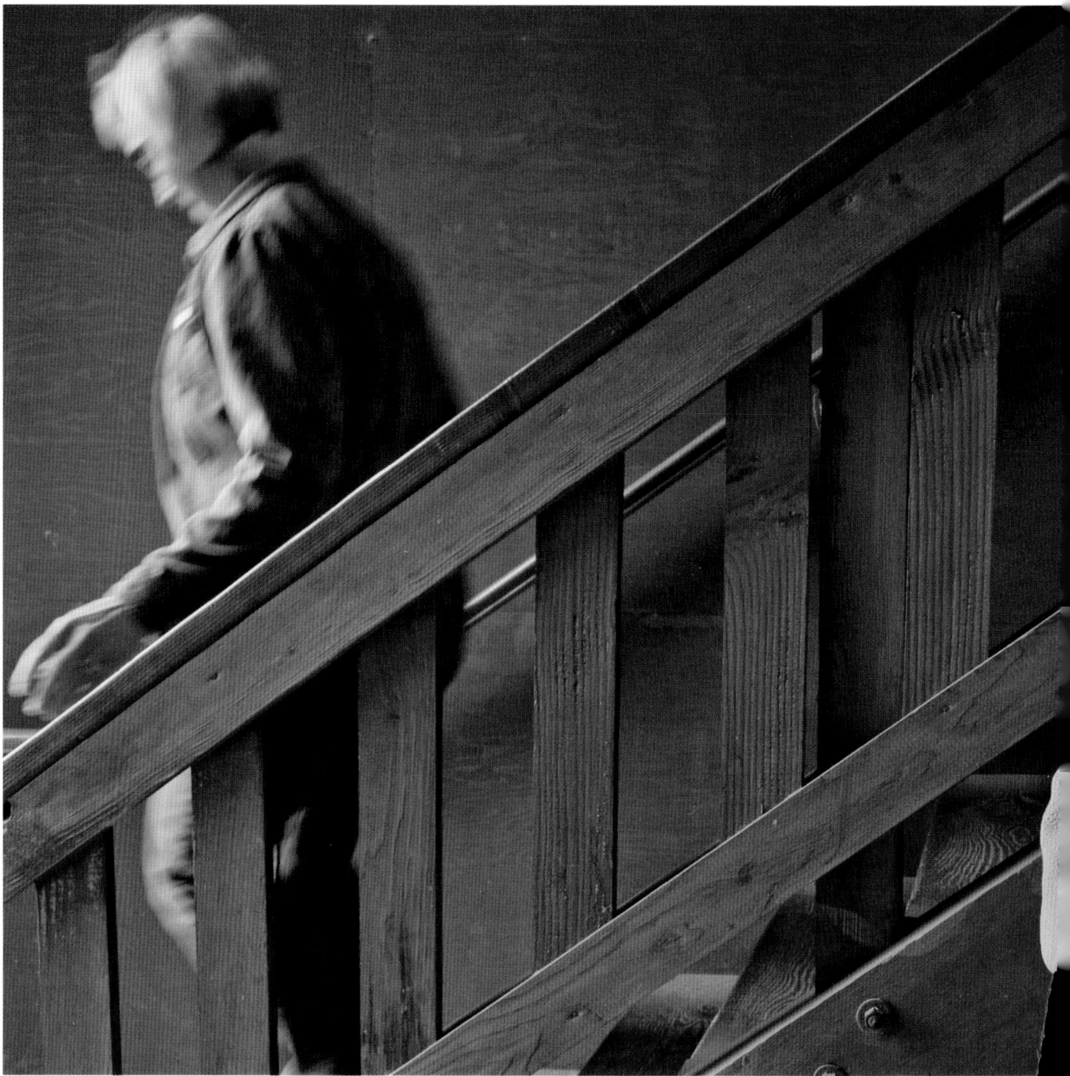

wines. The Meritage is aged mostly in American oak. A second, and more complex, Bordeaux blend, Mariner, first made in 2004 and employing all five varieties, is aged in 50 percent new barriques. At the top of the line is a Cabernet, first made in 1997 and called Endeavour, which comes from a vineyard that the winery has planted in the southeast sector of the valley. It is aged for 30 months in new French oak. This is the winery's most expensive release—and the fact that it costs

Above: David Stare, who founded the first winery in Dry Creek Valley since Prohibition, now run by his daughter and son-in-law

about the same as some entry-level Napa Cabernets confirms the excellent value that Dry Creek Vineyard has always offered.

FINEST WINES

(Tasted 2008–10)

White wines

2007 Chenin Blanc [V] Muted, appley nose. Medium-bodied, fresh, and lively, not complex but dry, vibrant, and balanced.

2009 Fumé Blanc [V] Fresh, grapefruity nose. Lean, citric, with fine attack and concentration, clean and brisk, with moderate length.

2008 Taylor's Vineyard Sauvignon Musqué Floral nose: honeysuckle. Opulent, supple, and creamy, with surprising verve as well as weight.

Bordeaux-style reds

2006 Cabernet Sauvignon Dense, chocolaty, black-cherry nose. Firm, chunky, and concentrated, with earthy black-fruit flavors and a long finish.

2006 Mariner★ Powerful, oaky nose, with ripe black-currant and blackberry aromas. Bold and fleshy, with tannic power as well as imposing fruit. Spicy, minty, savory, complex, and long.

2005 Mariner Lush, spicy nose, with intense blackberry fruit and some smoky oak. Rich, broad, and rounded on the palate, with weight and concentration and sufficient vigor to give considerable persistence.

2005 Endeavour Toasty, smoky, black-fruit nose, with power and spice. Full-bodied and sleek, with well-integrated tannins and no excessive extraction. Has an appealing and fairly long chocolaty finish.

Zinfandel

2007 Heritage Ripe, lush, blackberry nose. Rich and broad, with palate weight yet little tannins and fresh acidity. Delicious, balanced, and long.

2006 Old Vine Dense, chunky, strawberry fruit—quite different from the Heritage Zin. Dense, burly, and spicy, but with a long, sweet finish.

2007 Somers Ranch Dense, black-fruit and vanilla nose. Rounded and juicy, with moderate structure and less flair than the Heritage. Less impressive than the 2004 Somers Ranch, which had both opulence and vibrancy.

Dry Creek Vineyard
Area under vine: 200 acres (80ha)
Average production: 1.5 million bottles
3770 Lambert Bridge Road, Healdsburg, CA 95448
Tel: (707) 433-1000
www.drycreekvineyard.com

Dutton-Goldfield

Dutton Ranch is one of Sonoma's largest commercial vineyards. It was founded in 1967 by Warren Dutton, who planted Colombard and some of Russian River's first Chardonnay. The Ranch's 1,000 acres (400ha), of which half are planted with Chardonnay, are dispersed into almost 50 blocks in various parts of Russian River, including Green Valley. For decades, Dutton has supplied many top wineries such as Kistler with excellent fruit. Today, the property is run by two brothers, Joe and Steve Dutton, and in the 1990s each brother developed his own winery.

Joe Dutton established Sebastopol Vineyards, renamed Dutton Estate in 2005, using fruit solely from the ranch. Steve formed a joint venture with winemaker Dan Goldfield. Their backgrounds are very different. Steve Dutton is a fifth-generation Sonoma farmer, while Goldfield began his professional life as a research chemist at Berkeley. Fascinated by great Burgundies, he enrolled at UC Davis, graduating in 1986. Thereafter, he worked at various wineries, including Mondavi, Schramsberg, La Crema, and Hartford, where he sourced grapes, as well as making wines. Dan is lean and wiry, no doubt the consequence of spending a great deal of time riding a bicycle at high speed.

The first vintage at Dutton-Goldfield was 1998, and the winery operates on a different principle from Dutton Estate. Although much of the fruit does come from the Dutton Ranch, Goldfield buys it on the same commercial terms as any other client winery. He admits that he has an inside track: should a particular block show great promise, his partner Steve may well tip him off. Dan also buys fruit from outside sources. About 80 percent of production consists of two blended wines—a Chardonnay and a Pinot Noir—and the remainder consists of vineyard-designated wines made in quantities that range from 200 to 500 cases.

Right: Dan Goldfield, whose intelligent grape sourcing and winemaking have helped to take his wines into the top flight

The winemaking style has not altered much, so Dutton-Goldfield has a very consistent hallmark. The wines are certainly at the leaner, more elegant end of the spectrum. Good acidity gives the wines their cut and edge

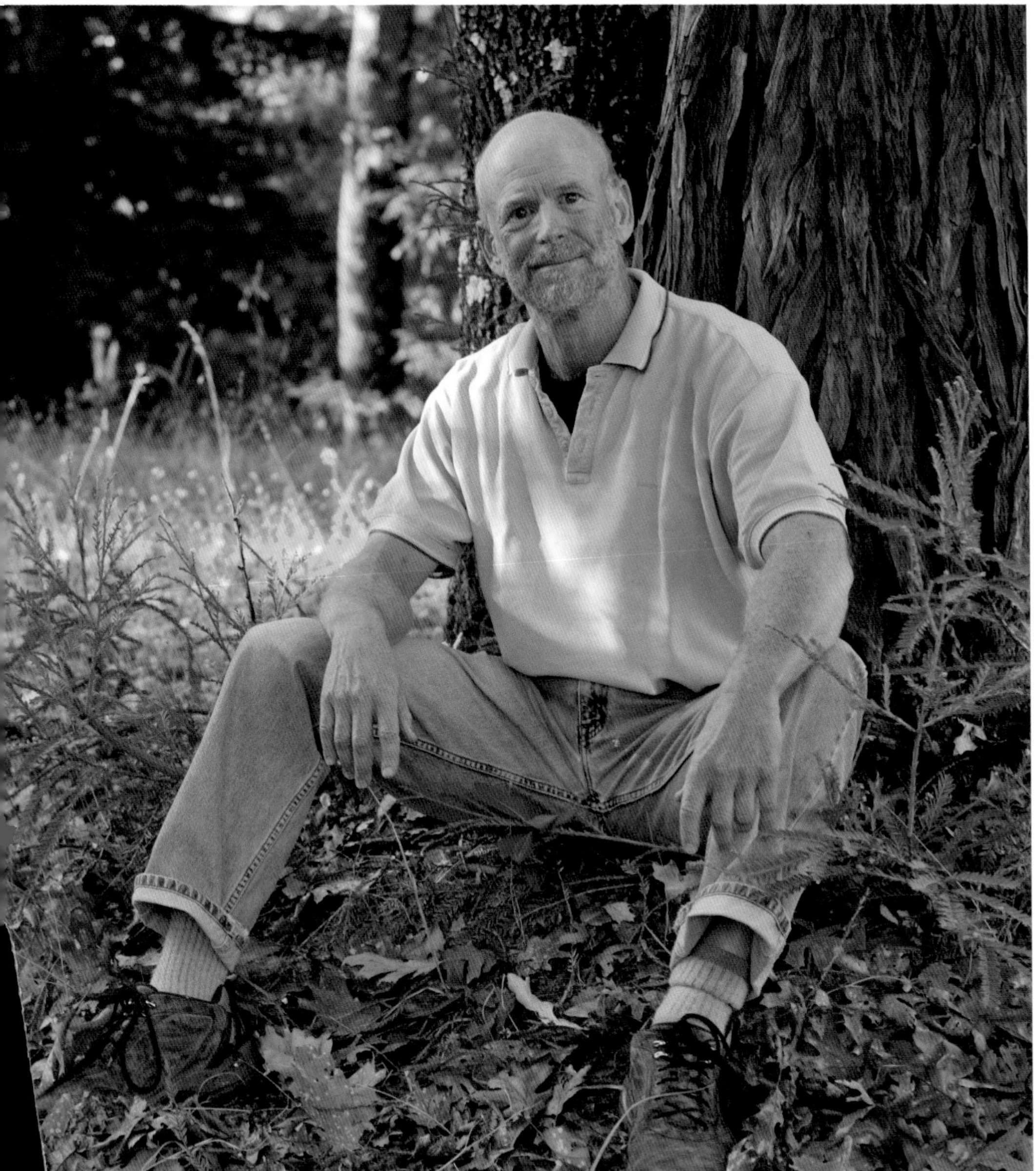

Although Russian River is a cool area, it can easily deliver, in the hands of certain winemakers, big, voluptuous Chardonnays. Goldfield aims for a very different, steelier style. To achieve this, he has specific criteria for the fruit he buys. He likes old vines because they give naturally lower yields without draconian interventions in the vineyard. He favors five specific blocks on the Dutton Ranch because the fruit routinely has high acidity, which gives backbone to the wines. He also favors east-facing sites that receive more morning than afternoon sun, thus avoiding rapid sugar accumulation. All the Chardonnays are barrel-fermented, with the proportion of new oak ranging from 30 to 50 percent, and because of the high acidity, full malolactic fermentation is de rigueur here. His only rule when deciding the proportion of new wood is, "When in doubt, use less."

Pinot Noir comes from around seven sites, chosen for their ability to ripen fruit at lowish Brix levels. The grapes are destemmed but not always crushed. After a six-day cold soak under dry ice, the must is inoculated with yeast; during fermentation, the cap is punched down, and there is usually a post-fermentation maceration of up to seven days. The proportion of new oak is slightly higher than for Chardonnay, and the wines are generally aged up to 16 months in barrel. Goldfield aims to keep alcohol levels below 14%, because he wants the varietal character to shine through. "If Pinot Noir isn't beautiful, it isn't Pinot Noir," he says.

The winemaking style has not altered much, so Dutton-Goldfield has a very consistent hallmark. The wines are certainly at the leaner, more elegant end of the spectrum. Good acidity gives them their cut and edge. The most extreme wine, in this regard, is the Pinot Noir from Devil's Gulch Vineyard in Marin County. This county, just north of San Francisco, is better known for its population of hot-tub-loving, New Age–infused suburbanites than for vineyards, but its proximity to the ocean means that even when grapes ripen, they are high in acidity. That is certainly true of this property, which sells grapes only to Dan Goldfield and to Sean Thackrey.

Careful and intelligent vineyard sourcing and meticulous winemaking have pushed Dutton-Goldfield, in just a few years, into the top ranks of Burgundian-style producers in Sonoma.

FINEST WINES

(Tasted 2008–10)

Chardonnay

2007 Dutton Ranch Rued Vineyard★ Vibrant and complex pear nose, oaky and with a salty minerality. Very rich and concentrated stone-fruit flavors, and weighty without being heavy, the oak giving grip rather than overt oakiness. Long.

Pinot Noir

2007 Devil's Gulch Marin County Rich raspberry nose. Lean and medium-bodied, with red-curranty fruit, high acidity, grip, and elegance.

2007 Dutton Ranch Freestone Hill Vineyard★ Intense, smoky nose, with spearmint, thyme, and red fruits. Lean, sleek, and concentrated, with fairly lush cherry fruit, integrated tannins, and ample spice and acidity on the finish. Still youthful. Long.

2007 McDougall Vineyard Stern nose, fairly closed, with hints of dried fruit. Dense, full-bodied, weighty, and brooding; a tannic style, but complex, vigorous, and long. Clearly needs time.

2006 Dutton Ranch Sanchietti Vineyard Delicate nose: red fruits and tomato. Concentrated, with marked tannins and plenty of spice; not the most elegant Pinot, but it has vigor and abundant fruit.

Syrah

2007 Dutton Ranch Cherry Ridge Muted, blueberry nose. Fairly rich but also limpid and intense, a cool-climate style with tangy red-fruit flavors and a long, sweet, peppery finish. The 2006 is equally fine, but richer and plumper.

Dutton-Goldfield
No vineyards
Average production: 60,000 bottles
3100 Gravenstein Highway N, Sebastopol, CA 95472
Tel: (707) 823-3887
www.duttongoldfield.com

Ferrari-Carano

If a Las Vegas casino operator were to come to California and create a winery in the image of his hometown, it would probably look like Ferrari-Carano. In reality, proprietor Don Carano comes from Reno, Nevada, where he is a lawyer, hotelier, and casino owner. He visited Sonoma in 1978 with a view to purchasing a supply of wines for his hotels and restaurants. He liked the area so much that he and his wife Rhonda bought a house here in Dry Creek Valley. There were 30 acres (12ha) of vineyards attached to the property, so he made some wine, soon realized the area's potential, and bought more vineyards. In 1981, the first vintage of Ferrari-Carano was produced.

The winery was built with practical advice from George Bursick, who was the winemaker here from 1985 to 2004. From the beginning it was equipped with some of the latest technology, such as Italian rotary fermenters.

It is misleading to think of Ferrari-Carano as a Dry Creek property, since its immense vineyard holdings are spread across 19 sites—from Alexander Valley to Carneros

In 1992, the Caranos began to construct the immense Villa Fiore, a Tuscan-style villa that functions as a tasting room and hospitality center. It was completed only in 1997. The structure is too grandiose to appeal to fastidious tastes, with its profusion of faux-marble columns, pastel cherubs flittering around a dome, and an excess of paintings and tapestries. But no one would dispute that the gardens, designed by Rhonda Carano, are beautiful indeed. It is no wonder that throngs of visitors regularly make their way up to these northern stretches of the Dry Creek Valley.

In the early days—the first Chardonnay was made in 1985—Ferrari-Carano was best known for its white wines. The Fumé Blanc was a pure Sauvignon drawn from various Sonoma regions and aged six months in French oak. The Reserve was given the full new-oak treatment and was sumptuous indeed. The Chardonnays, based on Alexander Valley fruit, were equally opulent; and a Reserve, using mostly Carneros fruit, was later added. Capitalizing on their reputation for fine white wines, the Caranos have added five single-vineyard wines from Russian River Valley. The reds faltered for a while. There were serviceable bottlings of Merlot and Cabernet, but phylloxera put a temporary halt to Cabernet production in the mid-1990s. Vineyards were replanted in Alexander Valley, and the first vintage of the reborn Cabernet was in 2001.

It is misleading to think of the current Ferrari-Carano as a Dry Creek property, since its immense vineyard holdings are spread across 19 sites—from Alexander Valley in the north, to Carneros in the south, as well as a ranch in Mendocino's Anderson Valley, which is the source of the single-vineyard Sky High Ranch Pinot Noir. The main focus these days seems to be on Alexander Valley, where the Caranos have planted vineyards at a fairly high elevation, allowing them to launch a new range of wines called PreVail.

Indeed, by 2009 the range had become quite complicated. Bursick had retired, and a new team of winemakers was in place, with Aaron Piotter responsible for red-wine production. Moreover, in 2003, consultant winemaker Philippe Melka, more prominent in Napa than in Sonoma, came on board. The classic varietal range was still being produced, but in addition there were several limited-release wines. Siena was initially a blend of Cabernet Sauvignon and Sangiovese, but the formula has been modified over the years. The 2007 Siena married 78 percent Sangiovese with 22 percent Malbec, and the wine was aged in Hungarian as well as French oak; it is made in

an easy-drinking style. Trésor was a proprietary Bordeaux-style blend from Alexander Valley and Dry Creek fruit. There are also two late-harvest wines: Eldorado Gold from Sauvignon Blanc and Semillon; and Eldorado Noir from Black Muscat.

But it is the PreVail range, created by Piotter and Melka with its first vintage in 2003, that has rightly attracted a fresh wave of attention. It consists of just two wines, West Face and Back Forty, both made from estate vineyards planted to a high density on the slopes above Alexander Valley at an elevation ranging from 700 to 1,200ft (210–370m). A new gravity-flow winery, complete with wine caves, has been constructed in the valley to process the fruit and age the wines. Back Forty began as a blend of Cabernet and Syrah but, from 2004, became a pure Cabernet, aged predominantly in new oak. West Face is Cabernet Sauvignon with 30 percent Syrah, aged in about 60 percent new oak. For both wines, yields are very low, at around 2 tons per acre; the fruit is picked at night, sorted, fermented without crushing, and given extended maceration.

The Ferrari-Carano wines are serious and always have been. Moreover, the Caranos clearly have no intention of resting on their laurels

The garishness of the winery and villa would lead one to suppose that Ferrari-Carano is essentially an excuse for a country jaunt, but the wines are serious and always have been. Moreover, the Caranos clearly have no intention of resting on their laurels, and the winery has always been developing and evolving in new directions, as the PreVail project confirms.

Left: Don and Rhonda Carano at Villa Fiore, their Dry Creek showcase, though they also own many vineyards elsewhere

FINEST WINES

(Tasted 2008–10)

2007 Carneros Chardonnay Reserve
Sweet, oaky nose, exotic and buttery. Full-bodied, oaky, and peachy on the palate; a bit heavy-handed though not at all blowsy, thanks to a lively and persistent finish.

2005 PreVail Back Forty
Dense, sumptuous, and brooding on the nose, with dense black fruit and coffee aromas as well as evident new oak. Voluptuous, full-bodied, and concentrated on the palate, with big, ripe tannins, much spicy oak, and torrefied flavors balanced by fair acidity. The 2004 has the same combination of power and vigor, but with more chocolaty richness and less Cabernet typicity.

2005 PreVail West Face★
Sweet, smoky, toasty nose, very intense and refined. Very rich and dense, spicy and tight, on the palate, with a vibrancy derived from the good acidity. This manages to have structure and finesse and very good length.

2006 Russian River Pinot Noir
Dumb nose, but a touch overripe on the palate, though balanced by some acidity; intense rather than complex.

2006 Cabernet Sauvignon
Smoky black-currant nose, with attractive herbal and tobacco tones. Medium-bodied, fresh, and limpid, ripe but with ample lift and spice; not a big wine, but balanced and refined.

2006 Trésor
Flamboyant black-currant nose, with some toasty oak. Suave and concentrated black fruits on the palate, which shows density and grip. This has flair, vigor, character, and persistence. Impeccably balanced and very long.

Ferrari-Carano
Area under vine: 1,400 acres (570ha)
Average production: 2.4 million bottles
8761 Dry Creek Road, Healdsburg, CA 95448
Tel: (707) 433-6700
www.ferrari-carano.com
www.prevailwines.com

Gallo Family Vineyards

The Gallo wine operation is a beast with two heads. The first is the vast Central Valley processing center in Modesto, with a winery the size of a small town, a bottle-manufacturing plant that never ceases production, and an output roughly equivalent to the whole of Australia. The second is what used to be called Gallo of Sonoma, based on vineyards established in prime areas of the county, resulting in attractively priced single-vineyard wines (even if some of the vineyards are very large) and with approachable family members such as Gina and Matt Gallo running the show—in stark contrast to the once highly secretive Gallo elders who hunkered down in Modesto.

The Modesto plant roars on, epitomizing industrial winemaking rather than fine-wine making, and does not pretend otherwise. In Sonoma, however, the family has confounded its critics by turning out wines of a very high standard. In the 1970s, the Gallos were still buying vast quantities of fruit from Napa; the high-priced juice that today is turned into $100 wines was once sold in bulk to the family. There was room for further expansion in Sonoma, so in 1977 Gallo bought the Frei and Laguna ranches. Frei already contained a large winery, but Laguna was an apple ranch. The driving force behind the move into Sonoma, which alarmed many old-time growers, was Julio Gallo, who knew some of the other growers of Italian ancestry in the county and understood its potential. Once he persuaded his brother Ernest, Gallo of Sonoma was born in 1984. Over the next ten years, they snapped up old ranches from which they had been buying fruit since the 1940s. These were known quantities, and the family was sure of their potential.

In came the bulldozers, and large tracts of land were transformed into vineyards. Ridge tops were flattened, earth was shifted and replaced, gullies and valleys carved out. Yet the worst fears of the critics were not realized, and the Gallos were careful to respect biodiversity. Their Sonoma vineyards do not resemble the vast grape farms of Monterey or Santa Barbara, which are essentially monuments to monoculture. The ranches are studded with woodlands, which attract wildlife. Indeed, most of these vineyards were also managed sustainably, and others were farmed organically. The first vintage to come on to the market was 1991.

The vineyard structure is complex, not least because there has been much replanting and reorganization. The Frei vineyard (Dry Creek) has been in existence since 1885 and is now planted mostly with red varieties; originally 200 acres (80ha), it has been expanded to over 600 (240ha). The 318-acre (128ha) Laguna Ranch (Russian River) was planted in 1980 and is a source of Chardonnay, Sauvignon Blanc, and Pinot Noir. Barrelli Creek (Alexander Valley) was bought in 1989 and planted from 1991 with a wide range of red varieties. Chiotti Vineyard (Dry Creek) consists of 54 acres (22ha) of Zinfandel and Merlot, planted from 1992. Stefani Vineyard (Dry Creek), replanted in 1989, is made up of 195 acres (79ha) of Zinfandel, Cabernet, and Chardonnay. In 2001, the 391-acre (158ha) Two Rock Ranch, a very cool site near Cotati, was planted with Pinot Noir, Chardonnay, and Pinot Gris.

Other properties formed the base for other brands in the Sonoma portfolio. MacMurray Ranch in Russian River, bought in 1996, consists of 427 acres (173ha) planted mostly with Pinot Noir and lends its name to a label devoted to Pinot Noir and Pinot Gris. Rancho Zabaco is a Zinfandel brand, and since the Gallos acquired Louis Martini in Napa Valley and its vineyards, it has been able to draw on the magnificent Monte Rosso vineyard in the Mayacamas Mountains. Of less commercial significance is the Winemaker's Signature Sonoma County range, which lets the company's individual winemakers amuse themselves with small-volume wines from a range of varieties and sources.

Right: MacMurray Ranch in Russian River, bought by the Gallo family in 1996 and planted with Pinot Noir and Pinot Gris

At the top of the pyramid is the Estate Range, which bears the Northern Sonoma appellation, allowing Gallo to blend as it sees fit from the finest lots, whatever their origin. The Chardonnay tends to come from Laguna; the Cabernet, from Frei.

With such a large and varied range of wines, it would be asking too much to expect each wine to be of the highest quality. But as an exercise in rejigging a fairly wretched image, Gallo of Sonoma has been a success, and individual wines can be very good indeed. It would be cynical to attribute the venture solely to the family's wish to escape its reputation for mediocre jug wines and products targeted specifically at America's poorest communities, even if that may have been one of the motives. Gallo Family Vineyards has shown that farming and winemaking on a substantial scale need not be incompatible with high quality.

FINEST WINES

White

2005 Northern Sonoma Estate Chardonnay
Discreetly toasty nose, with apple-compote and pear aromas. Creamy but not overblown, with apple and citrus flavors; a tight, refined style that still has a future.

2006 Two Rock Sonoma Coast Chardonnay
Appley nose, with a whiff of oak. Full-bodied, with considerable weight and power, though not to excess. Not structured, but forthright and balanced, with fairly good length. Has personality.

2006 Laguna Ranch Chardonnay [V]
Delicate, toasty, stone-fruit nose. Suave and less oaky than the nose, with appley flavors and plenty of spice. There's an appealing graininess to the texture, and the finish is long if not especially complex.

2008 MacMurray Ranch Sonoma Coast Pinot Gris
Ripe and flowery apple-compote nose. Medium-bodied but surprisingly intense, with apple and apricot flavors and lively acidity. A good example of a maligned variety.

Red

2002 Frei Zinfandel
Ripe cherry nose, rather jammy. Soft, rounded, and juicy, with flavors of black fruits and mocha, with a long but peppery and slightly alcoholic finish.

2003 Frei Cabernet Sauvignon
Sweet blackberry-and-mint nose, with some coffee tones. Plump and generous, broad-shouldered, and still quite tannic, with a long spicy finish.

2003 Winemaker's Signature Monte Rosso Cabernet Franc
Dried-herbs-and-tobacco nose. Full-bodied and creamy in texture, with black-fruit flavors and light tannins. Dense and gnarled for Cabernet Franc.

2004 Northern Sonoma Estate Cabernet Sauvignon
Dense but stylish cedary black-currant nose. Broad but concentrated, suave yet spicy, with delicate tannins giving some structure. Relatively undeveloped and needs more bottle age.

2004 Winemaker's Signature Petit Verdot
Dense black-cherry nose, quite oaky. Rich and concentrated, but rather one-dimensional and lacking in acidity. Softened with Merlot, which undermines the point of a varietal Petit Verdot.

2005 Barrelli Creek Cabernet Sauvignon
Very dense nose, black fruits and tobacco. Full-bodied and lush, but lacks some depth and vigor; finishes with a lot of tannin and savory tones.

2006 Rancho Zabaco Monte Rosso Vineyard Zinfandel★
Splendid nose, very ripe, with some red fruits and tobacco. Juicy, full-bodied, and vigorous, with an attractive earthiness and good length. Not refined, but appealingly boisterous.

2007 MacMurray Ranch Sonoma Coast Pinot Noir
Lush, spicy black-cherry nose, very aromatic and smoky. Rich and far from subtle, but concentrated, with plenty of flavor and drive and bright acidity.

Gallo Family Vineyards
Area under vine: 2,800 acres (1,135ha)
Average production: 5 million bottles
3387 Dry Creek Road, Healdsburg, CA 95448
Tel: (707) 431-5500
www.gallosonoma.com

Hanzell

Hanzell is a name to conjure with in the history of postwar California wine, especially from Burgundian varieties. Yet its history has been checkered, with some lapses in quality and direction. However, a new team is in place that clearly intends to maintain what is best about the Hanzell tradition, without being chained down by the past.

James Zellerbach made a fortune in the paper business and then enjoyed a new career as American ambassador to Italy. His wine tastes led him to Burgundy more than Tuscany, and after his return to the United States, he resolved to plant Chardonnay and Pinot Noir, both of which were scarcely known in the US in the early 1950s. He had bought some 200 acres (80ha) of land at the southern end of Sonoma Valley, with San Pablo Bay just visible in the distance. In 1953, he terraced 6 acres (2.5ha) of his land and began to plant vines. No one seems certain about the clonal origin of those first Pinot plantings. Some suggest it was the Mount Eden selection, which may be the same as the Paul Masson clone that originated in the late 19th century. Wherever it came from, it has now won its own identity as the Hanzell clone.

Brad Webb was the initial winemaker, and he was as innovative as his employer. He acquired stainless-steel fermenters in 1956, at a time when fermentation was always done in redwood tanks or concrete vats. Even Haut-Brion in Bordeaux had yet to install its pioneering steel tanks. He also introduced temperature control for white-wine fermentation and imported barrels directly from Sirugue in Burgundy, though some maintain that Martin Ray was doing this before Webb sent in his order. He adopted punching down of the cap for the Pinot Noir at a time when the handful of other Pinot producers were pumping over, as they would for any other red wine. If the equipment and techniques at Hanzell were well in advance of their times, the actual structure of the winery paid homage to the past; it was designed as a replica of the presshouse at Clos de Vougeot in Burgundy. The first vintage was 1957, and production never exceeded 1,000 cases.

James Zellerbach died in 1963. His widow Hana, despite lending her name to that of the winery, had no interest in the venture and sold off all the stock, including wines still in barrel. (They were bought by Barney Rhodes in Napa, then bottled and sold by Joe Heitz under his own name.) No wine at all was made in 1963 and 1964. The following year, she sold the property to retired businessman Douglas Day, and in 1976 it was acquired by Barbara de Brye, who was Australian-born but married to a Parisian banker. After de Brye's death in 1991, her son Alex took charge. Since he lives in London, Jean Arnold, who is married to former winemaker Bob Sessions, directs Hanzell's management.

Sessions made the wines from 1973 to 2001 and crafted the ageworthy style for which Hanzell became renowned. After he retired in 2001, a succession of new winemakers followed, and the incumbent is Michael McNeill.

The vineyards are steep and rise to a height of 860ft (260m), so fog intrusions are variable. The reddish soils have fairly low fertility but are water-retentive yet well drained. Of the 46 acres (18.5ha) under vine, one-third is Pinot Noir. Four of those Pinot acres are the original 1953 plantings, and there are also 4 acres (1.6ha) of Chardonnay planted in the same year. Cabernet Sauvignon was grown and vinified here from 1983 to 1992, but because it ripened with difficulty, it was taken out. However, there are reports that some of those vintages aged very well. (I certainly enjoyed the 1981 when I encountered it in a blind tasting in 1988.)

There have been changes, other than of winemaker, at Hanzell in recent years. Wine caves were built in the early 2000s, and the original winery was shut down, both because TCA problems had developed there in 1999 and 2000 and because

of fears of asbestos contamination. The original winery has been preserved as a museum, complete with those 50-year-old square steel vats. Beneath them was enough space to wheel in a vertical press, so that the pomace didn't need to be pumped out.

Yields are very low: for Chardonnay, no more than 20hl/ha, or 1.5 tons per acre. The grapes are sorted, whole-cluster pressed, and then fermented in a mixture of steel tanks and barrels. Brad Webb's Chardonnays were fermented only in tanks and did not go through malolactic fermentation, which may help account for their longevity. Today, about one-third of the wine does go through malolactic, and the Chardonnay is aged for 18 months in one-third new barriques.

The early Pinots were very tannic wines, both because of the way the vines were farmed and because of overextraction in the winery. But the more recent Hanzell winemakers concede that even with gentler modern winemaking techniques, the Pinot can still be a tannic wine. Although it is fashionable now to use whole-cluster fermentation, at Hanzell the grapes are usually crushed to give more structured wines. Selected yeasts are inoculated, and fermentation takes place in open-top steel vats. The wine remains in tanks until the spring and is then aged for two years in up to 50 percent new oak, with minimal racking.

The TCA problem has been dealt with, but Hanzell was obliged to remove the tainted 1999 Pinot Noir and 2000 Chardonnay vintages from the market. The vineyard has gradually been expanded since the original plantings, so there are now some additional wines in the range. Sebella is the second-label Chardonnay, for declassified lots. The Ambassador's Chardonnay, in contrast, is a cuvée made solely from the 1953 plantings; no more than 100 cases are made, and sales are limited to the members of the Hanzell wine club.

Left: Jean Arnold, who manages Hanzell for owner Alex de Brye, with her husband, the former winemaker, Bob Sessions

Hanzell remains faithful to its ideal: long-lived wines that are modeled on, but do not attempt to replicate slavishly, the top wines of Burgundy. For a start, Sonoma Valley is far warmer than the Côte d'Or. The Chardonnay could stand side by side with, perhaps, a Meursault Charmes; the Pinot Noir, with a fine Gevrey-Chambertin. But in their structure and power they nonetheless remain fully Californian.

FINEST WINES

(Tasted 2006–09)

Chardonnay

2003 Rich, honeyed nose, lush and quite toasty. Plump and full-bodied, but it has a fine thread of acidity on the mid-palate and a spicy aftertaste. It is a touch heavy, but the high alcohol is not perceptible, thanks to the richness and weight of the wine. Good length.

2004 Firm, oaky nose, robust, nutty, and mineral. Full-bodied and concentrated, with lemon-zest acidity and apricot flavors. Very good length, with a brisk, pure finish.

2006★ Imposing, waxy, peachy nose, with hazelnut aromas. Very concentrated and luxurious; textured and layered despite a slight lack of acidity and some graininess on the finish. The 15% alcohol doesn't show.

Pinot Noir

2002 Rich smoky-bacon nose, a touch charred, with raspberry and pomegranate aromas emerging after aeration. Full-bodied and velvety, with firm but not harsh tannins, tight with good underlying acidity. This is not a fruit-forward style but is structured and long.

2006★ Spicy nose, more earthy than fruity. Dense, plump, and concentrated, with earthy tannins alongside fine acidity; has weight and warmth without being overtly fruity. Good length, but a slightly dry finish. Needs time.

Hanzell
Area under vine: 46 acres (18.5ha)
Average production: 80,000 bottles
18596 Lomita Avenue, Sonoma, CA 95476
Tel: (707) 996-3860
www.hanzell.com

Hartford Family Winery

The Hartford winery is one of the most remote in Russian River Valley. It was built for Domaine Laurier, but the owner died before construction could be completed. In 1993, it was acquired by Kendall-Jackson, and it forms part of Jackson Family Estates, though Don Hartford runs it as an independent entity within the group. Hartford grew up in Massachusetts and, while studying law, married Jess Jackson's daughter Jennifer (before her father set up his first winery).

The winery's focus has been clear from the outset. Dan Goldfield, now of Dutton-Goldfield, helped by locating exceptional vineyards for its program, which was restricted to cool-climate Chardonnay and Pinot Noir and to small lots of vineyard-designated Russian River Zinfandel. Well-known winemakers Merry Edwards and Steve Test were also involved in some early vintages; and in 1998, Mike Sullivan, who had worked at Landmark in Sonoma Valley, was appointed as winemaker. Since 2006, the post has been filled by the modest but very able Jeff Mangahas, who had an earlier career as a cancer-research scientist before succumbing to the seductions of a career in food and wine and enrolling at UC Davis.

The organization is quite complex. A few of the vineyards are owned by the Hartfords; others supply grapes on a contract basis; while yet others are owned by the Jackson group but with agreements that give Hartford exclusive access to the fruit. Of the 20 wines made in 2007, 16 carry vineyard or cuvée names. For a vineyard to feature on the label, it must have defining characteristics that recur in most vintages. Larger-volume wines are made under the Sonoma Coast appellation. An additional—and surely needless—complication is that wines from Burgundian varieties are released under the Hartford Court label, while Zinfandels are released simply as Hartford wines.

Since the winery is so devoted to terroir-based wines, it may be worth describing each of them briefly, beginning with Chardonnay sites. All Chardonnays are picked after four or five passes through the vineyard, then sorted at the winery, barrel-fermented, aged in roughly 50 percent new French oak, and bottled without fining or filtration.

- Seascape is planted on a ridge near Occidental. Being close to the Pacific, ripening is slow, and the harvest often takes place in November. The grapes have high acidity.
- Laura's is not from a single site but is a blend of vineyards located near Dehlinger with vines up to 40 years old.
- Three Jacks is part of the Dutton Ranch in Green Valley.
- Stone Côte is a sector south of Sonoma and forms part of the Durrel vineyards. Grape clusters from here tend to be very small.
- Four Hearts is a Russian River Valley blend, from vineyards planted with heritage clones such as Old Wente and Rued.

The Pinot Noir is often picked at night, again with selective harvesting. The grapes are destemmed and given a prolonged cold soak under dry ice. Fermentation takes place in small open-top tanks, mostly with natural yeasts, with manual punching down of the cap. As with the Chardonnay, about 50–60 percent new oak is used; there is usually a single racking, and then the wine is bottled without fining or filtration.

- Arrendell is an estate vineyard 3 miles (5km) south of the winery in Green Valley. This exceptionally cool site is planted with the Martini clone and gives very low yields.
- Hailey's Block is a parcel within Arrendell that is planted with Dijon clones and is sometimes vinified and bottled separately.
- Sevens Bench is a Carneros vineyard planted with Dijon clones.
- Velvet Sisters is an Anderson Valley vineyard,

Right: Don Hartford, under whose direction the company produces excellent Chardonnay, Pinot Noir, and Zinfandel

not far from Roederer, and is also planted with Dijon clones.

- Land's Edge is a blend from various Sonoma Coast ridge tops but mostly from the Jackson family's Annapolis vineyard.
- Fog Dance is from Green Valley; a blend of the Ross and Arrendell vineyards, which are close to each other and planted with Dijon clones.
- Jennifer's is a blend from various cool, windy vineyards in the Sebastopol Hills.

Because the Zinfandel sites can be marginal, Hartford cannot be sure of releasing all of them as vineyard-designated wines each year. When a site doesn't demonstrate its typicity, it is blended into the Russian River Valley Zinfandel. The wines are made in the same way as the Pinot Noirs, with a cold soak and whole-berry fermentation with manual punch-downs. The single-vineyard wines are Fanucchi-Wood Road (centenarian vines, organically farmed), the estate-owned Hartford (7 acres [2.8ha]), Highwire (planted 1906), Jolene's (80–100-year-old vines), and Diana (4 acres [1.6ha]). These vineyards lie on either side of Route 101, just north of Santa Rosa. They are dry-farmed and cropped at no more than 2 tons per acre, and often much less. All the grapes are bought by Hartford.

Zinfandel tends to fare better in areas such as the Dry Creek and Alexander valleys, but in the warmer corners of Russian River it can deliver wines just as good but in a slightly leaner style, lying more at the red-fruit than black-fruit end of the spectrum. Hartford is one of the few wineries to offer a collection of fine wines from old-vine Zinfandel sites in Russian River. The Chardonnay and Pinot Noir are beautifully crafted wines, quite full-bodied yet aiming for the maximum finesse compatible with fairly high ripeness levels.

Hartford may not be quite as well known as wineries such as Dehlinger or Kosta Browne, but its wines are at the highest level.

FINEST WINES

(Tasted 2009)

Chardonnay

2007 Four Hearts Broad, rich, toasty nose. Creamy and full-bodied, with ripe citrus and pear flavors, and ample spice and grip. Quite long.

2007 Laura's Chardonnay Toasty apricot nose. Fresh attack on the palate, yet creamy and concentrated, both tight and opulent, though weight of fruit rather than high acidity gives persistence. Long nutty finish.

2007 Seascape★ Stern, toasty, pineapple nose. Medium-bodied, but sleek and silky, showing a light touch, with fine acidity and a pure, rapier-like texture. Refined and long.

Pinot Noir

2007 Hailey's Block Delicate, toasty, raspberry nose, with clovelike spice. Supple but concentrated, with a seductive texture and delicate acidity. The silky texture is utterly beguiling. Quite long.

2007 Fog Dance★ Floral nose, with violets, rose petals, and crystallized fruit. Lush, full-bodied, and very concentrated. This already shows weight, complexity, and a velvety texture. Fine length.

2007 Land's Edge Discreet nose of cherries, mint, and coffee. Sleek and silky, but a rugged quality, too, giving some youthful austerity. Good length.

2007 Arrendell Subdued herbal nose, with a light savory tone. Rich and broad, with heft and spice and powerful cherry fruit. Good length, but tannic.

Zinfandel

2007 Russian River Valley Muted raspberry-and-coffee nose. Surprisingly delicate, despite the evident richness of fruit, quite tannic and peppery, with firm acidity. Rather blunt on the finish.

2007 Hartford Vineyard Dense, lush, smoky nose, blackberry fruit. Big and opulent, but redeemed by fine acidity. Concentrated, with a bright, lifted finish.

2007 Highwire Vineyard Dense black-fruit-and-coffee nose. Voluptuous and very concentrated, with powerful but ripe tannins, clove spice, a touch of chocolate, and fine acidity on the long finish.

Hartford Family Winery
Area under vine: 45 acres (18ha)
Average production: 165,000 bottles
8075 Martinelli Road, Forestville, CA 95436
Tel: (707) 887-8012
www.hartfordwines.com

Marimar Estate

Marimar is Marimar Torres, sister of Miguel Torres, who has become synonymous with the finest wines of Catalonia while at the same time producing very large quantities of commercial wines to a high and consistent standard. Perhaps there was little room within the family structure at Torres wines in Penedès for another free spirit, so in her late 20s, Marimar headed for California, where she was married to a wine journalist for a while. She spent two years in the early 1980s looking throughout the state for a property she could develop and, in 1982, found a former apple orchard in Green Valley. She bought it in 1983 and planted it with Chardonnay from 1986 onward, carefully using phylloxera-resistant rootstocks. Two years later, she added Pinot Noir, though specialists at UC Davis warned her there was no demand for the variety.

Miguel Torres worried that his sister had paid too much for the land and that it wasn't a good spot for grapes either. But the sandy loam soils had both good water retention and good drainage, and with high-density plantings of around 2,000 vines per acre, Marimar was sure she could succeed. She was to be proved right. Moreover, she was soon able to dry-farm the vines, planted along the contours of an undulating slope. In 2006, the vineyard was certified organic, and she is now running biodynamic trials in some parcels. Since 2008, the winery has been operated by solar power.

With little room for expansion at the Green Valley property, in 2000 Marimar Torres acquired a slope between Freestone and Occidental, closer to the coast. Here she planted both Pommard and Dijon clones of Pinot Noir at 435–625ft (130–190m). Despite the cool location just 7 miles (11km) from the ocean, the soils are quite vigorous. The vineyard gave her a good deal of trouble, and there was much replanting and regrafting before she was satisfied with a property she subsequently named the Doña Margarita Vineyard.

The first vintage was the 1989 Chardonnay, though the Marimar winery was only completed in 1992, which was the year of the first Pinot Noir bottling. The Chardonnay is made from a small selection of heritage clones, which are fermented separately. It is whole-cluster pressed, then fermented in about one-third new Burgundian oak and aged for around 11 months. The wine goes through full malolactic fermentation, but lees-stirring is halted after the malo is completed.

Since 2003, the Pinot has been sorted at the winery. It is crushed, and for many years, about 20 percent whole clusters were retained. Since 2006, however, all the fruit has been destemmed. After a cold soak, the must is fermented in open-top vats with hydraulic punch-downs three times daily. The Pinot is aged for ten months in one-third new French oak. Since 1997 there has been no filtration.

Because grapes are now grown in two different sites, there have been new labels at Marimar. The Estate Pinot Noir has been renamed La Masía since 2006. The top 20 barrels are bottled separately and named after Marimar's daughter Cristina; this is aged in about two-thirds new oak. The Pinot from the Doña Margarita Vineyard is called Mas Cavalls, a reference to the equestrian center on the property. In 1992, a top barrel selection was released as Vineyard Selection but has not been made since.

The Chardonnay range has also expanded. In 1998, Marimar and her winemaker Bill Dyer first made Dobles Lías, a wine given extended lees aging by adding the lees from barrels of the previous vintage, these having been separated from the wine just before bottling. The process is quite expensive, since there is considerable loss of wine. Dobles Lías spends 16 months in 50 percent new oak and is bottled without filtration. At the other end of the spectrum is an unoaked Chardonnay called Acero.

Though she has now lived in California for more than 30 years, Marimar Torres remains proudly Catalan and is the author of several Catalan cookbooks. Privileged visitors to the property are sometimes treated to a home-cooked feast to accompany a tasting of the wines, and the design of the buildings and their furnishings are also inspired by and taken from her beloved homeland. The wines, too, are European in style, though bolder and a touch higher in alcohol than their European counterparts. However, they are certainly not blockbusters.

FINEST WINES

(Tasted 2009-10)

Chardonnay

2007 Acero Vivid lime-and-apricot nose. Lively and concentrated on the palate, with good acidity and appley fruit. Not complex, but delicious and long.

2006 Estate Light, toasty nose. Spicy but reticent, elegant rather than flamboyant, with fine acidity and persistence.

2005 Estate Flamboyant nose: lime and apricot, and a dash of oak. Creamy and concentrated, but with lemony acidity and ample vigor and length.

2005 Dobles Lías Yeasty nose, less exuberant than the Estate wine. Broad and a touch heavy, and it lacks the freshness of the Estate. A trade-off: greater richness, less zest.

2003 Estate Firm apple-and-apricot nose. Broad and spicy and has unusual weight for this property. Concentrated, but has only moderate acidity and length on the finish.

1999 Estate★ Light, toasty nose; delicate, apricot fruit but not tiring. Silky, lush, and concentrated on the palate, with a fine thread of acidity; balanced, elegant, and long.

1996 Estate Discreet apple-and-apricot nose, light toastiness. Suave texture, ripe stone fruits, concentrated and with firm acidity, but still supple.

Pinot Noir

2006 Mas Cavalls Fresh zesty raspberry nose. Lean, bright, and silky, concentrated but tight, piquant, and lively. Quite long.

2006 La Masía Very ripe, lush, fruity cherry nose; cloves. Rich, plump, and full-bodied but not heavy; has complexity and balance, with good acidity, as well as length.

2005 Cristina★ Lean, spicy, red-fruit nose. Silky, opulent, and concentrated, and it has depth, with discreet power and more spice and elegance than the 2004. Long.

2004 Cristina Rich, toasty, smoky nose, sumptuous and generous, with admirable ripeness and body. But it lacks a little zest and persistence.

2002 Estate Sweet, intense, cherry-and-mint nose. Lean, graceful, and stylish, but quite tannic. Lively acidity and good length.

2001 Estate Discreet, smoky nose, a bit leathery and mushroomy now. Quite rich, juicy, and concentrated, with surprisingly chewy tannins; forthright and long, but lacks some finesse.

2000 Estate Reticent herbal nose, cherries and

mint. Supple and juicy, but lacks a little drive, with rather subdued fruit. Pleasant enough, but lacks some personality. Less complete than 2001.

1996 Estate Evolved color. Slightly stewed cherry nose. Medium-bodied but concentrated, with sleek cherry fruit, fine acidity, and reasonable length of flavor.

1994 Estate Slightly evolved nose, with charming leafy aromas, herbal but not green. Compact, with ripe tannins, good acidity, and cherry fruit. Has finesse and a grainy finish.

1992 Vineyard Selection Moderate russet red. Sweet, leafy, mushroomy nose; cherry pie. Soft, rounded, and gentle; quite spicy, silky, and still delicious, with marked acidity, but fully ready and not especially long.

Above: Marimar Torres, who moved to California in her 20s and confounded the skeptics by producing successful wines

Marimar Estate
Area under vine: 80 acres (32ha)
Average production: 180,000 bottles
11400 Graton Road, Sebastopol, CA 95472
Tel: (707) 823-4365
www.marimarestate.com

Ravenswood

Joel Peterson was a biochemist by training and an immunologist in cancer cases by profession (until he retired from medicine in 1987). It was in the mid-1970s that he realized he needed to focus on the positive side of human experience, as well as its darker side. His father had always given him good wines to drink, especially Bordeaux, and had educated his palate, so he felt that winemaking would combine the artistic and scientific sides of his nature. One of the winemakers he encountered as his interest grew was Joe Swan, who was known for the excellence of his Sonoma Zinfandels, so Peterson spent his spare time working for him.

In 1976, he bought a batch of grapes and made 327 cases of his own wine, borrowing space at the Swan winery. Production steadily increased until, in 1979, he assembled a partnership to raise funds and moved into a former garage south of the town of Sonoma. Here he was to stay for ten years. He made some good Merlots and Cabernets, but his main passion was for old-vine Zinfandel. He was fascinated by the gnarled old vineyards and the field blends of Zinfandel and other traditional varieties still found in various spots in Sonoma and Napa, but he also made a bread-and-butter wine in the form of his Vintners Blend, also known informally as Chateau Cash-Flow.

At a time when much Zinfandel was being made from overripe fruit and aged in American oak, Peterson was treating the variety with respect. He assessed the fruit from each site on fruit flavors rather than sugar levels, and he avoided desiccated fruit that was likely to result in Porty flavors and very high alcohols. He always maintained that his role was to extract as much flavor as he could from the grapes and to enhance that flavor—but not too much. He saw his job as preserving the integrity of the splendid fruit he was buying.

After a brief cold soak, the grapes are fermented with native yeasts and given a fairly lengthy maceration. The single-vineyard wines are punched down at least three times a day and are aged for 14–18 months in French oak, with varying proportions of new wood, depending on the character of the wine. Fining and filtration are the exception rather than the rule. All the single-vineyard wines are made in essentially the same way, though there are always slight variations in maceration periods and the length of oak aging.

By the late 1990s, Ravenswood was firmly established as one of the outstanding producers of Zinfandel. The wines were superbly consistent and reasonably priced for the quality. So maybe it was not surprising that in 2001 the wine group now known as Constellation pounced and swallowed up Ravenswood for $148 million. Everyone feared the worst: that production would be ratcheted up to the extent that the winery would lose its identity. In the 1980s, Peterson told me that he didn't want to produce more than 15,000 cases each year, so that he could retain control over the winemaking process; but by 2008, the production had risen to more than 400,000 cases. The new bosses, however, have left the core of the business untouched. Production of the Vintners Blend range was certainly hugely expanded, as was the County series—that is, the Zinfandel blends from Lodi, Amador, Mendocino, and Sonoma. Joel Peterson remains at the helm, though the daily winemaking tasks are now in the hands of an accomplished team.

On a mock tombstone near the tasting room is the following inscription:

To Err is Human
But to Zin is D'vine
Here lies the Last Wimpy Wine.

"No wimpy wines" is the Ravenswood motto, emblazoned on T-shirts and other merchandise (in Japanese, as well as English). It's a great slogan, and it amuses the visitors who flock to the tasting room each weekend. But it actually does the Ravenswood

Right: Joel Peterson, who has long demonstrated Zinfandel's fine-wine potential and still produces some of the very best

RADOUX
2008
013757
2008
BARRICIA
017135

wines a disservice. Unlike many other Zinfandels, those from Ravenswood have considerable purity and elegance; they are not monsters of overripeness and extraction. It's possible that the folksiness of the Ravenswood marketing has led to the wines being underestimated—or perhaps merely being taken for granted. They remain unquestionably among California's finest expressions of Zinfandel.

It may be useful to summarize the principal vineyards that have regularly supplied Ravenswood with fruit.

Barricia East side of Sonoma Valley, from 12 acres (5ha) of vines planted from 1895 to 1905. The field blend has about 20 percent Petite Sirah.

Dickerson Mid-Napa Valley. A pure Zinfandel vineyard of 10 acres (4ha) planted from 1930 onwards.

Belloni A cool vineyard near Fulton in Russian River Valley, with vines planted between 1900 and 1908. A field blend, with 80 percent Zinfandel, plus Carignane, Alicante, and Petite Sirah, which are co-fermented.

Big River In Alexander Valley, east of Healdsburg: 14 acres (5.5ha) of pure Zinfandel, planted in 1900.

Teldeschi A dry-farmed vineyard in Dry Creek Valley, planted from 1900 to 1920. Zinfandel, plus Petite Sirah and Carignane.

Old Hill Ranch A valley-floor Sonoma Valley vineyard of 14 acres (5.5ha) south of Glen Ellen. An organically farmed 19th-century vineyard containing 14 different varieties.

Cooke A hillside vineyard in Sonoma Valley, with fairly young vines.

Wood Road From 90-year-old vines near Fulton in Russian River Valley.

A new addition to the range is a wine called Icon, made from pre-1905 vines from eight sites. Only half the fruit is Zinfandel. The idea is to re-create a traditional blend that Italian growers might have made a century ago.

FINEST WINES

(Tasted 2009–10)

County Zinfandels

The Lodi Old Vine is the most accessible of the county wines, with a splendid and often smoky black-fruit nose. It offers delicious, quaffable fruit rather than complexity and persistence. The Napa bottlings seem to vary most from year to year; the 2006 was particularly successful. The Sonoma Old Vine is consistently the most characterful of the county wines, with a fresh spicy nose and plenty of grip and vigor on the palate.

Vineyard-Designated Zinfandels

2007 Teldeschi Dense nose, plums and coffee. Very rich, with spicy black fruits; good acidity and tannins, but not heavy or extracted. Long.

2006 Barricia Rich, dense cherry nose, compact and toasty. Pungent, powerful, and tannic, structured and enlivened by good acidity; spicy and peppery if a touch too alcoholic.

2006 Teldeschi★ Blackberries and licorice on the nose. Succulent, very concentrated, and boldly flavored; sumptuous and spicy. Very long, with vanilla and cloves on the finish.

2006 Dickerson Lush, oaky, red-fruit nose, a touch confected. Medium-bodied but sleek and fresh, though not lacking in density and tannins, and showing good grip and sweetness on the finish.

2006 Belloni Complex nose, with cloves and eucalyptus. Plump, concentrated cherry fruit, with chewy tannins but a long, limpid finish.

2006 Old Hill Very ripe and slightly confected nose: plums and pepper. Sleek, cool, and concentrated, and with a stylish finish, despite its firm tannins.

2005 Teldeschi Discreet, black-cherry and blackberry nose, with smoky oak. Concentrated and rugged but has complexity, finesse, and length.

Icon

2007 Dense, oaky, black-fruit nose. Rich, plump, and fleshy, with freshness, elegance, and length.

2006 Dense, black-cherry nose. Concentrated and suave, with persistent black-fruit flavors.

Ravenswood Winery
Area under vine: 13 acres (5ha)
Average production: 5 million bottles
18701 Gehricke Road, Sonoma, CA 94576
Tel: (707) 933-2332
www.ravenswoodwinery.com

Chateau St. Jean

Students of hagiography will know that there is no such American saint as St. Jean. Jean was the name of the wife of one of the founders; quite what she did to merit her sainthood is not clear. The founders were Bob and Ed Merzoian (his wife was Jean) and Ken Sheffield, who were grape farmers from the Central Valley. They constructed the winery near the existing "chateau" of 1920 in the northern part of Sonoma Valley, and it was completed in 1976. In 1984, the partners were losing money on the table-grape business in San Joaquin Valley, though Chateau St. Jean itself was profitable. They had no choice but to sell up, and the business was sold to Suntory of Japan, which invested heavily in the winery. In 1996, Suntory sold Chateau St. Jean to Beringer, and today the winery is part of the vast Foster's Wine Estates group of Australia.

The initial winemaker was Richard Arrowood, who now has his own winery a short distance away. He embarked on a highly ambitious program, focusing on single-vineyard wines, which were uncommon for white wines at the time: in the 1970s, he would routinely make up to nine different Chardonnays and a number of Fumé Blancs, too. Although there was some dabbling with fruit from Mendocino, Arrowood soon concentrated on the wide range of fruit available in Sonoma County. He also made a style of wine that few large wineries (Joseph Phelps apart) were producing: TBA-style wines from Riesling and Gewurztraminer. Labeled as Individual Bunch Selected Late Harvest wines, they showed astonishing intensity and viscosity; they aged faster than their European equivalents but were magnificent acts of homage to the great sweet wines of Germany and Alsace. Furthermore, they came about by accident. In 1974, a well-known Alexander Valley grower, Robert Young, apologized for some mold on his Riesling, but Arrowood recognized it as botrytis and told him to bring in the lot. The wine was successful, despite its high price, especially for a barely recognized wine style.

The public and the winemakers may have loved this panoply of fine wines, but the corporate owners were less enthusiastic and put pressure on Arrowood to trim the range while maintaining production, which by 1982 had risen to 100,000 cases. He was not very happy about this and, by the mid-1980s, was establishing his own winery. In 1990, he left Chateau St. Jean for good. His assistant winemaker, Don Van Staaveren, took over, staying in place until 1997, when he was replaced by Steve Reeder, formerly one of the chief winemakers at Kendall-Jackson. After he left in 2003, it was Van Staaveren's wife, Margo, who took over.

Below: The 1920s "chateau" in Sonoma Valley, named after Jean Merzoian, the wife of one of the three original founders

R622
09 Pinot Noir

The winery has to purchase most of its fruit. It owns almost 100 acres (40ha) around the winery, a replanting of the original vineyard, which had been dug up during Prohibition. In 1989, it bought La Petite Etoile in Windsor, just within the Russian River Valley, and has vineyards in other parts of the county. Of the many vineyards from which Arrowood sourced his grapes, some have been dug up to make way for housing; others were dropped after the range was trimmed. After he left, there was also a change in style. The Arrowood wines were dramatic, oaky, and high in alcohol, but they did not always age well. Van Staaveren and Reeder aimed for a less powerful and more elegant style. The two surviving single-vineyard Chardonnays are from Robert Young and Belle Terre vineyards, both in Alexander Valley

Today the hierarchy of wines begins with basic fruit-driven Sonoma County bottlings; then there are the few surviving vineyard-designated wines and a handful of estate wines from Viognier, Merlot, Cabernet Franc, and Malbec; and at the top of the range are Reserves from Chardonnay, Merlot, and Cabernet Sauvignon, as well as the successful Bordeaux blend called Cinq Cépages. The red Reserves are aged for two years in new French oak.

The Special Select Late Harvest Riesling lives on. Botrytis is induced by sprinklers in the Belle Terre Vineyard, and infected grapes are picked individually. Bunches with only moderate infection levels are picked whole and used for the Select Late Harvest wine, which has less intensity. Clearly such wines are highly dependent on vintage conditions and cannot be made every year.

Margo Van Staaveren continues to innovate, producing small volumes of wine from Rhône varieties. The main county ranges are well made but commercial, but Chateau St. Jean knows how to pique the interest of the many visitors to its tasting room with these special bottlings. Unquestionably, a certain blandness has crept into the range now that the winery must play its part in the staid corporate drama of brewery ownership, but at the top level the wines remain both very good and very consistent.

Left: Margo Van Staaveren, Chateau St. Jean's winemaker, who has added Rhône-style wines to the extensive range

FINEST WINES

(Tasted 2009–10)

White

2007 Robert Young Vineyard Chardonnay Firm mineral nose with a hint of tropical fruit. Quite rich and full-bodied, with tropical fruit flavors, but good acidity too, giving moderate persistence. A better, more typical expression than the 2006.

2007 Le Petite Etoile Sauvignon Blanc Rich grapefruit and lime nose. A broad, fleshy, very Californian style of Sauvignon, concentrated and weighty, with moderate acidity and length.

2006 Special Select Late Harvest Belle Terre Riesling Rich, powerful, apricot nose. Very sweet and succulent (with 256g/l RS), yet it's also silky and graceful, with good acidity and a deliciously tangy finish, which is exceptionally long.

2006 Sonoma County Reserve Chardonnay Oaky, tropical fruit nose. Broad, creamy, and heavily oaky on the palate, too. A crowd-pleasing style, however, with opulence in place of finesse.

Red

2005 Cinq Cépages (about 75% CS) Fine, elegant, oaky nose, quite minty, with lift and purity. Suave and elegant, this is no blockbuster, though it has concentration, complexity, and persistence and luxuriates in very fine-grained tannins.

2004 Sonoma County Reserve Cabernet Sauvignon ★ Dense black-currant and blackberry nose, opulent and powerful. Suave and textured, with fine-grained tannins and moderate acidity; a tight, oaky wine that's stylish as well as balanced and long. Both the oak and the alcohol (14.8%) are well integrated. Fresher and less overbearing than the 2003, which is broader, richer, and more savory.

Chateau St. Jean
Area under vine: 250 acres (100ha)
Average production: 5 million bottles
8555 Sonoma Highway, Kenwood, CA 95452
Tel: (707) 833-4134
www.chateaustjean.com

Seghesio

Few families represent the progress of Italian immigrant winemakers as clearly as the Seghesios. Edoardo Seghesio came to Sonoma from Piedmont in the 1880s and worked for the Italian Swiss Colony, the major winemaking venture in the north of the county. He planted his own Zinfandel vineyard (the 190-acre [77ha] Home Ranch) in 1895 and founded his winery in 1902. The business consisted of selling bulk wines to other wineries such as Gallo. Just before Prohibition, Edoardo took the bold step of buying the Italian Swiss Colony and its 1,100 acres (445ha) of vineyards. Great idea, poor timing. By the time of Repeal, his debts had become too great, and despite having taken on partners, Edoardo sold his share. By the 1970s, the Seghesios were in trouble: the Gallos were sourcing fruit elsewhere and were developing their own vineyards, and there was little demand for the enormous quantities of Chenin Blanc, French Colombard, and Carignane the family was churning out. In 1979, they stopped producing bulk wines and adapted the winery to higher-quality production. Sacramento wine merchant Darrel Corti had offered to buy three vintages in succession, helping the business get off the ground. In 1983, the Seghesios launched wines under their own label.

Production grew steadily so that by the early 1990s they were producing 130,000 cases a year, but they were increasingly unhappy with the quality. The present winemaker, Ted Seghesio, recalls that his father was a frugal man, reluctant to make investments in improvements such as drip irrigation, bunch-thinning, or better-quality tanks. Ted persuaded the family of the necessity to ratchet up the quality, and at the same time production was ruthlessly cut to 40,000 cases. Ted's good sense and the support of his family, all of whom were involved in the business, turned out to be exactly what was required. With help from consultants such as Phil Freese and Alberto Antonini, the quality of the fruit soared. Ted wanted vibrancy of fruit both in his vineyards and in his wines, and by the late 1990s he was getting it.

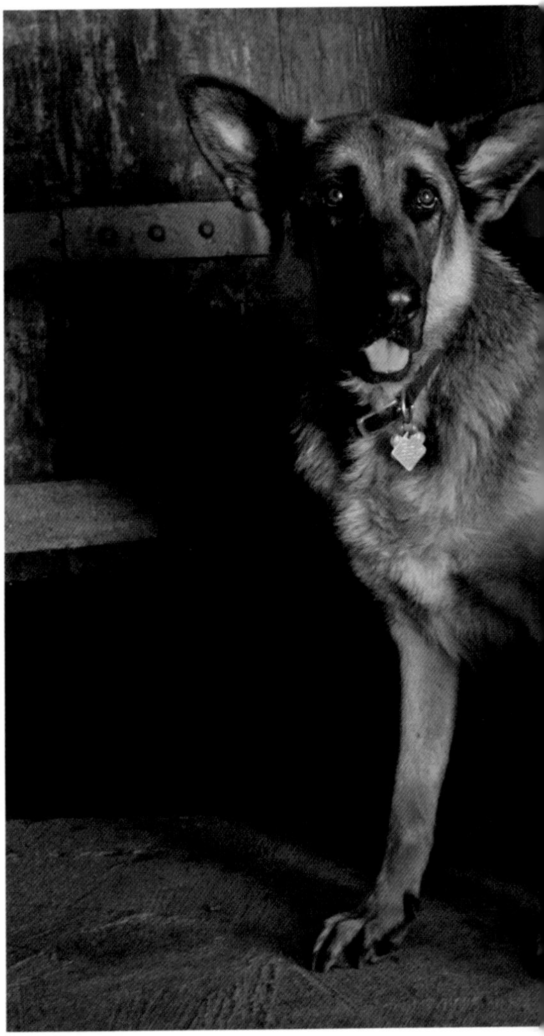

Above: Ted Seghesio, who led his family's shift up-market and continually strives to improve his already impressive wines

The Seghesios own substantial vineyards in the Alexander, Dry Creek, and Russian River valleys

Despite the acclaim, Ted Seghesio is relentlessly self-questioning and always trying to improve quality further. The Seghesios are a modest family, and it is quality alone, rather than clever marketing, that has won them their reputation

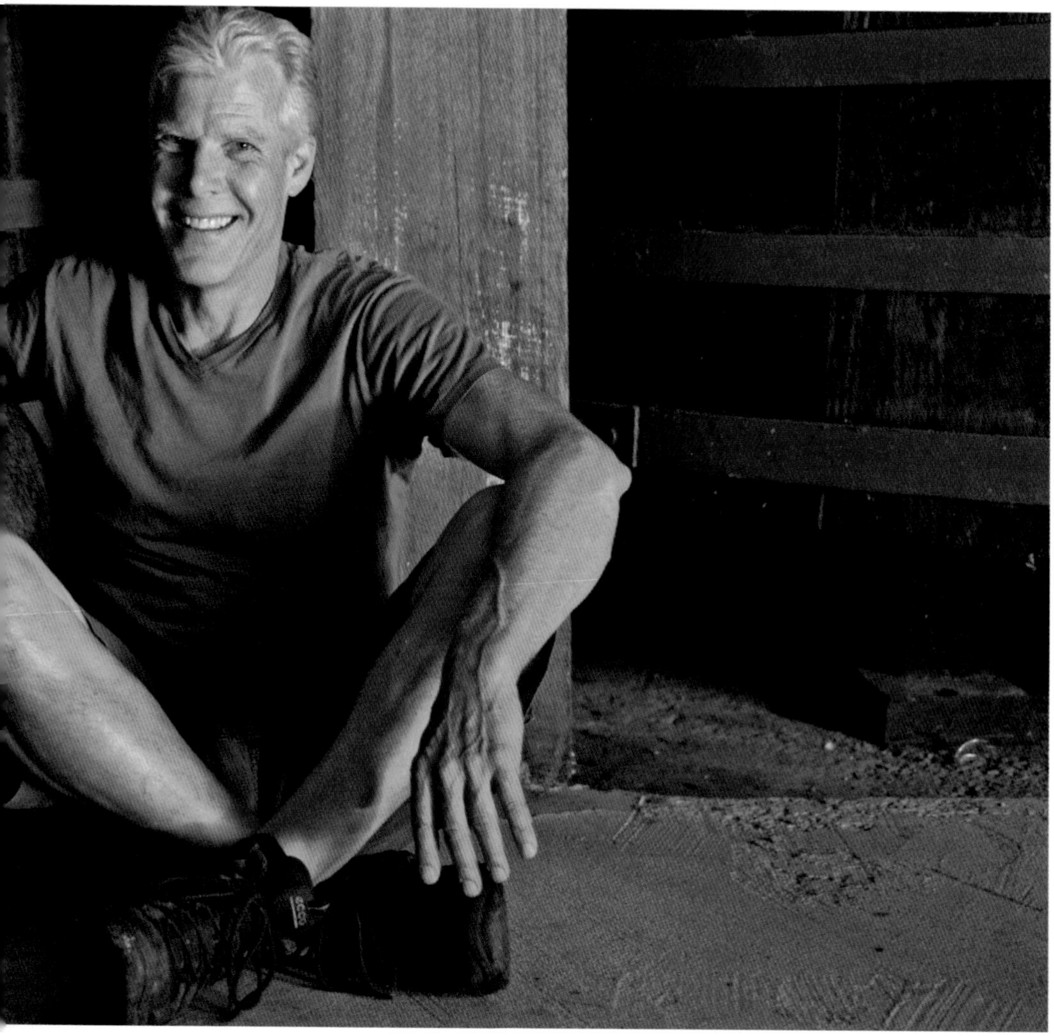

and also buy fruit from 100 more acres (40ha), working very closely with the growers. Although the company is best known for its Zinfandels, it grows some of the oldest Sangiovese in California, the original plantings dating from 1910. Chianti Station is a field blend made mostly from the surviving 2 acres (0.8ha) of 1910 Sangiovese but also includes Canaiolo, Malvasia, and Trebbiano in the mix. From cuttings taken from those old vines and planted in the 1980s, Seghesio produces a Sangiovese called Nonno's Clones; a third Sangiovese called Venom is made from a massal selection from the 1910 vines, using only a selection with pea-sized berries.

Barbera is sourced from Mendocino and Lake County, as well as Geyserville. Seghesio was among the first to plant Pinot Grigio in Russian River; Arneis was introduced in 2005, and there will be a Fiano once the vines are mature. Another new addition to the Italian range is an Aglianico, first made in 2002. Finally, since 1995 Ted Seghesio has made Omaggio, a blend of Barbera, Sangiovese, Merlot, and Cabernet Sauvignon, aged in new oak.

The basic Zinfandel is the Sonoma County wine, made from purchased fruit and mostly vinified in rotary fermenters to extract the maximum fruit and minimal tannin. It is aged in mostly American oak and 50,000 cases are made (about half the winery's current total). A distinct step up in quality is the Old Vine Zinfandel, made from a range of vineyards with an average age of 80 years. With this wine, French oak dominates. There are also four single-vineyard Zinfandels, aged in about one-third new oak, mostly or exclusively French:

Home Ranch Located in a hot part of Alexander Valley, the ranch contains vines planted in 1895. The microclimate gives wines with lower acidity and supple tannins.

San Lorenzo Planted in the 1890s just north of Healdsburg, this 32-acre (13ha) vineyard has been in the family since 1956. It's a field blend that supplements Zinfandel with 12 percent Petite Sirah, plus Alicante and Carignane.

Cortina This 56-acre (22.5ha) Russian River vineyard dates from 1960. It has higher acidity than most other sites, giving the wine a red-fruit character. The wine was first made in 1998.

Rockpile Located in the fairly new Rockpile AVA, this was only planted in the late 1990s, so the vines are young. This is not an estate vineyard.

Despite the acclaim for the Zinfandel, Ted Seghesio is relentlessly self-questioning and always trying to improve quality further. A sorting table was acquired in 2008, though the principal improvements are being made in the vineyard. The Seghesios are a modest family, and it is quality alone, rather than clever marketing, that has won them their reputation.

FINEST WINES

(Tasted 2009–2010)

Zinfandel

2007 Old Vine [V] Muted nose, minty and vibrant. Voluptuous and very concentrated, with integrated tannins and sweet cherry fruit; harmonious and balanced, with a spicy, complex finish. Quintessence of Zinfandel!

2007 Home Ranch Dense, plummy nose, some mint aromas. Soft, rich, and full-bodied, with black-cherry and plum flavors; fine concentration and acidity, but a touch too high in alcohol. Quite long.

2007 Cortina ★ Brooding, plummy nose, some mint and licorice. Very concentrated, tannic, yet suave; chocolaty, dense, but not too formidable, and still very youthful. Excellent length.

2007 Rockpile Dense plum-and-chocolate nose. Bright, assertive, very concentrated; it may not have much depth of flavor, but it's vibrant and delicious. Quite long.

2006 Old Vine Heady blackberry-and-blueberry nose, minty and intense. Bright and vigorous, tangy and vibrant, this still has good tannic structure, and the acidity gives it a welcome lean finish.

2006 Cortina Muted but peppery nose, with blueberry fruit. Medium-bodied but fleshy, quite tannic, concentrated; high in alcohol, but with no burn on the finish.

Other wines

2008 Arneis Firm, mineral, appley nose. Very ripe and soft, but there is good underlying acidity and a fine texture. Moderate length.

2007 Barbera Lush, lively red-fruit nose, piquant. Concentrated and zesty, with fine acidity and ample ripe fruit. Good length.

Seghesio Family Vineyards
Area under vine: 400 acres (160ha)
Average production: 1.2 million bottles
14730 Grove Street, Healdsburg, CA 95448
Tel: (707) 433-3579
www.seghesio.com

Williams Selyem

In the 1980s, Pinot Noir was still something of a niche product in Russian River Valley. Producers such as Davis Bynum and Rochioli had won a high reputation for their wines, and vineyards such as those owned by the Allens and Rochiolis were becoming well known; vineyard-designated wines from these sites were much sought after. But if there was a single winery that put Russian River Pinot on the map, it was Williams Selyem.

It was established in 1981 by a former typesetter named Burt Williams and a wine buyer and accountant named Ed Selyem, who had already teamed up as hobby winemakers. The first name of the winery was the romantic Hacienda del Rio, but a winery with a similar name forced a change, so in 1984 the proprietors simply melded their surnames. Throughout the 1980s, the partners operated out of a converted garage on River Road. Then, in 1989, the owner of the Allen Vineyard, Howard Allen, built a winery for them on his land.

Williams Selyem owned no vineyards but was able to buy fruit from some of the county's most celebrated sites: Olivet Lane, Rochioli's Riverblock, Allen, and Hirsch and Summa in the coastal ridge tops. Eyebrows were raised when the winery became the first in California to release a Pinot Noir (the 1991 Summa) at $100 a bottle. But there was no shortage of mailing-list customers and top restaurants anxious to snap up whatever the winery could produce. Williams seemed to have a magic touch, extracting all the perfume, silkiness, and finesse one would hope for from a fine Pinot Noir.

But by the late 1990s, the partners were tiring. Selyem had back problems and wanted to call it a day. In 1998, they sold the business to grape grower John Dyson, though Williams agreed to stay on for two years as winemaker. Dyson was a well-known figure in the world of viticulture and had, with Dr. Richard Smart, created the Smart Dyson trellising system. He also owned vineyards in New York State and Tuscany. When Williams retired in late 1999, Bob Cabral, who had been a winemaker at Hartford, took his place. He was told from the outset that the vineyard sources and styles were to remain unaltered, but as the years went by, changes were inevitable.

Dyson bought land near Guerneville in 1999 and then created the Drake Vineyard, with some 40 acres (16ha) devoted mostly to Pinot Noir, with some parcels of Chardonnay, too. He bought more land on Westside Road in Russian River to create Litton Estate, planting Pinot that came on-stream in 2005. Since the winery was being leased from the Allens, Dyson sought a more permanent solution, and a new winery should be up and running by 2011.

Williams Selyem also produced a number of vineyard-designated Chardonnays, though they were less acclaimed than the Pinots. They made Zinfandels, too, and by 2008 there were four of them. Any single vineyards that underperformed had their wine declassified into a Russian River blend. There were oddities, too: a rather flabby Muscat Canelli and an intensely sweet botrytized Gewurztraminer from San Benito in the Central Coast. Such ventures tended to dilute the profile of the winery.

Cabral, with Dyson's encouragement, has kept standards high, and in some vintages the equivalent of up to 2,000 cases is sold off in bulk. The winemaking preserves the basic principles established by Williams. The fruit is sorted, chilled overnight, then fermented in former milk tanks, which are shallow enough to permit foot-treading and manual punch-downs (which in 2006 were replaced by mechanical punch-downs). Cabral covers the fermenting must with nitrogen to protect it from oxygen, which was never one of Williams' practices. Williams favored a high proportion of new oak, but Cabral keeps it at between 40 and 70 percent. There is just a single racking and no pumping, fining, or filtration. Cabral makes all the wines in the same way, to allow the differences in terroir to emerge more clearly. The wines are less alcoholic than in the past, when some Chardonnays were released with around 16% alcohol and were, frankly, close to undrinkable.

Pinot Noir remains the strength here, and Cabral produces a large number, including one from Ferrington Vineyard in Anderson Valley and a blend from neighboring vineyards called Westside Road Neighbors, allowing him to produce a wine of high quality from top sites but in reasonable quantities. Small quantities of wine continue to be made from outstanding vineyards such as Hirsch, Peay, and Allen. Perhaps Williams Selyem is no longer in the very top ranks of Sonoma's Pinot producers—there is far more competition than in the founders' time—but quality is consistent and dependable.

FINEST WINES

(Tasted 2007–09)

Pinot Noir

2007 Russian River Valley Subtle cherry nose, already quite leafy. Supple, juicy, and concentrated, this has generosity of fruit and a tight structure. Not very nuanced at the moment, but this needs a year or two to show more complexity. Quite long.

2007 Westside Road Neighbors Powerful nose of cherries and cola. Suave, concentrated, and spicy, yet the finish is delicate and charming.

1996 Rochioli Riverblock★ Medium red, showing slight evolution. Rich, mulchy, leafy nose, raspberry and vanilla, mature but still intense. Velvety and concentrated, with fine acidity and a seamless texture and far from tiring. Still fresh and an impeccable example of how good Russian River Pinot can be.

Right: Winemaker Bob Cabral, who has kept standards high, prioritizing terroir by making the various wines the same way

Williams Selyem Winery
Area under vine: 70 acres (28ha)
Average production: 180,000 bottles
6575 Westside Road, Healdsburg, CA 95448
Tel: (707) 433-6425
www.williamsselyem.com

In the 1980s, Pinot Noir was still something of a niche product in Russian River Valley. But if there was a single winery that put Russian River Pinot on the map, it was Williams Selyem

SONOMA

Arrowood

Richard Arrowood was born in 1945. After obtaining a degree in enology from Fresno State University, he began his career working for sparkling-wine producer Korbel. By 1974, he was installed at Chateau St. Jean in Sonoma Valley, where he began producing a number of remarkable wines. He was one of the first winemakers in Sonoma to focus on single-vineyard white wines, sourcing Chardonnay and Sauvignon Blanc from top vineyards. His labels gave detailed information about the sites and the winemaking, justifying the profusion of wines from the same grape variety. He also made some astounding late-harvest wines, in Beerenauslese and Trockenbeerenauslese (TBA) styles, from Riesling and Gewurztraminer. The TBA-style

Arrowood owns few vineyards of his own but seems to have his pick of some of the best sites in the county. He particularly favors high-elevation vineyards

Riesling was the first of its kind in California. It was a way of testing the limits of what could be grown in Sonoma, and Arrowood should take credit for raising the county's profile as long ago as the 1970s.

In 1986, Arrowood started making wine under his own name, with help from his wife Alis, since he was still occupied with Chateau St. Jean. However, by 1990 he had left that winery and was able to focus exclusively on his own label. The strategy was different. He continued to produce exemplary Chardonnay but also made a good deal of red wine, which was rarely the case at Chateau St. Jean. His range of white wines was expanded to include Pinot Blanc and Viognier.

Arrowood owns few vineyards of his own but seems to have his pick of some of the best sites in the county. He particularly favors high-elevation vineyards. He makes the wines, or most of them, in a big, bold style, mirroring his approach at Chateau St. Jean. He likes a good deal of oak and barrel-fermentation for whites, though the Viognier is partially fermented in steel tanks. Reserves tend to be barrel selections that usually receive additional oak aging, which can be as long as 30 months for the most structured wines.

In 1992, Arrowood produced one of California's first Malbecs, from vines planted in 1986 in his own vineyard. It was a plump but pungent wine, with a good deal of personality. Today, the emphasis is on Cabernet Sauvignon and Merlot, and he has a long-standing interest in Syrah, which he first made in 1994, co-fermenting the wine with a little Viognier. There have been occasional late-harvest Rieslings and Viogniers. Sumptuous Special Select Late Harvest Rieslings were made from Alexander Valley fruit in 2000, 2001, 2004, and 2005.

It was, no doubt, Arrowood's consistency, as well as quality, that appealed to the Mondavis when they were in acquisition mode in 2000. The company paid $45 million for the brand, but Richard Arrowood stayed on as winemaker. In 2005, Mondavi sold the winery to a company called Legacy Estates; but soon after, Legacy filed for bankruptcy and Arrowood changed hands once again, this time landing in the lap of Jess Jackson and Jackson Family Wines. Jackson seems content to let Arrowood get on with what he does best.

Perhaps fretting under the constraints that come with corporate ownership, Arrowood has launched another personal label called Amapola Creek. For this venture, he buys centenarian Zinfandel from the great Monte Rosso vineyard on the Sonoma side of the Mayacamas Mountains and has his own vineyard, planted mostly with Cabernet Sauvignon, next door. Eventually, Rhône varieties will be added to the range. Initial releases in 2005—a total of 3,000 cases—were magnificent, though expensive.

FINEST WINES

Above: Richard Arrowood, who continues to innovate, despite changes in corporate ownership, and now has his own brand

(Tasted 2009–10)

Cabernet Sauvignon

2005 Sonoma County Sweet, intense, black-currant nose. Lush, powerful, and concentrated on the palate, but also sleek and textured, with splendid black cherry and black-currant fruit. Weighty but lacks a little vivacity, as does the 2004, which is in a similar style.

2005 Monte Rosso Forceful, oaky, black-currant nose, with more purity than the 2004. Rounded, tannic, and concentrated, this is a formidable style, with some heat on the finish. Nonetheless, there's power and grandeur here, with a less rugged vigor than in the previous vintage.

2004 Réserve Spéciale★ Lush, spicy fruitcake nose, showing a good deal of oak and mint; more exuberant than Monte Rosso. Full-bodied, dense, and deep, and certainly less austere than the mountain fruit from Monte Rosso. Spicy and complex, this should evolve well and has the greatest persistence of the trio.

Arrowood
Area under vine: 9 acres (3.5ha)
Average production: 250,000 bottles
14347 Sonoma Highway, Glen Ellen, CA 94542
Tel: (707) 938-5170
www.arrowoodvineyards.com

Dehlinger

Tom Dehlinger is a legendary name in Russian River Valley, but he keeps very much to himself. Attempts to visit the winery over almost two decades were always politely rebuffed. A chance encounter at a Pinot Noir seminar gave me the opportunity to pounce and request an appointment, which he readily agreed to, even though it was on a weekend. He explained that for many years he had done all the work at the property himself—viticulture, as well as winemaking—so he never had much time to receive visitors. I suspect old-fashioned shyness has as much to do with it. In person, Tom Dehlinger is precise, courteous, quietly opinionated, yet not very forthcoming. Clearly, he is happier in the vineyard or winery than in the company of writers and other intrusive visitors.

The property near Sebastopol, some 13 miles (21km) from the Pacific, was bought in 1973 by Tom's father, Dr. Klaus Dehlinger, a radiologist from UC Berkeley. There were no vines on the land, which was devoted, like much of the valley at that time, to growing apples. After studying at UC Davis, Tom Dehlinger planted grapes and made his first vintage in 1975, though the fruit was mostly Cabernet Sauvignon bought from Alexander Valley and elsewhere. The estate vineyard came on-stream only in 1978, and five years later Tom Dehlinger was able to stop buying fruit.

The original varieties planted were Cabernet Sauvignon, Chardonnay, and Pinot Noir. Merlot and Cabernet Franc were added subsequently and then pulled out, because Tom Dehlinger felt they had been planted in the wrong spot. It has to be remembered that this part of the Russian River Valley is cool and not ideally suited to Bordeaux varieties, though one of Dehlinger's achievements has been to show that it is indeed possible to make good Cabernet Sauvignon, as well as Pinot Noir.

The vines are planted on AxR-1 rootstocks, so there are some concerns that phylloxera could put in an unwelcome appearance. For that reason Dehlinger is installing some drip irrigation, which can deter the louse, even though almost the entire vineyard has been dry-farmed until now. Various trellising systems are employed, including lyre to split the canopy and reduce the vigor of the rootstock. No fertilizers are used, but the property is not fully organic. Dehlinger says, "My goal is simple: to farm for flavor." He is also happy to have contrasting varieties in the vineyard, since some vintages favor Cabernet and others favor Pinot Noir. And because they ripen at different times, there is no competition for space in fermentation vats.

In the 1990s Dehlinger offered about five Pinot Noir bottlings, but in recent years the range has been trimmed down to just two wines: Estate, the top wine; and Goldridge. Dehlinger used to make his Pinots in large barrels of about 500 liters, partially for economic reasons. But in recent years he has reverted to standard barriques. The wine is aged for about 20 months and racked only once, before bottling. Puncheons are retained, however, for aging the Syrah, which he first planted in 1989.

Fermentation of the Chardonnay in puncheons was also abandoned because the temperature sometimes rose too high for comfort. Fermentation takes place with whole clusters, with more native yeasts than in the past, and at least 60 percent of the wine goes through malolactic fermentation. About 40 percent new oak is used, though the natural acidity of the wine means that the oak is rarely discernible as such.

It always amazes those who taste them for the first time that the Cabernets are as good as they are. Dehlinger admits that only certain blocks are suitable for growing the variety and that blocks at a lower elevation would give unacceptably herbaceous wines. It's the fairly regular Indian summers that the valley often enjoys that make a good Cabernet vintage possible, and on really hot days he will use overhead sprinklers to refresh the bunches and deter raisining.

Above: The attractive family property near Sebastopol, where Tom Dehlinger and his two daughters "farm for flavor"

Tom Dehlinger is nothing if not meticulous. He has closely mapped his vineyards so that he can give the most careful consideration to what to plant and how to farm. There is an almost Germanic precision to his wines, giving one the feeling that nothing other than nature itself is left to chance. In 2008, his two daughters joined the family business, which, he admits, will permit him to become slightly less of a recluse.

FINEST WINES

(Tasted 2009)

2006

The Estate Pinot Noir is the wine Dehlinger is best known for. The nose is rich and heady, with ripe cherry and raspberry fruit, but nothing here is overblown. Medium-bodied in weight, it is nonetheless concentrated and has a light tannic grip; fleshy and opulent, it carries the 14.9% alcohol well, and the finish is restrained, elegant, precise, and long. The Syrah has ripe, sunny plum aromas that leap from the glass, with no savory or meaty tones. Only medium-bodied, it has a light chocolaty tone, but with fine, balancing acidity and a long, fresh finish. The Cabernet Sauvignon has remarkable aromatic purity, with lifted black-currant aromas. No blockbuster, it's graceful and bright, though there is no lack of tannin and structure; it's elegant and persistent and shows no greenness. The Estate Chardonnay has a fragrant appley nose that has great charm. It's fresh on the palate, concentrated, and tight, with fine acidity and a tangy mineral core. This is not a fruit-forward style, but it's dry, assertive, and remarkably long.

Dehlinger
Area under vine: 45 acres (18ha)
Average production: 80,000 bottles
4101 Vine Hill Road, Sebastopol, CA 95472
Tel: (707) 823-2378
www.dehlingerwinery.com

Iron Horse

There were vineyards on this spot in Green Valley in the 1870s, and they took their name from the railroad that hauled logs to and from Forestville. Vineyards were replanted in 1971 by a grower named Forrest Tancer on behalf of the Rodney Strong winery. However, Strong ran into financial difficulties and sold the property in 1976 to Barry and Audrey Sterling. They found the vines in poor shape: disease was rampant, and there was no frost protection—a grave drawback in an area as cool and marginal as Green Valley. In 1979, Forrest Tancer went into partnership with Barry Sterling, and they agreed that the site would be ideal for high-quality sparkling wine. The partnership was more than a business arrangement, and a decade later Tancer married Sterling's daughter Joy, a former television journalist. The marriage did not last, but Joy is still at Iron Horse and has been running the company since 2006.

Forrest Tancer had his own vineyards in Alexander Valley, called the T Bar T Ranch, and he pooled these resources with Iron Horse. The 60-acre (24ha) ranch grew Cabernet Sauvignon and Merlot, as well as Sauvignon Blanc, for which the winery developed a good reputation in the 1980s. He grew Sangiovese there, too, but this proved less successful. Tancer also made Pinot Noir and Chardonnay at Iron Horse.

The structure of the winery changed radically in 2002, when Forrest Tancer sold his vineyards to Kathryn Hall. Iron Horse had a lease on the vineyards until 2006 but no longer contracts for the fruit. At about the same time, Joy's brother Laurence took over the management of the estate. David Munksgard had been taken on as winemaker in 1996, so Tancer's departure had little effect on continuity. However, Laurence Sterling and Munksgard had ideas of their own, which they swiftly implemented.

Iron Horse is still an important producer of sparkling wine, though there are no vineyards specifically dedicated to the style. Sterling says it is the vineyard that determines the style of the wine in each vintage. He recalls certain rows of Pinot Noir vines in which one side was used to produce still red wine, while the other, with presumably less sun exposure, was used for sparkling wine. All the grapes for sparkling wine are estate-grown so as to give the wines a family identity, and the wines are all vintage-dated.

The sparkling wines do not go through malolactic fermentation and are machine-riddled, though the rosé, which tends to have a higher solids content, is sometimes riddled by hand. The *dosage* is about 10 grams per liter. Ideally, the character the Sterlings are looking for is a marriage of forward fruit and good acidity, with complexity obtained by prolonged aging on the lees, generally four to five years.

The Brut is dominated by Pinot Noir, and there is also a Brut Rosé. The Blanc de Blancs is disgorged to order, and there is a Blanc de Noirs called Wedding Cuvée. The Ultra Brut has a *dosage* of only 6 grams, and at the other end of the range is a Russian Cuvée with about 20 grams. Brut LD (late disgorged) spends almost six years on the yeast. A recent addition is Joy, which is aged for 10–15 years and bottled only in magnums. All the wines are intended to be drinkable on release.

As for still wines, now that there is no longer any access to Alexander Valley fruit, the emphasis is entirely on Chardonnay and Pinot Noir. Laurence Sterling has mapped the vineyards with great precision so as to learn how the sites vary. In such a cool region, ripening can vary dramatically, and the goal of the farming here is to try to ensure as much even ripening as possible. The mapping also allows him to determine how much irrigation each block requires, because vines on these sandy loam soils could struggle to ripen if dry-farmed.

The determining factor in the different cuvées of the Chardonnay and Pinot Noir is clonal selection. The rather complicated range of Pinots established by Tancer has been swept away in favor of two wines: the Estate Pinot from a mix of Martini and Pommard clones; and the Q Pinot, which is made solely from the Pommard clone.

The same is true of the Chardonnays, which are made from UC Davis clones and from smaller-berried heritage clones such as Old Wente and Rued. The winemaking is simple enough, with whole-cluster pressing and barrel-fermentation. The lees are stirred, but rather surprisingly, given the cool climate here, there is no malolactic fermentation. Munksgard fears that, by using malolactic fermentation, the differences between individual wines would be obscured. The bottlings, other than an unoaked version and the regular estate wine, are based on clonal origin: the Heritage Clone Chardonnay is from the Stony Hill selection; there is also a Rued clone bottling and a Corral Vineyard Old Wente bottling, which is aged in new French oak.

Iron Horse's identity is clearer and more transparent now that it has abandoned excursions into the Bordeaux varieties. The wines are not crowd-pleasers, but they are beautifully crafted and can be very elegant. The sparkling wines that are the house specialty are among California's finest.

FINEST WINES

(Tasted 2007–10)

Sparkling wines

The Blanc de Blancs is impeccable: lean, crisp, and melony, but with sufficient weight to give a long, tangy finish. It has much more precision than the Brut, which is made in a broader style, no doubt reflecting the 70 percent of Pinot Noir in the blend; nor does it have the length of the Blanc de Blancs. The Ultra Brut is finely tuned, too, and despite a hint of earthiness on the nose, it has a long, tangy finish. The Wedding Cuvée is lush and plump—a fruit-forward style that is more of a crowd-pleaser than the more austere Blanc de Blancs.

2007 Chardonnays

The Unoaked Chardonnay has delicate lime aromas, while the palate is supple and juicy, with fine acidity. All it lacks is complexity. The Estate has more complex aromas, with orange peel, as well as lime, and is more lavish and creamy on the palate, while the oak is kept in check. It is long and well balanced. The Heritage Clone bottling has a firm, nutty nose, with ripe citrus aromas; it's creamy, concentrated, and shows a lot of zest and fine length. The Rued Clone is more opulent, with lychee aromas and a lusher palate (which is also discernible on the 2005), though pronounced acidity cuts the richness. The finest wine is the Corral Vineyard, with similar aromas to the Estate but more body and intensity and exceptional length.

Pinot Noir

The 2005 Estate has a perfumed nose, with pure, refined red fruits; the palate is sleek and lively, with raspberry fruit and good, though not exceptional, length. The same aromatic charm is evident in the 2007 and 2008, which show a touch more weight and intensity. The 2006 Q is very different, with toasty cherry aromas and more richness on the palate, which shows darker fruit than the Estate wine and has splendid length.

Iron Horse Vineyards
Area under vine: 160 acres (65ha)
Average production: 250,000 bottles
9786 Ross Station Road, Sebastopol, CA 95472
Tel: (707) 887-1507
www.ironhorsevineyards.com

Kistler

In the mid-1970s, two young men who had met as students at Fresno University—Steve Kistler and Mark Bixler—teamed up to purchase a vineyard. This was the beginning of a partnership that would result in Steve Kistler becoming synonymous with fine California Chardonnay. Bixler has been the public face of the winery, insofar as it has one, as Kistler prefers to remain in the background, focusing on the winemaking. In over two decades of visiting California wineries, I had never met him and never even seen a photograph.

On my first visit to the Kistler property, in the early 1990s, I met up with Mark Bixler, who was affable enough as we tasted from barrel and bottle. On my return visit to research this book, I had an appointment with Bixler but was startled on arrival to be told that he had just left for San Francisco. The receptionist said she would try to contact him on his cell phone. As we were talking, a tall, studious, gray-haired man came into the reception area and looked through some papers, then vanished. I said I would wait outside in the sunshine.

Five minutes later, the receptionist ushered me back in. There had been a muddle, she explained, and my appointment was not with Bixler but with Kistler. I was gestured into an office, where the tall, studious, gray-haired man was seated. Whether there had been a genuine mix-up, or whether Kistler had made an anonymous and silent foray into the reception area to check me out before admitting me, I have no idea. It would not do to make a fuss. It felt like having an appointment with a cardinal at the Vatican, then finding oneself face to face with the pontiff—not an opportunity to be squandered.

It didn't take long to see why Kistler keeps to himself. He is exceedingly shy. Ask a question, and it takes him an age to complete his answer as he gropes for the right words. Nevertheless, with some perseverance I did manage to piece together the winery's story, and we then tasted a range of wines in the lab.

Bixler's first career had been as a college chemistry teacher, and Kistler, who already had a degree in English literature, had been one of his students. After Kistler graduated, he studied winemaking at UC Davis in the early 1970s, before working at Ridge from 1975. Bixler, meanwhile, worked for Fetzer in Mendocino, while continuing to teach. Kistler had been steeped in wine, as it were, from his youth, since his grandfather collected fine French wines. While at Ridge, he joined a tasting group to learn about Burgundian winemaking techniques, then little understood in California.

Bixler and Kistler had stayed in touch and began their search for a vineyard on the Sonoma side of the Mayacamas Mountains. In the late 1970s, they bought a former pig farm 1,650ft (500m) up in the mountains and began planting some 30 acres (12ha) with Chardonnay and Cabernet Sauvignon. Their first vintage, 1979, was produced from fruit bought from Warren Dutton and other growers. In the 1980s, they continued to use estate-grown grapes and fruit purchased from top vineyards. In 1992, they built a new winery in Sebastopol.

From the outset, Kistler had experimented: with picking at different sugar levels, trying varied stirring regimens, conducting yeast trials and clone evaluations, and altering the amount of solids left in the wine during barrel aging. Unlike many California winemakers, he was not primarily interested in fruit-driven wines but preferred to find the minerality derived from the soil, arguing that fruit itself was simply a transitory feature of any wine. His models were Burgundian: Coche-Dury, Lafon, Sauzet. He came to prefer heritage selections of Chardonnay to fashionable Dijon clones, which he found too floral and too productive.

By the 2000s, he was clear about the right way to make Chardonnay in California: whole-cluster pressing, native yeast fermentation, less stirring that had been common in the 1990s, full malolactic fermentation, moderate use of new oak (about

50 percent), and no fining or filtration. He applied the same analytical, empirical approach to Pinot Noir. Winemaking techniques needed to vary depending on the source of the fruit. Thus, grapes from vineyards close to the Pacific don't need cold-soaking or frequent punch-downs, whereas the reverse is true of much Russian River Valley fruit. There is no one-size-fits-all approach at Kistler. The Pinots are aged in about 50 percent new oak, without racking, fining, or filtration. Kistler did make Cabernet Sauvignon for some years, but it was often rather austere, and it was no surprise when he abandoned its production in 1993.

By 2008, fruit sources had changed as contracts came and went. The Kistler Vineyard that he and Bixler planted in 1979 is still in production, now 35 acres (14ha) of Chardonnay from Mount Eden cuttings. Near the winery is the Vine Hill Vineyard, bought in 1996 and planted in 1998 with Chardonnay. Other sources are Durell, in a foggy spot planted in southern Sonoma Valley with the Old Wente clone; Stone Flat near Durell; McCrea on the east side of Sonoma Mountain, old-clone Chardonnay farmed by Kistler since 1993; Dutton Ranch, with 35-year-old Chardonnay; Hirsch, high in the Sonoma Coast ridges; Silver Belt (Cuvée Natalie) from young vines east of Occidental; Hudson in Carneros, where Kistler always receives fruit from the E Block, planted with the Old Wente clone; and Hyde, also in Carneros. In 2008, he produced nine different Chardonnays.

The wines can be hard to find, despite the substantial production, since most of them are sold through the mailing list or end up on the wine lists of top restaurants. Do they live up to their exalted reputation? That is a difficult question. In the 1980s, I found the wines quite rich and powerful, impressive but not that different from other good California Chardonnays. In the early to mid-1990s, the wines had taken on another dimension; they had great concentration but often also had fine balancing acidity, as well as depth, spiciness, and glorious length. Then, in the late 1990s, the wines became broader and even showed some flabbiness. It was as though Kistler had reverted to the school of Chardonnay represented by Helen Turley: super-ripe, big, and buttery. Bizarrely, I almost always felt a preference for his Pinot Noirs: the 1995 Hirsch Vineyard was mesmerizing in its floral perfumes and concentration of flavor.

I have not, however, been able to follow the wines from vintage to vintage. My experiences of them are snapshots. As current releases confirm, they remain of high quality, whatever reservations one may have about some stylistic nuances.

FINEST WINES

2006 Chardonnay

Vine Hill Rich, voluptuous, toasty nose, with hazelnut and tropical-fruit aromas. Very ripe and silky on the palate, almost sweet, but does have grip on the mid-palate, moderate acidity, and length.

Hudson Discreet, nutty nose; reticent. Full-bodied and reasonably concentrated, with fine acidity and some phenolic grip and extract on the long finish.

Stone Flat Very ripe, oaky nose; quite mineral but also exhibiting tropical fruit such as pineapple. Creamy, with ample weight but also a mineral tang and a slight saltiness, though it lacks persistence.

2006 Pinot Noir

Kistler Vineyard Ripe and subtle nose of cherries, vanilla, and herbs. Suave and concentrated, juicy without being showy, abundant cherry and red-fruit flavors, and with firm tannins and fine acidity on the finish. Delicious and long.

Silver Belt Cuvée Natalie★ Lean, elegant, herbal nose, cherry fruit. Medium-bodied, bright, fresh, and lively, and though tannic, there is no harshness. A tight, invigorating style, with very good length.

Kistler Vineyards
Area under vine: 120 acres (48.5ha)
Average production: 300,000 bottles
4707 Vine Hill Road, Sebastopol, CA 95472
Tel: (707) 823-5603
www.kistlervineyards.com

Kosta Browne

Dan Kosta and Michael Browne met in 1992 at the John Ash restaurant in Santa Rosa, where they were both sommeliers. They had a shared urge to make wine but also had empty pockets in common. By 1997, however, they had saved enough to buy some grapes and made a barrel of wine that was mostly sold at the restaurant where they were working.

A year later, the pair found investors and began making wine in larger quantities, including 4,000 cases of Lake County Sauvignon Blanc that at least generated cash flow and allowed them to buy out their investors. They had their eyes on Pinot Noir, and their first attempt was in 2000. They managed to raise more money and were able to focus exclusively on Pinot Noir, primarily from the Russian River Valley. They rented a former apple warehouse and converted it into their winery.

Admirers of the wines enjoy the lush fruit, the kick of flavor, the immediate drinkability. They are as far, stylistically, as one can get from Burgundy—but this is Sonoma, not Volnay

Kosta and Browne have never owned vineyards but have worked closely with the growers they bought from. Dan Kosta handled the commercial side and promotional activities; Michael was the winemaker. Most of the wines are from single vineyards; the Russian River and Sonoma Coast bottlings are blends, but the team insists they also come from very good sites. Sonoma Coast is a vast AVA, but the fruit Michael Browne chooses comes mostly from the cool Petaluma Gap and Annapolis.

Browne is flexible in his winemaking so that the portion of whole clusters in the vats will vary, as will the use of native yeasts. The grapes are hand-sorted, given a cold soak, and fermented at fairly cool temperatures with punch-downs. The wines are aged for around 16 months in about 45 percent new French oak from up to 14 coopers. There is no racking.

The style has proved controversial. Kosta and Browne admit they like intense flavors in their wines and harvest when the grapes are fully ripe, which in practice means that they pick at between 25 and 27° Brix. The American wine press, in general, is besotted with these Pinots, though wine writers with a more European perspective have been critical of their super-ripeness and high alcohol levels. Although Michael Browne claims to prefer vintages such as 2007, when sugar and pH levels, and thus alcohol levels, were lower, these are nonetheless big wines, with alcohols, even in 2007, hovering around the 15% mark, though given the laxity of American labeling laws, possibly a little higher still.

Admirers of the wines enjoy the lush fruit, the kick of flavor, the immediate drinkability. They are as far, stylistically, as one can get from Burgundy—but this is, after all, Sonoma, not Volnay. However, the wines are, as it were, true to themselves and consistent in style. They find great favor with American consumers, and they can give abundant pleasure if you accept that weight of fruit means more to you than subtlety and finesse. The heaviest, ripest bottlings tend to win the greatest acclaim, but I have often preferred the blends, which seem less effortful and better balanced overall.

In 2009, Kosta Browne was bought for $40 million by a private-equity group. It's a remarkable price, given that the founders own neither vineyards nor a winery. The new owners have bought a brand and its stock. At present, Dan Kosta and Michael Browne are staying on, so the style and range of wines are unlikely to change much in the immediate future.

Above: Michael Browne, whose fashionable Pinot Noirs allowed him and partner Dan Kosta to fetch a high price for their brand

FINEST WINES

(Tasted 2009)

2007 Pinot Noir

Russian River Lean raspberry nose, quite elegant. Medium-bodied but quite tight, with perky acidity and a fresh, lively finish. Not profound, but well balanced.

Sonoma Coast★ Lean, tight, red-fruit nose, with brightness and vibrancy. Fresh attack, excellent balance, and doesn't lack concentration or grip. Fine acidity gives elegance and length. I prefer this to some single-vineyard bottlings.

Keefer Ranch From Green Valley. Rich cherry-and-cranberry nose. Suave and concentrated, this shows some spicy oak, and although one-dimensional at present, it is still youthful.

Amber Ridge From near Windsor. Smoky nose: cherries and tobacco. Full-bodied and concentrated, with firm tannins; very ripe and weighty, yet has a refreshing tang on the long finish.

Koplen From Olivet Lane within Russian River. Reserved nose of plums and cherries. Quite exotic for Pinot, fairly tannic and spicy; skeletal now, with good grip and concentration, but clearly youthful.

Kanzler From Petaluma Gap. Rich cherry nose, but a touch heady, though there are floral tones, too. Suave and concentrated, big and bold, super-ripe and rather extracted, with a long but Porty finish.

Rosella's From Santa Lucia Highlands, Monterey. Heady nose of plums and fruitcake. Bold and assertive but lacks varietal typicity; muscular and weighty, with a slight bitterness on the finish. This is too big for its own good.

Garys' From Santa Lucia Highlands. Lean, intense nose: raspberry and mint. Dense and tannic, rather burly and massive for Pinot, extracted, and fairly hot and tarry.

Kosta Browne
No vineyards
Average production: 130,000 bottles
PO Box 1555, Sebastopol, CA 95473
Tel: (707) 823-7430
www.kostabrowne.com

Littorai

There is surely no California winemaker more steeped in the mores and values of Burgundy than Ted Lemon. A modest, soft-spoken but eloquent man, he has forceful views on winemaking but seems to have no wish to impose them on others. He simply leads by example.

He studied enology at the University of Dijon, graduating in 1981. Thereafter, he worked at some of the leading properties in the Côte de Nuits, including Roumier and Dujac, before landing a job as winemaker at Domaine Roulot in Meursault. That made him the first American to be appointed as a full-time winemaker in the hallowed ground of Burgundy. In 1984, he left Roulot and returned to California, where he became involved in a slightly bizarre project. The Woltner family had been the majority shareholders in Château La Mission Haut-Brion until they sold it in 1983 to the Dillon family of Haut-Brion. Instead of embracing retirement, the Woltners bought a 19th-century winery high on Howell Mountain. Here, they specialized in Chardonnay and hired Lemon to make the wines. But the site was not that well suited to the variety, and the wines were generally overpriced. They got a mixed reception, and in 2000 the property was sold.

By then Lemon had moved on, and in the early to mid-1990s he acted as consultant to a wide range of estates in Napa and founded his own winery in 1993, using a small winery on Howell Mountain as his base. A new winery was built in 2008 on green principles, using solar power and other natural technologies. Gradually he has assembled a portfolio of vineyards, either by leasing specific blocks from existing vineyards or by planting on sites he had purchased. All vineyards that he either owns or leases are farmed biodynamically, and blocks he buys from are certified organic.

Most of the grapes come from the Sonoma Coast, but he also uses fruit from Anderson Valley: Roman, at 1,100ft (330m) in Navarro, is a leased Pinot Noir vineyard; Savoy Vineyard, in a warmer spot just north of Philo, was planted in 1991 with a range of Pinot Noir clones. On the Sonoma Coast, he leases blocks at Thieriot in the Occidental area and buys Pinot Noir from Hirsch in the coastal ridges. Mays Canyon is from the Porter Bass property and a source of both Chardonnay and Pinot Noir; it is located near Guerneville in Russian River Valley. An estate vineyard called The Haven is close to Jenner along the Pacific Coast and is planted with Pinot Noir (as well as tiny parcels of Sauvignon Blanc and Gewurztraminer, from which he makes Lemon's Folly). Also along the Sonoma Coast is the Heintz Vineyard, planted in 1983 with Wente clones of Chardonnay. Larger-volume blends are the Sonoma Coast Pinot Noir and Les Larmes Anderson Valley Pinot Noir.

The winemaking is both meticulous and minimalist. Lemon believes that clonal selection in the vineyard is of great importance; he also feels strongly that yields need to be kept low. Grapes are sorted carefully, with the Pinot Noir sorted again after destemming. The Chardonnay is whole-cluster pressed, and after overnight settling the must is fermented in barriques and 450-liter barrels, though 10 percent of the wine is aged in steel drums to retain freshness. No cultivated yeasts are used, either for primary or malolactic fermentation. The lees are rarely stirred, since Lemon isn't looking to produce fat wines. Nor is he in a rush for the malolactic fermentation to finish, and he's willing to let the wine move at its own pace. Use of new oak is also moderate, at around 30 percent for Chardonnay.

The Pinots are given a cold soak, which can be quite prolonged, then fermented in both open-top and closed vats, retaining a varying proportion of whole clusters, depending on the quality of the fruit. The length of maceration can also vary, for the same reason. Malolactic fermentation takes place in the barrels, and press wine is not usually included in the blend. The proportion of new oak used ranges from 30 to 50 percent. There is no filtration.

The trend toward prolonging hang-times in pursuit of maximum phenolic ripeness is anathema to Lemon. When he shares a vineyard with other winemakers, he notices that he is often among the first to pick, because he wants to retain freshness in the wines, as well as moderate alcohol. Finesse and balance are the priorities. Lemon argues that the last thing he wants is to pick raisined fruit: "One raisin tastes much the same as any other raisin, and using raisined berries simply obliterates the terroir I am trying to highlight in the first place."

Littorai has a strong following, and most of the wine is sold to restaurants and private customers through the mailing list. Quantities, after all, are modest. Lemon is confident of his tastes and abilities, and of the tastes of his customers, so he doesn't bother much with the tasting circuit or with large press tastings.

More than one winemaker has told me that he considers Lemon to be the finest exponent of Pinot Noir in California. Despite his Burgundian experience, Littorai is no slavish attempt to replicate Puligny and Vosne in coastal California. Nonetheless, I suspect that in a blind tasting it would be easy to confuse some Littorai wines with good Burgundy, simply because their intensity, finesse, and minerality are no different from the qualities that many top Burgundian winemakers are striving for.

FINEST WINES

(Tasted 2009–10)

Chardonnay

2008 Thieriot★ Ripe, heady, apricot nose, with well-integrated oak. Tight, fresh, and concentrated, with apple and apricot flavors, elegant oak, and excellent balance and length. More expressive than the fine but understated 2004.

2008 Heintz Discreet, citric nose. Concentrated and textured, with fine oak and more texture than the Thieriot but a similar fruit profile, fine acidity, and a long, sweet finish.

2006 The Gift A one-off, probably, being a botrytized wine with just 7% alcohol and 45° Brix of residual sugar. Thickly honeyed nose, and viscous, full-bodied, and creamy on the palate, with ripe citrus flavors, fine acidity, and a long, luscious finish.

Pinot Noir

2007 The Haven Flesh, opulent, cherry and raspberry nose. Medium-bodied, but blends the sweetness of cherry fruit with marked acidity; concentrated but expansive, and still youthful.

2007 Thieriot Subdued cherry aromas, rather closed. But the attack is sharp and lean, with distinct tannins balanced by sweet fruit on the palate. Refreshing acidity and admirable length.

2006 Mays Canyon★ Lean, reticent, minty nose. Medium-bodied but quite tannic and tight, with a slight tone of bonbons balanced by fine acidity that gives a long, racy finish.

2004 Hirsch Delicate and very stylish raspberry nose. Silky, pure, and fresh, with the weight and substance so often found in Hirsch, but with lift and acidity (and surprisingly gentle tannins) on the finish.

Littorai
Area under vine: 12 acres (5ha)
Average production: 36,000 bottles
788 Gold Ridge Road, Sebastopol, CA 95472
Tel: (707) 823-9586
www.littorai.com

Peter Michael Winery

Sir Peter Michael is a British tycoon who created an electronics business and sold it for a great deal of money in 1989, by which time he was already deeply involved in his Knights Valley wine estate. During the 1970s, he had lived in California and often visited the wine country. For his own estate he sought land with vineyard potential, a house, and enough room to build a winery. Five years went by before he found what he wanted in Knights Valley in 1981. There were no wineries in the valley, but soil analyses confirmed that the volcanic soils should produce outstanding wine, because they were rocky and well drained, with a high mineral content.

Over the years, the Peter Michael team planted at altitudes of up to 2,000ft (600m), where ripening could occur four weeks later than on the hot valley floor. While waiting for the vineyards to mature, and even after, the estate purchased grapes from other sources. The estate is now farmed biodynamically.

The first vintage was 1987 and the inaugural winemaker the now-much-lauded Helen Turley. But there were personality clashes, and in 1991 she was replaced by Mark Aubert, who stayed until 1999, when he left to establish his own winery. Vanessa Wong stepped in for two years, and then in 2001, Luc Morlet, who had been the winemaker at Newton, took over, to be succeeded in 2005 by his brother Nicolas. Despite the many changes in winemaker, the overall style of the Peter Michael wines has remained consistent.

The winemaking is essentially non-interventionist, with only indigenous yeasts used since 2001. Since 2002, the grapes have been sorted at the winery. Chardonnay and Pinot Noir spend up to 14 months in oak; Les Pavots and Point Blanc, from Bordeaux varieties, up to 22 months in about 50 percent new oak. With the sole exception of the Sauvignon Blanc, no wine is filtered, even if this means a discernible level of turbidity in some of the Chardonnays.

The vineyard sources have become quite complex. In addition to the plantings in Knights Valley, there is a vineyard in Alexander Valley, and a further 30 acres (12ha) along the Sonoma Coast. Some grapes are also bought from Monterey. In late 2009, the winery acquired the 26-acre (10.5ha) Showket Vineyard in Oakville, with a view to making a second Bordeaux blend. The result is a long list of wines, of which the principal are:

Après-Midi Sauvignon Blanc, originally sourced from Howell Mountain, but now estate-grown. About a third of the grapes are the Musqué clone. Little new oak is used.

Coeur à Coeur An equal blend of Sauvignon Blanc and Semillon, estate-grown and barrique-fermented in 20 percent new oak.

Mon Plaisir A Chardonnay from Alexander Valley grapes planted at over 1,400ft (430m). Aged for 12 months in heavily toasted barrels.

Belle Côte An estate Chardonnay from heritage-clone vines planted in 1990 at 1,850ft (560m).

Ma Belle-Fille Chardonnay from heritage-clone vines planted in 1999 at over 1,800ft (550m).

Clos du Ciel Chardonnay sourced from Howell Mountain at 1,700ft (520m). Barrel-fermented and aged in 50 percent new oak.

La Carrière Estate-grown Chardonnay from a vertically planted steep vineyard of 5 acres (2ha) with a majority of Dijon clones.

Cuvée Indigène A barrel-selection Chardonnay from wines made from Alexander Valley Mountain Vineyard fruit. Aged 16 months in oak.

Point Rouge The winery's top Chardonnay, a barrel selection aged in 100 percent new oak.

Le Caprice A Pinot Noir from the Sonoma Coast, planted in 2003 and first made in 2006.

Le Moulin Rouge A Pinot Noir made with fruit bought from Pisoni Vineyard in Monterey's Santa Lucia Highlands.

Les Pavots Originally a pure Cabernet Sauvignon, but since 1992 a Bordeaux blend, from Cabernet

Sauvignon, Merlot, and Cabernet Franc, made from vines planted at 1,100–1,400ft (340–430m), using cuttings from some of Napa's top vineyards.

L'Esprit des Pavots A Bordeaux blend from another sector of the vineyard that produces Les Pavots. Merlot accounts for 20 percent of the blend, the two Cabernets 40 percent each. Aged in new oak. The first vintage was 2001.

Point Blanc The winery's top red, from 45 percent Merlot, 38 percent Cabernet Franc, and 17 percent Cabernet Sauvignon. Aged in new oak and given two years' bottle age before release.

Despite having been exposed to the Peter Michael wines for more than ten years, I find these names utterly confusing. It seems perverse to call a Chardonnay Point Rouge and a Bordeaux blend Point Blanc. The profusion of French names suggests that the wines aim for a more European style, or perhaps a dash of European pretension, especially since the proprietor is a collector of top wines from Bordeaux and Burgundy. However, few wines are more intrinsically Californian in their boldness than those from Peter Michael. Sometimes all that power comes into focus, and the wine is a triumph of concentration and drive; at other times, the wines seem merely clumsy and overblown.

They earn their place in this book on the back of acclaim from American wine critics, who find in them all the qualities that I find lacking. Nicolas Morlet finds an elegance in his wines that eludes me, and he, and many critics, point to a minerality that, again, I simply can't discern. The red wines often have alarmingly high pHs, well over 4.0, which, although not uncommon in California, are often taken as a warning sign that the wines are unlikely to age. Morlet also disputes this.

No expense has been spared by Sir Peter. Planting costs on the steep slopes of his estate are exceedingly high, and yields can be very low. This, presumably, is the justification for the very high prices he demands for most of his wines.

FINEST WINES

(Tasted 2008–09)

Chardonnay

2006 Belle Côte Ripe, spicy nose, very oaky yet poised. Creamy and full-bodied, with moderate acidity and surprising delicacy. Quite good length.

2006 La Carrière Lively, spicy, citric nose. Creamy, super-ripe, and succulent; fleshy and concentrated, but almost sweet. Quite good length.

2007 Mon Plaisir Voluptuous apricot nose, with integrated oak. Lush, rounded, and heavy, with some mineral bite, but also some heat on the finish, which is soft and lacking in zest.

2007 Ma Belle-Fille Luxurious, oaky nose: apple compote. Soft, creamy, and concentrated, enlivened by toastiness more than acidity. Moderate length.

2007 Point Rouge★ Very ripe, toasty nose: grilled nuts, apples, and stone fruits. Extremely lush and concentrated, imposing and spicy, with a powerful finish and a welcome tightness of structure.

Les Pavots

2006 Very rich plum-and-chocolate nose. Dense, tannic, and chocolaty, with grip and structure; a burly style rather low in acidity, yet the 15.5% alcohol is not really noticeable. Quite long.

2005 Massive, black-fruit nose, black pepper and licorice. Very rich, yet soft and plump, concentrated and chocolaty, with a fairly blunt finish that lacks lift and persistence.

Other wines

2007 Le Caprice Pinot Noir Voluptuous cherry-and-raspberry nose. Medium-bodied but very concentrated, dense, and tannic. Shows little complexity but has some acidity on the finish.

2007 Le Moulin Rouge Pinot Noir Perfumed and dramatic nose, with sumptuous cherry and raspberry fruit. Very concentrated, juicy, and mouth-filling. An imposing wine, with individuality; very Californian; quite long and warm.

2006 Coeur à Coeur Big, waxy, melony nose. Rich, soft, and velvety, luxuriously textured, and has spice to balance the weight but is warm on the finish.

Peter Michael Winery
Area under vine: 150 acres (60ha)
Average production: 180,000 bottles
12400 Ida Clayton Road, Calistoga, CA 94515
Tel: (707) 942-3200
www.petermichaelwinery.com

Ramey Wine Cellars

David Ramey has had a long, diverse, and very distinguished career as a California winemaker. At the Matanzas Creek and Chalk Hill wineries in Sonoma, he produced Chardonnays of remarkable complexity; and at Dominus in the early 1990s (after an earlier spell at Pétrus in 1979), he was responsible for such excellent vintages as 1991 and 1994. Then, in 1998, he was hired by Leslie Rudd as the winemaker for the new Rudd winery. Rudd was rich, ambitious, and very keen on wine, so Ramey should have had carte blanche. But by 2001 he had departed to develop his own label, which he had founded in 1996. At first, he worked out of rented premises, but he subsequently built his own winery in Healdsburg. He owns no vineyards (yet) but sources grapes from well-known sites in Sonoma and Napa.

Ramey is meticulous and precise. One always has the impression that he knows exactly what he is looking for and exactly how to achieve it. As a Chardonnay specialist, he is clearly not enamored of some of the bigger, lusher styles that find favor with most American critics, though he is not trying to create Burgundy lookalikes. When I once remarked on the generous (though not excessive) alcohols of some of his Chardonnays, he was quick to reply: "Don't you think the Burgundians would be ecstatic to have the kind of ripeness levels that come easily in California?" He was not about to apologize for California's benign climate.

He makes no fewer than six Chardonnays. Three are regional blends: from Sonoma Coast, Russian River Valley, and Carneros. Although they differ in their geographical origins, they are all made from the standard California Clone 4 of Chardonnay, which can give good results, provided that yields are moderate. He much prefers the Old Wente clone, which, he finds, has no ungainly tropical-fruit tones and can better withstand aging in new oak. The three single-vineyard Chardonnays are cropped at lower yields and come from three outstanding sites: Hyde and Hudson in Carneros, and Ritchie in Russian River Valley. Both Hyde and Hudson come from blocks planted with the Old Wente clone.

All the Chardonnays are made in a similar way: whole-cluster pressing, fermentation with natural yeasts, no inoculation for malolactic fermentation (which is completed), and aging in oak with stirring but no racking or filtration. The regional blends are aged for around 12 months in 25–40 percent new oak; the vineyard-designated wines spend 20 months in 70 percent new oak.

Some years ago, Ramey invited me to compare barrel samples of the 1999 Hyde and Hudson Chardonnays. Both were excellent, but I preferred the more elegant Hyde to the more muscular Hudson. My response amused Ramey, who said it was typical of most British tasters, whereas American critics tended to prefer the Hudson.

While at Rudd, Ramey bought Cabernet from a Calistoga vineyard called Jericho Canyon. He made a 2001 wine from the vineyard under his own label, but by 2006 the vineyard had set up its own winery, so that source was closed to him. Instead, he buys red grapes from the J Davies blocks at Schramsberg and blends them with other grapes to create a proprietary blend called Annum. There is also a Napa blend and an Oakville Cabernet from the Pedregal Vineyard. These top reds have no press wine in the blend, whereas the second wine, known simply as Claret, does. There are also two Sonoma Mountain Syrahs, from Rodgers Creek and Shanel Vineyard; both contain 5 percent Viognier.

Ramey, though no braggart, doesn't lack self-confidence. It shows in the wines, especially the Chardonnays, which are invariably balanced and satisfying. Having followed the wines since the very first releases, I don't recall any duds or any wines marred by excesses of one kind or another. They show restraint while remaining unmistakably Californian.

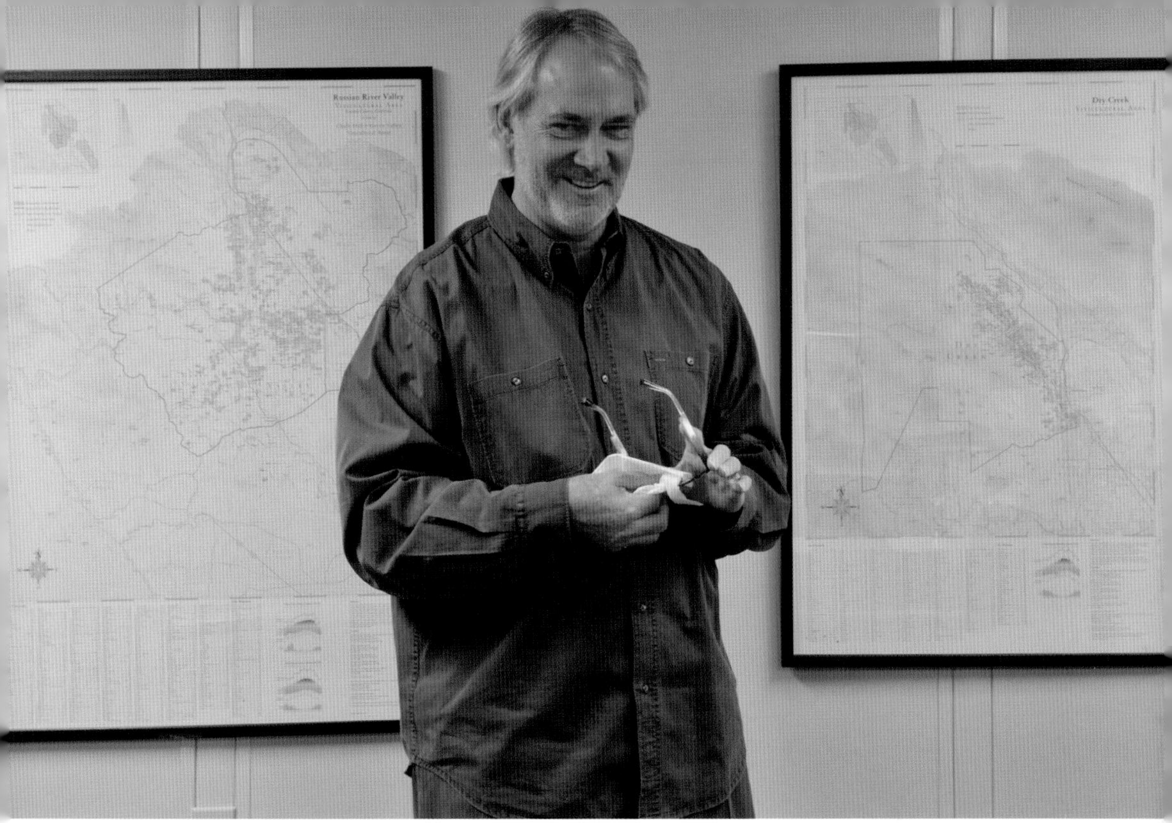

Above: David Ramey, the brilliantly consistent, experienced winemaker best known for restrained but stylish Chardonnays

FINEST WINES

(Tasted 2009)

Chardonnay

2007 Russian River Valley [V] Lean, stylish, smoky nose, with apple and apricot aromas. Rich and juicy on the palate but sustained by a fine thread of acidity. Broad and concentrated, yet also has lift and persistence. (This is, to me, the best of the regional blends; the Carneros is my least favorite.)

2006 Ritchie Discreet, toasty appley nose. Rich and concentrated on the palate; lush without being heavy; still tight and shows plenty of spice and toastiness on the long finish.

2006 Hyde★ Subdued, toasty, stone-fruit nose. Supple and concentrated, with ample minerality and bite; quite oaky, but has charm and balance and excellent acidity on the finish. Impeccable.

2006 Hudson Bold, burly, toasty nose, with appley fruit. Broad and creamy, the most opulent of this trio has depth and some power. It may lack a little elegance but has a long, oaky finish.

2001 Hyde Heady, oaky nose, a touch oily, with apricot aromas. Full-bodied and weighty, very concentrated, but no flab; long, and with a spicy finish. Still going strong.

2000 Russian River Valley Dried-apricot nose. Plump, lush, and a bit heavy. Beginning to tire.

Red

2006 Larkmead Cabernet Sauvignon Sweet, spicy nose, with some mint and black-currant aromas. Medium-bodied and fresh, yet concentrated and spicy; still tight, with fine acidity and finesse. Good length on the finish.

2006 Annum Opulent, spicy black-cherry nose. Very rich and plump on the palate, with black-fruit flavors; lightly savory, with forthright tannins and a chewy finish.

2006 Pedregal Sweet, refined black-currant nose. Lean and stylish, with considerable sweetness of fruit behind the grip. Poised and long.

2006 Rodgers Creek Syrah Very ripe, toasty nose, sweet and intense. Rich and very concentrated, but exuberant and lively, tannic and robust, with a long, *sauvage* finish.

Ramey Wine Cellars
No vineyards
Average production: 420,000 bottles
25 Healdsburg Avenue, Healdsburg, CA 95448
Tel: (707) 433-0870
www.rameywine.com

St. Francis

St. Francis was founded in the early 1970s as a commercial vineyard by furniture-store tycoon Joseph Martin. The property lies on the eastern side of the Sonoma Valley floor, and a winery was built only in 1979. Since 1983, the winemaker has been Tom Mackey, who established St. Francis's reputation for excellent Merlot. A new winery in landscaped grounds was built in 1999, allowing Mackey to vinify many more small lots than in the past. He also established a separate winemaking team to handle small-lot bottlings and the Reserves. Although Joseph Martin retains a share of the property, the major shareholder for some years has been the Kobrand company.

The winery strikes exactly the right balance between sound and balanced varietal wines and a collection of more concentrated and individual bottlings

Over the years, the vineyard holdings have been expanded to 600 acres (240ha), and there are also 45 vineyards from which they regularly buy fruit on a contract basis, with Mackey's team keeping a careful eye on their viticultural practices.

This is a large-scale operation, and winemaking programs play it fairly safe. Cultivated yeasts are routinely used, and large rotary fermenters are used for their larger bottlings, which also tend to be aged in a substantial proportion of American oak. Though the wines are often quite muscular, favoring rich fruit and fairly high alcohol, Mackey is careful not to let them become overblown, and he dislikes practices such as watering the musts in order to reduce alcohol. He would rather pick at a more moderate Brix level that obviates the need to tamper with the wine during production.

Both Merlot and Cabernet Sauvignon remain among the strengths at St. Francis. Both are made in regular and single-vineyard bottlings, the latter aged for about two years in oak, of which a growing proportion is French. The King's Ridge Cabernet Sauvignon comes from one of the few sites in the Sonoma Coast ridge tops warm enough to ripen that variety. From the Behler Vineyard, with its rich gravel soils, comes the Behler Merlot. There used to be Reserve bottlings, but Mackey felt the term had become tired and meaningless, so in its place he created the Wild Oak range, which is a selection of the best parcels and barrels.

Although other Sonoma properties are better known for Zinfandel than St. Francis, the winery sometimes releases as many as eight different bottlings in a year. The Old Vines Zinfandel is a blend from 22 dry-farmed vineyards, with vines from 60 to 100 years old. The top Zinfandel is usually a powerful bottling from the Pagani Vineyard, whose vines are well over a century old.

St. Francis offers wines of good value, and its large but relatively tranquil tasting room draws many visitors. The winery, it seems to me, strikes exactly the right balance between sound and balanced varietal wines and a collection of more concentrated and individual bottlings that nonetheless offer quite a good value.

FINEST WINES

(Tasted 2009–10)

2007 Old Vines Zinfandel [V]
Very ripe cherry nose, yet light and fresh. Although medium-bodied, this gains weight on the mid-palate, leading to a long, spicy, and quite powerful finish, with just a touch of heat (15.5% ABV).

2006 Bacchi Vineyard Russian River Zinfandel
(Vines from 1910) Sweet, spicy, herbal nose, thyme and eucalyptus. Supple and concentrated, yet has firm tannins; surprisingly elegant—and no sign of the high alcohol (16.1%) on the finish.

2005 Sonoma County Cabernet Sauvignon
Rich, dense, black-fruit nose, plus licorice and some savory tones. Full-bodied, with firm tannins;

a serious wine, with structure, given the 70,000 cases produced. Just lacks a little intensity and length on the finish.

2005 Wild Oak Cabernet Sauvignon
Bright black-currant-and-cherry nose. Medium-bodied and lively, quite tannic but not harsh, concentrated and sustained by quite good acidity, which gives it persistence.

2005 Wild Oak Zinfandel
Opulent, savory, oaky nose. Sumptuous and full-bodied, concentrated and spicy, with a delicious minty finish and no hint of rusticity. Long.

2004 Cuvée Lago
(70% CS, 30% Syrah) Super-ripe cherry nose, yet some brightness. Plump and very ripe, with supple tannins; a crowd-pleasing style, with some spice and vigor, but it lacks a little intensity and grip.

Above: Tom Mackey, winemaker at St. Francis since 1983, who oversees the broad range of Merlot, Cabernet, and Zinfandel

2006 Pagani Vineyard Zinfandel★
Intense berry fruit on the nose, which is pure and minty. Very concentrated and tannic, dense and powerful, yet suave in texture and full of character. Long, peppery finish.

St. Francis Winery & Vineyards
Area under vine: 600 acres (240ha)
Average production: 2.5 million bottles
500 Pythian Road, Santa Rosa, CA 95409
Tel: (707) 933-2332
www.stfranciswine.com

Stonestreet

On the slopes above Alexander Valley is a substantial vineyard known as the Alexander Mountain estate. It used to be known as the Gauer Ranch, when a clothing retailer called Edward Gauer bought a ranch here in 1968, rearing cattle and horses. Then, in 1971, he began planting vines, and by the mid-1980s, 400 acres (160ha) were under cultivation. Wines made from the ranch were often of outstanding quality, but in 1989 Gauer sold most of the property. It seemed likely that much of the land would be used for residential developments, but in 1995 Jess Jackson bought the estate and saved its vineyards.

The founding of Stonestreet in 1989 pre-dated the purchase by Jackson, and although various Jackson brands used Alexander Mountain fruit for their wines, it was logical that Stonestreet should be the main winery to make the most of this fruit. The vineyards are varied, ranging in elevation from 400 to 2,400ft (120–730m). Although the soils inevitably vary, too, they are mostly rocky, with clay, loam, and gravel. The soil and microclimate tend to stress the vines, which is why Alexander Mountain fruit has little in common with grapes grown on the more fertile soils of the valley floor. The property has been expanded since the Jackson purchase, and today there are 900 acres (365ha) under vine, with much of the fruit still being sold to other wineries. The grapes planted are the five Bordeaux varieties and Chardonnay. The estate includes 4,000 acres (1,620ha) of unplanted land, deliberately retained to encourage a diversity of flora and fauna.

Former Stonestreet winemaker Steve Test used to have to negotiate with Kendall-Jackson's chief winemaker, Randy Ullom, about who would have access to specific blocks. Today, under South African winemaker Graham Weerts, it seems understood that Stonestreet gets much of the best fruit. Weerts is extremely impressed by the Alexander Mountain vineyard, pointing out that the elevation of the higher vineyards gives complex acidity and marveling at the differences made by the angle at which sunlight hits the bunches. In general, berries are very small, and crop levels rarely exceed 2.5 tons per acre.

The vineyards are divided into different blocks, some of which give their names to the special cuvées for which Stonestreet has become known, such as the Upper Barn Chardonnay and Black Cougar Ridge Cabernet Sauvignon. The Stonestreet wines are rich and broad, with impressive weight and concentration. There is nothing dainty about them. They may not be subtle, but they do convey the density of fruit that these mountain vineyards give from year to year.

The winemaking is fairly conventional, though the red grapes are sorted by machine rather than by hand. After a cold soak, there is a two-week maceration. The top reds are aged in French oak. Some years ago, there were problems with Brettanomyces, but this is no longer an issue.

There are no fewer than five Chardonnays, as well as an occasional late-harvest version. There's an opulent Merlot, aged in 40 percent new oak. Stonestreet offers four Cabernets and two Bordeaux blends. The winery was in a bit of a quandary after the film *Sideways* almost killed the market for Merlot, so a new blend called Fifth Ridge was devised, which was a surreptitious way of using up some of the Merlot, blending it with Cabernet Sauvignon. The top wine is Legacy, which has been produced since the end of the 1980s. Most of the grapes come from the Alexander Mountain estate, supplemented by batches from the valley floor. Cabernet Sauvignon always dominates, and the wine is aged almost entirely in new French oak.

Like other wineries aiming for high quality, Stonestreet has been steadily lowering production. The actual winery is vast—a great slab of a shed laid across a lower slope of the foothills—but much of it is used for custom crushing for other producers.

Above: Graham Weerts, Stonestreet's South African winemaker, who makes the most of his intense Alexander Mountain fruit

FINEST WINES

(Tasted 2007–10)

Cabernet Sauvignon

2005 Alexander Mountain Estate Vivid and intense minty nose. Full-bodied and spicy; packs a punch but has surprising vigor and minerality, too, though time is needed to resolve the tannins. Long.

2005 Christopher's★ Muted nose, savory and chocolaty. Suave and very concentrated, this is formidable yet has elegance and acidity, as well as power. Finishes tannic and long.

2003 Three Block Opulent nose of plums and chocolate. Rich, rounded, and bracingly earthy, with robust tannins, moderate acidity, and quite good length.

2001 Cougar Ridge Very rich black-currant nose. Spicy, very concentrated, and rugged, with powerful imposing tannins and a good deal of grip. Moderate acidity but good length.

2005 Cougar Ridge Ripe yet herbal and savory nose. Bold and assertive, very concentrated, with firm tannins and impressive weight and power. Good length and a chocolaty finish.

Other wines

2005 Alexander Valley Chardonnay Fresh citric nose, crisp and lively. Fresh, concentrated, and vigorous, with unusual zest for Alexander Valley and a long, lemony finish.

2004 Broken Road Chardonnay Sweet nose that's both buttery and delicate. Juicy and plump, with a good deal of toastiness, yet far from monolithic or overbearing. Quite long.

2006 Fifth Ridge Spicy, savory nose, with chocolate and licorice. Rich but blunt and rather chunky, lacking the persistence of the Cabernet-dominated wines.

2005 Legacy Dense, meaty, chocolaty nose, with black fruits. Sumptuous and very rich, and although massive, there's a transparency of structure. The tannins are huge and the finish chewy, so this is still in its infancy.

2003 Legacy Dense, plummy, oaky nose. Very rich and concentrated, dense and chewy, with some charred oak to give complexity. Good length.

Stonestreet Wines
Area under vine: 900 acres (365ha)
Average production: 200,000 bottles
7111 Highway 128, Healdsburg, CA 95448
Tel: (707) 433-9463
www.stonestreetwines.com

Sbragia Family Vineyards

Ed Sbragia was the legendary winemaker at Beringer in Napa Valley for almost three decades, celebrated for his opulent Private Reserve bottlings, which were generally fashioned on the same massive scale as Sbragia himself. All good things come to an end, and Sbragia is no longer involved full time at Beringer, though he stays on as the rather grandly titled winemaster emeritus.

But Sbragia did not feel ready for complete retirement and turned his gaze to the family property. His grandfather had come to California a century ago as an immigrant from Italy, bringing with him the traditions of his Tuscan home. His father owned Zinfandel vineyards near Healdsburg, and Ed grew up with wine on the dinner table each night. So it seemed natural for him to return to Dry Creek Valley, where he has inherited or developed five vineyards. He built a winery at the northern end of the valley, and most of his family is involved one way or another, especially his son Adam, who assists him as winemaker. In addition to using his own grapes, he has been using his contacts to buy fruit from other outstanding sites in Napa, as well as Sonoma. These include the great Monte Rosso Vineyard on the Sonoma side of the Mayacamas Mountains, Rancho del Oso and Cimarossa vineyards on Howell Mountain, Andolsen in Dry Creek Valley, and Wall Vineyard on Mount Veeder.

Sbragia has never been afraid of oak. At Beringer, some of his wines could be too burly for their own good; here at his own winery, the reds are big and fleshy but never overblown

The main estate vineyards are Italo's, with very old Zinfandel vines and some Petite Sirah; Gino's, planted in 1959, with Carignane and Petite Sirah, as well as Zinfandel; and La Promessa, planted with Zinfandel as recently as 1999. Sbragia has never been afraid of oak, and he uses entirely new oak on his Zinfandels. However, the wines are very well balanced. At Beringer, some of his wines, especially the Chardonnays, could be too burly for their own good; here at his own winery, the reds are big and fleshy but never overblown.

FINEST WINES

(Tasted 2009)

Cabernet Sauvignon

2005 Andolsen Bright, intense, black-currant nose, vibrant and pure. Suave and quite concentrated, with ripe tannins, as well as fruit, and with a long, spicy, slightly warm finish.

2005 Monte Rosso★ Rich, smoky, oaky nose, black fruits and coffee, a bit overwhelming. Rich and broad, but has a tight structure and a spicy finish.

2005 Cimarossa Dense, oaky nose: black-currant, rubber, and spice. Broad, rounded, and concentrated, this is tannic and chunky, with spice and vigor, yet lacks some complexity.

2005 Wall Super-ripe nose: new oak and coffee. Plump and full-bodied, sumptuous black fruits and chocolate, with a burst of tannin on the finish.

2004 Rancho del Oso Sweet, ripe nose, close to jammy. Broad, juicy, and concentrated, but balanced by vigor and powerful tannins. Long.

Zinfandel

2006 La Promessa Lean, spicy, red-fruit nose, with upfront fruit and some charred oak. Rounded, juicy, concentrated, and peppery; has vigor and persistence and a piquant finish, with a touch of raisins. Quite long.

2006 Italo's Intense, dusty, raspberry nose, the new oak well integrated. Medium-bodied, reasonably concentrated, lovely acidity; zesty and peppery but not raisiny. Quite long.

2006 Gino's Sweet red-fruit nose, some caramel tones. Supple and medium-bodied, yet with firm tannins and dried-fruit flavors; perked up by good acidity.

Sbragia Family Vineyards
Area under vine: 45 acres (18ha)
Average production: 140,000 bottles
9990 Dry Creek Road, Geyserville, CA 95441
Tel: (707) 473-2992
www.sbragia.com

Sonoma Coast Wineries

In the mid-1990s, the prestigious area in which to grow Pinot Noir in Sonoma County was along Westside Road in Russian River Valley. Vineyards such as Rochioli and Allen acquired immense prestige, and the vineyard-designated bottlings from Williams Selyem, Davis Bynum, and Gary Farrell won great acclaim—and with good reason.

Ten years later, however, the focus of attention had switched to a different part of the county: the high coastal ridges a few miles inland from the Pacific shore. It's a large area, stretching from Annapolis and Fort Ross in the north, to as far south as Freestone and Bodega. This was an area with a handful of vineyards and hardly any wineries.

Ross Cobb is making Pinot Noirs with 13% alcohol or less, to demonstrate that, despite the current mantra that California Pinot must have at least 14%, this need not be the case

Flowers was the only estate of note, and its pure, intense Pinots and Chardonnays were typical of the region. The much smaller Marcassin property of Helen Turley also enjoyed a strong reputation, though for a fuller, richer style of Chardonnay.

Properties have proliferated, both along the ridge tops and also slightly farther inland, in Green Valley and around Occidental and Forestville; what they all have in common is elevation and considerable maritime influence. It's not necessarily the case that the ridge tops are cooler than, say, the Westside Road area of Russian River Valley. But elevation and impoverished soils provide a terroir in which the grapes struggle to ripen and do so regularly only thanks to rigorous viticultural practices. The result is wines that generally have more angularity and edge than those from farther inland.

During the 2000s, larger wineries also began planting vineyards in the coastal areas: Joseph Phelps with its Freestone estate, Peter Michael, Kendall-Jackson, Pahlmeyer, Marimar Torres, and others. This coastal band is still an area with few wineries but many labels. Producers such as Kosta Browne, Hartford, Radio Coteau, DeLoach, and Siduri bottle vineyard-designated wines from this area, though the number of small-scale estate wineries is gradually rising.

Most are too small to require individual entries in this book, excellent though the wines are. Kosta Browne, Hartford, and Littorai are represented, but others are worthy of note. Hirsch Vineyard, long a source of outstanding fruit to Littorai, Kistler, and others, has been bottling part of its Pinot production for some years. Ehren Jordan, the winemaker at Turley in Napa, has a coastal ridge-top vineyard from which he produces his Failla wines: Chardonnay, Pinot Noir, and Syrah. Vanessa Wong, formerly winemaker at Peter Michael, and her husband Nick Peay, have planted Peay Vineyards in a foggy spot just 4 miles (6km) from the ocean and also specialize in Chardonnay, Pinot Noir, and Syrah.

A particularly fascinating experiment has been conducted by Ross Cobb from his own and other vineyards near Occidental, which are lower than the ridge tops but even closer to the ocean and more imbued with direct maritime influence. Cobb is currently making his Pinot Noirs with alcohol levels of 13% or even lower, to demonstrate that, despite the current mantra that California Pinot must have at least 14% if it is to be considered fully ripe, this need not be the case. His wines can have fragrance and intensity but also a hint of greenness that some American palates might find disconcerting. Other names to look out for include Freeman, WH Smith, Keller (farther south in the equally cool Petaluma Gap), and Porter Bass.

Sierra Foothills

Head east from the San Francisco Bay past Sacramento, and you climb into the Sierra Foothills, the prelude to the Sierra Nevada. In the 1850s, this was Gold Rush country, with prospectors crowding into the hills in search of gold and sudden wealth. Viticulture was a support industry, but an important one, and by 1860 there were 10,000 acres (4,000ha) of vineyards here—more than in Napa or Sonoma. Today, the region is popular with tourists, including those on their way to Reno and the Sierra ski resorts.

There is no doubting the potential of the region. The soils, with their substantial granite content, are well suited to grape growing. Elevations vary from 1,000 to 3,000ft (300–900m), which explains the diversity of grape varieties grown here on some 5,700 acres (2,300ha). It's a warm area, but cold air descends from the high Sierras at night and helps retain acidity in the grapes. However, by the 1970s, the area, better known for its orchards than its wines, had become moribund. Then some sharp-eyed producers noticed that the Foothills, and Amador County in particular, had a profusion of old-vine Zinfandel, including vines planted in the 1860s. They were recognized as a precious resource, but it became clear that many other grapes do well here, especially Syrah, Barbera, and, occasionally, Cabernet Sauvignon. Pockets of the old Mission grape (Criolla) and Muscats survive, so dessert and Port-style wines are also still produced.

The Foothills are a world away from the glitz of Napa and Sonoma. Growers and producers, mostly family businesses, seem to pride themselves on a certain rusticity, though one or two have invested in elaborate tasting rooms, and the Kautz winery offers visitors wine, gastronomy, and a gold museum. It is possible to taste big, flavory wines with personality, and simply awful wines that can be oxidized, overly tannic, or overly alcoholic—or a combination of all the above. Inconsistency at individual wineries is another problem.

In terms of consumer recognition, the Foothills are better known for their counties than for some of their AVAs. Thus, the major counties are Placer, Amador, El Dorado, and Calaveras, as well as Yuba. Of these, only El Dorado has an AVA; the other AVAs are subregions within counties. Amador is the most important region, celebrated for its Zinfandel, with its old vineyards clinging to life thanks to a dry climate that deters disease. Calaveras, farther south, is cooler and known for white wines as well as reds. The actual AVAs are:

El Dorado County (AVA from 1983) Scarcely any vines existed here until 1972, when the Boeger winery planted its vineyards. These are high sites, at up to 3,500ft (1,000m), giving wines with a less jammy character than many from Amador County. The Bordeaux varieties also do well here.

Fair Play (AVA from 2001) This subregion of El Dorado County has vineyards at 2,000–3,000ft (600–900m), 350 acres (140ha) under vine, and 11 wineries. Zinfandel is the most important variety.

Fiddletown (AVA from 1983) Slightly higher than Shenandoah Valley, this Amador subregion of 325 acres (130ha) gives marginally leaner and more stylish Zinfandels than its neighbor.

North Yuba (AVA from 1985) A single winery dominates this rocky little region: Renaissance, with vines planted at 1,700–2,300ft (500–700m).

Shenandoah Valley (AVA from 1987) An important area, with 2,000 acres (800ha) in production and about 25 wineries. It is best known for Zinfandel and is home to the region's oldest vineyard, the Grandpère near Plymouth. Sauvignon Blanc can do well, and Vino Noceto is renowned for Sangiovese.

Right: The rugged beauty of the Sierra Foothills is reflected in its best wines, many of which come from old-vine Zinfandel

Domaine de la Terre Rouge

Tall, white-haired, and self-assured, William Easton was a wine merchant near San Francisco who, at the same time, had developed a custom-crush business, producing wines for clients from 1985. He founded his own label in 1987 and in 1994 sold his retail business and moved to Shenandoah Valley, producing his first vintage at Terre Rouge in 1995. There are two labels: Terre Rouge, reserved for Rhône varieties, and Easton, for Zinfandel and other wines. Although he owns only 12 acres (5ha) of vines, he farms considerably more and has exclusive contracts with the vineyards from which he purchases fruit. He particularly favors high sites, with some vineyards at over 3,000ft (900m). Fruit is sourced from four different counties.

His Sauvignon Blanc comes principally from vineyards east of Auburn at 2,500ft (760m). Viognier is grown in Fiddletown on decomposed granite soils. Notoma is a barrel-fermented blend primarily of Sauvignon Blanc, with additions of Semillon and Viognier. Another white blend is Enigma, from Marsanne, Viognier, and Roussanne, grown at 3,000ft. This, too, is barrel-fermented and aged on the fine lees. His varietal Roussanne is made in the same way.

For Syrah and Zinfandel, Easton begins fermentation with indigenous yeasts but usually completes it with selected yeasts. The cap is punched down by hand. The wines are aged in Burgundian barrels, with little racking. Although some wines can show signs of reduction, Easton is untroubled, observing that he is making wines for the long term and some initial reduction is nothing to worry about. Indeed, he routinely gives his best wines considerable bottle age before release. Thus, in 2009, some of the wines offered were from the 2003 and 2004 vintages.

The Zinfandels are much more refined than the often-rustic norm of some of his neighbors in Amador County. He dislikes overripe fruit and high alcohol, and he ages the wines entirely in French oak. The basic Zinfandel is the Amador County, a blend from different sites. The Fiddletown Zinfandel comes from vines planted in the 1860s. There is also an Estate Zinfandel made from bush vines and aged for 18 months in one-third new oak. Overall, the Cabernets are less persuasive than the other serious wines from Easton.

The Terre Rouge range is complex. As well as the white wines already mentioned, there is a barrel-fermented Vin Gris d'Amador from equal measures of Grenache and Mourvèdre. Tête-à-Tête is a light Rhône-style blend that emphasizes primary fruit and is not intended to be aged. Noir Grande Année is a Châteauneuf-style blend from old-vine Grenache, plus Mourvèdre and Syrah.

In some vintages there are no fewer than seven Syrahs. Côtes de l'Ouest is the lightest and comes from Lodi rather than the Foothills. There is a Sierra Foothills bottling, aged for 18 months in barriques; and High Slopes, from vineyards at over 3,000ft. In 1991, Bill made the first vintage of Sentinel Oak Vineyard Pyramid Block, from vines planted in 1984. This wine is aged for two years in one-third new oak. The top—or at any rate most expensive—Syrah is Ascent, a blend of top sites aged for two years in mostly new barriques; it was first made in 1999.

Bill Easton is a sophisticated operator, and by carefully selecting his fruit sources, he has made sure that each wine is the best possible expression of its terroir. It would be difficult to produce such a wide range of wines from a single estate, so his long-term contracts in various parts of the region give him great flexibility. It shows in the wines, which are probably the finest made in the Foothills. The Syrahs have all the weight and complexity one could hope for, and the Zinfandels have a rare finesse, with no raisiny character. They also age splendidly.

Right: Former wine merchant Bill Easton, who crafts a broad range of refined and stylish wines from carefully sourced fruit

FINEST WINES

(Tasted 2009)

Terre Rouge

2007 Enigma Lush tropical-fruit nose. Plump and rounded, this lacks vivacity, though there is sufficient acidity to sustain a fairly long finish.

2004 Pyramid Block Syrah Sumptuous yet reticent nose, with aromas of plums and black pepper. Spicy and tight on the palate, with ripe tannins and fresh acidity. Still closed, but the finish is lively and quite long.

2001 Pyramid Block Syrah★ Vibrant plum and black-pepper nose. Creamy and intense, with fine acidity and robust but not tough tannins. Long.

2001 Ascent Syrah Rich blackberry nose. Medium-bodied but sleek and very concentrated, with pronounced chocolaty tones. Though the fruit is clearly very ripe, the wine is not overblown, showing considerable elegance and excellent length.

1999 Pyramid Block Syrah Intense, heady nose, with sweet oriental spices and red fruits. Very rich and opulent, this has admirable concentration of sweet fruit, with ample freshness and zest. The tannins are still hefty but well integrated.

Easton

2007 Amador County Zinfandel Very spicy, lively black-cherry nose. Suave and spicy, with no jamminess; a fruit-forward style, with a lively finish. This lacks structure, but the fruit is forthright and the wine completely accessible. Moderate length.

2004 Estate Zinfandel★ Intense brambly nose: raspberries and pepper. Rich but sprightly, with delicious bright fruit and no Portiness. Peppery and lively, with excellent balance and length.

2002 Estate Zinfandel Raspberry and pepper nose. Lean, fresh, and bright; a lively but discreet style, with ripe tannins, fine acidity, and decent length.

1999 Estate Zinfandel Fairly deep red. Ripe, elegant red-fruit nose, with few secondary aromas. Rich and svelte on the palate, with little sign of age; concentrated and spicy, and also airy. The finish is quite long, with slightly dry tannins.

Domaine de la Terre Rouge
Area under vine: 12 acres (5ha)
Average production: 250,000 bottles
10801 Dickson Road, Fiddletown, CA 95629
Tel: (209) 245-3117
www.terrerougewines.com

Sobon Estate / Shenandoah Vineyards

In the 1970s, Leon Sobon was a research scientist living in Los Altos in the San Francisco Bay area with his wife Shirley and six children. Although he had a good career working for Lockheed, he found himself increasingly bored with working on government contracts. Sobon was drawn to a different kind of life and was already a hobby winemaker, sharing grape supplies with four of his colleagues. In 1977 he bought more than 70 acres (28ha) in Shenandoah Valley, where he planted a vineyard and developed a winery called Shenandoah Vineyards. The first few years were difficult, since Sobon had to hand-sell his unknown wines by filling his car with bottles and calling on potential customers in the Bay Area. But when, in the 1980s, prices for Zinfandel rose steeply, he bought a second property, this time planted with 70 acres of the variety, which has since been replanted. This property, acquired in 1989, he named after himself.

Although the Sobon range is more expensive than the Shenandoah Vineyards wines, they are still offered at very fair prices, especially compared with Zinfandels from Sonoma

Today, Leon Sobon has handed over daily winemaking duties to his son Paul, though he and Shirley are still very much involved in the winery. They have maintained separate identities for their two properties: Shenandoah Vineyards concentrates on less expensive wines from a wide range of varieties, and Sobon focuses on more expensive wines made to more exacting standards.

The Sobon vineyard is dry-farmed, and about one-third of it is planted with Rhône varieties, with Barbera vines draped over the highest sector. Sobon has named two separate Zinfandel vineyards: Cougar Hill and Rocky Top. There are two other Zinfandels: a basic bottling called Old Vines; and the winery's top wine, Fiddletown, from the 15-acre (6ha) Lubenko Vineyard planted in 1903. Of the two estate vineyards, Sobon himself expresses a slight preference for Rocky Top, though both wines are made the same way, with fermentation in small vats, or even in barrels, and manual punch-downs. The oak is mostly American.

Sobon also produces Viognier and Roussanne, which are fermented half in older barrels, half in tanks. These tend to be less successful than the reds. The Amador County Syrah can be very good, but some vintages have proved disappointing. There are also wines he calls ReZerve, made in small quantities from Primitivo as well as Zinfandel. Although the Sobon range is more expensive than the Shenandoah Vineyards wines, they are still offered at very fair prices, especially when compared with single-vineyard Zinfandels from Sonoma. Another range is called Nobos (a reversal of the family name) and consists of varietal wines from grapes that Paul Sobon sources from outside Shenandoah Valley.

When the Sobons bought the property that bears their name, the estate included one of California's most historic wineries. In 1856, a Swiss pioneer named Adam Uhlinger had gouged a small winery into the hillside, and it was subsequently named the D'Agostini Winery. The Sobons have carefully restored it and turned it into a museum. It still contains the old redwood oval casks that were made on the property in the 19th century. As the oldest winery in Amador County, it is well worth a visit.

FINEST WINES

(Tasted 2009)

2008 Roussanne

Stewed apricot nose. Medium-bodied, supple, and creamy, with a slight phenolic graininess and only moderate length.

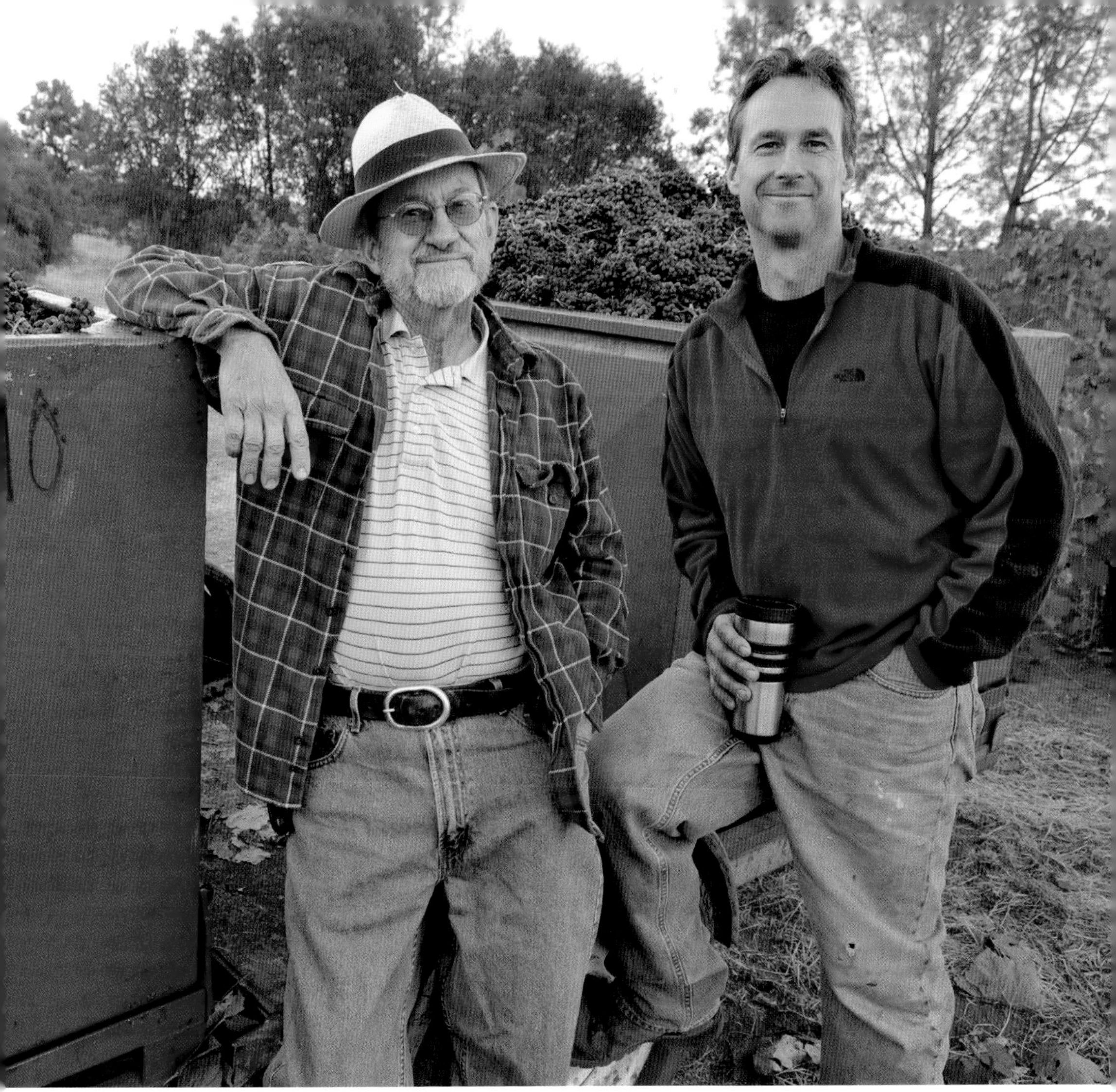

Above: Leon Sobon and his son Paul, whose family firm offers very reasonably priced Rhône varietals and Zinfandels

2007 Viognier
Honeysuckle nose. Juicy and reasonably concentrated, this has attractive fruit, but the acidity is a touch low, and there is some hollowness on the mid-palate and finish.

2007 Cougar Hill Zinfandel [V]
Lean and delicate red-currant nose. Concentrated on the palate, with a suave texture, ample richness, and spice. It has complexity and vigor.

2007 Fiddletown Zinfandel (Lubenko Vineyard)★
Very spicy red-fruit nose. Rich, full-bodied, and concentrated, with more density than the other Zinfandels. But there is no heaviness, and the finish is long and spicy. The 15.5% ABV doesn't jar.

2006 Rocky Top Zinfandel
Lean nose, with red-fruit and cherry aromas. Medium-bodied, moderately concentrated, and sleek, with bright acidity, this is made in a forward style. But it's well balanced.

Sobon Estate
Area under vine: 96 acres (39ha)
Average production: 350,000 bottles
14430 Shenandoah Road, Plymouth, CA 95669
Tel: (209) 245-6554
www.sobonwine.com

Santa Cruz Mountains

Now enclosed within the larger envelope of the San Francisco Bay AVA, Santa Cruz Mountains is an AVA created in 1981. Along with its neighbor Santa Clara, it is a region with a long history. Santa Clara has almost been driven out of existence by the encroachments of Silicon Valley. Santa Cruz Mountains is also a diminished region, with just below 400 acres (160ha) under vine, and topography is the limiting factor, though it is a large area spilling across three counties—San Mateo, Santa Cruz, and Santa Clara.

The coastal ranges south of San Francisco are steep, and carving out space for vineyards has never been easy. A surprising number of wineries operate within the region, but many of them buy grapes or wines from elsewhere. Thus, the well-established David Bruce winery in Los Gatos only owns 16 acres (6.5ha) within the appellation but buys extensively from Paso Robles, Russian River Valley, and other areas.

Every wine-drinking American knows about Napa and Sonoma, but few associate Santa Cruz Mountains with fine wine, even though some of the state's finest bottles have come from here

In the 19th century, logging was the major industry in these coastal ranges. Once the most prized stands of redwood trees had been chopped down, many logging companies moved out of the area—but they left the roads they had built, which made possible agricultural development within the region. That included viticulture. The first vineyards went in the ground in the late 1860s. The celebrated Monte Bello vineyard was established in 1892, and a few years later, Paul Masson started the company that would make him famous, though the good name has since been debased after corporate acquisitions. The single-minded Martin Ray subsequently bought the Masson vineyards, which he then sold in 1943, when he began to establish his own property on the site now occupied by Mount Eden. Ray was a perfectionist, producing small quantities of Chardonnay, Pinot Noir, and Cabernet Sauvignon that he was able to sell for high prices as futures (en primeur). At a time when a varietal wine needed to contain only 51 per cent of wine from the named variety, Ray defiantly made pure varietal bottlings. A difficult and quarrelsome man, he went out of business in 1972, but the site lives on.

It is difficult to generalize about Santa Cruz Mountains microclimates and soil types, because elevations and exposures are so varied. Rainfall can also vary greatly. The area is defined by elevation, since it lies above the fog line. As a general rule, Pinot Noir is often planted on the side of the ridges facing the Pacific, whereas Bordeaux varieties are planted on the east-facing slopes that look onto the San Francisco Bay.

A decade or so ago, it seemed doubtful whether the region would survive. Every wine-drinking American knows about Napa and Sonoma, but few associate Santa Cruz Mountains with fine wine, even though some of the state's finest bottles have come from here over the past century or more. Yet despite urban sprawl and tough growing conditions, with low yields the norm, the vineyards and wineries are hanging on. Even so, individual brands such as Ridge are better known than the region in which they are located.

Although the San Francisco Bay AVA was created in 1999, it is fairly meaningless—except in the sense that earlier AVAs now subsumed within it probably have even less consumer recognition than the Bay. While few consumers outside California could confidently pinpoint on a map areas such as Livermore Valley, Pacheco Pass, or Santa Cruz Mountains, the chic San Francisco Bay is well known to all.

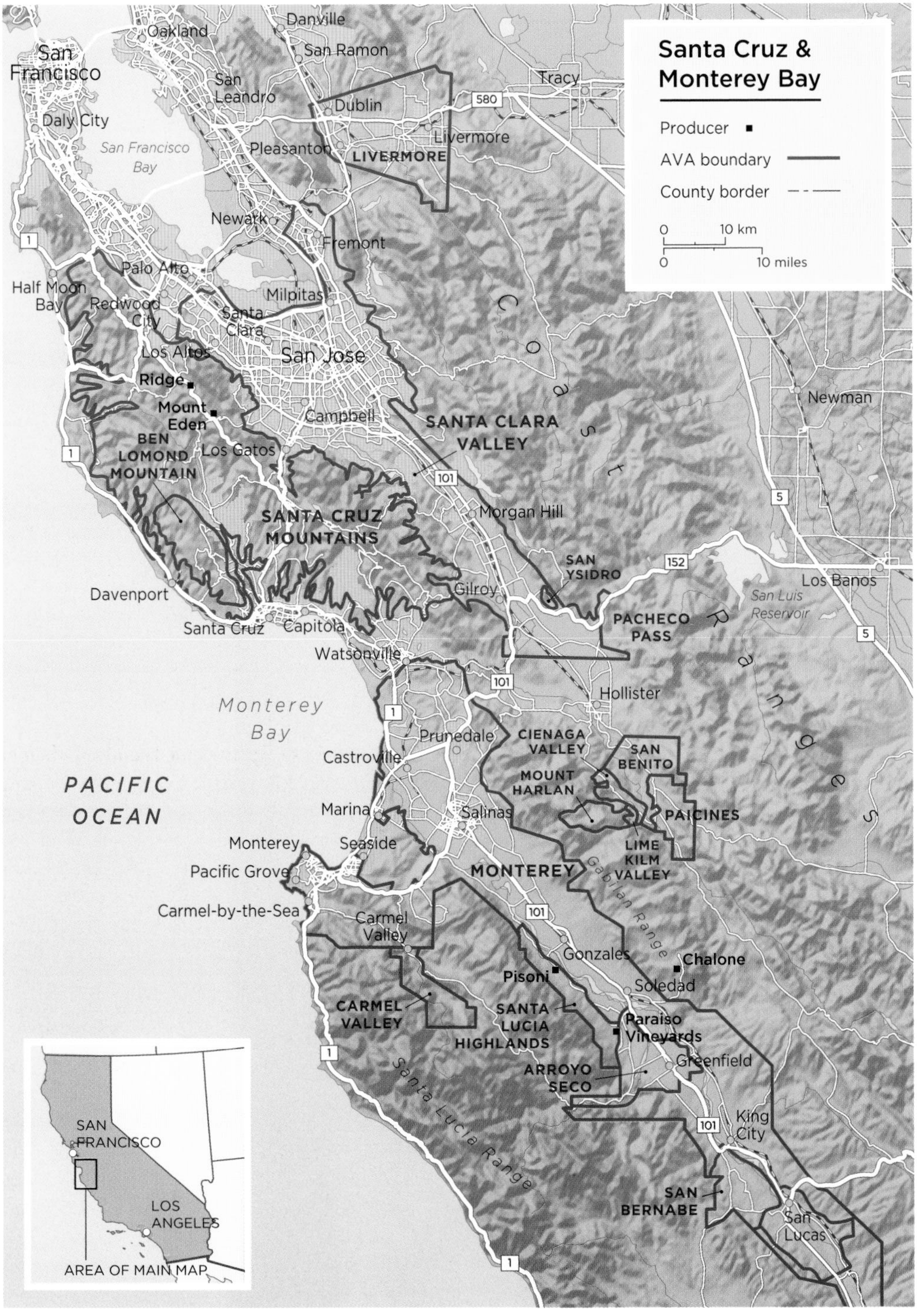
Santa Cruz & Monterey Bay
Producer
AVA boundary
County border
0 10 km
0 10 miles
San Francisco
Oakland
Danville
San Ramon
San Leandro
Dublin
Tracy
580
Daly City
Livermore
San Francisco Bay
Pleasanton
LIVERMORE
Newark
Fremont
Palo Alto
Half Moon Bay
Redwood City
Milpitas
Santa Clara
Los Altos
San Jose
Ridge
Mount Eden
Campbell
SANTA CLARA VALLEY
BEN LOMOND MOUNTAIN
Los Gatos
101
Coast Ranges
Newman
Morgan Hill
5
SANTA CRUZ MOUNTAINS
SAN YSIDRO
152
Los Banos
Davenport
Gilroy
San Luis Reservoir
PACHECO PASS
Santa Cruz
Capitola
Watsonville
Hollister
Monterey Bay
Prunedale
CIENAGA VALLEY
SAN BENITO
Castroville
MOUNT HARLAN
PACIFIC OCEAN
Marina
PAICINES
Salinas
Monterey
Seaside
LIME KILM VALLEY
Pacific Grove
MONTEREY
Gabilan Range
Carmel-by-the-Sea
Carmel Valley
Gonzales
Chalone
Pisoni
Soledad
CARMEL VALLEY
SANTA LUCIA HIGHLANDS
Paraiso Vineyards
Greenfield
ARROYO SECO
Santa Lucia Range
King City
SAN BERNABE
San Lucas
SAN FRANCISCO
LOS ANGELES
AREA OF MAIN MAP

Mount Eden Vineyards

The Mount Eden vineyards were created by Martin Ray, who first planted vines on these lofty slopes in 1943. The first vintage of Chardonnay and Pinot Noir here was in 1946. After Martin Ray lost control of the vineyards in 1972, the vineyard was divided, with the upper portion becoming Mount Eden, the Ray family retaining a lower section with just 5 acres (2ha) of Chardonnay. The Mount Eden shareholders entrusted the daily management to a series of mostly youthful winemakers. Deterred by the isolated location and low wages, they tended not to last long. In the early 1980s, Jeff Patterson, a young man from Berkeley and a graduate of UC Davis, took a winemaking job here, and his wife Eleanor became Mount Eden's sales manager. In 1988, Patterson became a shareholder—and 20 years later, he and his wife became the majority shareholders.

A long private road climbs a mountainside near Saratoga and eventually reaches the property, which lies at 2,000ft (600m), well above the fog line. Martin Ray's original winery is still in use as a barrel room for the Cabernet Sauvignon, but caves have been tunneled into the hillside for storing the Chardonnay and Pinot Noir, which need more precise temperature and humidity control than the original winery can provide.

Hardly any of the old vineyards survive. Only half the old Chardonnay is still in production, the other vines having been replanted. Of the 7 acres (2.8ha) of Pinot Noir, most were replanted in 1997, and the Cabernet Sauvignon dates from the early 1980s. Yields are extremely modest, because the shale soils are very low in nutrients and the older vineyards are dry-farmed. Foraging deer and erosion are the main obstacles to viticulture, but on the positive side, the soils are well drained and there is no frost and little disease. Jeff Patterson is emphatic: he is not interested in making obviously fruity wines but wants them to have power, length of flavor, *nervosité*, and longevity. Indeed, he finds that the Chardonnays often age even better than the Pinot Noirs. Nor does he want wines high in alcohol: they usually range from 13% to 14.2%.

The Chardonnay is barrel fermented with natural yeasts and spends about ten months in 50 percent new French oak. The wine goes through full malolactic fermentation, but there is no lees stirring. Patterson is convinced that the wine's mineral flavors come from the clone rather than the soil. It is probable that Paul Masson, who came from Beaune, brought cuttings from Burgundy, and these grew into vines from which Martin Ray took cuttings when he planted here.

A second Chardonnay is made from Edna Valley fruit. It used to be known as MEV, and the fruit came from the MacGregor Vineyard, which has some of the oldest Chardonnay in Edna Valley. In 1999, Jean-Pierre Wolff bought the vineyard and renamed it, and it remains the source for the Mount Eden Edna Valley wine. It exhibits lush tropical-fruit flavors that, it could be argued, are the polar opposite of the mountain fruit from Santa Cruz.

For Pinot Noir, Patterson looks for moderate ripeness. The grapes are partially destemmed, receive a cold soak, and are fermented with natural yeasts and regular punch-downs. The wine used to be aged in all new oak, but today the proportion is 50 percent, and the aging period has been reduced from about 18 months to 11. There is little racking, and the wines are bottled without fining or filtration.

The 20 acres (8ha) of Cabernet Sauvignon are planted lower down, at around 1,400ft (425m). There are also small blocks of Merlot and Cabernet Franc, and the blend usually contains about 75 percent Cabernet. This wine spends 18 months in oak, and until 2000 an Old Vine Reserve bottling was sometimes produced from

Right: Jeff Patterson, who came to Mount Eden in the 1980s and is now, with his wife Eleanor, the majority shareholder.

the original vines planted in the 1950s, but they have now had to be pulled out.

Only about one-third of the Mount Eden production is of the trio of Estate wines. Another third is taken up with the Edna Valley wine, and in 2004 Patterson introduced the Saratoga Cuvées. These are blends of declassified lots of the Estate wines, with fruit purchased from neighboring vineyards. The wines have the typicity of Santa Cruz Mountain fruit but are only partially made from the estate vineyards. Considerably cheaper than the Estate wines, they offer good value.

Even though venerable vines make up only a relatively small proportion of the fruit these days, the wines remain superb. They do not always show that well when young, because they are deliberately made in a restrained style. There is nothing flashy or fruit-forward about them. Mount Eden's regular customers know that these are wines that do not show their full potential or complexity on release but repay cellaring. Moreover, since the mid-1980s, the wines have been better than ever; some older vintages were distinctly vegetal, as a consequence of the large, sprawling canopies that were standard in the preceding decades. Patterson introduced leaf-pulling and proper canopy management, and today herbaceous characters, while not entirely eliminated (nor should they be) are kept firmly in the background.

Above: Mount Eden is still an isolated vantage point, from which Patterson can look down with great satisfaction

FINEST WINES

Chardonnay

2006 Saratoga Cuvée Stone-fruit nose. Plump and concentrated; less racy than the Estate wine but has good acidity and lift, especially on the finish.

2006 Estate★ Pure apricot nose; really elegant if not markedly mineral. Lean, tight, and citric, with high acidity—a Burgundian style with fine length.

2005 Estate Rich, oily, Chardonnay nose, quite oaky; plumper than 2006. Rich and weighty but has fine acidity to cut the fat; stylish and intense, with a long, citric finish.

1997 Estate Rich, toasty, waxy nose; apricot fruit. Rich and full-bodied but retains good acidity; stylish and tangy, with little sign of age. Quite long on the finish.

Pinot Noir

2006 Saratoga Cuvée [V] Warm, spicy cherry nose, upfront and not that complex. Medium-bodied, fresh, and lively, with fine acidity. It shows less depth and subtlety than the Estate wine but is still delicious and vibrant, with a long, earthy finish.

2006 Estate Slightly earthy nose, with some raspberry fruit in the background. Concentrated, yet fresh and delicate, with light tannins, pure red-fruit flavors, and a structure that's balanced and graceful.

2005 Estate Smoky raspberry nose. Supple but concentrated, with more flesh than the 2006, speckled with delicate red-fruit acidity. An understated style, with good length.
2000 Estate Undergrowth and mulch on the nose, which is distinctly Burgundian, with cherry and clove aromas. Sweet attack, with bright acidity that keeps it fresh and lively. Both precise and stylish, with intense red-fruit flavors on the long finish.

Cabernet Sauvignon
2006 Estate Rich, stylish nose; quite leafy but not herbaceous, with black-cherry fruit. Medium-bodied and quite intense, yet lacks a little flesh. A lean style, pretty but a touch light, with assertive acidity that gives it freshness, vibrancy, and length.
2005 Saratoga Cuvée Sweet, cedary, undergrowth nose. Plump, juicy, and accessible but doesn't lack concentration; shows black fruits and spice on the palate, if not great complexity.
2005 Estate Firm, oaky, leafy nose; quite dense. Medium-bodied, with firm tannins and a good deal of weight, extract, and persistence. Not overblown, but lean, balanced, and long.
2001 Estate Slightly sweaty nose, with rich black-currant aromas and a touch of mint. Suave in texture, delicious, and lively, with fine-grained tannins and a long, delicate, black-curranty finish.

Mount Eden Vineyards
Area under vine: 40 acres (16ha)
Average production: 180,000 bottles
22020 Mount Eden Road, Saratoga, CA 95070
Tel: (888) 865-9463
www.mounteden.com

Ridge Vineyards

There cannot be many historic wineries that have been resuscitated with the same success as the property now known simply as Ridge. In the 1880s, Dr. Osea Perrone bought 180 acres (73ha) of land high in the mountains above Saratoga and planted the Monte Bello vineyard. Phylloxera and Prohibition, that deadly pair, did for Monte Bello as for so many other vineyards. That would have been the end of the story had not a few scientists from Stanford University clubbed together in 1959 to buy land with a view to creating a vacation home for their families. The land they bought included Monte Bello, where they found a few old Cabernet vines still clinging to life. The new owners picked the grapes and vinified them, and they were astonished by how good the wine was. They gradually set up a winery and, in 1969, invited Paul Draper, a young winemaker with a philosophy degree and an inquiring mind, as well as experience producing wine in Chile, to take charge of the property. Once he had tasted the 1962 (the first vintage labeled as Monte Bello) and 1964, it was apparent to him that the vineyard had remarkable potential.

Draper was struck by the soil at Monte Bello, because just below the surface is a thick layer of fractured limestone, which is rare in California. There were other soil types on the property that seemed to bear some resemblance to Côte Brune in Côte Rôtie. In any case, the site was clearly of great interest. Some walls remained from the Perrone winery, and a new winery was built incorporating those remnants. The present winery is a multilevel warren sunk deep into the limestone, but not all the Ridge wines are vinified or stored here—the business has grown too much for that to be feasible. In 1967, before Draper arrived, production was no more than 3,000 cases, including wine made from bought-in grapes. Under Draper, Ridge expanded. Its celebrated Sonoma Zinfandels are now produced at a winery near Healdsburg.

Paul Draper is still at the helm, though the daily winemaking tasks are now undertaken or supervised by Eric Baugher, who has filled this role since 1994. As well as the Santa Cruz Mountain wines, there is the extensive range of Zinfandels that Ridge has been producing for many years.

The 125-acre (50ha) Monte Bello vineyard has been farmed organically since 1999, and missing vines are replaced by massal selections. The vines are planted at 2,300–2,600ft (700–800m), so not surprisingly this is a cool site—as cool as Bordeaux, but spared the Atlantic rains. The grapes do ripen, but slowly and steadily, and sugar accumulation is never as dramatic as in Napa or Sonoma. Thus, alcohol levels are fairly low, and acidity and tannins high. As Baugher remarks, "The site restricts excesses of style, such as overripeness." The wine is slow to evolve but will keep, in good vintages, for decades. Vine age varies considerably, but the average is 30 years. Draper finds that different parcels ripen at different speeds, so before harvest it is essential for the Ridge team to taste repeatedly in all parts of the vineyard. Early vintages of the red wine were pure Cabernet, but certainly by the late 1970s other Bordeaux varieties—first Merlot and then Petit Verdot—were being blended in.

The winemaking at Ridge is meticulous. Since 2008, the grapes are sorted before and after destemming and are fermented with natural yeasts. Draper and Baugher are extremely vigilant about extraction, taking enormous care not to overextract or to indulge in too prolonged a maceration, since the wine tends to be naturally tannic. Each vintage needs different handling to achieve the balance and harmony that Draper is seeking. There is no formula at work here. Blending of the various lots (there can be more than 30) takes place fairly early. What differentiates Monte Bello from California's other great Cabernets is that

Right: Paul Draper, who has been at Ridge since 1969 but who still approaches each vintage with an open and inquiring mind

it is aged—or 85 percent is aged—in American oak. Monte Bello may be the most claret-like of American Cabernets, but Draper is adamant that he wants to make an American wine and not a Bordeaux lookalike. Of course, the oak is air-dried and of the highest quality.

The second wine is the Santa Cruz Mountains Cabernet. It is not necessarily a blend of weaker lots, and the vinification is identical to that for Monte Bello. But Monte Bello demands a certain weight and structure, and some lots, however delicious, don't make the cut. Five percent of the vineyard is planted with Chardonnay, a variety that has been produced from the outset. From 1999, the best Chardonnay is bottled as Monte Bello, with Santa Cruz Mountains as the second wine. For many years, the wine was aged in equal proportions of French and American oak, but Draper, persuaded by the overall improvement in quality of the native wood, now ages the Chardonnay entirely in American oak.

Draper is fascinated by Zinfandel and has, over the years, sourced grapes from 35 vineyards, vinifying them and selecting the most interesting or characterful. The Zinfandels are made with the same care as the Cabernet, and again American oak is used, though little of it is new. The two most celebrated Zinfandels are Geyserville and Lytton Springs, both in Sonoma. Geyserville is a leased vineyard in Alexander Valley with some very old Zinfandel, Carignane, and Petite Sirah; Ridge first made this wine in 1966. Lytton Springs, first made in 1972, is about 4 miles (6km) from Geyserville, just across the border in Dry Creek Valley. It, too, is a field blend, with a significant proportion of very old vines. The climate is slightly hotter, so the wine, though robust, is usually less elegant than Geyserville. There is also a pure Zinfandel from Paso Robles, from vines planted in 1923; a delicious wine, it is, however, less structured than the Sonoma wines and best enjoyed young.

There are more wines. From York Creek, a vineyard on Spring Mountain in Napa, come a Petite Sirah and a Zinfandel. (The York Creek Cabernet was last produced in 1993.) Other Zinfandels come from the Ponzo Vineyard in Russian River Valley and from the mostly centenarian Pagani Ranch in Sonoma Valley.

Ridge is astonishingly consistent. Inevitably, some vintages are better than others, but I don't recall drinking a poor or mediocre wine under the Ridge label. Paul Draper, for all his experience and knowledge, seems to reflect freshly on each year, deliberating on the best way to harvest, vinify, and age the wines. In Monte Bello he has created an American classic, though the vineyard was already making excellent wines before his arrival in 1969. But nothing is taken for granted. In 1997, I arrived at the winery to visit Draper and, rather to my surprise, was ushered into the tasting room and asked to do some work. The team was assessing two blends of Lytton Springs—one with Petite Sirah, the other without. We tasted, scored, and discussed. We were all unanimous in recognizing the wine with Petite Sirah, and we were all wrong. Perplexed, Draper ordered a rerun, so the winemakers could figure out why their experienced palates were out of tune. Alas, I was not present for the second tasting. At Ridge, as at all great wineries, all major decisions are made by tasting the wines, not by analysis. Draper doesn't scorn the use of science, but science is at the service of the wine. Taste is paramount.

FINEST WINES

Monte Bello

2006★ Sumptuous black-cherry and black-currant nose, with vanilla tones. Very rich, concentrated, and mouth-filling, the black-fruited opulence balanced by fine acidity. Very long.

2002 Firm black-currant nose, with a pronounced minerality. Lively attack, almost racy for Cabernet; skeletal now but bright and fresh, so should age well.

Above: Eric Baugher, who has supervised daily winemaking tasks since 1994, shares Draper's ideals of balance and harmony

1996 Resplendent, black-fruit nose, savory, with coffee tones. Medium-bodied and lightly herbaceous, with splendid concentration, intense red-fruit flavors, and remarkable persistence and balance.
1994 Very deep red. Discreet black-currant nose, with graphite and cedar tones. Sleek and concentrated, with supple tannins and a charming silkiness. No heavyweight but has a long, bright finish.
1990 Deep red, with little evolution. Delicate black-currant nose, but quite savory and balsamic. Sweet attack, with great intensity, purity of fruit, and immense concentration. Superbly balanced, very elegant, and very long.
1981 Deep red; quite evolved. Discreet, smoky nose, with red-fruit and black-currant aromas. A touch of Brettanomyces, but not excessive. Lean, lively, and still fresh—an elegant wine with integrated tannins and considerable charm.
1974★ Deep and still youthful color. Ripe and powerful nose, with a fruitiness that suggests a much younger wine. Plump, sweet, and flamboyant, wonderfully concentrated, and with little sign of age. Drinks well now, but so well balanced it should stay on this plateau for many years yet.
1964 Pre-Draper. Deep red, with considerable maturity. Mushroomy, cedary nose, mature but not tired. Although a touch musty on the palate, it still has freshness and zest. Some sweetness and intensity remain, though it is becoming lean and attenuated now.

Zinfandel
2006 Lytton Springs Ripe, red-fruit nose. Suave and creamy, with fine concentration and tannins. Quite long.
2006 Geyserville★ Elegant cherry nose; has lift and freshness. Medium-bodied but concentrated, with discreet tannins and a peppery, tangy finish. Good length.
1999 Lytton Springs Coffee, plums, and meat on the nose. Soft yet full-bodied and concentrated; quite evolved, but sumptuous, with coffee on the persistent finish.
1999 Geyserville Earthy, smoky, leathery nose. Suave, velvety, and delicious, with integrated tannins and a lift of acidity on the finish. Long.

Ridge Vineyards
Area under vine: 525 acres (212ha)
Average production: 1,000,000 bottles
17100 Monte Bello Road, Saratoga, CA 95014
Tel: (408) 867-3233
www.ridgewine.com

Monterey

By far the most important of the county's grape-growing areas is the Salinas Valley, a 5-mile- (8km-) wide expanse southeast of the town of Monterey that is entirely dependent on irrigation for its agricultural productivity. Much of the valley is devoted to vegetable production, and at any time of the year you can see teams of Hispanic laborers bent over endless rows of cabbages and lettuce. In the northern stretches of the broad valley, around the towns of Gonzalez and Soledad, grapes tend to be confined to the less fertile benchlands; farther south, around King City and San Lucas, they invade the valley floor itself. The valley runs from north to south for over 80 miles (130km), growing considerably warmer as you move southward.

Compared to most other California wine regions, Monterey is a recent arrival, with hardly any land planted with grapes until the early 1960s. By 1970, 2,000 acres (800ha) were under vine, but the boom was only just getting under way, and by 1975 an extraordinary 35,000 acres (14,000ha) were planted, not far short of the 2008 total. Unlike Napa or Sonoma, the valley was planted by large wineries or consortia, often as tax shelters. Kendall-Jackson and Mondavi planted thousands of acres here, while Hess, Gallo, and Caymus also established vineyards. An insurance company provided the funds to set up the colossal San Bernabe vineyard, which is the world's largest single vineyard. Most of the Monterey fruit is trucked out of the county to provide inexpensive but generally reliable fruit to some of California's largest producers.

Climatic studies at UC Davis first identified the potential suitability of the Salinas Valley for viticulture. The loamy soils are fairly light and well drained, and the growing season for grapes is prolonged. The Davis professors were right about many things but wrong about the varieties that should be planted. They recommended Cabernet Sauvignon, and although the degree days (the units of sunshine that measured a region's warmth) seemed to match, the initial planters failed to take into account the maritime influence in the valley, notably summertime fogs and the fierce winds that can blow down it during the afternoons—both factors that inhibited ripening and could even shut down the vines. The result was a phenomenon that became known as the "Monterey veggies"—in short, very green tannins. Excessive irrigation, and immense yields as a consequence, certainly didn't help. Today, Cabernet Sauvignon is largely absent from the Salinas Valley, though it does well elsewhere in the county.

Growers were swift to correct their errors. Monterey has proved to be excellent Chardonnay country, and almost half the vines in the county are of that variety. Over recent years, Cabernet has declined from around 5,000 to 3,665 acres (2,000 to 1,500ha), and Pinot Noir has almost doubled to 5,760 acres (2,330ha); there has been a slight increase in Riesling, Viognier, Malbec, and Syrah, while Chenin and Pinot Blanc plantings have plummeted. Merlot remains at around 5,000 acres.

The county is far from uniform. Most of its eight AVAs lie in the Salinas Valley, but not all. Some of the outlying regions, such as Chalone and Carmel Valley, produce the most characterful wines.

Arroyo Seco (AVA from 1983) An area of sandy and rocky soils that covers over 5,000 acres between Soledad and King City. Pioneers such as Wente and Jekel made the area known for its Rieslings, but today Chardonnay is far more important. Doug Meador planted the Ventana Vineyard, which sells fruit to producers all over the state. His claim, often substantiated by his own wines, is that high quality can be compatible with high yields, if certain viticultural practices are followed.

Carmel Valley (AVA from 1983) An anomaly within the county: a sheltered and temperate valley, parallel to the Salinas Valley but protected from the ocean by a coastal range and thus capable of ripening varieties such as Cabernet Sauvignon and Merlot. Grapes were first planted in 1968 by what is now known as the Heller estate. Wetter, steeper, higher, and less windy than Salinas, the valley also supports a number of individual wineries that benefit from the excursions of tourists from the popular resorts of Monterey and Carmel. Yet very few wineries have established more than a local reputation, possibly because only 300 acres (120ha) are planted.

Chalone (AVA from 1982) Essentially a one-estate AVA but one that is fully justified. Its 300 acres (120ha) flourish at an elevation of 1,200–2,300ft (360–700m).

Hames Valley (AVA from 1994) The most southerly region in Monterey, warm enough to grow Bordeaux and Port varieties. 2,200 acres (890ha) are planted.

San Antonio (AVA from 2006) A recent AVA, and a warm one, with about 800 acres (320 ha) under vine on gravelly loam soils. It shows promise for the Cabernets and Syrah.

San Bernabe (AVA from 2004) Delicato, the present owners of this colossal 5,000-acre (2,000ha) vineyard, successfully petitioned for the creation of an AVA to match. Just about everything is grown here, and this is the source of some delicious and inexpensive Syrah.

San Lucas (AVA from 1997) A southerly region with some pedigree, having been developed by Almaden in 1970. Summers can be brutally hot, but overall temperatures are more moderate. Lockwood is a major grower here, and there are about 8,000 acres (3,200ha) under vine.

Santa Lucia Highlands (AVA from 1992) This region lies on benches and alluvial fans on the western side of Salinas Valley, and much of it is just above the fog line. About 5,000 acres (2,000ha) are planted. The highlands, which do not rise above 1,400ft (400m), have attracted more attention than any other Monterey AVA in recent times. Caymus's Mer Soleil vineyard is here, producing lush Chardonnays, while Paraiso is better known for its crisper whites and for Pinot Noir. The latter grape, as well as Syrah, has helped put a few relatively small vineyards on the map: Pisoni, Franscioni, and Garys' are the best known, and their grapes are eagerly sought by wineries all over California. The Pinot lies at the richer, more powerful end of the spectrum, though much depends on the individual requirements of regular purchasers.

Chalone

It's a long, steep drive up from Soledad to the Chalone vineyards. Vines were planted here in the Gavilan mountains in the early 20th century, long before vineyards were established in the valley below. A new owner, John Dyer, planted vines in 1919 that are still, just, in existence. New partners bought the property and planted additional varieties such as Chardonnay and Pinot Noir in 1946, and the fruit was sold to wineries such as Wente and Almaden. The first vintage to be estate-bottled was the 1960, and the winemaker was Philip Togni, who recalls having to make repeated trips down to Salinas and back during harvest just to buy ice blocks with which to cool the fermenting vats. No paved road existed until 1980.

The modern era at Chalone began when Dick Graff bought and expanded the estate in 1965. He soon established a terrific reputation for the wines: barrel-fermented Pinot Blanc and Chenin, as well as Chardonnay and Pinot Noir. In the 1990s, the structure of the estate became complicated, with Graff's acquisition of other properties, such as Acacia and Carmenet, and with the involvement of the Château Lafite group in a cross-shareholding arrangement. Graff died in a plane crash in 1998, and by 2005, the assets of the Chalone group were acquired by the giant drinks group Diageo. There was also a succession of winemakers: Michael Michaud, who ran Chalone from 1983 to 1998; then Dan Karlsen; and from 2007, Robert Cook.

Despite the vineyard's elevation, at 1,600–2,000ft (490–610m), the site is warmer than the Salinas Valley because there is less maritime influence. There can be morning fog, but by 10 o'clock it has usually burned off. Chalone's individuality derives from its soils—a mixture of limestone and volcanic soils that may explain why the site appealed to its French founder a century ago. The result is wines that are structured and that can be long-lived, especially the Reserve bottlings. There was a period in the late 1990s when the wines were scarred by Brettanomyces and TCA infection, and some vintages were not released. It took a few years for Karlsen to wrestle with and overcome the problems, which seem to have disappeared entirely.

Unfortunately, corporate ownership, under Diageo since 2005, has done Chalone no favors. The celebrated Reserves, from the oldest vines, have been phased out and replaced by bottlings called Heritage, which are aged in new oak and sold only at the tasting room. As a consequence, many of the wines for which Chalone was best known have vanished from the marketplace. Equally grievously, a new label has been created: Chalone Vineyards Monterey County. This range is produced in substantial quantities from purchased fruit. Although a back label showing the location of the estate vineyard is attached to each bottle, little or no wine for this range is actually grown on the estate. Moreover, the typography echoes that of the estate-wine labels. Any consumer could be forgiven for assuming, wrongly, that the Monterey County range is simply a new incarnation of the Chalone brand, not a complete departure from it. Moreover, some unscrupulous restaurateurs list these wines at the far higher estate-wine prices, and few consumers have the detailed knowledge to realize they are being cheated. In the 1990s, Chalone also marketed lesser ranges but used other names, like Gavilan and Echelon, to differentiate them from the estate wines. Diageo has been less discriminating.

However, some good estate wines are still being made. The Pinot Blanc comes from vines planted in 1973 and 1990, but as elsewhere in California, some of those vines may in fact be Melon. The 8 acres (3ha) of Chenin Blanc planted in 1919 still cling on, though there are many missing vines. The wine goes through malolactic fermentation, is aged in older barrels, and, unlike many California Chenins, is fully dry. The Chardonnay is lush and spicy, though only the Heritage bottling has real

distinction. The Pinot Noir used to be aged in oak for up to two years and could develop leathery tones. More recent bottlings see less wood and are generally fresher and more refined. Since 2000, Syrah and Grenache have been added to the range. Such wines earn Chalone its place in this book—but alarm bells are ringing.

FINEST WINES

(Tasted 2009)

White

2007 Chardonnay Delicate apple-and-apricot nose. Supple and not especially concentrated, and despite some welcome acidity on the finish, rather bland overall. Moderate length.

2007 Heritage Chardonnay★ Rich, oaky, grilled-nut nose. Full-bodied, with depth of fruit and fine concentration, this is a dry style, with fine extract and a long, nutty finish.

2006 Chenin Blanc [V] Firm nose, with aromas of nuts and bruised apples; surprisingly oaky. Rich but quite nutty and austere, with extract and character. Good length, with a firm, dry finish.

2006 Pinot Blanc Nutty, leesy nose; quite austere. Rich, creamy, and less earthy than the Chenin, but it has a comparable nuttiness and extract and some appley flavors. Long.

Above: The craggy peaks of the Gavilan Mountains form a dramatic backdrop to Chalone, and also inspired its labels

Red

2007 Heritage Pinot Noir Dense, chocolaty nose, black cherries, and a little Pinot typicity. Juicy and rounded but shows a touch of flab. It has less character than the 2005, being in a somewhat tannic and overripe style.

2006 Pinot Noir Light cherry nose, with lift and fragrance. Sleek and quite concentrated, this also has some grip and spice yet doesn't lack extract and persistence.

2006 Syrah Dense, tarry nose; chocolate mints and plums. Broad and juicy, hefty without being too extracted; balanced by good acidity and length.

2005 Heritage Pinot Noir (250 cases) Dense nose, with aromas of cherry compote and vanilla. Medium-bodied but bright and concentrated, not especially tannic, and culminates in a long, spicy, earthy finish.

Chalone Vineyard
Area under vine: 260 acres (105ha)
Average production (estate wines): 360,000 bottles
Stonewall Canyon Road, Soledad, CA 93960
Tel: (831) 678-1717
www.chalonevineyard.com

Paraiso Vineyards

Rich Smith and his partners were quick off the blocks in Soledad, planting vineyards in the Santa Lucia Highlands in 1973. In 1987, Smith bought out the other investors, and he has gradually expanded his holdings. He began releasing his own wines from 1988, but no winery was constructed until 1995. Today, he farms about 3,000 acres (1,200ha) of vineyards in the county, and 2,000 (800ha) of them are Chardonnay. Only 400 acres (160ha) lie within the Santa Lucia Highlands, and only 90 of those are used for the Paraiso label. His son-in-law David Fleming is the winemaker, and Rich's son Jason is also part of the team.

The Smiths' primary expertise is as growers. They have found that exposure to wind, in particular, retards ripening, and there can be four weeks' difference in harvesting dates within the Paraiso vineyards. The varietal configuration is always altering, reflecting not only the quality of fruit but the commercial realities of supply and demand. Thus, Pinot Blanc and Gewurztraminer have been pulled out, while Souzao has gone in as a "Port" variety. Syrah is a fairly new recruit, having been planted in 1989. Of the original vines from 1973, some Martini-clone Pinot Noir, Wente-clone Chardonnay, and Riesling are still in production.

The Paraiso wines are not in the front rank of California's finest, but they are honest wines, and they have been improving. In the 1990s, the label was Paraiso Springs and quality was humdrum, though prices were inexpensive. In 2001, the wines were rebranded as Paraiso, and quality has increased. Fleming doesn't take shortcuts and uses mostly French oak, though some American and Hungarian barrels are used for Syrah. At least half the production is of Pinot Noir. There are some special cuvées made from the oldest vines or most concentrated lots from the best parcels; they are the Eagles' Perch Chardonnay, the West Terrace Pinot Noir, and the Wedding Hill Syrah. To amuse themselves, Smith and Fleming also produce a small quantity of super-ripe Pinot called Faite, made in a point-scoring style that they personally don't much like. But they like to show they can do it if they want to, and the wine critics have responded with gratifyingly high scores.

FINEST WINES

(Tasted 2009)

White

2007 Riesling [V] Scented lime nose. Quite rich, concentrated, and lively—an essentially dry style, with some extract, lifted fruit of great charm, and good length.

2007 Chardonnay Lean, appley nose. Ripe and concentrated, with fine acidity giving the palate precision. Balanced and long—and exemplary value for the money.

2007 Eagles Perch Chardonnay Broad pear and apricot nose. Juicy and vibrant, with fine acidity and concentration, and a tighter, more persistent structure than the regular bottling.

Red

2007 Pinot Noir Lush cherry nose. Medium-bodied and ripe—indeed, a touch sweet from the oak; spicy and accessible if not very complex.

2006 West Terrace Pinot Noir Ripe cherry nose. Full-bodied for Pinot, with depth and weight and a pleasing spiciness, thanks to good acidity. Quite good length.

2006 Faite Pinot Noir Muted black-cherry nose. Very ripe and juicy, with a rounded texture and moderate acidity. A bit stolid but not too extracted. A dense, soft style that lacks a little zest and typicity.

2005 Syrah★ Vibrant and perfumed cherry-and-cola nose. Luxurious, but tempered with fine acidity that gives it drive. A pure and ripe style, with a long peppery finish.

Right: Rich Smith, son Jason, daughter-in-law Jennifer Murphy-Smith, and son-in-law David Fleming, together raising tandards

Paraiso Vineyards
Area under vine: 3,000 acres (1,215ha)
Average production (estate wines): 300,000 bottles
38060 Paraiso Springs Road, Soledad, CA 93960
Tel: (831) 678-0300
www.paraisovineyards.com

Pisoni Vineyards

It is no coincidence that Monterey's most prestigious vineyards all lie along the benches and slopes of the Santa Lucia Highlands. The Smiths of Paraiso and Chuck Wagner of Caymus all recognized long ago that this particular sliver of the Salinas Valley could deliver exceptional fruit. Initially, the emphasis was on Chardonnay, but over the past decade Pinot Noir has become just as important, if not more so. In the 1980s, some Italian families—expert farmers and enthusiastic wine lovers—bought and planted land here. The quality of their fruit soon attracted attention, especially from the many négociant wineries (Siduri, Testarossa, Arcadian, and Patz & Hall, among others) seeking outstanding parcels of fruit.

Before long, four vineyards stood out: Franscioni, Rosella's, Garys', and Pisoni. Garys' was an unusual venture in camaraderie, being jointly owned by the two leading, and no doubt competing, families: the Franscionis and the Pisonis. The main business of both families is farming and selling grapes, but both have established small wineries. The Franscioni label is called Roar (their wines are made for them by Adam Lee of Siduri), though, rather confusingly, some of the wines come from the Pisoni vineyard. The Pisonis stuck to their own name. Mark Pisoni farms the vineyard, and his brother Jeff, who is located in Santa Rosa, makes the wines. Since the operation is a small one, it is easy for Jeff to make numerous small batches of wines from different parcels. The grapes are sorted, dropped into the vats by gravity, and after aging in barriques with minimal or no racking, the wines are bottled without fining or filtration. The amount of new oak varies but is generally about 25 percent for Syrah and 45 percent for Pinot Noir.

The Pisonis don't make enough wine to have a formal tasting room, so I sampled the wines beneath a shady arbor next to a shack. When I arrived, the barbecue grill was still smoldering, and empty bottles were strewn about, while others were lined up on a wooden trellis. Clearly some good parties are held here. I was on my own, though, until I saw an ancient Jeep clatter down the dirt road toward me. Mark Pisoni gave me an enthralling tour, at breakneck speed, of the property, which at some points rises to an elevation of 1,400ft (425m), before returning to the "tasting room." The vineyards are divided into numerous blocks with many different exposures; the wineries that are regular, long-standing purchasers earmarked their favorites long ago. Mark seems thoroughly attached to these undulating vineyards. "We're not going anywhere," he told me emphatically. "As a family, we are attached to this land."

The Pisoni label consists of a single wine: estate Pinot Noir. Under the Lucia label are a Pinot from Garys' Vineyard, two Syrahs, and a Chardonnay.

FINEST WINES

(Tasted 2009)

2007 Lucia Chardonnay
Elegant lemony nose. The palate is full-bodied, very ripe, and juicy, showing both tropical fruit and ripe citrus flavors. Pungent in its vigor and unctuous in its texture, this is a complex wine made from the Old Wente clone.

2007 Lucia Garys' Vineyard Pinot Noir★
Bright cherry nose; a good deal of oak. Ripe and concentrated, but supple, with refreshing acidity backing the delicious, peppery cherry fruit. Long.

Above: Mark Pisoni directs his family firm's main business, farming and selling grapes, while brother Jeff makes the wines

2006 Pisoni Vineyard Pinot Noir
Lush, smoky-bacon-like nose. Rich and broad, a touch big and heavy, with distinct muscularity. Spicy and quite tannic, but it lacks a little finesse.

2006 Lucia Susan's Hill Pisoni Vineyard Syrah
Ripe fleshy plummy nose. Rich and supple, but not heavy or overblown, with concentrated black-fruit flavors punching through to a long, stylish finish.

Pisoni Vineyards
Area under vine: 45 acres (18ha)
Average production: 25,000 bottles
PO Box 908, Gonzales, CA 93926
Tel: (800) 270-2525
www.pisonivineyards.com

San Luis Obispo

This county is home to a number of different wine regions that have very little in common with each other. A generous sandwich filling between Monterey to the north and Santa Barbara to the south, San Luis Obispo is, overall, warmer than either, the exception being cool-climate Edna Valley. By far the most important subregion is Paso Robles, with vineyards fanning out on all sides from the town. South of Paso Robles, around the town of San Luis Obispo, are the other main regions: Edna Valley and Arroyo Grande.

Some vineyards were probably planted by missionaries in the late 18th century, but the first commercial winery was established in 1882 by what is today the York Mountain Winery. There was considerable vineyard expansion in the 1920s with the arrival of Italian immigrants, some of whose descendants are still farming grapes in the area. Luster was added to the region when the Polish pianist Ignace Jan Paderewski bought a farm west of Paso Robles and planted Zinfandel and Petite Sirah. Those were typical varieties around Paso Robles after Repeal, but it was Dr. Stanley Hoffman who, advised by André Tchelistcheff, planted Burgundian varieties on his ranch in the 1960s. Another important development was the planting in 1975 of Estrella River Vineyards by Gary Eberle, bringing Syrah to the region for the first time. Those plantings have not survived, and the vineyard now belongs to the vast Meridian winery, but Eberle is still making excellent wines at his eponymous winery east of Paso Robles.

There are four AVAs.

Arroyo Grande (AVA from 1990) Just south of Edna Valley, this area has lighter soils and fewer temperature swings than its neighbor. The valley extends for some 16 miles (26km), and there is some maritime influence. Talley has long demonstrated the area's suitability for Burgundian varieties. But Arroyo Grande is not uniform, and Zinfandel is successfully grown in the Saucelito Canyon subregion.

Edna Valley (AVA from 1987) A mostly flat area with marked maritime influence, with morning fogs and afternoon breezes. The soils are clay-based but not uniform. Chardonnay has always been the most important variety grown here, but Pinot Noir and Riesling are also present. The Chardonnays often show a pronounced tropical-fruit character, which can be highlighted when, as sometimes happens, there is also some botrytis infection. Plantings are said to be around 1,400 acres (570ha), though that may be an underestimate. Some corners of the valley are also capable of ripening Rhône varieties, as John Alban has definitively demonstrated.

Paso Robles (AVA from 1983, expanded in 1997 and again in 2009) This region, with 26,000 acres (10,520ha) under vine, has seen a substantial expansion in the 2000s. Its success with Zinfandel and Rhône varieties led to a rash of new plantings and the creation of what has now risen to a total of 180 wineries. This has all happened too rapidly, and many growers find they are unable to sell their fruit, which partly explains why some have set up small wineries and tasting rooms from which they can sell directly to the public.

There is a clear dividing line between the areas east of Highway 101 and those to the west. The area to the east is essentially a high plateau at up to 1,200ft (370m), which has permitted the plantings of large ranches such as Estrella River and many others. To the west and south of the city, the terrain is very different: undulating and in many places distinctly steep. Vineyards share the space with orchards, grazing land, and forest. The soils are different, too, with calcareous bands that are unusual in California as a whole, though varying combinations of loam, clay, silt, and shale are more widespread. To the west, rainfall is higher, too. Cool nights prolong

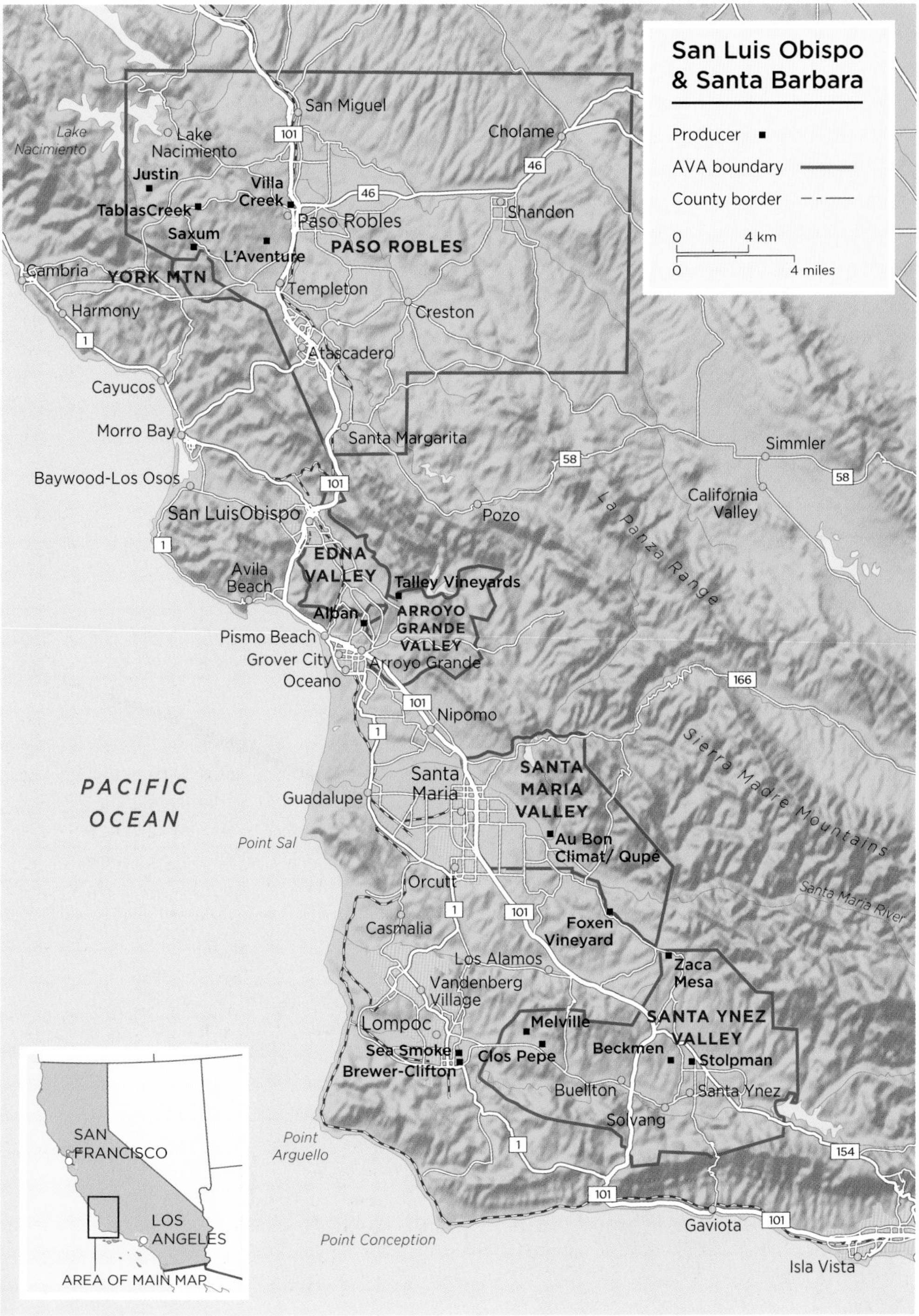
San Luis Obispo & Santa Barbara
Producer
AVA boundary
County border
0 4 km
0 4 miles
San Miguel
Lake Nacimiento
Lake Nacimiento
Cholame
Justin
Villa Creek
Tablas Creek
Paso Robles
Shandon
Saxum
L'Aventure
PASO ROBLES
Cambria
YORK MTN
Templeton
Harmony
Creston
Atascadero
Cayucos
Morro Bay
Santa Margarita
Simmler
Baywood-Los Osos
San Luis Obispo
Pozo
California Valley
La Panza Range
EDNA VALLEY
Avila Beach
Talley Vineyards
Alban
ARROYO GRANDE VALLEY
Pismo Beach
Grover City
Arroyo Grande
Oceano
Nipomo
Sierra Madre Mountains
PACIFIC OCEAN
Guadalupe
Santa Maria
SANTA MARIA VALLEY
Au Bon Climat/ Qupé
Point Sal
Orcutt
Santa Maria River
Casmalia
Foxen Vineyard
Los Alamos
Zaca Mesa
Vandenberg Village
Lompoc
Melville
SANTA YNEZ VALLEY
Sea Smoke
Clos Pepe
Brewer-Clifton
Beckmen
Stolpman
Buellton
Santa Ynez
Solvang
Point Arguello
Gaviota
Point Conception
Isla Vista
SAN FRANCISCO
LOS ANGELES
AREA OF MAIN MAP
101
46
1
58
166
154

Above: Arroyo Grande is a long valley whose climate is suitable for growing vegetables as well as vines, as here at Talley Vineyards

the growing season, and many growers are still harvesting into November. Though Syrah was first planted on the Eastside, it has achieved glory on the Westside. The Perrin family of Châteauneuf-du-Pape lifted the prestige of the Westside when they chose a ranch far out on Adelaida Road for their nursery and subsequent vineyard specializing in Rhône varieties. Named Tablas Creek, its vineyard is now mature, and the nursery supplies wineries all over California with virus-free plant material.

It has now become an article of faith that all the best wines in Paso Robles are made on the Westside. By and large, this is true, but the large Eastside vineyards are capable of producing delicious wines, especially Cabernet Sauvignon and Zinfandel, at sensible prices. It's true that their wines may not rise to great heights of complexity or subtlety, but they are supple and eminently drinkable, and economies of scale make those modest prices feasible. It is nonetheless also true that almost all the wines that have won the most acclaim come from the Westside. Justin Smith, whose family has been growing grapes for longer than most, observes that the terrain is complex, with varying soil types and exposures, and consequently not all the new vineyards have been planted well or in the right spots. Thus, Westside provenance is not a guarantee of good quality.

Moreover, winemaking quality has been, to put it politely, variable. Whereas the wineries featured here all make excellent wines, a chance visit to a Paso Robles tasting room could be a dismaying experience. The old-time winemakers—and some of the newer ones, too—were great characters, but their wines were full of volatile acidity and Brettanomyces. The Paso Robles heat easily results in high sugar accumulation and high alcohol, which greatly increase the risk of Brettanomyces and other infections. Vigilant winemaking and hygienic cellar practices are essential here.

Petitions are being circulated, arguing for the creation of up to three new AVAs for the Westside, including Adelaida Hills and, south of the city, Templeton Hills. So far, none has been approved.

York Mountain (AVA from 1983) A rather pointless AVA, which only came about when the owner of the sole winery, York Mountain Winery, refused to be included in the Paso Robles AVA. Only 7 miles (11km) from the Pacific Ocean, the region lies at a high elevation up to 1,800ft (550m), yet is susceptible to maritime fogs. Overall, it is quite wet and cool, and some varieties, such as Cabernet Sauvignon, can struggle to ripen in some vintages.

Alban Vineyards

Obsessions can be dangerous things, leading to unfulfilled careers that screech to a premature halt. But they can also be the driving force that leads to remarkable and innovative results, and that has clearly been the case with John Alban. His passion for Rhône wines began with a taste of Condrieu, which led to visits to the region and some spells working there. He also studied at Fresno and UC Davis. His career in wine began as a nurseryman, propagating Rhône-variety cuttings and refining them. It was in 1990 that he planted a property he purchased in Edna Valley with nothing but Rhône varieties, which must have raised eyebrows in the area. But he knew what he was doing—he had studied 40 years' worth of climatic data from that part of France and had developed a clear notion of where these varieties would fare best in California. He grafted over small blocks he had leased in various parts of California, including Santa Rita Hills and Hecker Pass, as well as Edna Valley. He knew he would have only one shot at planting a Rhône-variety vineyard, and he wanted to minimize the risk of failure. His first red release was a 1992 Syrah. Though he sells his wines for very high prices, production is very limited, so he has long sold fruit to other wineries; nowadays, however, he limits those sales to old friends who have long relied on his grapes.

John Alban's wines are demanding—on the palate, as well as on the pocket—but they are magnificent. Since the late 1990s he really hasn't put a foot wrong

"When I first planted here," he told me, "the neighbors all said I would never get any color on the grapes. They were wrong. They had tremendous extraction potential, and I wanted it all. I didn't destem and did long, cool fermentations with punch-downs. So in those early vintages, I was getting too much phenolic matter. Now I realize I don't need it all. Instead, I want to capture the maximum harmony in my wines."

To refine his understanding of viticulture and winemaking, he went off to Barolo in 1995, because he thought the problems of handling tannin and acidity in Syrah were not dissimilar from those difficulties with Nebbiolo. The experience made a strong impression. He began full destemming, relied on natural yeasts, and opted for shorter, hotter fermentations without pump-overs and completed fermentation in barrels. In recent years, he has modified the vinification further, preferring some pump-overs and limited punch-downs. But the major change has been the extension of barrel aging to up to 42 months. There is, unsurprisingly, no need for fining or filtration.

Though not organic—"I prefer to say we're Albanic"—he comes close. No herbicides are used, and sheep graze the cover crop and remove leaves; they also provide manure at the same time. Different grape varieties are planted on different soil types on the 250-acre (100ha) ranch. There are three separate Syrahs, and white varieties are planted on the soils best suited to them, as is Grenache, a variety at which Alban has always excelled. Recent additions to the range include Forsythe, a Mourvèdre, and Pandora, which is overwhelmingly from Grenache, with a dash of Syrah. Syrah has become the principal wine, though in early vintages white wines were equally important. Reva is grown on clay with gravel and gives wines rich in black fruits and tar. Lorraine is planted on stonier soils that heat up rapidly and give much earlier ripening and more red fruits than Reva. The scarcest of his Syrahs is Seymour's, named after his father and first made in 1998; grown on calcareous and schist soils, it also has, he finds, the most finesse. The 2002 vintage had 17% alcohol, which is ludicrously high, yet the wine is

so well structured that it shows no heat. Nonetheless, the prospect of finishing a bottle is daunting.

Made with low yields and almost constant sunshine, his wines can and do reach high alcohol levels, though fermentation in open-top vats and the use of indigenous yeasts reduces them slightly. Alban is unfazed. "I know high alcohol is not part of the French tradition, but we're not trying to mimic Rhône conditions here." Still, one is rarely aware of the alcohol in his wines.

In the late 1990s, the great Austrian winemaker Alois Kracher persuaded Alban that remarkable sweet wines could be made in California, too. The result was a TBA-style Roussanne called Rotten Luck, but the last vintage was 2005.

A slight figure, easing gracefully into middle age, John Alban is relaxed and modest but clearly with a strong will and sense of direction. His wines are demanding—on the palate, as well as the pocket—but they are magnificent. He has taken his fastidiously chosen piece of land and with each passing year explores its facets and possibilities with ever-increasing depth. There were a few duds, especially among the white wines, in his debut vintages, but since the late 1990s he really hasn't put a foot wrong.

FINEST WINES

(Tasted 2009)
The following wines were all tasted from barrel but shortly before bottling, so they were final blends.

2008 Estate Viognier (15.4% ABV)
Sumptuous, tropical-fruit nose: mango, banana, and mint leaf. Tight and concentrated, silky in texture, and with no heaviness, thanks to lively acidity. There's a slight sweetness from the alcohol but no burn. Quite long.

2007 Forsythe Mourvèdre
Complex nose of mint, plums, and mulberries. Ripe and dense, with great concentration yet supple tannins; some red-fruit flavors color the aftertaste, and the wine finishes with a light touch and a long, clean finish.

2006 Pandora (75% new oak)
Opaque red. Lush, oaky, chocolaty nose, quite peppery. Suave and deep, with rich black-cherry and chocolate fruit—very distinctive, and refreshed by good acidity and length.

2006 Reva Syrah (80% new oak)
Very deep red. Dense and gamey nose, meaty and minty. Intense attack but very rich and svelte; plump and plummy but has good underlying tannins and fine acidity and length.

2006 Lorraine Syrah★ (100% new oak)
Opaque red. Splendid nose of cherries and licorice. Dense, highly concentrated, with integrated tannins, fine acidity, and a long, chocolaty finish.

2006 Seymour's Vineyard Syrah
Opaque red. Vibrant aromas of smoked meat, bacon, and black pepper. Rich, dense, and tarry, this was rather closed and blunt, as well as being more austere and tannic than Reva or Lorraine. A more muscular, grippy wine, with dark-chocolate flavors on the long finish.

Left: John Alban, who has defied the skeptics and is making a range of wonderful wines from carefully sited Rhône varieties

Alban Vineyards
Area under vine: 66 acres (27ha)
Average production: 70,000 bottles
8575 Orcutt Road, Arroyo Grande, CA 93420
Tel: (805) 546-0305
www.albanvineyards.com

L'Aventure

Stephan Asséo (his first name seems to have dropped the final "e" on crossing the Atlantic) left France and his native St-Emilion, where his family owned La Fleur Cardinale and other properties, because he had grown frustrated by the refusal of the authorities (INAO) to permit unorthodox blends. It's an unusual explanation, since in Bordeaux there are no restrictions against blending at least six red varieties. However, he made the leap to California after looking at various countries, including Argentina and South Africa, and found what he was looking for just south of Paso Robles.

In 1997, he bought 126 unplanted acres (50ha) and had the soil analyzed to confirm his hunches. He discovered 18 different soil types, which offered sufficient diversity to support a full range of Rhône varieties, as well as Cabernet Sauvignon and Petit Verdot.

There is considerable limestone in the soil, which is water-retentive—a useful feature in so hot an area. Both the limestone elements and the cool nights help preserve acidity as a counterbalance to the inevitably high alcohols generated here. Each variety is planted on three sites, giving him more lots of wine with which to compose his blends. Asséo has planted to a high density, and pruning to only six bunches per vine, he keeps yields below 2.2 tons per acre (roughly equivalent to 35hl/ha). About half of the estate is now farmed biodynamically.

The first vintage of L'Aventure was 1998. Asséo had to purchase fruit at the beginning, but by 2008 his own vineyard was sufficiently extensive and mature for his production to be entirely estate-grown. More or less from the start, his wines made an impression on tasters; they were big and powerful, to be sure, but they also had tremendous intensity of flavor. I recall the ripe, spicy, leathery 1998 Syrah, and a juicy, forthright 1999 Zinfandel. Asséo insists on harvesting only at full phenolic ripeness, which largely accounts for the wines' high alcohol. The grapes are sorted, destemmed, and very lightly crushed. The red Rhône varieties are given a cold soak for a few days, and the fermentation then takes place with indigenous yeasts. The maceration lasts for between two and four weeks, and the wines are then aged in new oak.

The range has evolved considerably over the years, or, to put it less diplomatically, the wine list alters with irritating speed from vintage to vintage. Thus, a wine called Optimus, a roughly equal blend of Cabernet Sauvignon and Syrah (a kind of act of homage to Domaine de Trevallon in Les Baux) used to be the estate's top wine but by 2006 had been demoted to its most basic blend, accounting for roughly half of the total production. A wine called Côte à Côte used to be a Grenache/Syrah blend but by 2007 was composed of 40 percent each of Mourvèdre and Grenache, the rest being Syrah; it is aged in 45 percent new 500-liter barrels.

Though these shifting sands can certainly be perplexing even to those who follow L'Aventure closely, Asséo is clearly still feeling his way, finding what works best on his excellent steep terroir and adapting accordingly. He used to make Chardonnay, for example, but after 2002 decided to phase it out altogether in favor of Roussanne.

Though some of the wines are aged in a high proportion of new barrels, Asséo takes a pragmatic view, tailoring the *élevage* to the character of each wine; the Roussanne is fermented and aged in only 20 percent new oak.

The wine program clearly seems to reflect Asséo's own somewhat unruly personality. Perhaps this questing, restless character is, indeed, more at home in the relatively unexplored Westside of Paso Robles than among the certainties of St-Emilion.

Right: The restless, searching Stephan Asséo, who seems more at home in Paso Robles than in his native St-Emilion

CORK
SUPPLY
USA

Above: L'Aventure's carefully researched vineyards have up to 18 different soil types, permitting a broad range of wines

FINEST WINES

(Tasted 2009)

2008 Roussanne
(85% Roussanne, 15% Viognier)
Sweet, appley, apricot nose. Medium-bodied and initially neutral, but it develops spice and minerality on the mid-palate and has a long, peppery finish.

2007 Estate Cuvée★
(49% Syrah, 37% CS, 14% PV) Opaque red. Dense plum-and-chocolate nose. Sumptuous and concentrated, lush without being soupy, because it has some acidic bite; perhaps a bit one-dimensional in its flavor profile but has impressive energy and drive and a long, chocolaty finish.

2007 Estate Cabernet Sauvignon
(95% CS, 5% PV; 16% ABV) Opaque red. Very rich and aromatic black-currant nose, the fruit blaring out as though from a loudspeaker. Broad, fleshy, and powerful on the palate, with hefty tannins. It has some acidity but is still rather punishing.

2007 Côte à Côte
Opaque red. Very rich and tarry black-fruit nose. Plump and concentrated on the palate, with dark-chocolate flavors and powerful tannins, yet cut by bright acidity. Still rather alcoholic (16.5%) on the finish, which is rather blunt and lacks some persistence.

2006 Optimus
Opaque red. Sweet, gamey nose, dominated by Syrah. Dense and concentrated, quite meaty and chunky, but with good acidity, even if not quite the persistence one hopes for.

L'Aventure
Area under vine: 58 acres (23.5ha)
Average production: 100,000 bottles
2815 Live Oak Road, Paso Robles, CA 93446
Tel: (805) 227-1588
www.aventurewine.com

Tablas Creek Vineyard

Outside the tasting room at Tablas Creek is a sign reading, "Domaine de Beaucastel 9009km" [5,598 miles]. It is not there by chance: this is a joint venture between the Perrin family of Beaucastel, Châteauneuf-du-Pape, and the Haas family of Vermont, who imported the Perrins' wines. Back in the 1970s, they had pipe dreams about producing Rhône-style wines in California. It wasn't until the 1980s that the partners started looking for land in which to grow these varieties. They particularly wanted to find calcareous soil, which is rare in California. They searched in the Sierra Foothills and in other parts of Paso Robles. It gradually dawned on them that the Westside offered the soils and terrain they were looking for. However, such soils were hard to work, there was a risk of frost, and water was in short supply. In 1990, they found and bought 120 acres (50ha) of pasture land that they considered had exemplary potential. Their hunch was right. In 2003, a trench cut into the soil after six months without rain found sufficient moisture at 15ft (5m) below the surface.

That was just the beginning of the venture. The partners' idea was to import vines and rootstocks from France, but that entailed a three-year quarantine period while the US authorities established that the cuttings were virus-free. While waiting, in 1992 the families planted some 10 acres (4ha) of American source material, just to see whether the land was indeed suited to Rhône varieties. Gradually, some 60 acres (24ha) of French vines were planted between 1995 and 1997, and by 2004 most of the American vines had been grafted over to Perrin clones.

Today, there are more than 100 acres (40ha) under vine, and the property has been farmed organically since 2003 (as at Beaucastel). As well as producing its own wines, Tablas Creek has a nursery

Below: A sign to the Tablas Creek tasting room, where there is always a good buzz, and another to its source of inspiration

SYRAH
TCVS F.

that supplies numerous vineyards in California with virus-free vines. Robert Haas is now in his 80s, so the property is run by his energetic son Jason. Since 1998, the winemaker has been Neil Collins, and the first vintage was 1996.

Jason Haas believes his father's hunch was essentially correct. All the Rhône varieties do well here, though it is a bit warm for Viognier, which needs to be picked early to retain acidity. Counoise gives good results, and Grenache Blanc tends to have better acidity than in the Rhône. Haas admits the first vintages were a bit disappointing, since they tended to pick at ripeness levels that worked in the Rhône but not in the different climate of Paso Robles. He, François Perrin, and Neil Collins are very wary of new oak, and they age the red wines in large casks (*foudres*) rather than in barriques—the one exception being the Syrah.

The range has been fine-tuned over the years, but by now the owners have developed two ranges: the top blends, the white and red Esprit de Beaucastel; and the secondary Côtes de Tablas range, intended to be drunk soon after release. There are also varietal wines but in small quantities and available only from the winery. The red Esprit is a blend of Mourvèdre, Syrah, Grenache, and Counoise; the white is a blend of Roussanne, Grenache Blanc, and Picpoul. Collins also makes minute quantities of *vins de paille* (straw wines).

Since the 2000s, these have been excellent wines. The false starts of the earliest vintages have been corrected. The Tablas Creek team is careful to avoid the commonly encountered traps into which would-be Rhône-style producers frequently stumble. They steer clear of jamminess and high alcohol, though it cannot always be easy. There is always a good buzz in the Tablas Creek tasting room, suggesting the team really enjoys what it does—and it shows in the exuberance of the wines.

Left: Jason Haas at Tablas Creek, which sells vines throughout California, as well as making its own range of stylish wines

FINEST WINES

White

2008 Côtes de Tablas [V] Rich, floral honeysuckle nose. Silky in texture, yet spicy and lively, with considerable richness of fruit and moderate concentration and length.
2007 Roussanne Bright, lifted, apricot nose. Concentrated, velvety, and spicy, with delicious apricot and pear fruit. This is lightly mineral and persistent, and it shows exemplary balance.
2007 Esprit Subdued, waxy, stone-fruit nose. Rich, concentrated, and full-bodied, but with no trace of heaviness. Though the acidity is only moderate, the wine has lift, elegance, and quite good length.
2006 Esprit Opulent, peachy nose, but with some minerality, too. Rich, firm, and spicy, with tropical-fruit and orange-water flavors. Ripe, but with no rough edges or excessive alcohol. Quite long.
2006 Vin de Paille Quintessence Roussanne (8.6%) Straw gold. Honey-cake nose. Creamy and almost viscous, with flavors of honey and peaches and tropical fruit. Not cloying, and very long.

Red

2008 Rosé (58% Mourvèdre, 32% Grenache, 10% Counoise) Waxy, strawberry nose—a touch candied. Supple, juicy, and vinous; reasonably concentrated, with moderate acidity. Enjoyable and persistent.
2007 Côtes de Tablas Firm cherry nose; quite earthy. Rich, generous, juicy, and upfront; a quaffable wine, with a long, peppery finish.
2007 Esprit★ Sumptuous cherry fruit on the nose. Rich and mouth-filling, voluptuous without being jammy or heavy, this is nonetheless quite tannic and needs to age. Very concentrated, but not austere or extracted. Long, mineral finish.
2006 Grenache Succulent cherry-and-raspberry nose. Medium-bodied and reasonably fresh. Fairly simple wine with light tannins; no obtrusive alcohol despite being 15.3%, and a long, piquant finish.
2006 Esprit Dense, plum-and-blueberry nose. Full-bodied and lush, concentrated and quite tannic, but impeccably balanced, with no trace of harshness. Deft and long.

Tablas Creek Vineyard
Area under vine: 110 acres (45ha)
Average production: 200,000 bottles
9339 Adelaida Road, Paso Robles, CA 93446
Tel: (805) 237-1231
www.tablascreek.com

Justin

Justin and Deborah Baldwin may not have been the first outsiders to settle on one of the remote ridges west of Paso Robles, but they must have been among the most sophisticated. As a former investment banker, Justin could presumably have chosen a more glamorous spot in the North Coast, but the Baldwins were taken with this former barley farm in Adelaida Valley and bought it in 1981, planting their first vineyard the following year.

From the start, the Baldwins had a sense of style. The winery buildings were jaggedly painted in dashing and warm Mediterranean colors, the labels were modern and geometric, and the wine names showed a penchant for discreet punning. Despite the isolated location—today they have other distinguished estates, including Tablas Creek, for neighbors—the Baldwins even opened a tiny boutique hotel (the Just Inn) and restaurant. This marketing flair would not have counted for much had the wines not been good, but they were. The first vintage was 1987, and a Bordeaux blend from that year was delicious if oaky.

The land was not easy to cultivate. Elevations varied from 1,100 to 1,800ft (335–550m), and there were considerable variations of temperature, as well as fog and occasional frost to contend with. The soils varied, with sandy loam and clay topsoils over a base of limestone and shale. Yields were low—for red wines, not exceeding 2.5 tons per acre. Justin has been through a number of different winemakers, and each has left his mark. Jeff Branco, who was here until 2003, fine-tuned the viticulture, installing vertical trellising and gradually replanting to a high density. He also oversaw the construction of wine caves, which were completed in 2003 and were, at that time, the largest of their kind on the Central Coast. That was also the year of the Paso Robles earthquake, and Justin Baldwin lost a few hundred cases of wine and also broke his nose.

In that year, Branco was succeeded by Fred Holloway, who had been one of the top winemakers at Kendall-Jackson Artisanal Estates. Holloway has undertaken an extensive replanting program. Though the Westside has become known for its Syrahs, the Baldwins believe their patch of land is better suited to the Bordeaux varieties. So, they've seen off their Chardonnay, Sangiovese, and Syrah vines in favor of Cabernets Sauvignon and Franc and Merlot. Some of the vineyards are now farmed organically, and Holloway is trying out some biodynamic practices. The winery is thoroughly modern, and Justin is proud of his new and sophisticated Mistral grape-sorting machine.

Inevitably, the range of wines is constantly evolving. Good Syrah was made here in the 1990s, but it has been dropped from the roster. I was less sorry to see the Chardonnay go. The mainstay of the range is Isosceles, a Bordeaux blend dominated by Cabernet Sauvignon, which forms 70–85 percent of the blend; it is aged for two years in new barriques, without any press wine (as is the case with the other red wines). There is also an Isosceles Reserve, but quantities are tiny, and most of it is sold at the tasting room. Justification is an Ausone-style blend of Cabernet Franc and Merlot, and there is also a pure Cabernet Sauvignon and a Port-style wine, Obtuse, made from the same variety. A relatively new addition to the range is Savant, a blend of Syrah and Cabernet Sauvignon.

I do not know whether the Baldwins were savvy enough to foresee the bursting of the Syrah bubble on the Central Coast, but their focus on Bordelais wines has probably been commercially astute. They certainly excel at this style of wine, and no other Paso Robles property produces wines of comparable depth and complexity. It doesn't hurt that Deborah Baldwin is a gifted marketer with taste and flair, and the wines have nothing in common with some of the more rustic efforts that still proliferate in these hills.

Above: Justin Baldwin, the former investment banker now producing the most complex Bordelais wines in Paso Robles

FINEST WINES

(Tasted 2009)

2007 Justification
Intense black-currant-and-blackberry nose, but lightly herbaceous. Supple, with moderate concentration, light tannins, and attractive acidity; it's quite elegant but lacks a little drive. The 2006 was similar: rounded and accessible but lacking some complexity.

2007 Cabernet Sauvignon
Ripe, blackberry, plum, and vanilla nose. Approachable and lively, this has light tannins, fresh acidity, and moderate depth and persistence. The 2007 Reserve Cabernet Sauvignon has similar but denser aromas and more opulence. On the palate, there is more grip and spiciness, and more length, too.

2006 Reserve Cabernet Sauvignon
Sweet, fleshy, blackberry nose; very ripe, yet has charm. Rich and textured on the palate, with firm but ripe tannins and some spice and complexity. A wine that's juicy and accessible if not showing many nuances.

Isosceles
2006★ Rich, spicy, black-currant nose, with intensity and power and a good deal of sweet oak. Rich, creamy, and full-bodied, with admirable concentration and weight. Impressive, without being too extracted; a luxurious wine, with a long and fairly elegant finish. The Reserve is similar but has even more heft and power; but the alcohol does show, and overall the regular Isosceles seems the more balanced wine.
2005 Ripe but slightly tarry nose, savory and a touch herbaceous, too. Quite concentrated, but also attractively fleshy and forward. Quite good length. As in 2006, the Reserve shows a great deal of new oak and immense power; broad-framed and massive, it is also a bit hot and overpowering.

Justin
Area under vine: 72 acres (29ha)
Average production: 500,000 bottles
11680 Chimney Rock Road, Paso Robles, CA 93446
Tel: (805) 238-6932
www.justinwine.com

Saxum

Saxum is another example of a top grower turning his hand to winemaking. Even in the days when vineyard-designated wines were scarce in Paso Robles, the James Berry Vineyard had a certain cachet. Wineries such as Wild Horse would buy fruit from here and cite the vineyard on the label. Planted in 1981, shortly before Justin, it was the oldest of the "modern" Westside vineyards, since Zinfandel had been the grape of choice for decades before. At first, the Smith family put in Burgundian varieties, but in 1987 they planted some test blocks of Viognier and Mourvèdre for John Alban and Wild Horse. They soon realized that the complex shale and fractured limestone soils were particularly well suited to Rhône varieties, and in 1990 Syrah was planted for the first time.

For some years, the James Berry Vineyard and the Saxum label have been in the hands of the still youthful Justin Smith, who still sees himself primarily as a grape farmer. He likes to focus on the details of his terroir and has divided the hilly site into numerous blocks, each of which he manages individually. Though the ranch is not especially large, the micro-diversity is such that the vineyard takes up to six weeks to harvest. One of the best sectors is called Bone Rock, because fossils were found in the soil, and here the Syrah vines are trained up poles, Côte Rotie-style, since the curved and terraced site wouldn't permit the vines to be trained along wires. Smith attributes much of the quality of the fruit to the calcareous soil and the low (by California standards) pH that it gives the wines. Smith is pleased with the way Mourvèdre ripens here at relatively low potential alcohol, but he finds that Viognier is too rich and plump—Roussanne gives better results. He is also keen on Grenache, and his selection came from Château La Nerthe in Châteauneuf, via John Alban in Edna Valley. Since 2007, the vineyard has been farmed organically.

Justin Smith created Saxum as his own label in 2000. In addition to the James Berry Vineyard, he has planted two other sites, one of which is Heart Stone, a 7-acre (3ha) site that lies 2 miles (3km) north of the home farm. His basic blend is Broken Stones, made mostly from young Syrah vines, with 10 percent Grenache; it is aged in barriques for 16 months. The wine for which he is best known is Bone Rock, mostly Syrah from the block of the same name, plus some Mourvèdre.

Smith is sensitive to the fact that fully ripe grapes from the Westside often emerge with high alcohols: 16% is by no means unusual. For this reason, he sorts the bunches twice, so as to remove any raisined berries that would make the problem worse. After a cold soak, he likes to co-ferment the different varieties if the ripening schedule permits it, and he relies mostly on natural yeasts to complete the fermentation. There is no added acidity.

The cap is punched down, the grapes are basket-pressed, and during the barrel aging there is no racking, as well as no fining or filtration before bottling. In recent years, Smith has been making more use of 500-liter barrels in order to moderate any overt oakiness in the wines. There is no dealcoholization. High alcohol, says Smith, is just a reality here, and he doesn't want to alter the natural balance of the wines by using reverse osmosis or any other technique. However, it is rare that the alcohol is discernible on the nose or palate.

Another cuvée was added in 2003. Rocket Block is a blend of 50 percent Grenache, 40 percent Mourvèdre, and 10 percent Syrah; this is aged in older barrels. There are separate bottlings from the Heart Stone Vineyard and from Booker Vineyard (95 percent Syrah, aged in 75 percent new oak), as well as a blend from the James Berry Vineyard. Much of the fruit is still sold to other wineries.

Above: Justin Smith, who produces balanced if potent wines from carefully selected sites, including the famous James Berry Vineyard

FINEST WINES

(Tasted 2009)

2007 James Berry Vineyard
Ripe plums and pepper on the nose. Good attack on the palate and very concentrated; despite a leathery tone, there is fine underlying freshness and ample lift and energy. The tannins are well integrated and the 15.8% ABV is in check. Quite long.

2007 Booker Vineyard
Opaque red. Dense, jammy, leathery nose. Very rich, with sweetish fruit, though no evident residual sugar; very tannic, assertive, and muscular, and the finish is rather dry and alcoholic (15.5% ABV).

2006 James Berry Vineyard
(76% Syrah, 18% Mourvèdre, 6% Grenache) Dense nose of creosote, ink, and blackberry jam. Rich, broad, succulent, and surprisingly fresh for such a massive wine, with an open and limpid quality alongside the concentration of black fruits. But it is a bit hot on the finish (16.7% alcohol).

2005 Heart Stone Vineyard
(44% Syrah, 33% Grenache, 23% Mourvèdre) Very ripe, intense nose, with spicy black fruits, especially blackberries. Very dense and concentrated, tannic and a bit tarry, with the 15.7% ABV just about balanced, thanks to the density of fruit. Massive but has a long sweet finish.

2005 James Berry Vineyard★
(70% Syrah, 20% Mourvèdre, 10% Grenache) Opaque red. Dense, meaty, leathery nose, with powerful black fruits. Extremely rich and powerful on the palate, with tarry black fruits and chalky tannins, but it has some zest, and the 15.5% ABV is well integrated. *Sauvage*, exciting, and long.

Saxum
Area under vine: 62 acres (25ha)
Average production: 32,000 bottles
2810 Willow Creek Road, Paso Robles, CA 93446
Tel: (805) 610-0363
www.saxumvineyards.com

Talley Vineyards

The Talleys have been farming in Arroyo Grande, some 8 miles (13km) inland from the ocean, since 1948, growing vegetables. It was Don Talley who realized there could be potential for viticulture, too, and made some test plantings in 1982. Slopes once thick with avocado plants were planted with five grape varieties, and it became apparent that the local climate was too cool for Cabernet Sauvignon to ripen. A few years later, more than 100 acres (40ha) were planted, primarily with Chardonnay and Pinot Noir, and a little Sauvignon Blanc and Riesling. The first vintage was 1986, and some of the original plantings are still in production. For Chardonnay, Clone 4 dominates, but it gives smaller crops than its reputation would suggest, and there are also Wente and Mount Eden clones. As for Pinot Noir, there is the 2A Wadenswil clone, which thrives here, as well as some Dijon clones. Today the property is run by Bryan Talley, who has raised standards to a very high level. Yields are moderate and rarely exceed 3.5 tons/acre, leaf-pulling is routine, and use of drip irrigation and pesticides is minimal.

These are wines of considerable purity, made with a light touch, and invariably among the most elegant and consistent of Central Coast Chardonnays and Pinots

Morning fog keeps the site cool, which is why the Burgundian varieties do so well here. Since the mid-1990s, the Talleys have released single-vineyard wines, since the different soil types give different expressions of those varieties. Rincon is the largest site, with 89 acres (36ha) under vine on loam and clay soils over a limestone subsoil. To the west of Rincon is the 29-acre (12ha) Rosemary's Vineyard on rocky, fragmented sandstone—a cooler site that ripens later than Rincon. Over in Edna Valley, the Talleys have planted the 160-acre (65ha) Oliver's Vineyard (all Chardonnay) and, in collaboration with other growers, a Pinot vineyard called Stone Corral (first vintage 2004).

Harvesting has to be delayed until the naturally high acidity begins to drop, and the wines all undergo a leisurely malolactic fermentation, without which, say the Talleys, the wines would be undrinkable. The winemaking, supervised since 2005 by Leslie Mead, is classic. The Chardonnay is whole-cluster pressed and fermented in barriques with native yeasts. About one-third of the wood is new. As well as the single-vineyard bottlings, there is an Estate Chardonnay, blended from various sites. For the Pinot Noir, some stems are occasionally retained, and after a cold soak the must is fermented with native yeasts in open-top vats with punch-downs and no extended maceration. The barrel regimen is similar to that for Chardonnay, but the Pinot is aged for up to 17 months. Filtration is the exception, not the rule.

Overall, these are wines of considerable purity, made with a light touch, and invariably among the most elegant and consistent of Central Coast Chardonnays and Pinots.

FINEST WINES

(Tasted 2009)

Chardonnay

2007 Estate [V] Charming nose, with mango and pear. Medium-bodied, supple, with bright acidity and more charm than depth. Moderate length.

2007 Rincon Intense nose of lime and crushed herbs. Fine attack, with zesty acidity and apple and lime flavors. A mouthwatering wine, with excellent balance and length.

2007 Rosemary's Lightly oaky, citric nose, with tropical-fruit aromas. Fresh and juicy, yet with a light touch. Refreshing, with support and grip from the oak, but essentially delicate and long.

2007 Oliver's Lush, tropical fruit and pineapple nose. Juicy and creamy, a touch plump; a crowd-pleaser but lacks the finesse of the other vineyard-designated wines. In that sense, typical of Edna Valley.

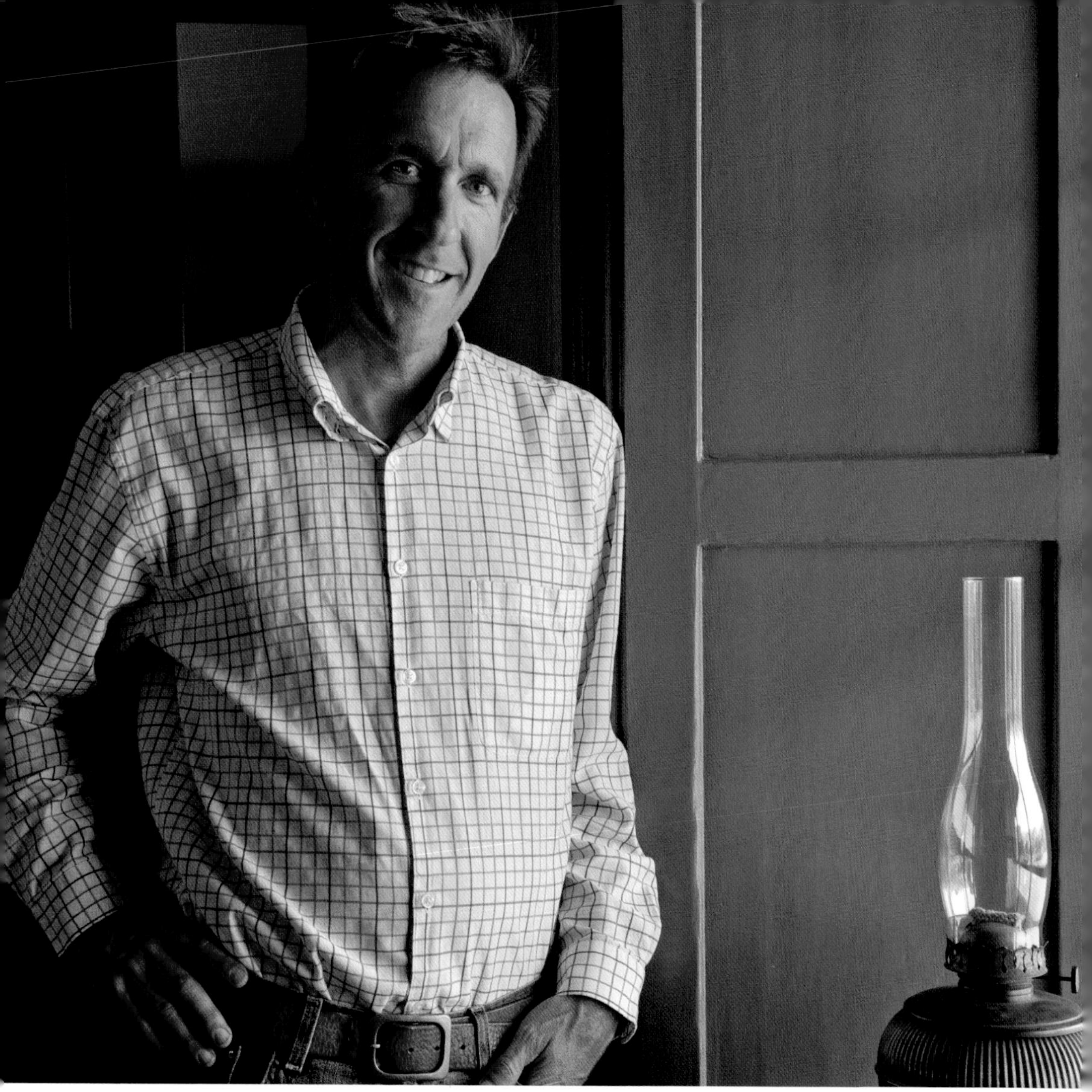

Above: Bryan Talley, who has raised already-high standards and is now producing some of Central Coast's most elegant wines

Pinot Noir

2007 Estate Delicate, sour-cherry nose. Medium-bodied and supple, with light tannins and not much depth. But balanced, delicate, and fresh, with good acidity on the finish.

2007 Rincon Rich, cherry nose. Sleek, medium-bodied, bright, and concentrated, with a light tannic backbone. The fruit is sweet and even slightly candied, but the wine has grip and length.

2007 Rosemary's★ Complex nose, with aromas of cherries, cola, and Indian spice. Rich, broad, and sleek, with bright acidity to give some piquancy. Very youthful and long.

2007 Stone Corral Rich, ripe, cherry nose, quite opulent. Rich and supple on the palate, with concentrated cherry fruit and moderate tannins and acidity. Relatively forward, and less persistent than the other Pinots.

Talley Vineyards
Area under vine: 225 acres (91ha)
Average production: 180,000 bottles
3031 Lopez Drive, Arroyo Grande, CA 93420
Tel: (805) 489-0446
www.talleyvineyards.com

Villa Creek

Cris Cherry and his wife JoAnn own the Villa Creek restaurant in downtown Paso Robles, which acts as a kind of urban headquarters for many local winemakers and vineyard owners. The food is eclectic but not nearly to the same extent as the wide-ranging wine list. Since 2001, the Cherrys have been buying small parcels of fruit from top Westside vineyards such as Denner and James Berry. Encouraged by the success of these wines, which were initially sold primarily at the restaurant, they plan to plant their own small vineyard in 2010 on their Westside property, which lies at an elevation of 1,400–1,800ft (425–550m). Cris Cherry oversees the winemaking, with assistance from Anthony Yount.

Winemaking is artisanal. All the wines are made to a consistently high standard, which cannot easily be said of many small Westside wineries

Their best-known wine is The Avenger, a Syrah-based blend, with additions of Grenache and Mourvèdre. It resembles a lively Côtes du Rhône. Vulture's Post is mostly Mourvèdre, plus Syrah and a dash of Grenache. High Road comes from the Smith family's James Berry Vineyard and is another SGM blend, as is Willow Creek Cuvée. La Boda is a blend, in equal parts, of Grenache and Mourvèdre, all from the Denner Vineyard. Damas Noir is a pure Mourvèdre. The Cherrys are also fond of Spanish varieties and produce a pure Garnacha from the Denner Vineyard, as well as Mas de Maha, a blend of Tempranillo, Grenache, and Mourvèdre. More recently they have produced a white blend from Grenache Blanc, Roussanne, and Viognier.

Winemaking is artisanal, in the best sense, with careful sorting before and after destemming, pressing in a basket press, and aging in both puncheons and barriques. All the wines are made to a consistently high standard, which cannot easily be said of many small Westside wineries. The sole drawback is that the proliferation of small-volume blends means that it will not be easy to find the wines outside the region.

FINEST WINES

(Tasted 2009)

2008 White★

Rich, flowery, peachy nose. A flamboyant palate, with admirable concentration knitting the stone-fruit and mandarin flavors. Delicious and long.

Above: Careful sorting of grapes, after as well as before destemming, is part of Villa Creek's artisinal but meticulous winemaking

2007 La Boda
Spicy, smoky, tobacco nose, with red-fruit aromas. Juicy cherry and raspberry fruit on the palate, with light tannins and a lively finish. Quite long.

2007 Garnacha
Dried herbs and plums on the nose. Though quite concentrated, with good acidity and an appealing herbal tone, this lacks some persistence and flesh.

2007 Willow Creek Cuvée
Rich, red-fruit nose, with some floral tones. A fresh and stylish wine, with ample spice, as well as some tannic grip. Quite long.

2007 Mas de Maha
The nose is sweet, spicy, and vibrant, with cherry aromas. Concentrated, with firm tannins coating the dried-fruit flavors, and a brisk and lively finish.

2006 The Avenger
Rich and dusty red-fruit nose; quite floral. A full-bodied and vigorous blend, with moderate acidity to keep it fresh. There is sufficient fruit to cover the alarming 15.6% ABV, which is not discernible (unless you drink too many glasses).

Villa Creek Cellars
Area under vine: 10 acres (4ha)
Average production: 36,000 bottles
5995 Peachy Canyon Road, Paso Robles, CA 93446
Tel: (805) 238-7145
www.villacreek.com

Santa Barbara

Santa Barbara County—at least when away from the coast—is a region of rolling grassy hills, often dotted with rather solitary trees. For decades it has been ranching land, as well as providing boltholes for the rich, such as the Neverland ranch of the late Michael Jackson. There was a small flurry of missionary planting in the late 18th century, but the modern history of the county's wines begins in the mid-1960s, when Uriel Nelson planted 100 acres (40ha) of Riesling, Chardonnay, and Cabernet Sauvignon. By 1975, there were no more than four wineries. Zaca Mesa and Firestone, in the Santa Ynez Valley, were among the first to establish vineyards on former cattle-ranching land. By the 1980s, however, there was a rush to plant. Tax loopholes encouraged investors to plant large vineyards, with Chardonnay usually the dominant variety. Fluctuations in demand for this new ocean of grapes forced some investors to sell up, and the purchasers tended to be the major wineries of the North Coast, such as Mondavi and Kendall-Jackson. Growers also recognized the potential of some areas, such as the Santa Maria Valley, for Pinot Noir, and by 1999 there were 1,200 acres (485ha) of Pinot under vine. Syrah would follow, with plantings scattered through various parts of the county. Today, there are 20,000 acres (8,000ha) under vine, of which 75 percent is planted with Chardonnay, Pinot Noir, and Syrah.

Santa Maria Valley is relatively cool, making it ideal for Burgundian varieties. However, site selection was crucial, since without sufficient exposure to sunlight, Pinot in particular could exhibit vegetal tones. Santa Ynez Valley varied greatly in temperature and growing conditions, growing steadily warmer as one moved east. So in the western parts of the valley, Pinot Noir gave excellent results, while to the east it was possible to ripen the Bordeaux varieties. Many of the large Chardonnay vineyards were located in the Los Alamos region, which straddled Highway 101 between Santa Maria and Los Olivos, but Los Alamos has never won its own AVA, even though around 6,000 acres (2,430ha) have been planted.

Given its climatic diversity, it has been difficult for Santa Barbara to establish a clear identity of its own. It is certainly capable of producing delicious Chardonnay and Pinot Noir, but its ability to produce exceptional Syrah and other Rhône varieties became evident just as demand for such wines plummeted. Stylistic footprints seem to be determined as much by individual choice in the vineyard and winery as by microclimatic conditions.

The initial growers planted by following their hunches. Although UC Davis had given its thumbs-up to Santa Barbara in the 1960s as an area with viticultural potential, there had been few studies to assess the best soil types and microclimatic conditions. So it is all the more surprising that so many delicious and even adventurous wines (such as a clutch of Cabernet Francs and an unusual Sylvaner from Rancho Sisquoc) were already being made here in the 1980s. Moreover, outstanding vineyards such as Sanford & Benedict and Bien Nacido were quick to win recognition. Today, as development in the burgeoning Santa Rita Hills AVA confirms, there is far greater understanding of the local conditions and a realization that the county's potential is only beginning to be fulfilled.

Happy Canyon (AVA from 2009) Like the Santa Rita Hills, Happy Canyon used to form part of the Santa Ynez Valley. It lies in the easternmost sector of that valley, so maritime influence is minimal. At present, some 550 acres (222ha) are planted, and both Rhône and Bordeaux varieties can ripen here. The best-known vineyards are Vogelzang and Star Lane.

Santa Maria Valley (AVA from 1981) The most prized vineyards of this region in the northern part of the county lie on the benchlands along southern slopes of the San Rafael Mountains. Elevation ranges from 300 to 800ft (90–245m). It's an area of large vineyards, such as the esteemed Bien Nacido, the enormous White Hills Vineyard, and Kendall-Jackson's Cambria. Morning fogs ensure a cool microclimate, and rainfall is sparse. Soils are essentially sandy loam and are well drained. Chardonnay is Santa Maria's mainstay, though the variety sometimes exhibits tropical-fruit flavors that can be too much of a good thing. Pinot Noir flourishes here, too, though it can sometimes be vegetal, and in certain spots, such as Bien Nacido, the Rhône varieties (white and red) can have both richness and elegance.

Santa Rita Hills (AVA from 2001) Two valleys run from the little town of Buellton toward Lompoc and the coast. The AVA consists almost entirely of what used to be the western sector of the Santa Ynez Valley. It was recognized some time ago that this subregion had quite a different microclimate from the rest of the valley: cooler and windier. The Sanford & Benedict Vineyard led the way, producing some excellent Chardonnay and Pinot Noir since the mid-1970s. Many new vineyards, planted especially with Pinot, have gone into the ground over the past decade or so, including hillside sites, whereas Sanford & Benedict and other early vineyards were on the valley floor. Today, there are some 5,000 acres (2,000ha) under vine on soils that contain both sand and clay, as well as some chalk and marl. Budbreak can be as early as February, giving the region a very long growing season; growth is also moderated by the steady winds. The drawback is that acidity levels can remain uncomfortably high until late into the fall, and by waiting until the acidity drops, growers risk picking at high sugar—and thus alcohol—levels. This explains the paradox of a genuinely cool region that nonetheless can produce rather alcoholic wines.

Some slopes near Lompoc are home to one of the most daring viticultural experiments in California. Evening Land Vineyards (ELV) is a project involving Dominique Lafon of Burgundy and local growers and winemakers in various sites in California and Oregon. Near Lompoc, 40 acres (16ha) of Pinot Noir have been planted, with the first crop in 2009. Instead of planting the fashionable Dijon clones, the American "heritage" clones have been chosen. Density is also very high: from 4,000 to 6,900 vines per acre. In addition, the soils are unusual, with shale and diatomaceous earth, as well as some limestone. Lafon and Sashi Moorman of Stolpman, who will run this part of the operation, are confident that the site will produce outstanding Pinot, but conditions here are extreme, so it is too early to say whether their hunch will be borne out. Still, it says much for the dynamism of the Santa Rita Hills that such a venture can even be contemplated.

Santa Ynez Valley (AVA from 1983) As has already been mentioned, the microclimates of this valley vary considerably, growing ever warmer as one moves eastward. The region, which is separated from Santa Maria Valley to the north by the San Rafael Mountains, has been "topped and tailed," now that Santa Rita Hills and Happy Canyon AVAs have been created at either end of the valley. The valley does benefit from some maritime influence in the mornings, but afternoons can be very hot, though usually tempered by breezes later in the afternoon. Ballard Canyon, a subregion between Solvang and Los Olivos, seems to have its own character, and vineyards such as Rusack, Jonata (under the same ownership as Screaming Eagle in Napa), Stolpman, and Beckmen produce some outstanding wines from Rhône varieties.

Au Bon Climat

There's a vast shed on the Santa Maria Valley floor that is the unphotogenic headquarters of Au Bon Climat (ABC) and some other labels. ABC was established in the early 1980s by Jim Clendenen and Adam Tolmach, who had both been winemakers at Zaca Mesa. In 1990, Tolmach left to set up his own Ojai label. His place was taken by Bob Lindquist, a pioneer of Rhône varieties in Santa Maria under his Qupé label. I doubt anyone knows for sure what goes on in this hangar. Some of Clendenen's labels, such as Vita Nova, Thumbs Up, and Podere Los Olivos, have come and gone, and he uses the facility to produce, among others, his Clendenen Family Vineyards wines, which specialize in Italian varieties.

The winery is more like the court of Clendenen. Most days, he cooks and hosts an excellent lunch for his staff and for any other winemakers, journalists, or retailers who happen to stop by. Bottles are distributed along the long trestle table, their contents depending on the interests of the guests or what Clendenen fancies trying that day. Any bottles not emptied go into the next day's cooking pots. The Clendenen terrier Emmy does her best to steal your food after jumping on your lap. As Clendenen observes, "The price for your lunch is the dry-cleaning bill for your pants."

Jim Clendenen cultivates his own image of flamboyance and exuberance. With long shoulder-length locks and an undeveloped dress sense, he still looks like an overgrown college student. But he is an astute operator, with a wide range of friends and colleagues on many continents, and he wields a razor-sharp mind that cuts through much of the nonsense spouted by other winemakers and critics. Too iconoclastic to claim status as a mentor, he is nonetheless a leading figure not just in Santa Barbara but in the entire California winemaking confraternity.

Despite the party atmosphere at ABC, Clendenen is a skilled and discerning winemaker, even if these days he is more like a general, supervising the troops and leaving the routine winemaking tasks to a squad of juniors led by the experienced Jim Adelman. Family tradition pointed Jim toward a career in law, but a spell working with Louis Jadot in Burgundy put a stop to all that. He proved a quick study, soon got to know the leading Burgundian winemakers of the day, and came back to California well versed in Burgundian winemaking techniques.

His long familiarity with the county and its vineyards gives Clendenen, and ABC, access to some excellent fruit, from sites such as Bien Nacido, Sanford & Benedict, and (in Arroyo Grande) Talley. Whether Chardonnay or Pinot Noir, they are bottled as vineyard-designated wines, and in addition there are blends such as Isabelle, which combines wines from different regions, and Knox Alexander, a high-quality blend from Bien Nacido fruit. Sources can vary from year to year, so there can be a bewildering profusion of labels. Clendenen's own vineyard, the organic Le Bon Climat, also supplies some of his brands.

Clendenen is steeped in Burgundy, and it shows. His wines don't aim to be Burgundy lookalikes—he is far too intelligent to find that an interesting goal—but he does seek a restraint and finesse typical of that great region. While the techniques he adopted are now standard practice in California, that was certainly not the case in the early 1980s. An ardent believer in barrel fermentation, punch-downs, some native-yeast fermentation, and malolactic fermentation, he is careful not to drown his wines in new oak, and he works hard with his growers to ensure that grapes are picked when balanced: he detests high-alcohol wines, arguing that they represent a failure to farm carefully. All this means that his wines are often underestimated, at least by the American wine press.

Right: Jim Clendenen, whose flamboyance is matched by his intelligence, which he uses to craft balanced, consistent wines

In 1996, he fashioned a Chardonnay in the style he personally dislikes: thickly textured and stuffed with lush, buttery fruit, aged in new oak. He called this deliberately Parkerized Chardonnay Nuits Blanches. It existed primarily as a caricature wine intended to irritate Robert Parker, which it apparently did. Parker refused to rise to the bait, scoring the wine low, but other tasters admire it.

Although best known for Chardonnay and Pinot Noir, Clendenen also has a passion for Italian wine, stimulated by a visit in the 1980s from the likes of Aldo Vajra, Josko Gravner, and Paolo di Marchi, who were all eager to learn about growing Chardonnay. He later visited some of these producers and returned to California bubbling with enthusiasm. At that time, Italian varieties were much abused in California, cropped overly generously and usually marketed as jug wines. Clendenen kept yields low and daringly produced varieties such as Arneis, Fiano, and Nebbiolo under his now-semi-defunct Podere Los Olivos label, which has in effect been replaced by a similar range under the Clendenen Family Vineyards label. He has also played around with wines from Mendocino and Oregon.

Given the scale of operation—and all the Clendenen brands combined must yield close to 50,000 cases—quality remains consistently high. The Au Bon Climat wines are never out of balance: the fruit retains freshness, the alcohol rarely exceeds 14%, and each bottle fulfills its primary role of quenching thirst and stimulating the appetite.

FINEST WINES

(Tasted 2008–10)

White

2006 Sanford & Benedict Chardonnay Lush, ripe nose. Rounded, but concentrated and spicy, with fresh acidity that keeps it tight, lively, and long.

2005 Sanford & Benedict Chardonnay★ Lean, lemony nose, quite oaky and severe. Still reticent and firm on the palate, almost earthy in its minerality, with good acidity and a long dry finish.

2004 Hildegard Spicy, oaky nose. Rich, broad, and juicy, packed with fruit, some of it tropical, but spicy and lively.

1983 Los Alamos Chardonnay Clendenen's first wine. Full straw. Stewed apricot nose, just a hint of oxidation. Plump and flamboyant, with apricot and passion-fruit flavors; a remarkable survivor, thanks to good acidity. Long.

Pinot Noir

2007 Santa Maria Valley Muted nose. Medium-bodied, fresh and zesty, with crunchy fruitiness and a lively finish. But there is little complexity and moderate length.

2006 La Bauge Delicate and pretty raspberry nose. Silky, concentrated, with light tannins, and a tight structure. A delicate style but will improve. Long.

2006 Knox Alexander Very fragrant nose, with cherry and raspberry aromas. Medium-bodied, supple, and understated, but admirably concentrated, with fine acidity and a long, delicate, oaky finish.

2006 Isabelle★ Rich, full, oaky, red-fruit nose. Plump, rounded, and full-bodied, with an almost earthy spiciness. Complex and long.

2005 Isabelle Intense and spicy cherry nose. Sleek and stylish, with ample tannins but no harshness. Very concentrated and voluptuous, with delicious fruit and persuasive acidity and length.

2005 Knox Alexander Spicy but atypical black-fruit nose, with herbal tones and a touch of licorice. Sleek and concentrated, quite tannic, with ample volume and weight but no excessive power. Long and surprisingly chocolaty finish.

2000 Knox Alexander Rich, smoky nose; cherries, cloves, and a touch of menthol. Lean, silky, still fresh, discreet but concentrated; flavors of cherries and café au lait. Delicate, balanced, and long.

1995 Isabelle Deep color, but some browning. Rich, sweet, leafy cappuccino nose; quite floral, too. Very concentrated on the palate, rich and spicy, with fine acidity keeping it lifted and vigorous. Complex and long.

Au Bon Climat
Area under vine: 62 acres (25ha)
Average production: 500,000 bottles
Santa Maria Mesa Road, Santa Maria, CA 93454
Tel: (805) 937-9801
Tasting room: 1672 Mission Drive, Solvang, CA 93463

Qupé

The modest, soft-spoken Bob Lindquist is totally different in personality from Jim Clendenen, with whom he has shared winery and lunch-table space at Au Bon Climat for 20 years. What they share, of course, is a passion for wine. Fortunately, they gaze in different directions: Clendenen has Burgundy firmly in his sights; Lindquist, the lusher slopes of the Rhône Valley. Their wine careers started in the same place, at Zaca Mesa winery, where in 1979 Lindquist was first a tour guide and then a cellar rat. He made his first Qupé wine in 1982 at Zaca Mesa, with grapes from Gary Eberle's Estrella River vineyard in Paso Robles. Thereafter, he used facilities at other Santa Barbara wineries before teaming up with Clendenen in 1989. Their winery, on land owned by the Miller family who own Bien Nacido Vineyard nearby, is a vast, unruly hangar that often has the atmosphere of a bohemian squat presided over by the loquacious Jim Clendenen.

The mainstay of Qupé is Syrah. Bob Lindquist has more experience of the variety than most. For decades he has leased or farmed land, much of it within the immense Bien Nacido vineyard close to the winery. Indeed, about half the Qupé wines come from here. Many blocks have been custom-planted for Lindquist, and the very finest wine, the Hillside Select, usually comes from a block planted to a higher density on a steep slope within Bien Nacido. The basic bottling is the blended Central Coast Syrah. The Syrahs are mostly destemmed and aged in about one-third new oak. The Hillside Select is partly barrel-fermented in new oak, but that portion is then blended in with the rest of the wine.

Below: Members of the fun-loving but hard-working Qupé team in the large shed it has shared with ABC since 1990

Dodgers

There are also single-vineyard wines from other sources, such as the Syrah and the Grenache from the Purisima Mountain Vineyard.

Lindquist produces some white wines, too: Chardonnays from Bien Nacido, a Roussanne and Viognier/Chardonnay from the same vineyard, and a surprisingly long-lived Marsanne from the Ibarra-Young Vineyard in Los Olivos.

The only vineyard Lindquist actually owns is a biodynamically farmed block across from Alban in Edna Valley. It is planted with Marsanne, Syrah, Grenache, Albariño, and Tempranillo, but the Spanish varieties are used by his wife Louisa Sawyer, who has her own label, Verdad.

The wines, whether white or red, are never flashy or overwrought but have a wonderful integrity and consistency. They remain among the very best

The wines are very successful at all levels. The simple Central Coast Syrah is both delicious and sensibly priced, even though it is naturally less layered and complex than the single-vineyard Syrahs. A vertical tasting in 1999 of the unorthodox Viognier/Chardonnay blend, going all the way back to the 1992 vintage, convincingly demonstrated the exemplary balance and consistency of that cuvée.

The wines, whether white or red, are never flashy or overwrought but have a wonderful integrity and, again, consistency. There has been an explosion in the production of massive, broad-shouldered, high-alcohol Syrahs in recent years, so the Qupé wines may have become slightly overshadowed by the proliferation of newcomers. But they remain among the very best.

Left: The soft-spoken but highly talented Bob Lindquist, who produces red and white wines of integrity and longevity

FINEST WINES

(Tasted 2008–09)

White

2007 Bien Nacido Viognier/Chardonnay
Spicy, aromatic nose, blending floral Viognier and firm Chardonnay. Rich and creamy, but with fine acidity and a long, tangy finish.

2007 Ibarra-Young Marsanne Fragrant apricot nose. Medium-bodied, precise, fresh, tangy, and long.

2006 Bien Nacido Roussanne Muted tropical fruit nose; mango. Rich, juicy, and spicy, but not overblown; precise, with good acidity and a perky lean finish that just lacks a little opulence.

1988 Marsanne Yellow straw. Lush, honeyed nose. Creamy, plump, and juicy, with ripe apricot fruit and surprising persistence. By no means over the hill.

Syrah

2007 Bien Nacido Hillside Select Vibrant plum and mint aromas. Very rich and full-bodied, but also spicy and fresh, with lively acidity and delicious black-fruit flavors. Long.

2006 Bien Nacido Sweet, delicate, intense floral nose. Medium-bodied, supple, and concentrated; still youthful, but lacks some vigor on the finish.

2005 Bien Nacido Hillside Select★ Reserved nose, plum and licorice aromas. Rich and full-bodied, with big, ripe tannins, but balanced and fresh with plenty of lift on the long finish. (14.5% ABV)

2001 Bien Nacido Hillside Select Lean and slightly herbaceous nose, with plum and espresso coffee. Medium-bodied and supple but doesn't lack tannins behind the silky texture. Flavors of black fruits and mint, and a spicy lifted finish. Refined and long.

2005 Bien Nacido X Block Dense, meaty nose; plums and licorice. Hefty and tannic, very concentrated and a bit tarry. Needs time to unwind. (14.8% ABV)

1998 Bien Nacido Hillside Select Very deep and unevolved color. Ripe, gamey nose, fresh and brisk, with some espresso aromas. Fairly rich and supple, juicy and vigorous, with delicate acidity. May lack some flesh and weight, but it's balanced and long.

Qupé
Area under vine: 40 acres (16ha)
Average production: 480,000 bottles
PO Box 440, Los Olivos, CA 93441
Tel: (805) 937-9801
Tasting room: 2963 Grand Avenue, Los Olivos, CA 93441
www.qupe.com

Beckmen Vineyards

Tom Beckmen, a music technology entrepreneur, bought and planted this property close to Los Olivos and, two years later, in 1996, created a more ambitious vineyard on Purisima Mountain in the Ballard Canyon area, hoping to attain the same high results as the neighboring Stolpman vineyard. It may have been luck, but Purisima Mountain Vineyard does seem to produce exceptional fruit—mostly from Rhône varieties but also some Sauvignon Blanc and very low-yielding Cabernet Sauvignon. Some of the fruit was sold to other wineries. As well as the mountain vineyard, which is the source of the best fruit, the original vineyard close to the winery is still in production.

Steve Beckmen is reserved and thoughtful. His wines are among the most consistent and satisfying expressions of the Rhône varieties in the Central Coast

Tom's son Steve has been running the property for some years. It has been through a number of changes. It's quite a complex site, with vines at elevations from 750 to 1,250ft (230–380m), and there are considerable variations in soil, since the upper sectors are calcareous, whereas lower down, sandstone dominates. Virused plant material has had to be replaced, and some Grenache has been converted from wire trellising to head-trained vines. In some places, the density of the Syrah vines is being doubled by interplanting between the rows. In 2006, the vineyard became biodynamic.

Steve Beckmen favors destemming and fairly short but hot fermentations, because he does not want any astringency in the wines. The latest addition to the winery is a sorting table introduced in 2009. The proportion of new barriques ranges from 30 to 60 percent, depending on the wines. Up to 100 lots are aged separately, giving Beckmen a huge range of blending material.

Beckmen is best known for its Syrah, of which there are three bottlings. The Estate wine is the basic version, aged in 35 percent new oak; Purisima Mountain blends the best blocks and sees more new oak; and Clone 1 comes from a gravelly parcel with sandstone, which gives tiny bunches and, thus, concentrated wines. The Grenache is also very good, aged in both barriques and 300-liter barrels. The white wines are whole-cluster pressed and fermented in older barrels.

Steve Beckmen is reserved and thoughtful and doesn't give much away, but his wines are among the most consistent and satisfying expressions of the Rhône varieties in the Central Coast.

FINEST WINES

(Tasted 2009)

2008 Grenache Rosé [V]
Delicate, strawberry-and-watermelon nose. Ripe and vinous, but reasonably fresh; a pretty and beguiling rosé for early drinking.

2007 Marsanne
(With 20% Roussanne) Strong, peachy nose, surprisingly aromatic for Marsanne. Quite rich and creamy, this has moderate acidity and flavors of ripe apricots, with some bite on the finish.

2007 Estate Grenache
Bright, red-fruit nose: strawberries and cherries. Medium-bodied and silky, this has moderate concentration and structure, and although the finish is slightly dry, it is also lively.

2007 Estate Syrah
Very peppery nose that leaps from the glass, with aromas of blackberries and a touch of tar. Plump, concentrated, and juicy, the fruit is backed by light tannins and has a sleek, peppery finish.

2007 Purisima Mountain Clone 1 Syrah
Rich, damson nose, with a good deal of spice: cinnamon and clove. Rich, broad, and lush, with considerable depth; it may lack a little finesse, but it has exuberance and drive, giving a long finish.

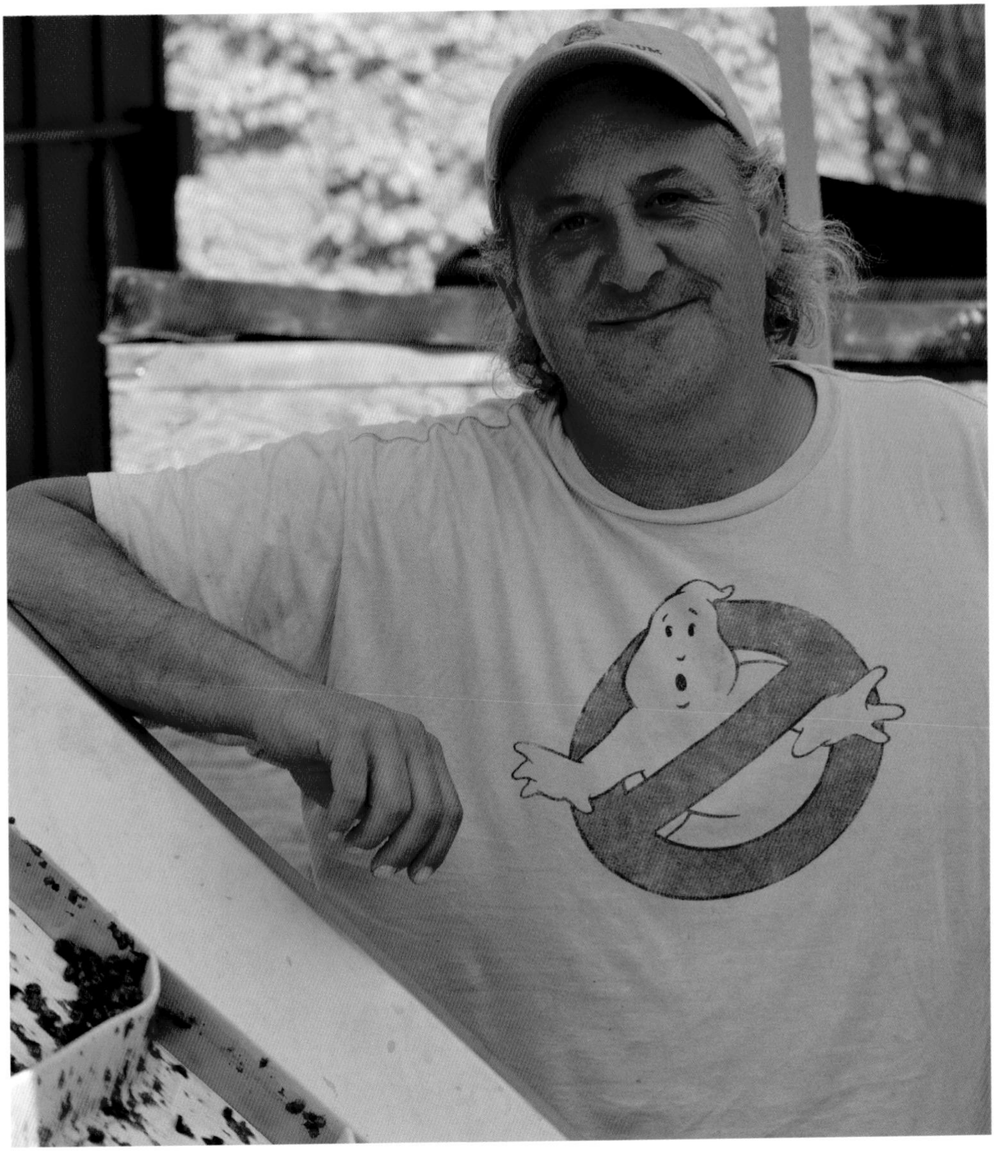

Above: Steve Beckmen, who crafts a range of stylish Rhône varietals, the best from the Purisima Mountain Vineyard

2007 Purisima Mountain Syrah ★

Gorgeous plum-and-blackberry nose, pure and focused, with lift and elegance. On the palate, this has a bright, luminous quality; sleek and harmonious, with discreet tannins on the long finish.

2006 Purisima Mountain Grenache

Rich, cherry nose, quite smoky. Full-bodied, suave, and concentrated, the lush fruit enlivened by fine acidity. It's harmonious, deep, and long.

Beckmen Vineyards
Area under vine: 150 acres (60ha)
Average production: 130,000 bottles
2670 Ontiveros Road, Los Olivos, CA 93441
Tel: (805) 688-8664
www.beckmenvineyards.com

Brewer-Clifton

Greg Brewer and Steve Clifton, equally passionate about wine, met in 1995 and founded this négociant winery a year later to produce a range of wines from Chardonnay and Pinot Noir. Brewer, lean and intense, had long experience in winemaking, at Santa Barbara Winery and later at Melville, while the more urbane Clifton's background was in the music and restaurant businesses. Steve Clifton also has his own label, Palmina, which focuses on Italian varieties and is run with his wife Chrystal.

Although at the beginning the partners bought fruit from individual vineyards that they considered full of character, they realized after a while that it would be impossible to maintain a consistent fruit supply, as growers either reduced their allocation or set up their own wineries. So Brewer and Clifton have developed 60 acres (24ha) of their own, mostly on land they have leased. Greg Brewer explains that most Santa Rita Hills vineyards form part of very large ranches, so it has not proved difficult to negotiate leases of small blocks that they can then plant with the rootstocks and clones of their choice. Their own vineyards include Mount Carmel (close to Sea Smoke), 3-D (planted to Chardonnay and Pinot Noir, and first made in 2009), Machado (near Clos Pepe), and the all-Chardonnay Gnesa. In 2007, Brewer-Clifton deviated from their single-vineyard program by producing appellation blends, since some lots were too small to be worth bottling separately.

All the wines are made in the same way, the only fluctuating element being the amount of malolactic fermentation. The partners want to highlight the specificity of individual vineyards, so maintaining a single style of winemaking allows the terroirs to be differentiated. The Chardonnays are all fermented with Montrachet yeasts and aged in Sirugue barrels that they buy from Hanzell. Although at first the Chardonnays were aged in about one-third new oak, today no new oak is used.

As for the Pinots, they are picked at quite high ripeness levels (Brewer likes to pick on flavor rather than by numbers), sorted in the vineyard, cold-soaked, and fermented as whole clusters in square steel bins, then given a maceration of about one month. There is no fining or filtration.

These are wines of strong individuality, as their makers intend, and Greg Brewer aims for a distinct minerality, which he defines in terms of a salty character. The wines, highly rated and scarce, have been difficult to find, but the new appellation blends should bring the forceful Brewer-Clifton style to a wider audience.

FINEST WINES

(Tasted 2009)

Chardonnay

2008 Santa Rita Hills Charming and pure, lifted nose, with apple and apricot aromas. Medium-bodied, with quite sharp acidity, giving a lean and assertive style that is tight and tangy but also rather strident. Needs time.

2007 Mount Carmel★ Rich, spicy, appley nose, discreet and stylish. Quite rich and concentrated on the palate but also has some racy citric acidity, and some depth and grip on the persistent finish.

Pinot Noir

2007 Santa Rita Hills Voluptuously ripe red fruits, especially strawberries, on the nose. Rounded and sappy on the palate, its opulence cut by a fine tannic grip. Still youthful, with a welcome austerity.

2007 Mount Carmel Sumptuous raspberry-and-cherry nose. Rich but luminous, with no heaviness despite the firm tannins. Although possibly lacking some depth, it has a pure, airy quality, a silky texture, and admirable length.

Above: Greg Brewer (right) and Steve Clifton, who produce a range of distinctive, mineral, highly rated Chardonnay and Pinot

Brewer-Clifton
Area under vine: 60 acres (24ha)
Average production: 90,000 bottles
329 North F Street, Lompoc, CA 93436
Tel: (805) 735-9184
www.brewerclifton.com

Foxen

The Foxen family received a Mexican land grant of some 9,000 acres (3,640ha) in 1837, and generations later a descendant, Dick Doré, still inhabits some of that land. Until the mid-1980s, he made his living as a banker but never really enjoyed a career in finance. So in 1986 he teamed up with Bill Wathen, who had been a vineyard manager at what is now the Cambria estate in Santa Maria Valley and had also worked at Chalone. Ever since, he has been the winemaker for Foxen. The Dorés own two small estate vineyards, but most of the fruit is purchased on long-term contracts from top Santa Barbara properties.

There seems to be a distinct leap in quality since the early 2000s. Today, the wines are consistently enjoyable and worthy of the hordes who descend on the old shack

The winery headquarters has long been a dilapidated roadside shack that for decades has drawn loyal visitors to the tasting room. When Foxen moved to a solar-powered winery nearby in 2009, it was tempting to tear down the shabby wooden hut, but it had become so associated with the winery that it earned a reprieve.

The mainstay of Foxen is Chardonnay and Pinot Noir, but there are other wines of interest. Chenin Blanc has been produced from the outset, from the Cambria Vineyard, and is aged in neutral oak for six months. One of the estate vineyards, Williamson-Doré, lies at the eastern end of Santa Ynez Valley, where the warm climate allows Rhône varieties to ripen. Cuvée Jeanne Marie comes from here—a blend of Grenache, Syrah, and Mourvèdre aged almost entirely in older barrels. There is also a Cabernet Sauvignon from the Vogelzang Vineyard in the new Happy Canyon AVA, and a Merlot/Cabernet called Range 30 West from the same area.

The Burgundian varieties come mostly from Bien Nacido, though Foxen is probably the only winery to source some Pinot Noir from Sea Smoke, because Bill Wathen helped lay out the vineyard. The winery used to buy from Sanford & Benedict, but that contract has been terminated. The Pinot Noir is destemmed and fermented with selected yeasts; manual punch-downs extract color and tannins. The single-vineyard Pinots are aged in up to 80 percent new oak but usually considerably less.

The wines were unremarkable in the early 1990s, but there seems to be a distinct leap in quality since the early 2000s. Today, they are consistently enjoyable and worthy of the approval of the hordes who routinely descend on the old shack to buy.

FINEST WINES

(Tasted 2008–09)

White

2008 Bien Nacido Block UU Chardonnay Discreet, oaky, appley nose. Rich and creamy, but has marked acidity and is still unformed. Moderate length.

2007 Wickenden Old Vine Chenin Blanc Reticent and delicate, lemony nose. Medium-bodied, with racy acidity balanced by a touch of residual sugar that doesn't obtrude on a tangy, citric finish.

2006 Bien Nacido Block UU Chardonnay Lean, tropical-fruit nose, with a light herbal tone. Quite lush, concentrated, and ripe, with an attractive texture and sufficient acidity to prevent the wine from seeming too weighty.

Red

2007 Bien Nacido Block 8 Pinot Noir Very oaky nose, with coffee aromas, as well as cherries and raspberries. Quite dense and concentrated, even burly for Pinot. It has good acidity yet lacks some finesse, and the tannins need time to integrate.

2007 Julia's Vineyard Pinot Noir★ Ripe, seductive, raspberry nose, quite leafy and savory. Very ripe, suave, and juicy, with excellent balance. No trace of extraction or manipulation and has good length.

2007 Sea Smoke Pinot Noir Rich, hefty, oaky nose, plums and black cherries, but it lacks some typicity. Rich and full-bodied, lush and opulent, concentrated, chocolaty, and peppery, with a dash of alcohol (15.5%) on the finish of moderate length.

Above: Dick Doré (left) and Bill Wathen, who produce a broad range of enjoyable, popular wines from top vineyards

2007 Jeanne Marie Bright, raspberry nose, with a touch of bacon. Fleshy, open, and juicy, with light tannins. Not a complex wine, but it has moderate acidity and length and is very enjoyable.
2006 Tinaquaic Syrah Rich, smoky, plummy nose. Rich, with chewy tannins and ample grip, this has persistence, despite only moderate acidity, and plenty of grip on the peppery finish.

2006 Williamson-Doré Syrah Ripe, meaty nose, cherries and cloves. Juicy, with bright acidity, good concentration, and a delicate, peppery finish.

Foxen
Area under vine: 16 acres (6.5ha)
Average production: 120,000 bottles
7200 Foxen Canyon Road, Santa Maria, CA 93454
Tel: (805) 937-4251
www.foxenvineyard.com

Sea Smoke Cellars

There have been many new plantings in the Santa Rita Hills over the past decade, but few are as ambitious as Bob Davids' Sea Smoke. The almost all-Pinot vineyard, divided into 24 blocks, sprawls along a clay slope with shallow soils at an elevation of 350 to 650ft (106–198m), looking down on the famous Sanford & Benedict Vineyard on the other side of the valley. It enjoys a south-facing exposure and ripens some two weeks earlier than the valley-floor vineyards. Yields can be very low—too much so for commercial comfort.

Owner Davids is a games inventor with a passion for Burgundy. He lives in the Caribbean and is a hands-off proprietor who did not even ask to see the plans for the new winery that was built in 2009. The initial winemaker—the first vintage was 2001—was Kris Curran (now at Foley), but she left in 2007. The general manager, Victor Gallegos, appropriately qualified with both a viticulture degree from UC Davis and an MBA from Berkeley, took over winemaking, as well as commercial responsibilities at Sea Smoke. He also makes wines in Priorat for his own label.

There have been many new plantings in the Santa Rita Hills over the past decade, but few are as ambitious as Bob Davids' Sea Smoke

The current range is three-tiered. The basic wine is called Botella (which is named after a dominant soil type), but quantities are small, and the main cuvée is Southing. The top wine is called Ten, so named because it consists of the best barrel from each of the ten clones planted. To this range has recently been added a single-barrel bottling called, aptly, One.

Admittedly, I have had a love/hate relationship with Sea Smoke from the start. I have admired the scale and ambition of the enterprise and the eagerness of Kris Curran to experiment with different vinification regimes to coax the maximum flavor from her grapes. And although the grapes were often late-harvested with high sugars, she was reluctant to pick at high pH levels because she did not want to acidify the wines (but would consider adding a little water to reduce the alcohol).

And yet the opaque, saturated color of these wines, their density and high alcohol, put me off. They were impressive and superbly concentrated, but were they really what one was looking for from Pinot Noir, even allowing for the fact that Santa Rita Hills Pinot was under no obligation to taste like Volnay? The grapes were chilled overnight, given a cold soak of up to four days, punched down three times a day, and aged for up to 20 months in a proportion of new oak that varied from 40 percent (Botella) to 100 percent (Ten). Alcohol was frequently just below or above 15%.

However, recent vintages have seen a welcome modification of the style. The Sea Smoke Pinots are still big and rich, but less new oak is being used, and the alcohols are lower, at around 14.5%. Consequently, the wines now strike me as better balanced and showing greater typicity, too.

A small quantity of Chardonnay is also produced, but most of it is actually given away to Sea Smoke's best customers and consequently called Gratis; it is of no commercial significance. However, the 2007 was surprisingly pungent and Chablisien on the nose, combining power and refreshment on the palate.

FINEST WINES

(Tasted 2008–09)

2007 Southing Fine, tight, oaky nose, with powerful if spicy Pinot aromas of cherries. Medium-bodied yet concentrated and tannic, spicy and peppery, with plenty of alcohol, yet not too hot. It has good acidity and a long, chewy aftertaste.

Above: The Sea Smoke vineyard, which ripens early due to its southerly exposure, but where yields are kept extremely low

2007 Ten★ Very ripe nose, almost jammy, with red-fruited fragrance and intensity. Rich, firm, and very concentrated, with pronounced acidity, a good deal of oak, and a long, spicy finish.
2007 One Very rich, flamboyant, raspberry nose, intense and perfumed. Rich, suave, and very concentrated; quite extracted, yet the tannins are held in check. Has depth and spiciness but is still overbearing and not as balanced as other cuvées.
2005 Botella Very ripe, almost Porty nose, with a hint of hard candy, as well as aromas of black cherries and beets. Plump, creamy, and full-bodied on the palate, this is a bit hot and heavy-handed and could use more acidity and length.
2005 Southing Firm, oaky nose, cherries and red fruits. Full-bodied, creamy, and quite tannic, showing some opulence and more typicity than Botella. Although there is more finesse, this is still a heavy-handed style of Pinot, with a long and distinctly sweet finish.
2005 Ten Dense, Porty, new-oak nose, with plummy fruit that resembles Syrah more than Pinot. Full-bodied and quite extracted, this has hefty tannins and only moderate acidity. Although the fruit is imposing, it lacks some lift and is muscular for Pinot Noir. Moderate length, with an earthy finish.

Sea Smoke Cellars
Area under vine: 100 acres (40ha)
Average production: 150,000 bottles
PO Box 1953, Lompoc, CA 93436
Tel: (805) 737-1600
www.seasmokecellars.com

Stolpman Vineyards

In the late 1980s, when the Ballard Canyon just south of Los Olivos was still not well known or recognized for vineyard potential, viticulturist Jeff Newton had an informed hunch that a former 220-acre (90ha) cattle ranch with clay-loam soils over an unusual limestone subsoil could produce exceptional grapes. It was one of the properties that the Perrins checked out before eventually settling on Tablas Creek for their Rhône-variety nursery and vineyard. After the Perrins turned it down, it was bought by Long Beach lawyer Tom Stolpman. At first, Stolpman and Newton planted Merlot and Cabernet Franc, but before too long these varieties were grafted over to Syrah at double the vine density. Today, the density is as high as 3,000 vines per acre (compared to the 870 vines of the original plantings). As an experiment, there is a parcel planted à la Côte Rôtie: own-rooted vines planted at 6,000 vines per acre and trained up sticks rather than trellised. This method gives more shading and thus protects the bunches from sunburn.

For the first decade, Stolpman was happy to grow and sell grapes to Ojai, Sine Qua Non, and other wineries. In the late 1990s, wines were made for him by local winemakers Craig Jaffurs and Brian Babcock. Then, in 2001, a former chef named Sashi Moorman, who had been making wine at Ojai, came on board, and so did Alberto Antonini, as a consultant. They oversaw the replanting of much of the site, with better clones, density, and exposition. The vineyard was divided into numerous small blocks, each of which could be cultivated and irrigated differently, though by 2009, 60 percent of the vineyard was dry-farmed. Moorman finds that the limestone subsoil gives the wines a distinctive vibrancy, though only if yields are kept below 2 tons per acre. He also found that the site, like many great vineyards, is marginal in terms of sugar accumulation, so in some years it can be a bit of a struggle to achieve sufficient ripeness. Surprisingly, there is some Cabernet here, which gives wines of finesse rather than power.

Stolpman is not solely focused on Rhône varieties and also produces wines from Nebbiolo and Sangiovese. This makes the range quite complex. Roussanne is blended with a little Viognier to create L'Avion, and there is a Roussanne/Viognier blend called La Coppa Blanc. Varietal Nebbiolo and Syrah are aged in new oak. As well as the blended Estate Syrah, there is a special cuvée called Hilltops. But Syrah is also blended with Sangiovese to give a blend called Croce. Angeli is a Bordeaux blend. If Moorman gives the wines a signature, it is one highlighting freshness and vigor, though some years ago the wines could be too marked by new oak. As a long-term aim, Moorman hopes to produce more inexpensive, or at least good-value, wines, which will increase case production slightly.

Moorman takes a modern approach to winemaking but adapts it to different varieties and blends. He favors a long cold soak, and begins fermentation with natural yeasts, though often some cultivated yeasts are added to complete the process satisfactorily. He likes a hot fermentation and vinifies some lots in barrels with the heads removed. Only French oak is used.

Moorman is an exceptionally intelligent and flexible winemaker and is also involved with the fascinating ELV project with Dominique Lafon. As for Stolpman, its excellent wines might be better appreciated if the range were more transparent.

FINEST WINES

(Tasted 2009)

2007 L'Avion Intense, apricot and lemon-curd nose. Creamy and voluptuous, with moderate acidity and integrated oak. Quite long.

2007 Sangiovese Cherry and coffee aromas on the nose. Medium-bodied and supple but concentrated, has vigor and bite, and though tannic, it's balanced and quite long.

Above: Sashi Moorman, the former chef who has proved an exceptionally skillful and successful winemaker at Stolpman since 2001

2007 La Croce Dense, chunky, oaky nose. Very ripe and rich, quite tannic and tight, but with good acidity to lift the palate. A touch overbearing, with a long, chocolaty finish.
2007 Estate Syrah★ Dense, plummy nose, oaky and voluptuous. Rich but not hefty, very concentrated yet fresh and lively, showing a light touch and a peppery finish.

Stolpman Vineyards
Area under vine: 140 acres (56ha)
Average production: 75,000 bottles
Tasting room: 2434 Alamo Pintado Avenue, Los Olivos, CA 93441
Tel: (805) 688-0400
www.stolpmanvineyards.com

Zaca Mesa

One of the first wineries to be established deep within Santa Ynez Valley, along with Firestone, Zaca Mesa was founded in 1972 by a group of investors headed by an oilman named Louis Ream. The vineyards were planted in 1973, and the winery was built five years later. The first vintage was 1975. More by accident than design, Zaca Mesa became the place where aspiring winemakers came to cut their teeth. Jim Clendenen and Bob Lindquist were here in the late 1970s, when Ken Brown, later of Byron, was the head winemaker. Other head winemakers have been Dan Gehrs, Clay Brock, and, currently, Eric Mohseni.

Ream expanded production too rapidly and ran into trouble when, by the early 1980s, the winery was releasing more than 100,000 cases. He sold Zaca Mesa in 1986, and real-estate tycoon John Cushman, one of the original partners, acquired the winery and remains the owner to this day.

By the mid-1990s it had become clear that this was an excellent location for Rhône varieties, and they remain the winery's forte. Moreover, Zaca Mesa continues to offer excellent value

The vineyards have also been through many phases. They are on elevated marine layers of sandy loam with a little limestone, at a height of 1,400–1,500ft (425–485m), which helps counter the heat in this part of the valley. The initial plantings were shotgun—no one in the early 1970s knew which varieties would flourish here—and many varieties, such as Chenin Blanc, Semillon, and Petite Sirah, were not even vinified. But by the early 1980s, they were planting what is thought to be the oldest Syrah in Santa Barbara County, now supplemented by new clones. Other varieties have been pulled out: Cabernet Sauvignon, Pinot Noir, and Zinfandel didn't give good results. Though many grapes used to be sold to other wineries, since the early 2000s all the Zaca Mesa wines are estate-grown. The acreage of Chardonnay has been reduced and that of Roussanne increased. About half the Chardonnay is vinified and aged in steel tanks, the remainder aged in older barrels, with no malolactic fermentation, all suggesting that the winemakers have to work hard to conserve freshness.

Zaca Mesa remains a large commercial winery, and there have been misses as well as hits. Rieslings and Chardonnays made in the late 1980s were generally disappointing. But by the mid-1990s it had become clear that this was an excellent location for Rhône varieties in general, and they remain the winery's forte. Moreover, Zaca Mesa continues to offer excellent value. Blends like Z Gris (a Grenache-based rosé) and Z Cuvée (a blend in the style of a Côtes du Rhône) may not be great wines, but they are well made, highly quaffable, and relatively inexpensive. In recent years, there have been some new additions to the range, such as Z Three, a blend of Syrah, Mourvèdre, and Grenache, aged for 20 months in 60 percent new barriques; and Z Blanc, a blend of mostly Roussanne, plus Grenache Blanc and a dash of Viognier.

The regular Syrah is co-fermented with Viognier and aged for 16 months in 25 percent new barriques. The Black Bear Block Syrah comes from a 3.5-acre (1.4ha) block planted in 1978; it was first made as a single-parcel wine in 1996. Each winemaker seems to have left his personal stamp on this Syrah, as well as on other Zaca Mesa wines, but the current versions are aged for 21 months in 80 percent new barriques.

While it would be foolish to make exaggerated claims for the Zaca Mesa wines, I have enjoyed many of them over two decades, and the Syrah and some of the blends have sometimes risen to considerable heights.

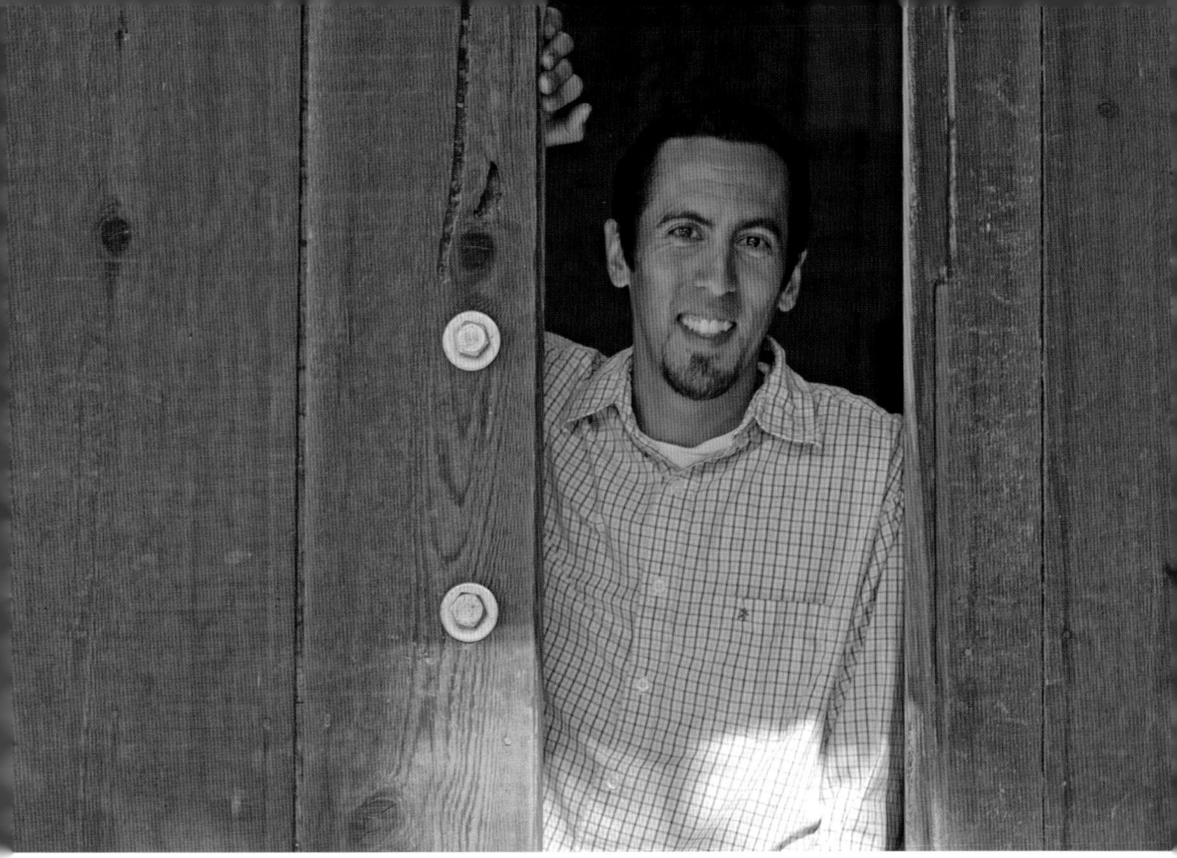

Above: Eric Mohseni, head winemaker at Zaca Mesa, where he produces a broad range of accessible, enjoyable, good-value wines

FINEST WINES

(Tasted 2008–09)

White

2007 Z Blanc Spicy, oaky nose, with apricot and melon. Creamy, concentrated, and suave, but sound underlying acidity gives the blend persistence.

2006 Viognier Rich, honeysuckle nose. Creamy, supple, and opulent, with moderate acidity to add charm to the weight of the wine. Well balanced.

2007 Chardonnay Bright, spicy, appley nose. Medium-bodied, with light acidity—a clean brisk style that's fresh if not complex.

2006 Roussanne Dense, oaky nose. Quite rich, plump, and concentrated, and less oaky than the nose; has flavors of stone fruits and melon, with fair acidity and quite good length.

Red

2008 Z Gris Smoky, red-fruit nose. Fresh, medium-bodied, with some dusty tannins and good acidity, as well as a discernible touch of residual sugar.

2006 Z Cuvée [V] Lean, spicy, red-fruit nose, with a touch of tobacco. Rich and full-bodied but has zest and freshness. Delicious, bright, and quite long.

2005 Z Three Smoky, spicy nose, plums and cocoa. Broad, fleshy, and concentrated; has heft and depth without being too extracted. Has integrated tannins, with berry fruit and pepper on the finish.

2005 Syrah Ripe nose, with bright blueberry aromas. Supple, juicy, and quite concentrated. Highly drinkable, well balanced, with a long, fresh finish.

2005 Black Bear Block Syrah★ Rich, spicy, and aromatic nose, with aromas of blueberries, mint, and plums. Rich and suave, with dense but ripe tannins, chocolaty but fresh. Still youthful, with a long, intense finish.

2004 Z Cuvée Smoky, oaky nose, with excellent fruit. Rich, juicy, and accessible, concentrated and quite tannic. Bags of fruit and a long, spicy finish.

2004 Syrah Smoky, black-fruit nose. Rich, formidable, and very concentrated; lush and swaggering; invigorating, exciting, and long.

Zaca Mesa
Area under vine: 200 acres (80ha)
Average production: 420,000 bottles
6905 Foxen Canyon Road, Los Olivos, CA 93441
Tel: (805) 688-9339
www.zacamesa.com

Clos Pepe

When Steve Pepe and his wife retired from their corporate-law practice, they decided to pursue a second career as grape farmers. They bought a piece of land in the Santa Rita Hills in 1994 and began planting it two years later. At first, they sold the grapes to other wineries, but in 2000 they began producing small quantities of their own Chardonnay and Pinot Noir. They were aided and abetted by their son-in-law Wes Hagen, who has his own very strong ideas about viticulture and winemaking. If there is a tendency at some Santa Rita Hills estates to produce powerful and burly wines, Hagen and Clos Pepe reflect the opposite tendency, striving to make wines of delicacy and finesse.

If there is a tendency at some Santa Rita Hills estates to produce powerful wines, Wes Hagen and Clos Pepe reflect the opposite tendency, striving to make wines of delicacy and finesse

Hagen says his primary focus is on the vineyards and that he is content to let the wines make themselves. His aim is to maximize even ripening. This is not easy in this spot, since the soils are of varying depth. He believes the soil composition, dominated by calcium and diatomaceous earth, gives the wine a distinct minerality. But that very individuality would be compromised if the wines were made in too rich a style. Yields are very low, never exceeding 2.5 tons per acre. The property is not organic, but Hagen uses sheep both to control the cover crop and to produce the raw material for the compost later spread over the vineyards.

The winemaking is simplicity itself, and the Chardonnay—a variety Hagen believes is underrated here because of the fashion for Santa Rita Hills Pinot—is aged only in older barrels. In contrast, the Pinot Noir, which is fermented with both natural and selected yeasts, is aged in about 40 percent new oak.

Hagen freely admits that the drawback of his taut, lean, often acidic wines, which are usually below 14% in alcohol, is that they do not show so well young and need to be aged, which is not what most American consumers are looking for. For that reason, he takes pains to make contact with his customers and to invite them to visit the vineyard and stay for lunch, so that they can understand the reasons behind the stylistic individuality of the wines.

FINEST WINES

(Tasted 2009)

Chardonnay

2008 Lean, fragrant lime nose. Tight and pungent, with high acidity and a long, sherbetty finish. Skeletal now and needs time.

2001 Delicate apple-and-apricot nose. Intense, lean, and refined, but definitely not a fruit-forward style. It retains its firm acidity and shows little evolution, but it has poise, finesse, and length.

Pinot Noir

2008 Intense and lifted red-curranty nose. Medium-bodied but concentrated, with light tannins and tight acidity. Lacks fruit expression now but has length and poise.

2007 Slightly candied raspberry nose, with finesse and intensity. Medium-bodied and fleshier than the 2008, with fine acidity and tannins. Still quite austere, but this gives grip and potential to the long finish.

2005★ Intense red-fruit nose, with just a hint of gaminess. Rich, full-bodied, and very concentrated; it's also spicy, vigorous, and impeccably balanced and complete. Shows as yet little evolution. Long.

Clos Pepe
Area under vine: 32 acres (13ha)
Average production: 12,000 bottles
4777 Highway 246, Lompoc, CA 93436
Tel: (805) 735-2196
www.clospepe.com

Melville

Ron Melville was in a bind. He was a grape grower in Knights Valley but increasingly fascinated by Pinot Noir, a variety definitely not on the recommended list for that corner of Sonoma. Encounters with Santa Rita Hills Pinots suggested to him that it was the ideal place to grow Pinot, so in 1996 he bought a property there and planted vines a year later. He intended to sell his grapes (and he still sells a great deal), but Greg Brewer persuaded him it would be a sound idea to produce his own wines. Greg was taken on as winemaker, and the first vintage was in 1999. Since 2000, all the wines have been estate-grown.

More than two-thirds of the vines are Pinot Noir, plus 20 percent Chardonnay; the remaining 10 percent consists of Viognier and Syrah planted on leased land in a warmer area, Cat Canyon in Los Alamos. There are 11 clones of Pinot, planted on seven rootstocks, as Melville tries to establish the selections that work best in his vineyard. Yields hover around 2 tons per acre for Pinot; those for Chardonnay are a bit higher.

The Melville wines are unusual in being kept away from new oak barrels. Pinot Noir used to be aged in about 30 percent new barriques, but since 2007 the proportion has been minimal, and the Chardonnay is aged only in neutral barrels. Instead of relying on wood to give the wines some tannic structure, Brewer prefers to retain some stems during fermentation. Moreover, from the start Melville produced a Chardonnay called Inox, since it was aged only in steel tanks. Today, quite a few wineries produce unoaked Chardonnay, but in 2000 it was a controversial move. Sommeliers loved the restraint of the wine, but consumers were baffled for a while, since Chardonnay had become synonymous with "oaked white wine."

As well as the Estate wines, Melville produces a few Pinots from specific blocks. The Terraces comes from a 5-acre (2ha) parcel near the winery; and in 2001, Carrie's was added, a wine from a different 4-acre (1.6ha) block on the same mesa. All the red wines are unfined and unfiltered.

Greg Brewer is a winemaker who likes purity and transparency in his wines. He picks according to flavor, so the harvest at Melville can take four weeks. As a result, Melville wines can be high in alcohol, but its presence is rarely discernible.

FINEST WINES

(Tasted 2008–09)

Chardonnay

2007 Clone 17 Inox Lean, tangy nose of lime and mango. Tight, lean, and assertive. Certainly racy and dry but also one-dimensional and rather raw.

2007 Estate Elegant nose, with a surprising toastiness that (suggests Greg Brewer) comes from lees contact; aromas of apples and brine. Medium-bodied, supple, and understated, it also has a tanginess linked to its vigorous acidity. A distinctive wine, quite austere now, and long. (14.9%)

2002 Estate Chardonnay Delicate, apricot-and-pineapple nose, a touch buttery. Sleek, lively, and still fresh, with fine acidity, though it lacks some complexity. Quite long. (15.2%)

Red

2007 Estate Pinot Noir Light, cherry nose, with purity and lift. Sleek, medium-bodied, with fresh raspberry fruit and welcome acidic bite that gives raciness, as well as impressive length. (15.3% ABV)

2007 The Terraces Pinot Noir Fairly rich, cherry-and-raspberry nose, discreet and stylish. Silky and delicate on the palate, yet with concentration, depth, and grip. Needs time. Long. (14.9% ABV)

2007 Carrie's Pinot Noir★ A more opulent nose than the other Pinots. Juicy and plump, but good acidity to cut. Long, earthy finish. (14.7% ABV)

2004 Estate Pinot Noir Fairly rich cherry nose, smoky and perfumed. Quite full-bodied and mouth-filling, with fine acidity to cut the opulence. Quite long, with delicate cherry fruit on the finish.

Melville
Area under vine: 250 acres (100ha)
Average production: 220,000 bottles
5185 Highway 246, Lompoc, CA 93436
Tel: (805) 735-7030
www.melvillewinery.com

Sean Thackrey

There can't be many antiquarian winemakers, but the tousled Sean Thackrey is certainly one of them. His primary career was in San Francisco as an art dealer specializing in 19th-century prints and photographs. He started to make wines as long ago as 1979 and, from the beginning, carved out his own idiosyncratic path. He is self-taught and learned how to make wine by reading about it. (This has never worked for me.) "That's how I learn about everything," he explained. "I happen to be very good at improvisation, so I was able to deal with things that went wrong, as they inevitably did." When I met him in 1997, he was wearing a custom-made vest that presented a quotation on the back from Le Gentil's 18th-century treatise on winemaking: *Je ne consulte que mon plaisir*. If that summarized Thackrey's philosophy at that time, it hardly seems to have changed. He just follows his taste buds wherever they lead, just as a chef simply tastes and adjusts a sauce he's preparing rather than sending it to a lab for analysis.

He began his adventure in wine by planting some vines near his house. Since he lives in the coastal town of Bolinas, which always seems shrouded in bone-chilling Pacific fog, it's not surprising that the vines did not flourish. He had no wish to follow the usual path of hobby winemakers by purchasing Concord grapes but managed to find a company in Berkeley that could offer him crushed fruit from good vineyards such as Fay in Stags Leap. He made his first wine from these grapes in 1979, just to test the water, and fell in love with the whole process. His first commercial release was a 1981 Merlot/Cabernet blend. Unsold stock could be poured at his gallery openings. The wine was a critical success, but for some years he couldn't afford to buy more grapes, so the next vintage was not until 1986.

In that year, he found a vineyard in Yountville owned by Arthur Schmidt. Schmidt used to sell his grapes to jug-wine producers, but Thackrey noticed a patch of old Syrah, which he bought every year to form a wine he called Orion. Unfortunately, Clarke Swanson, a rich proprietor in Napa, bought the vineyard, so Thackrey lost his supply. He replaced it in 1991, when he discovered the Andrew Rossi vineyard in St. Helena. Here, he found a block of bush vines, planted in 1905 and always dry-farmed. There are 11 varieties, and the dominant one appears to be Syrah—or at least Serine, a strain of Syrah that was once planted in Côte Rôtie. Yields are tiny, and this new incarnation of Orion is sufficiently concentrated to support aging in 100 percent new oak.

Thackrey's winery, close to his house, is artisanal, to put it mildly. Many barrels and the basket press are kept outdoors, with a tarpaulin casually tossed over them. He points out that, with the cool summers and mild falls, there is no problem with temperature control. In 2005, however, he bought a barn, now converted into a more conventional winery that's located in a more sheltered spot. There are few winemaking rules here. He does take great care over the fermentation, keeps the press wine separate, and never filters. Other than that, anything goes. "I always like to reinvent the wheel. A lot of my wines are one-offs, because I like challenging my own wine assumptions. If I make a certain wine in older barrels, I might change my mind the next year and try a lot of new oak—or the opposite. I'm an inveterate experimenter."

This makes it difficult to assess his wines, since the range can vary from year to year. Orion is the wine from the Rossi Vineyard. Andromeda is a Pinot Noir from the Devil's Gulch Vineyard in Marin County; Aquila, a Sangiovese from the Eaglepoint Ranch in Mendocino, which is also the source of the Petite Sirah called Sirius. He has experimented with white wines over the years but admits they are not yet his forte.

His best-known wine is Pleiades, a variable

blend that, he says, "is supposed to be complex, interesting, and delicious but easy to drink". The principal varieties are Syrah, Sangiovese, and Viognier. As a blend from various vineyards and different vintages, it is always released as a non-vintage wine. "It's like a chef's special. You trust the chef, so you're prepared to order the dish of the day." He assembles his blends by composing a proto-blend from most or all of the potential elements, and he then removes components that don't appeal to him.

Sean Thackrey remains very much a free spirit, making wines that please him and hoping that his loyal clientele will share his taste. "Wine has become part of the fashion industry, at the whim of sommeliers, critics, and bloggers. I find this very irritating. Fortunately, I have loyal customers who simply like my wines and trust me."

FINEST WINES

(Tasted 2009)

2007 Orion★
Rich, heady, plummy nose; sumptuously fruity, with aromas of chocolate mints. Suave and very concentrated; has a seamless texture and great depth of flavor, with plums and chocolate to the fore. Good length.

2006 Andromeda Devil's Gulch Pinot Noir
Bright but sturdy red-fruit nose, with intense raspberry aromas. Medium-bodied, silky, and delicate, but showing little complexity.

2003 Aquila
Reticent nose, with aromas of crystallized fruit and sour cherries. Medium-bodied, still quite tannic, has intensity and drive. Coffee tones underscore the cherry fruit, and the 15.2% ABV is not detectable.

2001 Andromeda Devil's Gulch Pinot Noir
Very spicy, aromatic nose, with aromas of red fruits and cherries; quite leafy, minty, and complex. Full-bodied, svelte, and spicy, this has a lot of vigor, and fine acidity comes through on the finish, along with some leafy undergrowth tones. Complex and long to finish.

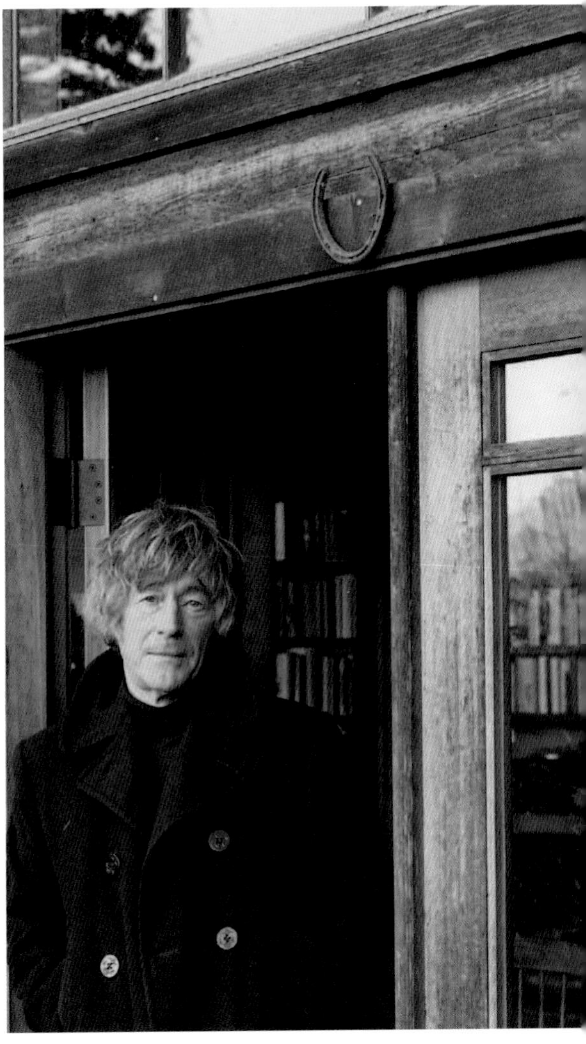

Above: The brilliant, idiosyncratic, self-confessed "inveterate experimenter" Sean Thackrey in the door of his Bolinas home

Sean Thackrey
No vineyards
Average production: 60,000 bottles
Bolinas, CA 94924
www.wine-maker.net

The Négociants

Given the high cost of vineyards in California, it is not surprising that many winemakers prefer to buy grapes from established growers rather than go to the expense and trouble of buying and then cultivating their own vineyards. These négociant winemakers aspire to build up long-term relationships with some outstanding growers, often buying each year from the same vineyard blocks. They will also negotiate a price based not on tonnage but on acreage. This means that if the winemaker wants the grower to reduce yields or pursue specific practices in the vineyard, then the grower will not suffer financially. The grower gets paid, and the winemaker ends up with the desired quality of fruit.

Such a relationship can be full of pitfalls, but it can also work extremely well. Many of the wineries discussed in previous pages have very satisfactory relationships with their growers. One example will suffice: Bob Lindquist of Qupé has been buying from Bien Nacido Vineyard in Santa Maria Valley for well over 20 years, and he has even had some blocks planted to his specifications.

Some of the wineries already discussed in these pages are essentially négociant wineries: Kosta Browne, Ramey, and Thackrey fall into this category, but I do not place them as négociant wineries because the owners' intention is to forge and maintain long-term contracts with those they buy from. The true négociant is a more fickle creature, often through no fault of his own. Although the goal may be to purchase from the same growers each year, that may be difficult to attain. Negotiations on grape prices may founder, or a grower may turn to a new client, or the winemaker may grow dissatisfied with the quality of the fruit he receives. Thus, vineyard sources tend to fluctuate—not radically but often significantly.

Because of this ever-shifting pattern of grape sources, I have decided not to profile individual négociant wineries. That decision should not be taken as implying that their wines are substandard. On the contrary, the best négociant wineries make wines of very high quality. By contracting out the very different activity of grape farming, such winemakers are free to focus on what they do best: selection, vinification, and *élevage*.

The following is a selection of some of the best négociant wineries of California.

Arcadian Joseph Davis worked in Burgundy with Jacques Seysses and started his own winery in 1996. He leases blocks of Chardonnay and Pinot Noir at Bien Nacido and Sleepy Hollow vineyards and also buys from Santa Lucia Highlands vineyards. He aims for a harmonious style with moderate alcohol but is not averse to a high proportion of new oak in some of his wines. www.arcadianwinery.com

Capiaux Sean Capiaux founded his winery in 1994, specializing in Pinot Noir from Sonoma and Santa Lucia Highlands. www.capiauxcellars.com

Copain Wells Guthrie's winery is in Healdsburg, but he buys grapes from Santa Barbara in the south, to Anderson Valley in the north. Anderson Valley is the source of all his Pinot Noirs. He also makes a range of Syrahs and a Rhône blend from James Berry Vineyard in Paso Robles. New oak and alcohol are kept to moderate levels. www.copainwines.com

Dashe Michael and Anne Dashe, both enologists (he spent most of the 1990s at Ridge), founded their winery in 1996, specializing in lush but balanced Cabernet Sauvignon and Zinfandel from Dry Creek and Alexander valleys. www.dashecellars.com

Kalin Cellars Terrance Leighton, a retired microbiologist, produces a wide range of wine styles but only releases the wines after giving them a great deal of bottle age. Thus, he still offers 1991 Chardonnay and 1997 Sauvignon Blanc. This is a somewhat eccentric venture that has attracted a cult following. www.kalincellars.com

Ojai Since 1984, Adam Tolmach, based in the Ventura area, has made a range of wines from Santa Barbara and Arroyo Grande, focusing mainly on Burgundian varieties and on Syrah and Viognier. Sources include Bien Nacido, Clos Pepe, and Roll Ranch. www.ojaivineyard.com

Patz & Hall Founded in 1988, this is a partnership between winemaker James Hall, sales director Donald Patz, and enologist Ann Moses. They specialize in Sonoma Chardonnay and Pinot Noir but also buy some grapes from Napa, from Pisoni Vineyard in Monterey, and from Alder Springs in Mendocino. In the past, some of their wines showed too much alcohol, but this has largely been corrected. www.patzhall.com

Radio Coteau Burgundy-trained Eric Sussman worked at Dehlinger Estate before founding his winery in 2002. He purchases a range of varieties from mostly organic vineyards in Sonoma County and Anderson Valley. The Pinot Noirs are usually his best wines. www.radiocoteau.com

Siduri Adam and Dianne Lee are self-taught winemakers from Texas. Their first vintage was in 1994, and by 2009 they were making 25 single-vineyard Pinot Noirs from Sonoma, Monterey, and Oregon. Adam takes an intense interest in the vineyards he buys from, visiting them repeatedly during the growing season. The wines tend to be made in a rich style, with considerable power and alcohol. www.siduri.com

Testarossa Founded in 1993 by Rob and Diana Jensen, Testarossa makes wines in the impressive old Novitiate winery in Los Gatos. The main varieties produced are Chardonnay, Pinot Noir, and Syrah. Grapes are sourced from Monterey (Rosella's, Garys', and Sleepy Hollow vineyards) and from Santa Barbara (Sanford & Benedict and Bien Nacido). www.testarossa.com

149
CHATEAU
MONTELENA
ESTABLISHED 1882
NAPA & ALEXANDER VALLEYS
CHARDONNAY
1973
Produced and Bottled by

Year by Year 2009–1990

2009

At the time of writing, it was too early to assess the vintage accurately. In Napa, the growing season was gratifying, and there was no sunburn, excessive stress, or raisining. Cool nights had preserved good levels of acidity. However, as harvest was getting under way, there was torrential rain on October 12. It had been forecast, so growers and winemakers were faced with a tricky decision: to pick before the storm, when the grapes might not yet have attained optimal ripeness, or to wait. Those who waited had to deal with rot and dilution, but much depended on how well each vineyard or estate had been managed.

In Sonoma, Burgundian varieties were picked before the rain. But earlier downpours, just before flowering, had reduced the crop. The summer was mild, but a mid-September heat spike accelerated ripening. In the Central Coast, too, yields were low.

2008

The North Coast experienced a troubled growing season. In Sonoma, the frosts were among the worst in living memory. In Napa, too, the spring was frosty, and in both counties this led to a smaller crop. The fruit set in May was also uneven, thanks in part to very strong winds. The summer was relatively cool, though it warmed up considerably in late August and early September. The harvest began in early September and continued into late October, depending on the variety. The wines were very concentrated but had good acidity.

In Sonoma, the summer was uneven, with alternating hot and cool spells, which meant the fruit ripened in spurts rather than evenly. The ten-day heat spike in late August, as in Napa, sped up maturation, and some growers were picking Pinot Noir by the end of that month. The quality of both red and white wines was high, but in many areas the crop was halved.

Left: California's best wines can age very well, including the Chardonnay that triumphed at the 1976 Judgment of Paris

In Paso Robles, the growing season was even, producing supple wines for fairly early drinking. Santa Barbara had a good vintage, though spring frosts caused damage and crop losses here, too.

2007

In Napa, the spring was warm and dry, and the growing season temperate and mild, though there was a heat spike in late August, which accelerated sugar development. Fortunately, cooler weather returned, so there was no raisining. White varieties were picked in excellent conditions. September was mild, with some rainstorms. Cool, wet weather returned in mid-October, but by then most fruit had been picked in Napa; the poor weather did not last long, so those who had not completed the harvest were able to do so at leisure. Even if the weather was not ideal, it was not a challenging harvest, and the Cabernet was of excellent quality.

Similar weather patterns prevailed in Sonoma. Heat spikes in early September boosted sugars, and the harvest began about two weeks earlier than usual. By the end of the third week of September, all whites and much of the Pinot Noir had been picked. Some rain in September did little damage but persuaded growers to complete the harvest quite rapidly, even though some of the cooler sites could have done with a longer growing season. Some growers considered the vintage to be the best since 2002, with beautifully ripe Pinots with small berries and thus high concentration; Zinfandels were lush and fruity, with little raisining.

In Santa Cruz, the harvest was early and excellent. Paso Robles growers were delighted with their lush but balanced reds, and Tablas Creek believed it was their best-ever vintage. Rhône varieties ripened beautifully, giving less tannic wines than in 2005. In Santa Barbara, problems at flowering led to a fairly small crop, which increased fruit concentration—impeccable, long-lived Chardonnay and Pinot Noir. A very good vintage in the Sierra Foothills, too.

2006

In Napa, the winter was wet and the spring cool, leading to a late flowering. June was warm, but there was a blistering heatwave in mid-July. Since it took place well before veraison, there was little sunburn or damage other than a shrinking of berry size, which only aided fruit concentration. August was cooler. Mild autumnal weather favored perfect ripening, especially of Cabernet Sauvignon. Maturation was slow, and growers needed to be patient. Tastings of the young Cabernets revealed well-balanced wines with moderate alcohols, though in some cases tannins were quite obtrusive, suggesting some wines would need time.

In Sonoma, rain led to rot in some Chardonnay, Pinot, and Zinfandel vineyards, which required vigilance, but warm weather returned in September, so quality was high and the crop was generous. Conditions in Mendocino were excellent, too.

The Central Coast also enjoyed excellent conditions and the same Indian summer as the North Coast. The reds were leaner, less alcoholic, and more tannic than the 2005s, with more elegance than power among, for example, Rhône varieties in Paso Robles. The one region that seemed to have had a disappointing year was the Sierra Foothills.

2005

After a normal winter in the North Coast, a cool, damp spring delayed budbreak. June was mild and wetter than usual, encouraging a spurt in vine growth and some disease, which needed to be treated. But the rest of the summer was mild, with unusually few very hot days. This meant the growing season was long, with even ripening, which a brief heat spike in late September did not perturb. The cool conditions resulted in elegant wines from Napa, which was welcome after the somewhat overblown 2004 Cabernets and Zinfandels. However, the crop was huge, even for growers who bunch-thinned during the summer. As a consequence, some wines, though very appealing, lacked structure and the potential for long aging. On the other hand, acidities remained high, giving the wines great freshness. The harvest continued into November in some areas. It was important for wineries to pace the harvest carefully to ensure there was sufficient tank space for what turned out to be a very large crop.

In Sonoma and the Central Coast, the Pinot Noir was structured and quite tannic, because yields were atypically low. It is a classic year for Sonoma Zinfandel, though the crop was large, and for Chardonnay, which shows good acidity. Paso Robles and Santa Barbara also enjoyed a long growing season, resulting in intense, powerful wines.

2004

In the North Coast, the summer was relatively cool, but the pattern was disturbed by very hot weather and drying winds in late August and early September. Conditions were more extreme in Napa than in Sonoma. Growers had to work hard to avoid raisining and very high sugar (and alcohol) levels. Not all succeeded, and there are several big, ungainly wines, especially Cabernet Sauvignon and Zinfandel, since much Chardonnay, Pinot, and Merlot had been picked before the heat spike took its toll. Top estates did their best to cull raisined berries, unless they specifically welcomed that style. The difficulty was that the heat spike, and the raisining that followed, meant that grapes needed to be picked very fast, which put pressure on growers and wineries that not all were able to handle. Many wines—Pinots, as well as Zinfandels and Cabernets—exhibit rather jammy characters.

Similar conditions prevailed in the Central Coast, giving rich, ripe red wines. The vintage was outstanding in the Sierra Foothills.

2003

The year got off to a tricky start. Stormy weather in the spring affected the flowering and thus the size of the crop. In Napa, Merlot suffered badly. The summer was uneven, with some heat spikes, as well as rainy spells in August. The weather seems to have been more temperate in Mendocino than farther south in Napa and Sonoma. Heat spikes in September blocked maturation, and an ensuing cold snap confused the vines further; but patience was rewarded with fine weather in October, which relieved the pressure to harvest in a hurry. Top estates like Rubicon picked their Cabernet in late October. Those who picked too soon may have ended up with an uncomfortable combination of greenness and jamminess.

It was a difficult year in Sonoma, too, with some poor flowering and early summer fogs that brought disease in their wake. August was cool; September, hotter, but also more stormy and windy. There was sunburn, and selection was advisable. Chardonnay and Pinot Noir were mostly picked during the latter half of September. The hot weather also drove up sugars in the Zinfandels, resulting in some high-alcohol wines. The unsettled weather caused some uneven ripening and dehydration, especially among Pinot Noir. But much depended on the responses of individual growers, so it is difficult to generalize.

In Monterey, there was a good deal of mildew, especially among Chardonnay, but overall quality was good. In Paso Robles, crops were down by about a third, but quality for Rhône varieties was high. Santa Barbara also suffered from mildew, wild temperature swings, and uneven ripening, which meant the vines were in disarray, but an Indian summer in October saved the crop.

2002

Spring frosts affected some North Coast vineyards, but not across the board. There was an uneven fruit-set and a growing season disturbed by heat spikes during the summer, which had the effect of making the uneven ripening even more marked and also caused some dehydration. July was average; August, fairly cool; September, normal for the season. Such conditions would not seem to herald a fine vintage, yet by the time it was over, hopes were high. In Sonoma, Chardonnay and Pinot Noir were very fine, though at some estates, such as Marimar, the white grapes were picked after the red. For Cabernet Sauvignon, selection in the vineyard was important, but scrupulous growers and winemakers ended up with exceptional wines, which many considered superior to both 2000 and 2001. The best are deeply colored, textured, tannic, and structured. It would also be a great vintage for Sonoma Zinfandel.

After a warm summer, Rhône varieties in the Central Coast gave exceptionally rich wines, but in Paso Robles the crop was reduced by about one-fifth. In Santa Barbara, the Pinot Noir had very small berries, which yielded much less wine than usual, as well as wines rich in tannin. Syrah ripened perfectly.

2001

After a warm March, budbreak was earlier than usual but was followed by sharp April frosts, which caused losses in Carneros, as well as in scattered locations across the North Coast. Overall, frost reduced the crop by about 15 percent. May and June were very hot, but the rest of the summer was cooler, which prolonged the growing season. It also kept acidity levels high, and in some areas, Chardonnay, of excellent quality, was picked later than Cabernet Sauvignon. Almost all varieties delivered fine results, with superb wines from Pinot Noir, Merlot, Syrah, and Zinfandel. The Cabernets benefited from a cool September, but patience was required to ensure the tannins were ripe and the acidity levels more friendly by the time harvesting teams were activated. The Cabernets were very ripe, and many winemakers compared the Cabernets to the great 1997 harvest, but alcohol levels were not as high.

Zinfandel from Napa and Sonoma benefited from the same benign conditions, giving wines with intense fruit and good acidity levels that have aged well, though they are less rich than the 2002s.

Wines from the Central Coast were also of very high quality, with conditions marginally better in Monterey and Santa Barbara than in Paso Robles.

2000

The growing season in the North Coast was cooler than average, though there was a very hot spell in June and another in late September, bringing a risk of dehydration. It was also more humid, with rain in late August, mid-September, and again in October. The summer rains were beneficial. It would prove a good year for earlier-ripening varieties such as Sauvignon Blanc, Chardonnay, and Pinot Noir, and Zinfandel also ripened quite early. Indeed, much North Coast Chardonnay was of exceptional quality. Temperatures dropped sharply in October, causing some problems for Cabernet Sauvignon that had not been picked, especially in vineyards where green harvesting had not been carried out. From the outset, it had been clear that the crop would be large and would require bunch-thinning. Mountain vineyards in particular suffered from the sudden change in the weather, and some grapes failed to ripen sufficiently. Napa Cabernet was rich and supple but less structured than in 1999, though some wines were distinctly tannic.

Sonoma enjoyed a growing season similar to Napa's, and it posed few problems. Regular fog incursions kept acidity levels satisfactory. Pinot Noir and then Chardonnay were picked in September and into early October. Both varieties showed considerable finesse. Zinfandel was quite patchy, because the vines suffered from the heat spikes.

The hot period in September accelerated ripening in Mendocino. There was some dehydration with Zinfandel, but it was a fine year for Pinot Noir, Chardonnay, and Rhône varieties.

The crop was large in Santa Cruz and the Central Coast, too, but quality was high, especially in Santa Barbara, despite some abrupt changes in weather during the summer. Chardonnay came through well in Monterey, and Bordeaux red varieties performed excellently in Paso Robles. In Santa Barbara, growers who had not thinned the abundant crop suffered during rainy spells at harvest. It was a fine year in the Sierra Foothills, despite some losses from spring frost and some uneven ripening.

1999

The hallmark of the vintage was the exceptionally cool summer, which provoked one of the longest growing seasons ever in California. The low temperatures simply delayed ripening, though a heat spike in late September gave maturation a welcome boost. In Sonoma, there was some frost in the spring and the fruit-set was poor, which resulted in a small crop. Throughout the North Coast, yields were down at least 15 percent. Because of the problems during the set, it was important to eliminate laggard bunches when green harvesting over the summer. Although quantities were small, Sonoma Chardonnay and Pinot Noir were of high quality. A mild October meant that growers of later-ripening varieties such as Cabernet Sauvignon could take their time and await optimal maturity.

The long growing season affected the Central Coast, too. In Monterey, the exceptionally cool spring and delayed budbreak led some growers to worry whether the fruit would ripen; an Indian summer and some rain in September saved the region from disaster, though few would make great claims for the vintage. In much of Santa Barbara the harvest continued into November, and in some cases December. Sugar and alcohol levels were below average, and some wines showed unripe characters. In the Sierra Foothills, the wines had unusually high acidity because of the cool summer, but quality was high, except where the vines had been overcropped.

1998

This was a year that some growers and winemakers would rather forget, though it was far from disastrous. In the North Coast, the spring was cold and wet, which delayed flowering. The set was very uneven, and there was quite a severe reduction in the crop. The summer was not too bad, though there was a heat spike in July and a good deal of rain in late September. But August was very warm, which helped with ripening. October had splendid weather, but by then many grapes had been picked. On the Napa Valley floor and in Sonoma, there was widespread fog during the harvest, and the cool, damp conditions caused some outbreaks of rot. Mountain vineyards were not affected.

The consequence of this difficult fall was that not all of the crop ripened fully. Zinfandel was particularly patchy, and some wines suffered from high tannins and high acidity—not the most delectable combination. Few of them aged well. White varieties were also unimpressive, with a frequent lack of concentration and weight.

In the Central Coast, conditions were not much better, though wineries in Paso Robles seemed reasonably happy. In Santa Barbara, the harvest was a few weeks later than usual, and overcropped vineyards did not ripen. However, where yields were kept to moderate levels, there was a fine Chardonnay harvest. Syrah also fared quite well, but it was difficult to coax Pinot Noir to full ripeness.

Rain in the Sierra Foothills made this a vintage to forget in that hilly area.

There was a tendency to write off the whole vintage, and some American tasters were savage in their dismissal. It is undoubtedly true that 1998 was one of the decade's weaker vintages, but as always, much depended on crop levels and viticultural skills. Many winemakers did produce enjoyable and balanced wines, but few merited long cellaring.

1997

This year will be remembered for its abundance, as well as for its quality. It was a precocious year, with early budbreak, an early veraison, and thus an early harvest. It was not all plain sailing: in the North Coast, rains in August and humid conditions led to outbreaks of rot, except in very well-managed vineyards. Sonoma Pinot Noir and Chardonnay were quite badly affected by rot, but its incidence was patchy. There was further rain in September, but warm, dry weather followed swiftly, so there was far less damage to the crop than in August. The Chardonnay yields were particularly high; those for Merlot and Cabernet only slightly above average. Growers in Carneros and elsewhere bunch-thinned conscientiously, but clusters remained large. The large crops tempted some critics to dismiss 1997, but in fact it was one of those years when copious quantities did not equate with mediocre quality. It was an easy harvest to pick and vinify, and most growers had completed the harvest by early October. Chardonnay was a particular success.

Zinfandel in some areas was affected by rot, and there were some tricky fermentations that failed to attain dryness. Yet overall the wines had ample flavor and generous alcohol. Although it was necessary to pick and choose, the best Zinfandels were superb. Initial reports on the Napa and Sonoma Cabernets were not optimistic; but as time went by, reports became increasingly enthusiastic, and many were comparing the vintage to 1994 in quality, crediting the fine end to the growing season. However, the Cabernets in general had quite high pHs and have not aged quite as well as anticipated.

In the Central Coast, the weather was drier than in the North Coast. The same was true in the Sierra Foothills, where winemakers were extremely happy with the quality, and the wines had excellent concentration. Yields were close to normal in Santa Barbara, but there was some rain and rot. In contrast, Monterey remained mostly dry.

1996

In Napa, the winter was mild, with ample rainfall, leading to an early budbreak. Spring was cool, and rain in May affected the fruit-set for Sauvignon, Chardonnay, and Cabernet. After a cool June, the weather improved and ripening sped up, only to slow down again after a cool spell in late August and early September. White varieties were picked in excellent conditions, though yields were below average. Sonoma Pinot Noir certainly ripened but was fairly soft; in many instances, the wines lacked structure. Zinfandel was patchy, with some thin wines. Mendocino also had a short crop for the same reasons, but the summer was hot and quality high.

In the Santa Cruz Mountains, Ridge reported very high tannin levels for Cabernet, yet skillful vinification kept the wine in balance. The Central Coast did not experience the same problems at flowering and set as the North Coast. In Paso Robles and Santa Barbara, the long, warm growing season culminated in an easy harvest of excellent quality.

1995

The vintage got off to a slow start in the North Coast, with a wet winter and damp, cool spring, which led to problems at flowering and a reduced crop. The summer was warm, and there were signs of dehydration by mid-September. Mendocino stayed in low gear for longer than Napa and Sonoma, since it only heated up in August but then remained warm. Yet the red wines turned out very well, with deep colors, supple tannins, and ample generosity of flavor. Pinot Noir was delicate rather than rich.

This was also an excellent vintage in the Sierra Foothills. Santa Cruz reported cooler temperatures than most other California wine regions. In Santa Barbara, the problem was quantity rather than quality, because the poor flowering resulted in much lower yields than normal.

1994

In the North Coast, a dry, sunny March led to an early budbreak, followed by a cool spring. The summer was warm, with only the first half of August hot. Maturation continued steadily, culminating in an uneventful harvest when sugar and acidity were in balance. Merlot and Cabernet were both exceptional, rivaling 1991 in quality and showing more structure than 1992 or 1993. There was no rush to pick, and the mild summer called for extended hang-time; Mondavi completed its harvest only in early November. Sonoma and Napa delivered wines of equal quality, with an outstanding balance of ripeness and acidity. This also applied to Zinfandel. This was a great vintage for Pinot Noir, too—a variety at last coming into its own in areas such as Russian River Valley and Carneros. Chardonnay also delivered rich and unusually complex wines.

The Central Coast did not enjoy the same benign conditions, with heavy rain that led to rot, especially in Chardonnay. Monterey fared better than regions farther south. Mendocino also had more rain than the rest of the North Coast. Some good wines were still produced, though not with the same consistency as Napa and Sonoma.

1993

Wind and rain in the early summer interfered with the flowering and set in the North Coast, so the crop was substantially reduced. The summer was perturbed, with alternating spells of hot and cool weather. There was some raisining after heat spikes in August and September, and the uneven weather conditions persisted through harvest, complicating the process. Nonetheless, some good Pinot Noir and Cabernet were produced, even if few wines were deemed capable of long aging. Many growers panicked and picked according to sugar levels, and in some cases phenolic ripeness lagged behind. Some well-known Cabernets, such as Caymus Special Selection and Dominus, were not made this year, since quality was not deemed up to standard. While it is true that some Cabernets lacked concentration and were too tannic for their slender frames, some perfectly acceptable wines were made, though most should probably have been drunk by now. The same is true of the Zinfandels.

The Central Coast escaped the problems that beset the North. Yields were normal, and plenty of rich, fruity wines were produced, especially Chardonnays and some first-rate Pinot Noirs.

1992

As often happens even in the generous California climate, flowering was blighted by cool weather, so the fruit-set was uneven. However, the summer was dry and hot, with the exception of late August in Napa, which was foggy. The fog was not problematic, since it allowed the Cabernet to ripen fully at a leisurely pace. The crop was quite large, and there was some dilution in wines made from vineyards that were not reined in. Excellent Pinot Noirs were made in Carneros, and the Burgundian varieties also fared well in Sonoma, especially Chardonnay. Some Zinfandel was overripe, but quality overall was above average. Cabernets from Sonoma were rich and structured. The weather in Mendocino was uniformly warm, allowing an early and successful harvest. The crop in the Central Coast was small.

This is a vintage that was probably underrated for Cabernet Sauvignon, coming, as it did, after the excellent 1991 vintage. Disappointments occurred with wines that were either insufficiently concentrated or too tannic.

1991

An excellent vintage in Napa, after an abundant fruit-set, a long, cool growing season (other than a very warm spell in July), and perfect conditions during harvesting. There was surprisingly little dilution, given that the crop was the largest since 1982, because conscientious growers did not hesitate to green harvest. White varieties were less favored, since acidity was fairly low, and there was some botrytis. Yields were high in Sonoma, too, leading to a late but successful harvest. For Cabernet Sauvignon, the vintage proved classic, with wines of excellent concentration and no pressure to pick before tannins were fully ripe. In Stags Leap, Clos du Val picked its Cabernet only on October 25, though stormy weather thereafter effectively put an end to the harvest. Acidities remained quite high, but there was little astringency. Some delicious Pinot Noir was made in Carneros, but the large crop caused some uneven ripening of Zinfandel, though the best wines, from Amador County and Dry Creek Valley, were rich and ripe.

Similar weather conditions prevailed in the Central Coast, but the crop was less generous than farther north. Much excellent Pinot Noir was produced in Santa Barbara. Growers who waited too long were confronted by unwelcome rains.

1990

Although Cabernet Sauvignon and Sauvignon Blanc had below-average yields, this was another fine year in the North Coast, thanks to a long, warm summer that ensured full maturation. All factors—fruit, acidity, tannin—were in balance, and the Cabernets and Zinfandels were soon hailed as the best since 1985. Pinot Noir and Chardonnay delivered lush, full-bodied wines in Carneros and Sonoma.

The Central Coast had more troubled conditions than the North, with some heavy rainfall during harvest in Santa Barbara. Nonetheless, some very attractive Chardonnays were produced. The Sierra Foothills were also out of luck, with a lackluster rather than poor vintage.

Wine lovers and critics continue to discuss whether 1990 or 1991 was the better vintage for Cabernet Sauvignon. The consensus seems to be that 1990 was the more consistent year, but many prefer the classic cool-climate character of 1991. It comes down to individual winemaking styles and to personal tastes.

Other fine vintages: 1987, 1985, 1980, 1978, 1974, 1970.

The Finest 100

Producers or wines appear in alphabetical order within their category.
A star (★) indicates what is, in my opinion, the finest of the fine.

Ten Best Zinfandels
Robert Biale Monte Rosso Vineyard
Domaine de la Terre Rouge Easton Estate
Dry Creek Vineyard Old Vine
Hartford Highwire Vineyard
Ravenswood Teldeschi Vineyard★
Ridge Geyserville
St. Francis Pagani Vineyard
Seghesio Old Vine
Sobon Lubenko Vineyard
Turley Hayne Vineyard

Ten Best Cabernet Sauvignons
Arrowood Réserve Spéciale
Dalla Valle Vineyards
Diamond Creek Vineyards Red Rock Terrace
Dunn Howell Mountain★
Harlan Estate
Heitz Wine Cellars Martha's Vineyard
Mayacamas Vineyards
Chateau Montelena Winery Estate
Spottswoode Estate Vineyard & Winery
Stag's Leap Wine Cellars SLV

Ten Best Bordeaux Blends
Araujo Estate Wines
Benziger Tribute
Cain Vineyard and Winery Cain Five
Dominus Estate
Ferrari-Carano Trésor
Justin Isosceles
Opus One
Ridge Monte Bello★
Rudd Oakville Estate
Viader Vineyards & Winery

Ten Best North Coast Chardonnays
Cakebread Cellars Anderson Valley
Dutton-Goldfield Rued
Flowers Sonoma Coast
Hanzell
Iron Horse Corral Vineyard
Kistler Hudson Vineyard
Littorai Mays Canyon★
Marimar Estate
Mayacamas Vineyards
Merryvale Vineyards Silhouette

Ten Best Central Coast Chardonnays
Au Bon Climat Sanford & Benedict Vineyard
Brewer & Clifton Mount Carmel Vineyard
Clos Pepe Estate
Foxen Bien Nacido Block UU
Melville Inox
Mount Eden Estate★
Paraiso Eagle's Perch
Ramey Hyde Vineyard
Ridge Monte Bello
Talley Rosemary's Vineyard

Ten Best North Coast Pinot Noirs
Dehlinger
Dutton-Goldfield Freestone Hill★
Hartford Fog Dance
Kistler Cuvée Natalie
Kosta Browne Koplen Vineyard
Littorai Hirsch Vineyard
Marimar La Masía
Saintsbury Toyon Farm
Siduri Hirsch Vineyard
Williams Selyem Westside Road Neighbors

Ten Best Central Coast Pinot Noirs
Arcadian Francesca
Au Bon Climat Isabel Morgan★
Brewer-Clifton Mount Carmel
Clos Pepe
Foxen Julia's Vineyard
Melville Carrie's
Mount Eden Estate
Sea Smoke Ten
Siduri Rosella's Vineyard
Talley Rosemary's Vineyard

Top Ten Syrahs
Alban Reva
Araujo Estate Wines
Beckmen Purisima Mountain
Dutton-Goldfield Cherry Ridge Vineyard
Qupé Bien Nacido Vineyard Hillside Select★
Saxum Bone Rock
Terre Rouge Pyramid Block
Thackrey Orion
Viader Vineyards & Winery
Zaca Mesa Black Bear Block

Ten Best Anything But Chardonnay/Cabernet
Alban Estate Viognier
Arrowood Estate Malbec
Beckmen Purisima Grenache
Benziger Paradiso de Maria Sauvignon Blanc
Foxen Wickenden Old Vine Chenin
Navarro Cluster Select Riesling★
Seghesio Barbera
Tablas Creek Vin de Paille Quintessence
Terre Rouge Roussanne
Togni Ca' Togni Black Muscat

Ten Best-Value Wineries
Beringer Vineyards
Dry Creek Vineyard★
Frog's Leap
Gallo Family Vineyards
Robert Mondavi Winery
Navarro
Ravenswood
St. Francis
Sobon Estate
Zaca Mesa

Glossary

biodynamic farming based on the phases of the moon and principles of homeopathic treatments; developed by Rudolf Steiner in the 1920s. Despite its eccentricity, the system has been adopted by leading estates in Burgundy, Alsace, and elsewhere in Europe, and, increasingly, in California

blush pale pink wine, usually quite sweet, from Zinfandel or other red grapes

Brix American measure of sugar content in grapes, also known as Balling, approximately equal to double the potential alcohol of the wine, if all the sugar is fermented. 19.3° Brix is equivalent to 10% ABV

cold soak fashionable technique of keeping grapes at cool temperatures before fermentation so as to extract more color and aroma

crush California term for the vintage

field-grafting method for converting established vines from one variety to another by grafting a bud of one variety onto an existing vine

free-run juice juice that flows from crushed grapes before pressing; usually mixed with pressed juice

jug wines pejorative term for standard wines sold in large bottles

Meritage red or white blends made from two or more Bordeaux varieties

Pierce's disease a disease spread by sharpshooter insects and hard to eradicate. Has inflicted huge damage on the southern California vineyards of Temecula

residual sugar the sugar that remains in a wine after incomplete fermentation

TCA wine contamination giving musty aromas and flavors caused either by corks or by barrels and other woodwork tainted by this chemical compound

whole-cluster pressing the practice of pressing white grapes, stems and all, as soon as they arrive at the winery. The advantage is a greater freshness in the wine, sometimes at the expense of complexity

Bibliography

William A. Ausmus,
Wines & Wineries of California's Central Coast (University of California Press, Berkeley; 2008)

Bruce Cass (editor),
The Oxford Companion to the Wines of North America
(Oxford University Press, Oxford; 2000)

John Winthrop Haeger,
North American Pinot Noir (University of California Press, Berkeley; 2004)

James Halliday,
Wine Atlas of California
(Viking, New York; 1993)

Matt Kramer,
New California Wine
(Running Press, Philadelphia; 2004)

James T. Lapsley,
Bottled Poetry
(University of California Press, Berkeley; 1996)

George M. Taber,
Judgment of Paris
(Scribner, New York; 2005)

Index